THE
RIVERSIDE
READER

JOSEPH TRIMMER
Ball State University

MAXINE HAIRSTON
University of Texas at Austin

The Riverside Reader

Volume 1

Second Edition

HOUGHTON MIFFLIN COMPANY BOSTON

Dallas   *Geneva, Ill.*   *Hopewell, N.J.*   *Palo Alto*   *London*

Publisher's Note

◆

The Riverside Reader consists of two volumes, each of which is revised every four years on a staggered schedule so that a revised volume is published every two years and both volumes are simultaneously available.

Printed in the U.S.A.

Library of Congress Catalog Card Number: 80-82759

ISBN: 0-395-35749-7
BCDEFGHIJ-FG-898765

Cover illustration: Albert Bierstadt, *Sunset in the Yosemite Valley,* 1868. Haggin Collection, The Haggin Museum, Stockton, California

Preface

———— ◆ ————

This second edition of Volume 1 of *The Riverside Reader* is, like the original edition, a collection of fifty-one essays drawn from a wide variety of sources. In purpose, strategy, and design this edition reflects its predecessor, but we have made several substantial revisions.

First, and most important, nineteen of the essays—almost forty percent of the total—are new to this edition. Among their authors are certain acknowledged masters of contemporary prose style—Malcolm Cowley, Lewis Thomas, Barbara Tuchman, Loren Eiseley—and also younger writers whose reputations continue to grow— Annie Dillard, Alice Walker, Barry Lopez, Patricia Hampl. The new essays are, of course, accompanied by new study questions.

Second, the introduction to the text offers an expanded discussion of thoughtful reading techniques and a more detailed analysis of a model essay—Virginia Woolf's "If Shakespeare Had Had a Sister."

Third, for those instructors who prefer to organize their courses in terms of themes or issues, an alternate thematic table of contents follows the annotated table of contents.

The ten sections in this reader are arranged in a sequence that is familiar to most writing teachers. The first eight sections group essays according to traditional writing strategies, beginning with narration and description, moving through the five expository patterns, and ending with argument. The last two sections are small anthologies—Essays for Further Reading (longer and more complex essays that employ several strategies) and Essays on Reading and Writing (essays that illuminate the reading and the writing processes).

The selections within each section have been chosen according to five criteria. *Length.* Most essays are brief, some as short as two pages, several as long as twelve to fourteen pages, but most are about five pages. *Level.* Within each section the essays are arranged in an order of ascending complexity: the essays at the beginning are short and simple; those near the end are longer and more complicated. *Accuracy.* The essays illustrate what the introductions say they illustrate: there are no strange hybrids or confusing models. *Variety.* We have chosen essays on a wide range of subjects and tested them for interest level with students. These essays were written by the best traditional and contemporary authors and include memorable selections by female, black, and ethnic writers. *Liveliness. The Riverside Reader* presents the essay at its best—graceful, witty, and illuminating. We are convinced that students and teachers will find our choices engaging and informative.

The introductions are written in simple, direct prose. The general introduction explains not only how to read an essay, but also how students can use the essay to improve their own writing. The introductions to individual sections explain how to identify an author's purpose, audience, and strategies when he or she is working within a specific form. The introductions to each writer (headnotes) contain basic biographical information. All this introductory material focuses on the five elements of the writing situation: *Who* wrote the essay? *What* kind of essay is it? *Why* was the essay written? To *whom* is the essay addressed? *How* does the author accomplish his or her purpose?

The study questions are placed at the end of each selection and are organized according to a clear and consistent pattern. There are Questions about Purpose, Questions about Audience, Questions about Strategies, and Questions for Discussion. The questions in the first three categories ask students to apply the information presented in the section introduction to specific essays. The questions in the last category ask students to extend and sharpen their thinking about each essay.

The writing assignments are placed at the end of each

section and are organized by four categories: Points to Consider, Prewriting Exercises, Topics for Writing in Class, and Topics for Writing Out of Class. The ultimate purpose of a college reader is to produce writing. For that reason, the writing assignments in *The Riverside Reader* have been designed as the culminating activity of each section. They grow out of and provide a natural purpose for every reading assignment.

We are grateful to the writing instructors and students across the country who have shared with us their responses to the first edition of *The Riverside Reader*. We especially want to thank the following individuals for their astute comments and suggestions for the development of this revision: Kirk H. Beetz, University of California at Davis; Franz Douskey, South Central Community College, Connecticut; Thomas Hamel, St. Olaf College; Sarah Harrison, Tyler Junior College, Texas; John Huxhold, St. Louis Community College at Meramec; Steven W. Lynn, University of South Carolina; Barry M. Maid, University of Arkansas at Little Rock; Larry Mapp, Middle Tennessee State University; Donovan J. Ochs, University of Iowa; James Thompson, University of North Carolina; and Elizabeth Williams, Pratt Institute.

Special thanks also go to Karen Taylor and Linda Batt for their help in manuscript preparation. And, as ever, we thank our students for their continuing role in our own educations.

Contents

◆

NARRATION

25

An American humorist recalls himself at fourteen—
"when the first rocks were just ahead"—and tells of an
evening on which he found out more than he wanted
to know about himself.

An essayist and author of children's books tells how he
did and did not recapture the past when he took his
son back to the scenes of his own childhood.

A disabled and disillusioned Vietnam veteran narrates
the chain of events that ended with frightened soldiers
killing helpless civilians.

A Chinese-American writer tells a story to dramatize the
cruelty that a woman who deviates from tradition must
endure in a rigid and primitive culture.

Contents

Contents

DEFINITION

293

CAUSE AND EFFECT

335

Contents

PERSUASION AND ARGUMENT

389

Contents

xv

ESSAYS ON READING AND WRITING

531

Alternate Thematic Table of
Contents

———— ◆ ————

III. THE MINORITY EXPERIENCE

IV. THE EDUCATION OF EXPERIENCE

V . TEACHING AND LEARNING

V I . READING AND WRITING

VII.   LEISURE AND THE ARTS

VIII.   WORK

IX.   THE MARKET PLACE

X.   SCIENCE AND TECHNOLOGY

XI. HEROES

XII. A SAMPLER OF CONTROVERSIAL ISSUES

---◆---

INTRODUCTION

---◆---

WHAT IS A COLLEGE READER?

A college reader for a composition course is a collection of essays chosen to illustrate effective writing on different topics for different purposes. For convenience, the essays are often grouped together to illustrate particular patterns of writing (that is, narration, classification, definition, argument, and so on). By organizing the book in this way, however, the editors are not suggesting that all writing can be classified according to these neat categories or that the authors of these essays set out to write exclusively in one pattern. Most writers begin with ideas and then develop them by using a variety of strategies to fulfill their purposes. Their writing may use several supporting strategies but exhibit an overall dominant pattern (such as comparison and contrast), as do the essays in *The Riverside Reader*, or it may mix the strategies of various patterns and exhibit no single discernible overall pattern.

Whatever the case, there are good reasons to organize this book around the commonly recognized dominant patterns. Such an arrangement makes it possible to see how writers go about carrying out typical kinds of writing tasks —defining terms, examining causes or effects, arguing beliefs, narrating what happened. And studying a pattern of writing in its relatively pure form before studying it as a component of a more complex product enables you to understand better its characteristic features and principal uses.

The editors of this reader, both of whom write and teach writing, provide analysis and questions that will help you understand the essays and the writing processes that produced them. They also suggest writing exercises and assignments that give you the opportunity to work at various kinds of writing.

WHO ARE THE WRITERS IN A COLLEGE READER?

The writers whose work is included in a college reader are chosen for their diverse subjects, styles, and reputations. Some of them are known for essays that are primarily informative or entertaining—for example, John McPhee, the master of numerous, divergent subjects, and Jean Shepherd, a quintessentially American humorist. Others, such as E. B. White and Joan Didion, are acknowledged masters of personal expression, often writing about the education that their experiences have given them. Still others represent an important group of writers whom you may not have encountered before: the writers of nonfiction articles and books that influence our culture and our lives. In any generation, the changes that take effect are frequently the result of *writing:* someone had an idea and wrote about it; someone felt strongly about prevailing conditions and wrote about them; someone discerned a pattern in events and wrote about it. Three good examples of this kind of writer are Loren Eisely, who writes about links in the mystery of evolution; Rachel Carson, who writes about the destruction of our environment; and Barbara Tuchman, who writes about patterns of behavior in history.

Most of these writers are not often famous in the way that best-selling novelists or songwriters are, but their writing is important because it reaches the thoughtful and mentally alert readers of any generation, and it contributes to those readers' understanding of their world. Furthermore, it provides the information and the intellectual stimulation that enable people in government, business, and the professions to make informed decisions. A college reader samples the best of this kind of writing, both old and new, and invites you to read not only for entertainment and information but also for the sheer pleasure of encountering new insights into the major issues of our time.

It is important to remember that professional writers work within a writing situation governed by three primary concerns. Those concerns are

1. *Their* PURPOSE *or reason for writing.* Writers must know, at least in general, the ideas they want to express or the questions they want to answer. Sometimes they have identified a problem for which they want to propose a solution. They must hold their purpose constantly in mind as they write, both to keep their ideas in order and to sustain their readers' attention.

2. *The nature of the* AUDIENCE *for whom they are writing.* What writers know about their readers seriously affects what and how they write. They

must consider the information and attitudes their readers are likely to bring to their reading; further, they must anticipate the questions for which those readers will want answers. And they must think about whether their readers have limitations in time or attention span.

3. *The* STRATEGIES *they will use as they write.* How can they best make their points? What type of organization will be most effective? What anecdotes or examples will help engage their readers' interest? Given certain assertions, what kind of evidence must they offer? Sometimes writers chart their strategies in advance of putting paragraphs on paper; sometimes they discover the strategies they need as they are writing. In either case, they do work with specific, knowable techniques—ways of putting their ideas across most effectively for the audience to whom they are writing.

WHAT IS THE PURPOSE OF A COLLEGE READER?

A college reader serves several purposes in a composition classroom. First, it provides examples of effective writing by accomplished, respected writers. By reading professional essays, you can discover how skilled writers use language to achieve their purposes. It is important to remember, however, that the essays in *The Riverside Reader* are not intended as absolute models for your writing and that you should not judge your writing by professional standards. Few people can write as well as E. B. White or Annie Dillard, and an inexperienced writer should no more compare his or her writing to the work of such authors than a high school basketball player should judge his or her performance by comparing it to that of Julius Erving. Such comparisons are unnecessary and self-defeating. Nevertheless, you do need to know what a good description or argument looks like if you are going to write one yourself. After all, if you hope to become a ballet dancer, you start by watching ballet dancers perform.

Second, a college reader gives you the opportunity to practice close, critical reading. Because the essays in a reader are usually short and are accompanied by questions for study and discussion, you can read them more carefully than you can most magazine articles or books. The study questions help you analyze what you are reading and understand what a writer is trying to accomplish and how he or she is trying to accomplish it. The questions in *The Riverside Reader* are especially helpful in coaching you to read actively—that is, to put yourself in the writer's place as you read and to be aware of all the concerns that the writer kept in mind when writing. For example, if you read Barry Lopez's "The Raven," which compares ravens and crows, you might imagine Lopez asking himself why his readers would confuse ravens with crows and, accordingly, wondering which details to include that would most vividly call out the differences between the two birds. Putting yourself in the writer's place also offers you the chance to come to know the writer. As one writing teacher has said, a piece of writing is a map to the mind of the person who wrote it. Learning to read closely helps you follow such maps accurately and with pleasure.

Third, a college reader can stimulate you to reflect on and evaluate your own experiences and opinions and to think about how you can use them in your own writing. Too often, unpracticed writers underestimate the value of their experiences, not realizing that they are worth writing about—or they assume that no one is interested in their opinions, so they rely on second-hand ideas or conventional arguments when writing. But if you examine the work of professional writers in terms of subject, ideas, and supporting evidence, you will almost certainly realize that you can find good material for writing in your own life. Read, for example, Alice Walker's "In Search of Our Mothers' Gardens," an essay that begins with an appreciation of her mother's creative talent and broadens to discuss the creative talent of all black women. This essay might stimulate a student to write about his father's hobby of woodworking, concentrating particularly on what it reveals about the man. Or read Carol Bly's "Getting Tired," an essay that speculates about the way intense physical labor affects one's perceptions of the world. Reading it might prompt a student to recall her own exhausting experiences on the job one summer, concentrating particularly on how those experiences colored her point of view toward her nonworking friends that season. The point is that seemingly unexceptional events are the common coin of everyone's life; writers have simply learned how to probe them for their deeper significance.

Finally, a college reader offers examples that you can analyze to learn what makes a good piece of writing work. If you want to improve your tennis game, you focus closely on the games played by the experts. So it is with writing: you can learn much from focusing on the techniques of the professionals. For example, even a casual reading of the essays in *The Riverside Reader* reveals how important *facts* are to good writing. Most of the essays work because their authors have done their research and have given their readers an abundance of concrete, specific information about their subjects—for example, William Styron's facts about smoking, or John McPhee's facts about grizzly bears. When most people read they want to learn something; writers meet that need by adding the *weight of facts* to their work.

Professional writers are often masters of metaphor and analogy, using them to reveal and enlighten as well as to invigorate their writing. Ellen Goodman, for example, dramatizes the rigor of the premedical curriculum by calling organic chemistry "the sieve into which was poured every premedical student in the university." Martin Luther King, Jr., emphasizes this country's mistreatment of blacks by writing "America has given the Negro people a bad check." By watching for such metaphors as you read you will become more aware of the power of the striking comparison.

Professional writers also know how to begin their essays with paragraphs that catch their readers' interest and give clear signals about what to expect. If you examine the essays in this reader and look at just the first paragraphs, you will probably be struck by how skillfully the writers have engaged your interest and made you want to read. You will find particularly good examples in George Orwell's "Marrakech," Ron Kovic's "On Patrol," and Joan Didion's "Migraines." Many other essays, too, will give you some ideas about the kinds of openings you might choose for your own writing.

When you establish the habit of reading to find out *how* a writer writes as well as to find out *what* he or she is saying, you are reading in two dimensions, simultaneously responding to the content of an essay or book and recognizing the writing techniques being used. The experience is similar to that of watching a good film by a talented director; you follow the action of the story as it unfolds, to be sure, but you also notice and admire the clever use of special effects, or the parody of other films, or the unusual camera angles. Such awareness enables you to see beyond the images on the screen—and when you bring a similar awareness to reading, you see beyond the words on the page. Reading becomes a richer experience that not only informs or entertains you but also gives you some understanding about the craft of writing.

WHO IS THE AUDIENCE FOR A COLLEGE READER?

The Two Audiences. The essays in a college reader have two audiences—an important fact to bear in mind. The *first* audience for each essay was made up of the readers who read it when it originally appeared in a magazine or book (or, in the case of speeches, those who first heard it).

For example, Barbara Tuchman's "An Inquiry into the Persistence of Unwisdom in Government" first appeared in *Esquire,* and John Brooks's "Dressing Down" was originally a chapter in a popular book about American customs and manners. These writers—and all the writers in *The Riverside Reader*—write with particular audiences in mind. They know the kinds of readers who are interested in their work, what those readers expect, and the kinds of books and magazines those readers read.

The *second* audience consists of students who, like you, are enrolled in writing courses. Student readers may have had comparatively few opportunities to read serious nonfiction, and they do not necessarily have the experience or background that the authors of the essays have assumed in their first audience. As a member of this second audience, you may occasionally find yourself at a disadvantage because you are not the reader the authors had in mind, and thus you may encounter unfamiliar allusions or vocabulary or feel uneasy because you don't know as much as an author seems to assume you do. Such a reading experience is understandably frustrating, but you should neither be discouraged nor give up in despair. Instead, realize that you are exploring new territory, just as you do in your other college courses, and that you need some help. This you can get in a number of ways: by learning to use the Guidelines for Reading an Essay (see pages 12–13); by giving serious attention to the introductions preceding and study questions following the essays in the reader; and by listening to and joining in class discussion.

Learning to Keep Both Audiences in Mind. If you learn to keep both audiences in mind as you read, you can sharpen your insights about the writing process. You can identify specific elements in an essay—such as word choice, tone, use of evidence, connotative or metaphorical language—and then try to deduce from those elements the characteristics of the author's first audience. You can analyze the strategies the writer used to appeal to that audience and speculate about why he or she chose those strategies. You can try to put yourself in the place of the original audience and imagine how those readers reacted to the writing.

This kind of exercise develops the quality that may be a writer's most valuable asset: *audience awareness.* Few practices can help a writer as much as cultivating the habit of asking, "What do I know about my audience? What do they expect of me? How much do they already know about my subject? How can I catch and hold their interest?" You can also use such questions to assess the audience for your college papers and related writing tasks. If you consider these questions before writing a term paper, applying for a scholarship, or requesting funds for research, you can learn to write effectively in different situations for a variety of reasons. In doing so, you will be following the model of professional writers—for professionals are, among other things, writers who have learned to adapt their writing to their audience.

HOW DOES ONE USE A COLLEGE READER?

You can read an essay in a college reader more effectively if you think about its *external,* nontextual features before you begin to read—that is, if you read *around* the essay. Start with the headnote, which will give you the essay's title, some pertinent facts about its author, and information about when and where the essay was first published.

Next, read the essay straight through, noting any headings or subheadings in the text, thinking about how the major strategy is being employed, and staying alert to how the content reflects the title of the essay. Watch particularly for key words and repeated phrases and pay attention to any names that keep appearing. In this first reading, you should try to see the essay as a whole and, at the end of it, ask yourself, "What is my first impression? What is the writer saying? How is he or she attempting to say it?

What is my response to the essay? Am I going to have to read it again to understand it fully?"

Almost certainly the answer to that last question will be "Yes." Most people need to read any serious piece of writing more than once to master its contents, but additional readings can yield more than information. As you go through an essay a second time, you should view it in terms of its parts rather than as a completed product. You should think about the *process* the writer went through to create the product. You should probe beneath the surface of the writing and ask what the writer was trying to say, to whom it was being said, and how the writer combined certain elements to produce the final effect.

If you develop the habit of asking your own strategy questions during a second or third reading—and also systematically answering the editors' study questions after you have finished several readings—you will begin to think like a writer. You will discover the process of a writer's craft—a process you can begin to work with in your own writing.

Finally, after you have studied and analyzed an essay, write a short response—perhaps a paragraph or so—that sums up your feelings about what you have read: "Did I enjoy the essay? Did I learn something from it? Did it change my attitudes? What questions would I like to ask the person who wrote it?" Writing such a response may help you discover what you think about an essay. In a way, you are talking back to an author while the essay is still fresh in your mind. It may also spark new ideas and associations that will give you momentum to begin your own writing assignments.

HOW TO USE *THE RIVERSIDE READER*

The Riverside Reader is designed to help you become a more active reader and more effective writer. The introductions that precede every section of essays, the headnotes that appear before each essay, the study questions that follow each essay, and the writing assignments that conclude each section are all arranged to call attention to the essential elements in any writing situation: AUTHOR, DEFINITION, PURPOSE, AUDIENCE, STRATEGIES. Another way to describe these elements is to ask WHO wrote the essay? WHAT kind of essay is it? WHY was it written? to WHOM is it addressed, and HOW does the author make it work? The consistent reference to these elements throughout the text encourages you to think critically about what you are reading and to plan intelligently for what you write.

The following pages provide an illustration of how these elements work. First, "Guidelines for Reading an Essay" lists those questions that the editors have addressed in their introductions, headnotes, and study questions and that you should consider as you read every essay. Second, "Sample Analysis of an Essay" provides brief answers to those questions as they apply to Virginia Woolf's essay "If Shakespeare Had Had a Sister." Third, the Woolf essay, complete with editorial annotations, suggests the way an active reader should mark strategies in essays throughout the text. And, finally, "About the Writing Assignments" explains how the writing assignments relate to the essays in each section.

Guidelines for Reading an Essay

I. WHO IS THE AUTHOR?

a. What is the author's age, sex, and ethnic background?

b. How does the author's educational background and work experience qualify him or her to write on this topic? What reasons might the author have for being biased?

c. When and where did the author first publish the essay? Is the subject still important?

II. WHAT KIND OF ESSAY IS IT?

a. What particular form of writing—narration, definition, argument, etc.—does the author use as the principal form for the essay?

b. What is there about the subject that makes using this form appropriate?

c. What other forms does the author employ?

III. WHY DID THE AUTHOR WRITE THIS ESSAY?

a. What is the general purpose of the essay—to inform, persuade, entertain? Is it a combination of these purposes?

b. Does the author state the purpose directly? If so, where?

c. If the author does not state the purpose directly, how does the reader learn it?

d. Does there seem to be a direct relationship between the purpose of the essay and the form the author chose to write in?

IV. TO WHOM IS THE ESSAY ADDRESSED?

a. What kind of knowledge and general experience does the author assume his or her original audience has?

b. What attitudes does the author anticipate the original audience has toward the subject of the essay?

c. What does an audience generally expect from this particular kind of essay—to find out how to do something, to learn what something looks and feels like, to share someone else's experience?

d. What major differences exist between the audience who read this essay in a particular book or magazine and the student audience who is studying it in a college reader?

V. HOW DOES THE AUTHOR USE CERTAIN STRATEGIES TO ACHIEVE HIS OR HER PURPOSE?

a. How does the author catch and hold the reader's interest?

b. How does the author organize and develop the main idea of the essay?

c. How does the author use the strategies of a particular form—e.g., pacing (narration), attributing characteristics (definition), citing authorities (argument)—to accomplish his or her purpose?

d. To what extent have these strategies been effective? Has the author accomplished his or her purpose?

---------- ◆ ----------

Sample Analysis of an Essay

The headnote that accompanies each essay provides pertinent information about the writer's life and works, as well as a general characterization of the essay that follows. The headnote below discusses Virginia Woolf, whose essay "If Shakespeare Had Had a Sister" is annotated and analyzed in the following pages.

Virginia Woolf (1882–1941) was born in London, England, the daughter of Victorian critic and philosopher Leslie Stephen. She educated herself in her father's magnificent library and, after his death, lived with her sister and two brothers in Bloomsbury, a district of London that later became identified with her and the group of writers and artists she entertained. In 1912 she married journalist Leonard Woolf and together they founded the Hogarth Press, which published the work of the Bloomsbury group, including Woolf's own novels. Woolf's adult life was tormented by intermittent periods of nervous depression; finally, she drowned herself in the river near her home at Rodmell. Her novels include Mrs. Dalloway *(1925),* To the Lighthouse *(1927),* Orlando *(1928),* The Waves *(1931), and* The Years *(1938). Woolf's many essays and reviews are collected in books such as* The Common Reader *(1925) and* The Death of the Moth and Other Essays *(1942). One of Woolf's most popular works is* A Room of One's Own *(1929), which grew out of a talk she gave on "Women and Fiction" to the Arts Society. In it, Woolf—an early feminist—offers a spirited analysis of the subject of women and creativity. In this selection, taken from that volume, Woolf creates a hypothetical argument to demonstrate the limitations encountered by women in Shakespeare's time.*

The annotations in the margins of the essay below call attention to the principal strategies Woolf employed in writing it. Following the essay is a brief analysis of how those strategies work. If you acquire the habit of marking the essays you read in this fashion and of consciously analyzing both what the writer says and how he or she says it, you will find that you are more involved in your reading and that you carry over what you learn to your own writing.

If Shakespeare Had Had a Sister

It is a perennial puzzle why no woman wrote a word of that extraordinary [Elizabethan] literature when every other man, it seemed, was capable of song or sonnet. What were the conditions in which women lived, I asked myself; for fiction, imaginative work that is, is not dropped like a pebble upon the ground, as science may be; fiction is like a spider's web, attached ever so lightly perhaps, but still attached to life at all four corners. Often the attachment is scarcely perceptible; Shakespeare's plays, for instance, seem to hang there complete by themselves. But when the web is pulled askew, hooked up at the edge, torn in the middle, one remembers that these webs are not spun in mid-air by incorporeal creatures, but are the work of suffering human beings, and are attached to grossly material things, like health and money and the house we live in.

But what I find ... is that nothing is known about women before the eighteenth century. I have no model in my mind to turn about this way and that. Here am I asking why women did not write poetry in the Elizabethan age, and I am not sure how they were educated; whether they were taught to write; whether they had sitting-rooms to themselves; how many women had children before they were twenty-one; what, in short,

Marginal annotations:

states problem: why didn't women write? what were conditions?

compares science and fiction

description: analogy of fiction and spider's web

cause/effect: writing affected by material things

looks for evidence, finds few facts

they did from eight in the morning till eight at night. They had <u>no money evidently; according to</u> *cites* <u>Professor Trevelyan</u> they were <u>married</u> whether ⎱ *authority:* they liked it or not <u>before they were out of the</u> ⎰ *historian* <u>nursery,</u> at fifteen or sixteen very likely. <u>It would</u> ⎱ *cause/effect* <u>have been extremely odd, even upon this showing,</u> <u>had one of them suddenly written the plays of</u> <u>Shakespeare, I concluded,</u> and I thought of that ⎰ old gentleman, who is dead now, but was a bishop, I think, who declared that it was impossible for any woman, past, present, or to come, to have the genius *ironic* of Shakespeare. He wrote to the papers about it. *citation of* He also told a lady who applied to him for informa- *oversimplified* tion that cats do not as a matter of fact go to *causal* heaven, though they have, he added, souls of a sort. *analysis* How much thinking those old gentlemen used to save one! How the borders of ignorance shrank back at their approach! Cats do not go to heaven. Women cannot write the plays of Shakespeare.

Be that as it may, I could not help thinking, as I looked at the works of Shakespeare on the shelf, that the bishop was right at least in this; it would have been impossible, completely and entirely, for any woman to have written the plays of Shake-speare in the age of Shakespeare. <u>Let me imagine,</u> *begins* <u>since facts are so hard to come by, what would have</u> *narrative* <u>happened had Shakespeare had a wonderfully gifted</u> <u>sister, called Judith, let us say.</u> Shakespeare him-self went, very probably—his mother was an heiress —to the grammar school, where he may have learnt Latin—Ovid, Virgil and Horace—and the elements of grammar and logic. He was, it is well known, a ⎱ wild boy who poached rabbits, perhaps shot a deer, and had, rather sooner than he should have done, to marry a woman in the neighbourhood, who bore him a child rather quicker than was right. That *divided* escapade sent him to <u>seek his fortune in London.</u> *comparison/* He had, it seemed, a taste for the theatre; he began *contrast:* by holding horses at the stage door. Very soon he *A: Shakespear* *description* got <u>work in the theatre,</u> became a successful actor, and <u>lived at the hub of the universe, meeting every-</u> <u>body,</u> knowing everybody, <u>practising his art on the</u> <u>boards, exercising his wits in the streets,</u> and even ⎰

getting access to the palace of the queen. Meanwhile his extraordinarily gifted sister, let us suppose, remained at home. She was as adventurous,
as imaginative, as agog to see the world as he was.

description But she was not sent to school. She had no chance
of learning grammar and logic, let alone of reading
Horace and Virgil. She picked up a book now and
then, one of her brother's perhaps, and read a few
pages. But then her parents came in and told her to
mend the stockings or mind the stew and not moon
about with books and papers. They would have
spoken sharply but kindly, for they were substantial
people who knew the conditions of life for a woman
and loved their daughter—indeed, more likely than
not she was the apple of her father's eye. Perhaps
she scribbled some pages up in an apple loft on
the sly, but was careful to hide them or set fire to
them. Soon, however, before she was out of her
teens, she was to be betrothed to the son of a
neighbouring wool-stapler. She cried out that marriage was hateful to her, and for that she was severely beaten by her father. Then he ceased to scold
her. He begged her instead not to hurt him, not to
shame him in this matter of her marriage. He
would give her a chain of beads or a fine petticoat,
he said; and there were tears in his eyes. How
could she disobey him? How could she break his
heart? The force of her own gift alone drove her
to it. She made up a small parcel of her belong-
ings, let herself down by a rope one summer's night
and took the road to London. She was not seventeen. The birds that sang in the hedge were not
comparisons more musical than she was. She had the quickest
fancy, a gift like her brother's, for the tune of
words. Like him, she had a taste for the theatre.
She stood at the stage door; she wanted to act, she
said. Men laughed in her face. The manager—a
fat, loose-lipped man—guffawed. He bellowed
something about poodles dancing and women acting
—no woman, he said, could possibly be an actress.
He hinted—you can imagine what. She could get
no training in her craft. Could she even seek her
causes dinner in a tavern or roam the streets at midnight?
that led Yet her genius was for fiction and lusted to feed

*B: Shakespeare'
sister*

*causes that
prompted sister
to leave*

*narrative:
sister's trip
and suicide*

to Judith Shakespeare's death abundantly upon the lives of men and women and the study of their ways. At last—for she was very young, oddly like Shakespeare the poet in her face, with the same grey eyes and rounded brows—at last Nick Greene the actor-manager took pity on her; she found herself with child by that gentleman and so—who shall measure the heat and violence of the poet's heart when caught and tangled in a woman's body?—killed herself one winter's night and lies buried at some cross-roads where the omnibuses now stop outside the Elephant and Castle. *effect of attempt to become actress*

moves from narrative to final argument That, more or less, is how the story would run, I think, if a woman in Shakespeare's day had had Shakespeare's genius. But for my part, I agree with the deceased bishop, if such he was—it is unthinkable that any woman in Shakespeare's day should have had Shakespeare's genius. For genius like Shakespeare's is not born among labouring, uneducated, servile people. It was not born in England among the Saxons and the Britons. It is not born today among the working classes. How, then, could it have been born among women whose work began, according to Professor Trevelyan, almost before they were out of the nursery, who were forced to it by their parents and held to it by all the power of law and custom? *deductive argument*

One can analyze Woolf's writing situation like this.

PURPOSE

Woolf's purpose in her talk and *A Room of One's Own* was to disprove the age-old sexist claim that women must be inherently less creative and talented than men because there have been so few famous women writers—or painters or musicians, for that matter. In this essay Woolf wants to explain why women in the sixteenth century created so few masterpieces, and she does so by devising a story that illustrates the conditions under which women lived.

AUDIENCE

Woolf's immediate audiences—those who heard her lecture and those who first read *A Room of One's Own*—were certainly people interested in the arts and in artists; otherwise they would not have attended a meeting of an Arts Society or read a book about women and creativity by a well-known novelist and critic. There were probably many women in both audiences, and they were likely to be especially sympathetic to Woolf's argument and willing to accept her claim that women in the Elizabethan age lived in the kind of society that made it virtually impossible for them to write. Her audience certainly knew of—indeed, probably had read widely in—Shakespeare's great plays and poems and probably knew something about his life. Likewise, they no doubt knew a little about life in the time of Elizabeth I.

The questions that Woolf's audience would have expected her to answer are these: How were the conditions for women in the Elizabethan age different from those for men? What evidence do you have that such conditions existed? How did such conditions affect women writers?

STRATEGIES

Woolf, who was known as a witty and effective speaker, clearly decided that her original listening audience would be more likely to accept her argument if she could personalize it somehow. Thus she created a story to dramatize her points, knowing that she could arouse her audience's sympathy for her imaginary character, Judith Shakespeare. She knew that these tactics would work well with her reading audience as well, and so she drew on her skill as a novelist to shape a compelling narrative enhanced by vivid description. But she also knew that she must appeal to the reason of her intelligent readers, so she concluded the essay with a logical argument.

The essay itself displays the strategies of a number of patterns of writing, but its overall pattern can be identified as ARGUMENT BY CAUSAL ANALYSIS. In it, Woolf proposes to answer the question that she poses in the first sentence: Why were there no women writers in an age of great literature that produced so many men writers? She begins her argument by refusing to DEFINE women as less talented than men; rather she says, in effect, literature necessarily grows out of a writer's life and must be affected by the material elements of that life: health, money, and living conditions. Therefore if we look at the conditions under which women live, we may be able to understand why they didn't write.

Woolf then looks for evidence to document what those conditions were. She finds that "nothing is known about women before the eighteenth century" but does cite the opinion of a historian of her time who wrote that Elizabethan women had no money of their own and were married by the time they were fifteen or sixteen. To supplement this evidence, Woolf creates a NARRATIVE in which she uses COMPARISON AND CONTRAST to show the difference between a boy's life and a girl's life at the time of Shakespeare. Boys were educated and were allowed to travel, to undertake adventures, and to act on the stage. Girls were not educated, were expected to work at home, and were married off without their consent. Woolf uses DESCRIPTION to suggest what would have happened to an Elizabethan girl who went to London by herself and tried to act on the stage.

At the end of the essay Woolf uses a logical argument to clinch her case. She has presented the CAUSES that drove the imaginary Judith Shakespeare to her death; now she turns from her story to analyze the implications or EFFECTS of those causes on women in the Elizabethan age. Her final paragraph employs deductive logic, which can be diagrammed like this:

Major premise: Genius like Shakespeare's is not born among laboring, uneducated, servile people.

Minor premise: In the Elizabethan age, women were laboring, uneducated, servile people.

Conclusion: Therefore genius was not born among women in the Elizabethan age.

But the heart of Woolf's essay—the message it delivers —is greater than its summary logical statement. Woolf has used multiple writing strategies to create an image that lingers in the reader's mind. The emotional effect of that image, buttressed by the rational evidence of the essay's concluding argument, convinces the reader that historical conditions of inequality, and not innate lack of talent, have hindered women's creative expression. Thus Woolf has achieved her purpose.

---- ♦ ----

About the Writing Assignments

The Riverside Reader emphasizes the productive relationship between *active* reading and *effective* writing. At the conclusion of each section of readings, the editors have provided writing assignments that contain the following features:

Points to Consider focuses on *three* elements of the writing situation: PURPOSE, AUDIENCE, STRATEGIES. These points summarize the information on those elements outlined in the introduction to each section.

Prewriting Exercises suggests activities that will generate ideas for writing. They are designed to help you get started on an assignment.

Topics for Writing in Class suggests short writing assignments that will usually allow you to complete a first draft in one class period. The topics are deliberately narrow in focus.

Topics for Writing out of Class suggests longer writing assignments that allow you to develop a topic more fully. They give you the chance to gather material and try various strategies.

The Riverside Reader has grown out of the strong belief that active reading and effective writing are related and are essential to the learning process. After all, as a college student today you are one of tomorrow's decision makers. Active reading will help you expand your knowledge and sharpen your judgment of the ideas that have shaped your life. Attempting to express that knowledge and judgment effectively in your own writing prepares you for a life of imaginative participation in and intelligent assessment of your own culture.

THE
RIVERSIDE
READER

NARRATION

DEFINITION

A narrative essay is a story that makes a point. It provides a detailed, personal account of some memorable experience—a first trip alone, a last-minute political victory, a picnic in the park. The experience is arranged in some kind of chronological sequence by the storyteller (usually called the *narrator*), who was involved in the events, either as a participant or an observer, and who wants to tell an audience what happened—I took a wrong turn, she made the right speech, we selected the perfect spot. The verb *to narrate* comes from the verb *to know*. A narrator, then, is someone who knows what happened, knows what the experience means, and knows how to tell a story about that experience so that its meaning is made clear.

PURPOSE

Narration, storytelling, is used for *three* purposes. In its simplest form, narration is used to introduce or illustrate a complicated subject. For example, a writer might begin an explanation of the energy crisis by recounting a personal anecdote (a little story) that dramatizes wastefulness. Or a writer might conclude an argument in favor of gun control by narrating an account of a tragic shooting accident.

In a more extended form, narration is used in the personal essay not as a single example but as primary evidence in the analysis of an issue or theme. A writer's whole essay might be devoted to the narration of a personal experience in a foreign country that produced a new awareness of patriotism. Even though the narrative material might provide the primary evidence for such an essay, the narrative purpose (what happened) might still be secondary to other purposes—to *explain* the causes of the new awareness (why it happened) or to *argue* the necessity of such an awareness (why all people should reach the same conclusion about what happened).

The most extensive use of narration appears in autobiography, biography, and fiction. In these forms narrative material is more than example or evidence. It is subject. Writers may want to *explain* why an event occurred as it did or to *argue* that such an event should never occur again, but they will usually imply rather than state such purposes. Their primary purpose is to tell what happened—to report the events of a minute, a week, or a lifetime that shaped or were shaped by people.

AUDIENCE

Writers of narrative essays must be concerned about how much they have to tell their readers. Because a narrative essay is based on a personal experience, few readers will know the story before it is narrated. They may know similar stories or have had similar experiences, but they do not know *this* story. Under these circumstances, writers must decide how much information their readers need to understand what happened. Do they need to know every detail of the story, only a summary of its action, or some mixture of detail and summary?

Storytellers answer such questions by assessing the alternatives within a story and by anticipating the expectations of their audience. They know they can tell the same story many ways, adding and deleting material to fit a particular situation. They know most audiences expect writers to take some time to develop a story—to describe the principal characters, to set up the major scene. But all writers know that audiences are quick to spot boring storytellers. There are certain telltale signs—an inability to distinguish between major and minor details; a tendency to get sidetracked on some unrelated issue; a knack for confusing dates, names, and the sequence of events; and the unalterable belief that simply because something happened to them, everybody will be fascinated to hear about it.

STRATEGIES

Good storytellers understand the expectations of their audience and so develop strategies to ensure the success of their narratives. For openers, good storytellers know that an experience and a story about that experience are not the same thing. Any experience, regardless of duration, seems disorganized and undefined; a successful story about that experience must be focused and purposeful.

The first step in transforming an experience into a narrative is to locate the *story* in the story, to identify the CONFLICT on which the action focuses. The conflict may be between (1) the narrator and himself, as in Jean Shepherd's reaction to his blind date; (2) the narrator and others, as in Maxine Hong Kingston's attempt to understand her family tradition; or (3) the narrator and the environment, as in E. B. White's story about the site of his summer vacations.

Once the conflict is identified, the narrative must be arranged so the reader knows how the conflict began, how it developed, and how it was resolved. PLOT is the sequence of events that forms the beginning, middle, and end of a story, but that sequence may not present the events of the story as they actually happened. Sometimes stories do follow a simple chronological pattern. Ron Kovic's account of a military patrol begins at the beginning and describes events as they occur. But other stories begin in the middle or even near the end. Alex Haley's narrative begins near the end and then works its way backward to the beginning as he searches for his ancestral roots. In each case, the pattern of the plot is determined by the purpose of the narrative: to describe the immediate causes of an event in the present or to discover the ultimate causes of the present in the events of the past.

Determining the beginning, middle, and end of a story helps establish how each event in these sections should be paced. PACE is the speed with which events are recounted. Some events can be narrated quickly. Details can be omitted, time compressed, experience summarized. For example, E. B. White summarizes his first summer at the lake in a single sentence. Other events, because they are vital to the author's purpose, require more deliberate pacing. Every detail must be included, time must be extended, and the situation, rather than being summarized, must be presented as a scene: the narrator must not only *tell* what happened but must actually *show* what happened. White creates such a scene at the conclusion of his narrative when he makes his readers see the afternoon thunderstorm and feel the cold, wet swimming suit.

After writers have identified the conflict, organized the plot, and determined the pace of their narratives, they must SELECT A POINT OF VIEW. In narration, point of view refers to the person and position of the narrator (point) and the attitude toward the narrative (view). *Person* means simply whether the author tells the story as "I" saw it (as in Maxine Hong Kingston's mother's story about "a no-name woman") or whether the author indicates how someone else, "he" or "she," saw it (as in Ron Kovic's third-person account of a military maneuver). *Position* means the narrator's proximity to the action in space and time. A narrator may be involved in the action of the narrative or may view it from the position of an observer; a narrator may tell about events as they are happening or many years after they have taken place. For example, Jean Shepherd (the adolescent) is the chief actor in his narrative, but Jean Shepherd (the author) is removed from those events by the passage of time. Person and place help create the narrator's *attitude*—how he or she feels about the actions to be presented and interpreted. The attitudes of the narrators in the following selections might be characterized as whimsical (Shepherd), pensive (White), perplexed (Kingston), detached (Kovic), and enthralled (Haley).

Point of view not only determines the presentation of a narrative but also establishes its point. Remember, a narrative essay is a story that makes a point. Mark Twain once said that a good story had to accomplish something and arrive somewhere. If writers know their story, know what it means, know how they feel about it, they are able to plot and pace it so that it makes its point. The essays in this section do not wander aimlessly into confusion, but proceed to their conclusions with absolute certainty.

The Endless Streetcar Ride into
the Night, and the Tinfoil Noose

JEAN SHEPHERD

———————— ◆ ————————

*Jean Shepherd was born in Chicago, Illinois, in 1929
and attended the University of Maryland and Indiana
University. He has had a varied career as an author,
actor, and radio and television personality. Shepherd's
articles in* Playboy *and* Car and Driver, *his all-night
radio programs on WOR (New York City), his television series for PBS, "Jean Shepherd's America," and
his feature film "The Christmas Story," all treat his
humorous misadventures growing up in the Midwest.
His books include* The America of George Ade *(1961);*
In God We Trust: All Others Pay Cash *(1967);* Wanda
Hicky's Night of Golden Memories and Other Dis-
asters *(1972);* The Ferrari in the Bedroom *(1973); and*
A Fistful of Fig Newtons *(1981). In "The Endless
Streetcar Ride into the Night, and the Tinfoil Noose"
(from* In God We Trust) *Shepherd tells a story about
a common experience, a blind date, that leads to a
moment of truth.*

Mewling, puking babes. That's the way we all start.   1
Damply clinging to someone's shoulder, burping weakly,
clawing our way into life. *All* of us. Then gradually,
surely, we begin to divide into two streams, all marching
together up that long yellow brick road of life, but on
opposite sides of the street. One crowd goes on to become
the Official people, peering out at us from television
screens; magazine covers. They are forever appearing in
newsreels, carrying attaché cases, surrounded by banks of
microphones while the world waits for their decisions and
statements. And the rest of us go on to become . . . just us.

They are the Prime Ministers, the Presidents, Cabinet 2
members, Stars, dynamic molders of the Universe, while
we remain forever the onlookers, the applauders of their
real lives.

Forever down in the dark dungeons of our souls we 3
ask ourselves:

"How did they get away from me? When did I make 4
that first misstep that took me forever to the wrong side
of the street, to become eternally part of the accursed,
anonymous Audience?"

It seems like one minute we're all playing around back 5
of the garage, kicking tin cans and yelling at girls, and the
next instant you find yourself doomed to exist as an office
boy in the Mail Room of Life, while another ex-mewling,
puking babe sends down Dicta, says "No comment" to the
Press, and lives a real, genuine *Life* on the screen of the
world.

Countless sufferers at this hour are spending billions 6
of dollars and endless man hours lying on analysts' couches,
trying to pinpoint the exact moment that they stepped off
the track and into the bushes forever.

It all hinges on one sinister reality that is rarely men- 7
tioned, no doubt due to its implacable, irreversible inevi-
tability. These decisions cannot be changed, no matter
how many brightly cheerful, buoyantly optimistic books
on HOW TO ACHIEVE A RICHER, FULLER, MORE BOUNTIFUL
LIFE or SEVEN MAGIC GOLDEN KEYS TO INSTANT DYNAMIC
SUCCESS or THE SECRET OF HOW TO BECOME A BILLIONAIRE
we read, or how many classes are attended for instruction
in handshaking, back-slapping, grinning, and making
After-Dinner speeches. Joseph Stalin was not a Dale Carnegie graduate. He went all the way. It is an unpleasant
truth that is swallowed, if at all, like a rancid, bitter pill.
A star is a star; a numberless cipher is a numberless cipher.

Even more eerie a fact is that the Great Divide is rarely 8
a matter of talent or personality. Or even luck. Adolf
Hitler had a notoriously weak handshake. His smile was,
if anything, a vapid mockery. But inevitably his star

zoomed higher and higher. Cinema luminaries of the first order are rarely blessed with even the modicum of Talent, and often their physical beauty leaves much to be desired. What is the difference between Us and Them, We and They, the Big Ones and the great, teeming rabble?

There are about four times in a man's life, or a woman's, 9 too, for that matter, when unexpectedly, from out of the darkness, the blazing carbon lamp, the cosmic searchlight of Truth shines full upon them. It is how we react to those moments that forever seals our fate. One crowd simply puts on its sunglasses, lights another cigar, and heads for the nearest plush French restaurant in the jazziest section of town, sits down and orders a drink, and ignores the whole thing. While we, the Doomed, caught in the brilliant glare of illumination, see ourselves inescapably for what we are, and from that day on skulk in the weeds, hoping no one else will spot us.

Those moments happen when we are least able to fend 10 them off. I caught the first one full in the face when I was fourteen. The fourteenth summer is a magic one for all kids. You have just slid out of the pupa stage, leaving your old baby skin behind, and have not yet become a grizzled, hardened, tax-paying beetle. At fourteen you are made of cellophane. You curl easily and everyone can see through you.

When I was fourteen, Life was flowing through me in 11 a deep, rich torrent of Castoria. How did I know that the first rocks were just ahead, and I was about to have my keel ripped out on the reef? Sometimes you feel as though you are alone in a rented rowboat, bailing like mad in the darkness with a leaky bailing can. It is important to know that there are at least two billion other ciphers in the same boat, bailing with the same leaky can. They all think they are alone and are crossed with an evil star. They are right.

I'm fourteen years old, in my sophomore year at high 12 school. One day Schwartz, my purported best friend, sidled up to me edgily outside of school while we were waiting on the steps to come in after lunch. He proceeded to outline his plan:

"Helen's old man won't let me take her out on a date [13] on Saturday night unless I get a date for her girlfriend. A double date. The old coot figures, I guess, that if there are four of us there won't be no monkey business. Well, how about it? Do you want to go on a blind date with this chick? I never seen her."

Well. For years I had this principle—absolutely *no* [14] blind dates. I was a man of perception and taste, and life was short. But there is a time in your life when you have to stop taking and begin to give just a little. For the first time the warmth of sweet Human Charity brought the roses to my cheeks. After all, Schwartz was my friend. It was little enough to do, have a blind date with some no doubt skinny, pimply girl for your best friend. I would do it for Schwartz. He would do as much for me.

"Okay. Okay, Schwartz." [15]

Then followed the usual ribald remarks, feckless boast- [16] ing, and dirty jokes about dates in general and girls in particular. It was decided that next Saturday we would go all the way. I had a morning paper route at the time, and my life savings stood at about $1.80. I was all set to blow it on one big night.

I will never forget that particular Saturday as long as [17] I live. The air was as soft as the finest of spun silk. The scent of lilacs hung heavy. The catalpa trees rustled in the early evening breeze from off the Lake. The inner Me itched in that nameless way, that indescribable way that only the fourteen-year-old Male fully knows.

All that afternoon I had carefully gone over my ward- [18] robe to select the proper symphony of sartorial brilliance. That night I set out wearing my magnificent electric blue sport coat, whose shoulders were so wide that they hung out over my frame like vast, drooping eaves, so wide I had difficulty going through an ordinary door head-on. The electric blue sport coat that draped voluminously almost to my knees, its wide lapels flapping soundlessly in the slightest breeze. My pleated gray flannel slacks began just below my breastbone and indeed chafed my armpits. High-belted, cascading down finally to grasp my ankles in a vise-like grip. My tie, indeed one of my most prized possessions, had been a gift from my Aunt Glenn upon the state occasion of graduation from eighth grade. It was of a beautiful silky fabric, silvery pearly colored, four inches wide at the fulcrum, and of such a length to endanger occasionally my zipper in moments of haste. Handpainted upon it was a magnificent blood-red snail.

I had spent fully two hours carefully arranging and rearranging my great mop of wavy hair, into which I had rubbed fully a pound and a half of Greasy Kid Stuff. 19

Helen and Schwartz waited on the corner under the streetlight at the streetcar stop near Junie Jo's home. Her name was Junie Jo Prewitt. I won't forget it quickly, although she has, no doubt, forgotten mine. I walked down the dark street alone, past houses set back off the street, through the darkness, past privet hedges, under elm trees, through air rich and ripe with promise. Her house stood back from the street even farther than the others. It sort of crouched in the darkness, looking out at me, kneeling. Pregnant with Girldom. A real Girlfriend house. 20

The first faint touch of nervousness filtered through the marrow of my skullbone as I knocked on the door of the screen-enclosed porch. No answer. I knocked again, louder. Through the murky screens I could see faint lights in the house itself. Still no answer. Then I found a small doorbell button buried in the sash. I pressed. From far off in the bowels of the house I heard two chimes "Bong" politely. It sure didn't sound like our doorbell. We had a real ripper that went off like a broken buzz saw, more of a BRRRAAAAKKK than a muffled Bong. This was a rich people's doorbell. 21

The door opened and there stood a real, genuine, gold-plated Father: potbelly, underwear shirt, suspenders, and all. 22

"Well?" he asked. 23

For one blinding moment of embarrassment I couldn't   24
remember her name. After all, she was a blind date. I
couldn't just say:

"I'm here to pick up some girl."   25

He turned back into the house and hollered: 26

"JUNIE JO! SOME KID'S HERE!"   27

"Heh, heh. . . ." I countered.   28

He led me into the living room. It was an itchy house,   29
sticky stucco walls of a dull orange color, and all over the
floor this Oriental rug with the design crawling around,
making loops and sworls. I sat on an overstuffed chair
covered in stiff green mohair that scratched even through
my slacks. Little twisty bridge lamps stood everywhere.
I instantly began to sweat down the back of my clean
white shirt. Like I said, it was a very itchy house. It had
little lamps sticking out of the walls that looked like
phony candles, with phony glass orange flames. The rug
started moaning to itself.

I sat on the edge of the chair and tried to talk to this   30
Father. He was a Cub fan. We struggled under water for
what seemed like an hour and a half, when suddenly I
heard someone coming down the stairs. First the feet;
then those legs, and there she was. She was magnificent!
The greatest-looking girl I ever saw in my life! I have hit
the double jackpot! And on a blind date! Great Scot!

My senses actually reeled as I clutched the arm of that   31
bilge-green chair for support. Junie Jo Prewitt made Cleo-
patra look like a Girl Scout!

Five minutes later we are sitting in the streetcar, head-   32
ing toward the bowling alley. I am sitting next to the most
fantastic creation in the Feminine department known
to Western man. There are the four of us in that long,
yellow-lit streetcar. No one else was aboard; just us four.
I, naturally, being a trained gentleman, sat on the aisle to
protect her from candy wrappers and cigar butts and such.
Directly ahead of me, also on the aisle, sat Schwartz, his
arm already flung affectionately in a death grip around
Helen's neck as we boomed and rattled through the night.

I casually flung my right foot up onto my left knee so 33
that she could see my crepe-soled, perforated, wing-toed,
Scotch bluchers with the two-toned laces. I started to
work my famous charm on her. Casually, with my practiced offhand, cynical, cutting, sardonic humor I told her
about how my Old Man had cracked the block in the
Oldsmobile, how the White Sox were going to have a good
year this year, how my kid brother wet his pants when
he saw a snake, how I figured it was going to rain, what
a great guy Schwartz was, what a good second baseman I
was, how I figured I might go out for football. On and
on I rolled, like Old Man River, pausing significantly for
her to pick up the conversation. Nothing.

Ahead of us Schwartz and Helen were almost indis- 34
tinguishable one from the other. They giggled, bit each
other's ears, whispered, clasped hands, and in general made
me itch even more.

From time to time Junie Jo would bend forward stiffly 35
from the waist and say something I could never quite
catch into Helen's right ear.

I told her my great story of the time that Uncle Carl 36
lost his false teeth down the airshaft. Still nothing. Out
of the corner of my eye I could see that she had her coat
collar turned up, hiding most of her face as she sat silently,
looking forward past Helen Weathers into nothingness.

I told her about this old lady on my paper route who 37
chews tobacco, and roller skates in the backyard every
morning. I still couldn't get through to her. Casually I
inched my right arm up over the back of the seat behind
her shoulders. The acid test. She leaned forward, avoid-
ing my arm, and stayed that way.

"Heh, heh, heh. . . ." 38

As nonchalantly as I could, I retrieved it, battling a 39
giant cramp in my right shoulder blade. I sat in silence
for a few seconds, sweating heavily as ahead Schwartz
and Helen are going at it hot and heavy.

It was then that I became aware of someone saying 40
something to me. It was an empty car. There was no one
else but us. I glanced around, and there it was. Above us
a line of car cards looked down on the empty streetcar.
One was speaking directly to me, to me alone.

DO YOU OFFEND?

Do I *offend*?! 41

With no warning, from up near the front of the car 42
where the motorman is steering I see this thing coming
down the aisle directly toward *me*. It's coming closer
and closer. I can't escape it. It's this blinding, fantastic,
brilliant, screaming blue light. I am spread-eagled in it.
There's a pin sticking through my thorax. I see it all
now.

I AM THE BLIND DATE! 43

ME!! 44

I'M the one they're being nice to! 45

I'm suddenly getting fatter, more itchy. My new shoes 46
are like bowling balls with laces; thick, rubber-crepe bowling balls. My great tie that Aunt Glenn gave me is two
feet wide, hanging down to the floor like some crinkly
tinfoil noose. My beautiful hand-painted snail is seven
feet high, sitting upon my shoulder, burping. Great Scot!
It is all clear to me in the searing white light of Truth.
My friend Schwartz, I can see him saying to Junie Jo:

"I got this crummy fat friend who never has a date. 47
Let's give him a break and...."

I AM THE BLIND DATE! 48

They are being nice to *me!* She is the one who is out 49
on a Blind Date. A Blind Date that didn't make it.

In the seat ahead, the merriment rose to a crescendo. 50
Helen tittered; Schwartz cackled. The marble statue next
to me stared gloomily out into the darkness as our streetcar rattled on. The ride went on and on.

I AM THE BLIND DATE! 51

I didn't say much the rest of the night. There wasn't 52
much to be said.

———— ◆ ————

For Study and Discussion

QUESTIONS ABOUT PURPOSE

1. What theory of fate does Shepherd propose to illustrate with his narrative?
2. What evidence does Shepherd's conclusion provide to confirm his theory?
3. What is Shepherd's purpose in illustrating this theory? Does he intend to persuade, inform, or entertain? Explain your answer.

QUESTIONS ABOUT AUDIENCE

1. Shepherd considers the question of audience in the first paragraph. Does he envision his readers as "official people" or "just us"?
2. What assumptions does Shepherd make about his audience in paragraphs 6, 7, and 8? Why does he think the information in these paragraphs will help his readers understand what happened?
3. Shepherd the character tells Junie Jo Prewitt several stories on their blind date. Why doesn't Shepherd the author repeat those stories in detail for his audience?

QUESTIONS ABOUT STRATEGIES

1. Where does Shepherd begin the narrative portion of his essay? How would you divide that narrative into beginning, middle, and end?
2. How does Shepherd pace various scenes in the narrative? For example, how does the pace of paragraph 18 or 33 contribute to his purpose?
3. How does Shepherd use the notion of "blind date"

to demonstrate a change of point of view in his conclusion?

QUESTIONS FOR DISCUSSION

1. How would you characterize the difference between Shepherd the adolescent and Shepherd the author?
2. How does Shepherd use exaggeration to illustrate certain details of his narrative? To what extent is exaggeration an appropriate technique for describing adolescent romance?
3. How do you respond to Shepherd's assertion that the Big Ones (important, official people) become Big Ones by ignoring moments of truth? What evidence could you offer to suggest that the opposite assertion is true—that is, that people must face such moments of truth in order to know enough about themselves to become Big Ones?

Once More to the Lake

E. B. WHITE

———— ◆ ————

E(lwyn) B(rooks) White was born in 1899 in Mt. Vernon, New York. He was educated at Cornell University, where he was taught English composition by William Strunk, Jr., whose textbook, the legendary Elements of Style, White later revised for trade publication. In 1927 White began his career in journalism, working on the staff of The New Yorker, contributing a column ("One Man's Meat") to Harper's (1938–1943), and developing the prose style that earned him the reputation as America's finest essayist. His books include The Second Tree From the Corner (1954), The Points of My Compass (1962), and three classic children's stories, Stuart Little (1945), Charlotte's Web (1952), and The Trumpet of the Swan (1970). "Once More to the Lake," reprinted from The Essays of E. B. White (1977), is a narrative reverie about White's trip with his son to the site of his own childhood vacations.

August 1941

One summer, along about 1904, my father rented a camp on a lake in Maine and took us all there for the month of August. We all got ringworm from some kittens and had to rub Pond's Extract on our arms and legs night and morning, and my father rolled over in a canoe with all his clothes on; but outside of that the vacation was a success and from then on none of us ever thought there was any place in the world like that lake in Maine. We returned summer after summer—always on August 1 for one month. I have since become a salt-water man, but sometimes in summer there are days when the restlessness of the tides and the fearful cold of the sea water and the incessant wind that blows across the afternoon and into the evening make me wish for the placidity of a lake in the woods. A few weeks ago this feeling got so strong I bought myself a couple of bass hooks and a spinner and returned to the lake where we used to go, for a week's fishing and to revisit old haunts.

I took along my son, who had never had any fresh 2 water up his nose and who had seen lily pads only from train windows. On the journey over to the lake I began to wonder what it would be like. I wondered how time would have marred this unique, this holy spot—the coves and streams, the hills that the sun set behind, the camps and the paths behind the camps. I was sure that the tarred road would have found it out, and I wondered in what other ways it would be desolated. It is strange how much you can remember about places like that once you allow your mind to return into the grooves that lead back. You remember one thing, and that suddenly reminds you of another thing. I guess I remembered clearest of all the early mornings, when the lake was cool and motionless, remembered how the bedroom smelled of the lumber it was made of and of the wet woods whose scent entered through the screen. The partitions in the camp were thin and did not extend clear to the top of the rooms, and as I was always the first up I would dress softly so as not to wake the others, and sneak out into the sweet outdoors and start out in the canoe, keeping close along the shore in the long shadows of the pines. I remembered being very careful never to rub my paddle against the gunwale for fear of disturbing the stillness of the cathedral.

The lake had never been what you would call a wild 3 lake. There were cottages sprinkled around the shores, and it was in farming country although the shores of the lake were quite heavily wooded. Some of the cottages were owned by nearby farmers, and you would live at the shore and eat your meals at the farmhouse. That's what our family did. But although it wasn't wild, it was a fairly large and undisturbed lake and there were places in it that, to a child at least, seemed infinitely remote and primeval.

I was right about the tar: it led to within half a mile 4
of the shore. But when I got back there, with my boy,
and we settled into a camp near a farmhouse and into
the kind of summertime I had known, I could tell that it
was going to be pretty much the same as it had been before—I knew it, lying in bed the first morning, smelling
the bedroom and hearing the boy sneak quietly out and
go off along the shore in a boat. I began to sustain the
illusion that he was I, and therefore, by simple transposi-
tion, that I was my father. This sensation persisted, kept
cropping up all the time we were there. It was not an
entirely new feeling, but in this setting it grew much
stronger. I seemed to be living a dual existence. I would
be in the middle of some simple act, I would be picking
up a bait box or laying down a table fork, or I would be
saying something, and suddenly it would be not I but my
father who was saying the words or making the gesture.
It gave me a creepy sensation.

We went fishing the first morning. I felt the same 5
damp moss covering the worms in the bait can, and saw
the dragonfly alight on the tip of my rod as it hovered a
few inches from the surface of the water. It was the arrival of this fly that convinced me beyond any doubt that
everything was as it always had been, that the years were
a mirage and that there had been no years. The small
waves were the same, chucking the rowboat under the
chin as we fished at anchor, and the boat was the same
boat, the same color green and the ribs broken in the
same places, and under the floorboards the same fresh-
water leavings and débris—the dead helgramite, the wisps
of moss, the rusty discarded fishhook, the dried blood from
yesterday's catch. We stared silently at the tips of our
rods, at the dragonflies that came and went. I lowered the
tip of mine into the water, tentatively, pensively dislodg-
ing the fly, which darted two feet away, poised, darted
two feet back, and came to rest again a little farther up
the rod. There had been no years between the ducking of

this dragonfly and the other one—the one that was part of memory. I looked at the boy, who was silently watching his fly, and it was my hands that held his rod, my eyes watching. I felt dizzy and didn't know which rod I was at the end of.

We caught two bass, hauling them in briskly as though they were mackerel, pulling them over the side of the boat in a businesslike manner without any landing net, and stunning them with a blow on the back of the head. When we got back for a swim before lunch, the lake was exactly where we had left it, the same number of inches from the dock, and there was only the merest suggestion of a breeze. This seemed an utterly enchanted sea, this lake you could leave to its own devices for a few hours and come back to, and find that it had not stirred, this constant and trustworthy body of water. In the shallows, the dark, water-soaked sticks and twigs, smooth and old, were undulating in clusters on the bottom against the clean ribbed sand, and the track of the mussel was plain. A school of minnows swam by, each minnow with its small individual shadow, doubling the attendance, so clear and sharp in the sunlight. Some of the other campers were in swimming, along the shore, one of them with a cake of soap, and the water felt thin and clear and unsubstantial. Over the years there had been this person with the cake of soap, this cultist, and here he was. There had been no years.

Up to the farmhouse to dinner through the teeming, dusty field, the road under our sneakers was only a two-track road. The middle track was missing, the one with the marks of the hooves and the splotches of dried, flaky manure. There had always been three tracks to choose from in choosing which track to walk in; now the choice was narrowed down to two. For a moment I missed terribly the middle alternative. But the way led past the tennis court, and something about the way it lay there in the sun reassured me; the tape had loosened along the backline, the alleys were green with plantains and other weeds,

6

7

and the net (installed in June and removed in September) sagged in the dry noon, and the whole place steamed with midday heat and hunger and emptiness. There was a choice of pie for dessert, and one was blueberry and one was apple, and the waitresses were the same country girls, there having been no passage of time, only the illusion of it as in a dropped curtain—the waitresses were still fifteen; their hair had been washed, that was the only difference —they had been to the movies and seen the pretty girls with the clean hair.

Summertime, oh, summertime, pattern of life indelible, the fade-proof lake, the woods unshatterable, the pasture with the sweetfern and the juniper forever and ever, summer without end; this was the background, and the life along the shore was the design, the cottages with their innocent and tranquil design, their tiny docks with the flagpole and the American flag floating against the white clouds in the blue sky, the little paths over the roots of the trees leading from camp to camp and the paths leading back to the outhouses and the can of lime for sprinkling, and at the souvenir counters at the store the miniature birch-bark canoes and the postcards that showed things looking a little better than they looked. This was the American family at play, escaping the city heat, wondering whether the newcomers in the camp at the head of the cove were "common" or "nice," wondering whether it was true that the people who drove up for Sunday dinner at the farmhouse were turned away because there wasn't enough chicken.

It seemed to me, as I kept remembering all this, that those times and those summers had been infinitely precious and worth saving. There had been jollity and peace and goodness. The arriving (at the beginning of August) had been so big a business in itself, at the railway station the farm wagon drawn up, the first smell of the pine-laden air, the first glimpse of the smiling farmer, and the great importance of the trunks and your father's enormous authority in such matters, and the feel of the wagon under

8

9

you for the long ten-mile haul, and at the top of the last long hill catching the first view of the lake after eleven months of not seeing this cherished body of water. The shouts and cries of the other campers when they saw you, and the trunks to be unpacked, to give up their rich burden. (Arriving was less exciting nowadays, when you sneaked up in your car and parked it under a tree near the camp and took out the bags and in five minutes it was all over, no fuss, no loud wonderful fuss about trunks.)

Peace and goodness and jollity. The only thing that   10
was wrong now, really, was the sound of the place, an unfamiliar nervous sound of the outboard motors. This was the note that jarred, the one thing that would sometimes break the illusion and set the years moving. In those other summertimes all motors were inboard; and when they were at a little distance, the noise they made was a sedative, an ingredient of summer sleep. They were one-cylinder and two-cylinder engines, and some were make-and-break and some were jump-spark, but they all made a sleepy sound across the lake. The one-lungers throbbed and fluttered, and the twin-cylinder ones purred and purred, and that was a quiet sound, too. But now the campers all had outboards. In the daytime, in the hot mornings, these motors made a petulant, irritable sound; at night, in the still evening when the afterglow lit the water, they whined about one's ears like mosquitoes. My boy loved our rented outboard, and his great desire was to achieve single-handed mastery over it, and authority, and he soon learned the trick of choking it a little (but not too much), and the adjustment of the needle valve. Watching him I would remember the things you could do with the old one-cylinder engine with the heavy flywheel, how you could have it eating out of your hand if you got really close to it spiritually. Motorboats in those days didn't have clutches, and you would make a landing by shutting off the motor at the proper time and coasting in with a dead rudder. But there was a way of reversing them, if you learned the trick, by cutting the switch and putting

it on again exactly on the final dying revolution of the flywheel, so that it would kick back against compression and begin reversing. Approaching a dock in a strong following breeze, it was difficult to slow up sufficiently by the ordinary coasting method, and if a boy felt he had complete mastery over his motor, he was tempted to keep it running beyond its time and then reverse it a few feet from the dock. It took a cool nerve, because if you threw the switch a twentieth of a second too soon you would catch the flywheel when it still had speed enough to go up past center, and the boat would leap ahead, charging bull-fashion at the dock.

We had a good week at the camp. The bass were biting 11 well and the sun shone endlessly, day after day. We would be tired at night and lie down in the accumulated heat of the little bedrooms after the long hot day and the breeze would stir almost imperceptibly outside and the smell of the swamp drift in through the rusty screens. Sleep would come easily and in the morning the red squirrel would be on the roof, tapping out his gay routine. I kept remembering everything, lying in bed in the mornings—the small steamboat that had a long rounded stern like the lip of a Ubangi, and how quietly she ran on the moonlight sails, when the older boys played their mandolins and the girls sang and we ate doughnuts dipped in sugar, and how sweet the music was on the water in the shining night, and what it had felt like to think about girls then. After breakfast we would go up to the store and the things were in the same place—the minnows in a bottle, the plugs and spinners disarranged and pawed over by the youngsters from the boys' camp, the Fig Newtons and the Beeman's gum. Outside, the road was tarred and cars stood in front of the store. Inside, all was just as it had always been, except there was more Coca-Cola and not so much Moxie and root beer and birch beer and sarsaparilla. We would walk out with the bottle of pop apiece and sometimes the pop would backfire up our noses and hurt. We explored the streams, quietly, where the turtles slid off the sunny logs and dug their way into the soft bottom; and we lay on the town wharf and fed worms to the tame bass. Everywhere we went I had trouble making out which was I, the one walking at my side, the one walking in my pants.

One afternoon while we were there at that lake a thunderstorm came up. It was like the revival of an old melodrama that I had seen long ago with childish awe. The second-act climax of the drama of the electrical disturbance over a lake in America had not changed in any important respect. This was the big scene, still the big scene. The whole thing was so familiar, the first feeling of oppression and heat and a general air around camp of not wanting to go very far away. In midafternoon (it was all the same) a curious darkening of the sky, and a lull in everything that had made life tick; and then the way the boats suddenly swung the other way at their moorings with the coming of a breeze out of the new quarter, and the premonitory rumble. Then the kettle drum, then the snare, then the bass drum and cymbals, then crackling light against the dark, and the gods grinning and licking their chops in the hills. Afterward the calm, the rain steadily rustling in the calm lake, the return of light and hope and spirits, and the campers running out in joy and relief to go swimming in the rain, their bright cries perpetuating the deathless joke about how they were getting simply drenched, and the children screaming with delight at the new sensation of bathing in the rain, and the joke about getting drenched linking the generations in a strong indestructible chain. And the comedian who waded in carrying an umbrella.

When the others went swimming, my son said he was going in, too. He pulled his dripping trunks from the line where they had hung all through the shower and wrung them out. Languidly, and with no thought of going in, I watched him, his hard little body, skinny and bare, saw him wince slightly as he pulled up around his vitals the small, soggy, icy garment. As he buckled the swollen belt, suddenly my groin felt the chill of death.

——— ◆ ———

For Study and Discussion

QUESTIONS ABOUT PURPOSE

1. Why does White return to the lake? What differences does he see between the lake and the seashore?
2. What theory about the pattern of summer life does White propose to illustrate with his narrative?
3. To what extent does the last paragraph alter that theory?

QUESTIONS ABOUT AUDIENCE

1. What kinds of common experiences does White assume he shares with his readers?
2. To what extent would people who have never spent a summer on a lake or been parents appreciate this essay?
3. White anticipated that his readers would be like himself. Did he anticipate that his readers would be like his son (that is, young people)? Explain your answer.

QUESTIONS ABOUT STRATEGIES

1. How much space does White devote to the lake as it is now and how much to the lake as it used to be? How does this decision emphasize his purpose?
2. How does White pace paragraph 5 or 8? What kind of mood does he create with this pacing?
3. What problem with point of view does White have throughout his stay at the lake? How does he use that problem to control the point of view of his essay?

QUESTIONS FOR DISCUSSION

1. In what way might White's description of the motor-boat "running beyond its time" provide a metaphor for the ideas in his essay?
2. Why do you think we remember summer experiences with such special fondness?
3. What does White's essay illustrate about the ability to repeat experiences? What has your experience been when you have attempted such experiments?

On Patrol

RON KOVIC

♦

Ron Kovic was born on the fourth of July, 1946, in Massapequa, Long Island, where his father worked in a supermarket. He lived out a typical all-American boyhood, dreaming of becoming a baseball star and leading men like John Wayne into combat. Kovic graduated from high school in 1963, enlisted in the Marines, and began the first of his two tours of duty in Vietnam. He was wounded during the second tour and returned home paralyzed from the chest down. His re-entry into everyday life was assisted by his work with Vietnam Veterans Against the War and by his writing of Born on the Fourth of July *(1976), one of the most powerful books to appear in the aftermath of Vietnam. "On Patrol," an excerpt from that book, recounts a single military action that reveals the confusion and brutality of war.*

He went out on patrol with the others the night of the ambush at exactly eight o'clock, loading a round into the chamber of his weapon before he walked outside the tent and into the dark and rain. As usual he had made all the men put on camouflage from head to toe, made sure they had all blackened their faces, and attached twigs and branches to their arms and legs with rubber bands.

One by one the scouts moved slowly past the thick barbed wire and began to walk along the bank of the river, heading toward the graveyard where the ambush would be set up. They were moving north exactly as planned, a line of shadows tightly bunched in the rain. Sometimes it would stop raining and they would spread out somewhat more, but mostly they continued to bunch up together, as if they were afraid of losing their way.

There was a rice paddy on the edge of the graveyard. 3 No one said a word as they walked through it and he thought he could hear voices from the village. He could smell the familiar smoke from the fires in the huts and he knew that the people who went out fishing each day must have come home. They were the people he watched every morning moving quietly in their small boats down toward the mouth of the river, heading out to the sea. Some of the older men reminded him of his father, going to work each morning and coming back home every night to sit by their fires with their children cooking their fish. They must talk about us sometimes, he thought. He wondered a lot what it was they thought about him and the men.

He remembered how difficult it had been when he had 4 first come to the war to tell the villagers from the enemy and sometimes it had seemed easier to hate all of them, but he had always tried very hard not to. He wished he could be sure they understood that he and the men were there because they were trying to help all of them save their country from the communists.

They were on a rice dike that bordered the graveyard. 5 The voices from the huts nearby seemed quite loud. He looked up ahead to where the lieutenant who had come along with them that night was standing. The lieutenant had sent one of the men, Molina, on across the rice dikes almost to the edge of the village. The cold rain was still coming down very hard and the men behind him were standing like a line of statues waiting for the next command.

But now something was wrong up ahead. He could see 6 Molina waving his hands excitedly trying to tell the lieutenant something. Stumbling over the dikes, almost crawling, Molina came back toward the lieutenant. He saw him

51

whisper something in his ear. And now the lieutenant turned and looked at him. "Sergeant," he said, "Molina and I are going to get a look up ahead. Stay here with the team."

Balancing on the dike, he turned around slowly after 7 the lieutenant had gone, motioning with his rifle for all of the men in back of him to get down. Each one, carefully, one after the other, squatted along the dike on one knee, waiting in the rain to move out again. They were all shivering from the cold.

They waited for what seemed a long time and then the 8 lieutenant and Molina appeared suddenly through the darkness. He could tell from their faces that they had seen something. They had seen something up ahead, he was sure, and they were going to tell him what they had just seen. He stood up, too excited to stay kneeling down on the dike.

"What is it?" he cried. 9

"Be quiet," whispered the lieutenant sharply, grabbing 10 his arm, almost throwing him into the paddy. He began talking very quickly and much louder than he should have. "I think we found them. I think we found them," he repeated, almost shouting.

He didn't know what the lieutenant meant. "What?" 11 he said.

"The sappers, the sappers! Let's go!" The lieutenant 12 was taking over now. He seemed very sure of himself, he was acting very confident. "Let's go, goddamn it!"

He clicked his rifle off safety and got his men up 13 quickly, urging them forward, following the lieutenant and Molina toward the edge of the village. They ran through the paddy, splashing like a family of ducks. This time he hoped and prayed it would be the real enemy. He would be ready for them this time. Here was another chance, he thought. He was so excited he ran straight into the lieutenant, bouncing clumsily off his chest.

"I'm sorry, sir," he said. 14

"Quiet! They're out there," the lieutenant whispered 15

to him, motioning to the rest of the men to get down on their hands and knees now. They crawled to the tree line, then along the back of the rice paddy through almost a foot of water, until the whole team lay in a long line pressed up against the dike, facing the village.

He saw a light, a fire he thought, flickering in the dis- 16 tance off to the right of the village, with little dark figures that seemed to be moving behind it. He could not tell how far away they were from there. It was very hard to tell distance in the dark.

The lieutenant moved next to him. "You see?" he 17 whispered. "Look," he said, very keyed up now. "They've got rifles. Can you see the rifles? Can you see them?" the lieutenant asked him.

He looked very hard through the rain. 18

"Can you see them?" 19

"Yes, I see them. I see them," he said. He was very 20 sure.

The lieutenant put his arm around him and whispered 21 in his ear. "Tell them down at the end to give me an illumination. I want this whole place lit up like a fucking Christmas tree."

Turning quickly to the man on his right, he told him 22 what the lieutenant had said. He told him to pass the instructions all the way to the end of the line, where a flare would be fired just above the small fire near the village.

Lying there in the mud behind the dike, he stared at 23 the fire that still flickered in the rain. He could still see the little figures moving back and forth against it like small shadows on a screen. He felt the whole line tense, then heard the WOOOORSHH of the flare cracking overhead in a tremendous ball of sputtering light turning night into day, arching over their heads toward the small fire that he now saw was burning inside an open hut.

Suddenly someone was firing from the end with his 24 rifle, and now the whole line opened up, roaring their weapons like thunder, pulling their triggers again and again without even thinking, emptying everything they had into the hut in a tremendous stream of bright orange tracers that crisscrossed each other in the night.

The flare arched its last sputtering bits into the village 25 and it became dark, and all he could see were the bright orange embers from the fire that had gone out.

And he could hear them. 26

There were voices screaming. 27

"What happened? Goddamn it, what happened?" yelled 28 the lieutenant.

The voices were screaming from inside the hut. 29

"Who gave the order to fire? I wanna know who gave 30 the order to fire."

The lieutenant was standing up now, looking up and 31 down the line of men still lying in the rain.

He found that he was shaking. It had all happened so 32 quickly.

"We better get a killer team out there," he heard 33 Molina say.

"All right, all right. Sergeant," the lieutenant said to 34 him, "get out there with Molina and tell me how many we got."

He got to his feet and quickly got five of the men to- 35 gether, leading them over the dike and through the water to the hut from where the screams were still coming. It was much closer than he had first thought. Now he could see very clearly the smoldering embers of the fire that had been blown out by the terrific blast of their rifles.

Molina turned the beam of his flashlight into the hut. 36 "Oh God," he said. "Oh Jesus Christ." He started to cry. "We just shot up a bunch of kids!"

The floor of the small hut was covered with them, 37 screaming and thrashing their arms back and forth, lying in pools of blood, crying wildly, screaming again and again. They were shot in the face, in the chest, in the legs, moaning and crying.

"Oh Jesus!" he cried. 38

He could hear the lieutenant shouting at them, want- 39 ing to know how many they had killed.

There was an old man in the corner with his head 40
blown off from his eyes up, his brains hanging out of his
head like jelly. He kept looking at the strange sight, he
had never seen anything like it before. A small boy next
to the old man was still alive, although he had been shot
many times. He was crying softly, lying in a large pool
of blood. His small foot had been shot almost completely
off and seemed to be hanging by a thread.

"What's happening? What's going on up there?" The 41
lieutenant was getting very impatient now.

Molina shouted for the lieutenant to come quickly. 42
"You better get up here. There's a lot of wounded people
up here."

He heard a small girl moaning now. She was shot 43
through the stomach and bleeding out of the rear end. All
he could see now was blood everywhere and he heard their
screams with his heart racing like it had never raced before. He felt crazy and weak as he stood there staring at
them with the rest of the men, staring down onto the floor
like it was a nightmare, like it was some kind of dream
and it really wasn't happening.

And then he could no longer stand watching. They 44
were people, he thought, children and old men, people,
people like himself, and he had to do something, he had
to move, he had to help, do something. He jerked the
green medical bag off his back, ripping it open and grabbing for bandages, yelling at Molina to please come and
help him. He knelt down in the middle of the screaming
bodies and began bandaging them, trying to cover the
holes where the blood was still spurting out. "It's gonna
be okay. It's gonna be okay," he tried to say, but he was
crying now, crying and still trying to bandage them all
up. He moved from body to body searching in the dark
with his fingers for the holes the bullets had made, bandaging each one as quickly as he could, his shaking hands
wet with the blood. It was raining into the hut and a cold
wind swept his face as he moved in the dark.

The lieutenant had just come up with the others. 45

"Help me!" he screamed. "Somebody help!" 46

"Well goddamn it sergeant! What's the matter? How 47
many did we kill?"

"They're children!" he screamed at the lieutenant. 48

"Children and old men!" cried Molina. 49

"Where are their rifles?" the lieutenant asked. 50

"There aren't any rifles," he said. 51

"Well, help him then!" screamed the lieutenant to the 52
rest of the men. The men stood in the entrance of the hut,
but they would not move. "Help him, help him. I'm
ordering you to help him!"

The men were not moving and some of them were cry- 53
ing now, dropping their rifles and sitting down on the wet
ground. They were weeping now with their hands against
their faces. "Oh Jesus, oh God, forgive us."

"Forgive us for what we've done!" he heard Molina cry. 54

"Get up," screamed the lieutenant. "What do you 55
think this is? I'm ordering you all to get up."

Some of the men began slowly crawling over the 56
bodies, grabbing for the bandages that were still left.

By now some of the villagers had gathered outside the 57
hut. He could hear them shouting angrily. He knew they
must be cursing them.

"You better get a fucking chopper in here," someone 58
was yelling.

"Where's the radio man? Get the radio man!" 59

"Hello Cactus Red. This is Red Light Two. Ahhh this 60
is Red Light Two. We need an emergency evac. We got a
lot of wounded ... ahh ... friendly wounded. A lot of
friendly wounded out here." He could hear the lieutenant
on the radio, trying to tell the helicopters where to come.

The men in the hut were just sitting there crying. 61
They could not move, and they did not listen to the lieutenant's orders. They just sat with the rain pouring down
on them through the roof, crying and not moving.

"You men! You men have got to start listening to me. 62
You gotta stop crying like babies and start acting like
marines!" The lieutenant who was off the radio now was

shoving the men, pleading with them to move. "You're men, not babies. It's all a mistake. It wasn't your fault. They got in the way. Don't you people understand—they got in the goddamn way!"

When the medivac chopper came, he picked up the 63 little boy who was lying next to the old man. His foot came off and he grabbed it up quickly and bandaged it against the bottom stump of the boy's leg. He held him looking into his frightened eyes and carried him up to the open door of the helicopter. The boy was still crying softly when he handed him to the gunner.

And when it was all over and all the wounded had 64 been loaded aboard, he helped the lieutenant move the men back on patrol. They walked away from the hut in the rain. And now he felt his body go numb and heavy, feeling awful and sick inside like the night the corporal had died, as they moved along in the dark and the rain behind the lieutenant toward the graveyard.

———— ◆ ————

For Study and Discussion

QUESTIONS ABOUT PURPOSE

1. What is Kovic's major purpose in this essay: to tell what happened on one maneuver, to illustrate what happened in one war, or to explain what happens in all wars? Explain your answer.
2. What very personal purpose might Kovic have in writing this essay?
3. What long-range purpose can such accounts serve?

QUESTIONS ABOUT AUDIENCE

1. What groups of people would you suspect Kovic has identified as the intended audience for this essay?

2. How much does Kovic think this group knows about the Vietnamese war?

3. What preconceptions about the rules of combat would Kovic expect his readers to have?

QUESTIONS ABOUT STRATEGIES

1. How does Kovic use the first and last paragraphs to comment on the events narrated in the body of this essay?

2. How does Kovic pace the narrative when the men enter the hut? Does the pace of the narrative match the pace of their feelings?

3. How does Kovic's selection of a point of view (the Sergeant) emphasize his purpose? How would the Lieutenant, the victims, or the villagers outside the hut have told this story?

QUESTIONS FOR DISCUSSION

1. What evidence in the narrative might help you explain the cause of this "accident"?

2. What images does the word *enemy* normally suggest? According to this essay, who is the enemy?

3. What does this essay reveal about the relationship of *fear* and *error*? How do people feel about mistakes they make when they are afraid? Do they feel *more* or *less* responsible for their actions?

No Name Woman

MAXINE HONG KINGSTON

———— ◆ ————

Maxine Hong Kingston was born in 1940 in Stockton, California, where her parents operated a laundry. After graduating from the University of California at Berkeley, she married actor Earll Kingston and began a career as a teacher of English and mathematics at several high schools in California and Hawaii. Since 1977 Kingston has taught creative writing at the University of Hawaii, Honolulu. **The Woman Warrior: Memories of a Girlhood Among Ghosts** *(1975), her first book, won the nonfiction award from the National Book Critics Circle for its vivid portrayal of life in a Chinese-American community. Her latest book is* **China Men** *(1980). In "No Name Woman," excerpted from* **The Woman Warrior,** *Kingston retells one of the stories her mother told her "to grow up on."*

"You must not tell anyone," my mother said, "what I am   1
about to tell you. In China your father had a sister who
killed herself. She jumped into the family well. We say
that your father has all brothers because it is as if she had
never been born.

"In 1924 just a few days after our village celebrated   2
seventeen hurry-up weddings—to make sure that every
young man who went 'out on the road' would responsibly
come home—your father and his brothers and your grandfather and his brothers and your aunt's new husband

sailed for America, the Gold Mountain. It was your grandfather's last trip. Those lucky enough to get contracts
waved good-bye from the decks. They fed and guarded the
stowaways and helped them off in Cuba, New York, Bali,
Hawaii. 'We'll meet in California next year,' they said.
All of them sent money home.

"I remember looking at your aunt one day when she   3
and I were dressing; I had not noticed before that she had
such a protruding melon of a stomach. But I did not think,
'She's pregnant,' until she began to look like other pregnant women, her shirt pulling and the white tops of her
black pants showing. She could not have been pregnant,
you see, because her husband had been gone for years. No
one said anything. We did not discuss it. In early summer she was ready to have the child, long after the time
when it could have been possible.

"The village had also been counting. On the night   4
the baby was to be born the villagers raided our house.
Some were crying. Like a great saw, teeth strung with
lights, files of people walked zigzag across our land, tearing the rice. Their lanterns doubled in the disturbed black
water, which drained away through the broken bunds. As
the villagers closed in, we could see that some of them,
probably men and women we knew well, wore white
masks. The people with long hair hung it over their faces.
Women with short hair made it stand up on end. Some
had tied white bands around their foreheads, arms, and
legs.

"At first they threw mud and rocks at the house. Then   5
they threw eggs and began slaughtering our stock. We
could hear the animals scream their deaths—the roosters,
the pigs, a last great roar from the ox. Familiar wild heads
flared in our night windows; the villagers encircled us.
Some of the faces stopped to peer at us, their eyes rushing
like searchlights. The hands flattened against the panes,
framed heads, and left red prints.

"The villagers broke in the front and the back doors   6
at the same time, even though we had not locked the doors

against them. Their knives dripped with the blood of our animals. They smeared blood on the doors and walls. One woman swung a chicken, whose throat she had slit, splattering blood in red arcs about her. We stood together in the middle of our house, in the family hall with the pictures and tables of the ancestors around us, and looked straight ahead.

"At that time the house had only two wings. When 7 the men came back, we would build two more to enclose our courtyard and a third one to begin a second courtyard. The villagers pushed through both wings, even your grandparents' rooms, to find your aunt's, which was also mine until the men returned. From this room a new wing for one of the younger families would grow. They ripped up her clothes and shoes and broke her combs, grinding them underfoot. They tore her work from the loom. They scattered the cooking fire and rolled the new weaving in it. We could hear them in the kitchen breaking our bowls and banging the pots. They overturned the great waist-high earthenware jugs; duck eggs, pickled fruits, vegetables burst out and mixed in acrid torrents. The old woman from the next field swept a broom through the air and loosed the spirits-of-the-broom over our heads. 'Pig.' 'Ghost.' 'Pig,' they sobbed and scolded while they ruined our house.

"When they left, they took sugar and oranges to bless 8 themselves. They cut pieces from the dead animals. Some of them took bowls that were not broken and clothes that were not torn. Afterward we swept up the rice and sewed it back up into sacks. But the smells from the spilled preserves lasted. Your aunt gave birth in the pigsty that night. The next morning when I went for the water, I found her and the baby plugging up the family well.

"Don't let your father know that I told you. He denies 9 her. Now that you have started to menstruate, what happened to her could happen to you. Don't humiliate us. You wouldn't like to be forgotten as if you had never been born. The villagers are watchful."

61

Whenever she had to warn us about life, my mother 10
told stories that ran like this one, a story to grow up on.
She tested our strength to establish realities. Those in the
emigrant generations who could not reassert brute survival
died young and far from home. Those of us in the first
American generations have had to figure out how the invisible world the emigrants built around our childhoods
fit in solid America.

The emigrants confused the gods by diverting their 11
curses, misleading them with crooked streets and false
names. They must try to confuse their offspring as well,
who, I suppose, threaten them in similar ways—always
trying to get things straight, always trying to name the unspeakable. The Chinese I know hide their names; sojourn-
ers take new names when their lives change and guard
their real names with silence.

Chinese-Americans, when you try to understand what 12
things in you are Chinese, how do you separate what is
peculiar to childhood, to poverty, insanities, one family,
your mother who marked your growing with stories, from
what is Chinese? What is Chinese tradition and what is
the movies?

If I want to learn what clothes my aunt wore, whether 13
flashy or ordinary, I would have to begin, "Remember
Father's drowned-in-the-well sister?" I cannot ask that. My
mother has told me once and for all the useful parts. She
will add nothing unless powered by Necessity, a riverbank
that guides her life. She plants vegetable gardens rather
than lawns; she carries the odd-shaped tomatoes home
from the fields and eats food left for the gods.

Whenever we did frivolous things, we used up energy; 14
we flew high kites. We children came up off the ground
over the melting cones our parents brought home from
work and the American movie on New Year's Day—*Oh,
You Beautiful Doll* with Betty Grable one year, and *She
Wore a Yellow Ribbon* with John Wayne another year.
After the one carnival ride each, we paid in guilt; our tired
father counted his change on the dark walk home.

Adultery is extravagance. Could people who hatch 15
their own chicks and eat the embryos and the heads for
delicacies and boil the feet in vinegar for party food, leaving only the gravel, eating even the gizzard lining—could
such people engender a prodigal aunt? To be a woman, to
have a daughter in starvation time was a waste enough.
My aunt could not have been the lone romantic who gave
up everything for sex. Women in the old China did not
choose. Some man had commanded her to lie with him
and be his secret evil. I wonder whether he masked himself when he joined the raid on her family.

Perhaps she encountered him in the fields or on the 16
mountain where the daughters-in-law collected fuel. Or
perhaps he first noticed her in the marketplace. He was
not a stranger because the village housed no strangers.
She had to have dealings with him other than sex. Perhaps he worked an adjoining field, or he sold her the cloth
for the dress she sewed and wore. His demand must have
surprised, then terrified her. She obeyed him; she always
did as she was told.

When the family found a young man in the next vil- 17
lage to be her husband, she stood tractably beside the best
rooster, his proxy, and promised before they met that she
would be his forever. She was lucky that he was her age
and she would be the first wife, an advantage secure now.
The night she first saw him, he had sex with her. Then he
left for America. She had almost forgotten what he looked
like. When she tried to envision him, she only saw the
black and white face in the group photograph the men had
had taken before leaving.

The other man was not, after all, much different from 18
her husband. They both gave orders: she followed. "If
you tell your family, I'll beat you. I'll kill you. Be here
again next week." No one talked sex, ever. And she might
have separated the rapes from the rest of living if only she
did not have to buy her oil from him or gather wood in the
same forest. I want her fear to have lasted just as long as
rape lasted so that the fear could have been contained. No

drawn-out fear. But women at sex hazarded birth and hence lifetimes. The fear did not stop but permeated everywhere. She told the man, "I think I'm pregnant." He organized the raid against her.

On nights when my mother and father talked about 19 their life back home, sometimes they mentioned an "outcast table" whose business they still seemed to be settling, their voices tight. In a commensal tradition, where food is precious, the powerful older people made wrongdoers eat alone. Instead of letting them start separate new lives like the Japanese, who could become samurais and geishas, the Chinese family, faces averted but eyes glowering sideways, hung on to the offenders and fed them leftovers. My aunt must have lived in the same house as my parents and eaten at an outcast table. My mother spoke about the raid as if she had seen it, when she and my aunt, a daughter-in-law to a different household, should not have been living together at all. Daughters-in-law lived with their husbands' parents, not their own; a synonym for marriage in Chinese is "taking a daughter-in-law." Her husband's parents could have sold her, mortgaged her, stoned her. But they had sent her back to her own mother and father, a mysterious act hinting at disgraces not told me. Perhaps they had thrown her out to deflect the avengers.

She was the only daughter; her four brothers went with 20 her father, husband, and uncles "out on the road" and for some years became western men. When the goods were divided among the family, three of the brothers took land, and the youngest, my father, chose an education. After my grandparents gave their daughter away to her husband's family, they had dispensed all the adventure and all the property. They expected her alone to keep the traditional ways, which her brothers, now among the barbarians, could fumble without detection. The heavy, deep-rooted women were to maintain the past against the flood, safe for returning. But the rare urge west had fixed upon our family, and so my aunt crossed boundaries not delineated in space.

The work of preservation demands that the feelings 21
playing about in one's guts not be turned into action. Just
watch their passing like cherry blossoms. But perhaps my
aunt, my forerunner, caught in a slow life, let dreams
grow and fade and after some months or years went toward what persisted. Fear at the enormities of the forbidden kept her desires delicate, wire and bone. She looked
at a man because she liked the way the hair was tucked
behind his ears, or she liked the question-mark line of a
long torso curving at the shoulder and straight at the hip.
For warm eyes or a soft voice or a slow walk—that's all—
a few hairs, a line, a brightness, a sound, a pace, she gave
up family. She offered us up for a charm that vanished
with tiredness, a pigtail that didn't toss when the wind
died. Why, the wrong lighting could erase the dearest
thing about him.

It could very well have been, however, that my aunt 22
did not take subtle enjoyment of her friend, but, a wild
woman, kept rollicking company. Imagining her free with
sex doesn't fit, though. I don't know any women like that,
or men either. Unless I see her life branching into mine,
she gives me no ancestral help.

To sustain her being in love, she often worked at her- 23
self in the mirror, guessing at the colors and shapes that
would interest him, changing them frequently in order to
hit on the right combination. She wanted him to look
back.

On a farm near the sea, a woman who tended her ap- 24
pearance reaped a reputation for eccentricity. All the
married women blunt-cut their hair in flaps about their
ears or pulled it back in tight buns. No nonsense. Neither
style blew easily into heart-catching tangles. And at their
weddings they displayed themselves in their long hair for
the last time. "It brushed the backs of my knees," my
mother tells me. "It was braided, and even so, it brushed
the backs of my knees."

At the mirror my aunt combed individuality into her 25
bob. A bun could have been contrived to escape into black

streamers blowing in the wind or in quiet wisps about her face, but only the older women in our picture album wear buns. She brushed her hair back from her forehead, tucking the flaps behind her ears. She looped a piece of thread, knotted into a circle between her index fingers and thumbs, and ran the double strand across her forehead. When she closed her fingers as if she were making a pair of shadow geese bite, the string twisted together catching the little hairs. Then she pulled the thread away from her skin, ripping the hairs out neatly, her eyes watering from the needles of pain. Opening her fingers, she cleaned the thread, then rolled it along her hairline and the tops of her eyebrows. My mother did the same to me and my sisters and herself. I used to believe that the expression "caught by the short hairs" meant a captive held with a depilatory string. It especially hurt at the temples, but my mother said we were lucky we didn't have to have our feet bound when we were seven. Sisters used to sit on their beds and cry together, she said, as their mothers or their slaves removed the bandages for a few minutes each night and let the blood gush back into their veins. I hope that the man my aunt loved appreciated a smooth brow, that he wasn't just a tits-and-ass man.

Once my aunt found a freckle on her chin, at a spot   26
that the almanac said predestined her for unhappiness. She dug it out with a hot needle and washed the wound with peroxide.

More attention to her looks than these pullings of   27
hairs and pickings at spots would have caused gossip among the villagers. They owned work clothes and good clothes, and they wore good clothes for feasting the new seasons. But since a woman combing her hair hexes beginnings, my aunt rarely found an occasion to look her best. Women looked like great sea snails—the corded wood, babies, and laundry they carried were the whorls on their backs. The Chinese did not admire a bent back; goddesses and warriors stood straight. Still there must

have been a marvelous freeing of beauty when a worker laid down her burden and stretched and arched.

Such commonplace loveliness, however, was not 28 enough for my aunt. She dreamed of a lover for the fifteen days of New Year's, the time for families to exchange visits, money, and food. She plied her secret comb. And sure enough she cursed the year, the family, the village, and herself.

Even as her hair lured her imminent lover, many other 29 men looked at her. Uncles, cousins, nephews, brothers would have looked, too, had they been home between journeys. Perhaps they had already been restraining their curiosity, and they left, fearful that their glances, like a field of nesting birds, might be startled and caught. Poverty hurt, and that was their first reason for leaving. But another, final reason for leaving the crowded house was the never-said.

She may have been unusually beloved, the precious 30 only daughter, spoiled and mirror gazing because of the affection the family lavished on her. When her husband left, they welcomed the chance to take her back from the in-laws; she could live like the little daughter for just a while longer. There are stories that my grandfather was different from other people, "crazy ever since the little Jap bayoneted him in the head." He used to put his naked penis on the dinner table, laughing. And one day he brought home a baby girl, wrapped up inside his brown western-style greatcoat. He had traded one of his sons, probably my father, the youngest, for her. My grandmother made him trade back. When he finally got a daughter of his own, he doted on her. They must have all loved her, except perhaps my father, the only brother who never went back to China, having once been traded for a girl.

Brothers and sisters, newly men and women, had to 31 efface their sexual color and present plain miens. Disturbing hair and eyes, a smile like no other threatened the ideal of five generations living under one roof. To focus blurs, people shouted face to face and yelled from room to room. The immigrants I know have loud voices, unmodulated to American tones even after years away from the village where they called their friendships out across the fields. I have not been able to stop my mother's screams in public libraries or over telephones. Walking erect (knees straight, toes pointed forward, not pigeon-toed, which is Chinese-feminine) and speaking in an inaudible voice, I have tried to turn myself American-feminine. Chinese communication was loud, public. Only sick people had to whisper. But at the dinner table, where the family members came nearest one another, no one could talk, not the outcasts nor any eaters. Every word that falls from the mouth is a coin lost. Silently they gave and accepted food with both hands. A preoccupied child who took his bowl with one hand got a sideways glare. A complete moment of total attention is due everyone alike. Children and lovers have no singularity here, but my aunt used a secret voice, a separate attentiveness.

She kept the man's name to herself throughout her 32 labor and dying; she did not accuse him that he be punished with her. To save her inseminator's name she gave silent birth.

He may have been somebody in her own household, 33 but intercourse with a man outside the family would have been no less abhorrent. All the village were kinsmen, and the titles shouted in loud country voices never let kinship be forgotten. Any man within visiting distance would have been neutralized as a lover—"brother," "younger brother," "older brother"—one hundred and fifteen relationship titles. Parents researched birth charts probably not so much to assure good fortune as to circumvent incest in a population that has but one hundred surnames. Everybody has eight million relatives. How useless then sexual mannerisms, how dangerous.

As if it came from an atavism deeper than fear, I used 34 to add "brother" silently to boys' names. It hexed the boys, who would or would not ask me to dance, and made them less scary and as familiar and deserving of benevolence as girls.

But, of course, I hexed myself also—no dates. I should have stood up, both arms waving, and shouted out across libraries, "Hey, you! Love me back." I had no idea, though, how to make attraction selective, how to control its direction and magnitude. If I made myself American-pretty so that the five or six Chinese boys in the class fell in love with me, everyone else—the Caucasian, Negro, and Japanese boys—would too. Sisterliness, dignified and honorable, made much more sense.

Attraction eludes control so stubbornly that whole societies designed to organize relationships among people cannot keep order, not even when they bind people to one another from childhood and raise them together. Among the very poor and the wealthy, brothers married their adopted sisters, like doves. Our family allowed some romance, paying adult brides' prices and providing dowries so that their sons and daughters could marry strangers. Marriage promises to turn strangers into friendly relatives —a nation of siblings.

In the village structure, spirits shimmered among the live creatures, balanced and held in equilibrium by time and land. But one human being flaring up into violence could open up a black hole, a maelstrom that pulled in the sky. The frightened villagers, who depended on one another to maintain the real, went to my aunt to show her a personal, physical representation of the break she had made in the "roundness." Misallying couples snapped off the future, which was to be embodied in true offspring. The villagers punished her for acting as if she could have a private life, secret and apart from them.

If my aunt had betrayed the family at a time of large grain yields and peace, when many boys were born, and wings were being built on many houses, perhaps she might have escaped such severe punishment. But the men— hungry, greedy, tired of planting in dry soil, cuckolded—

had had to leave the village in order to send food-money home. There were ghost plagues, bandit plagues, wars with the Japanese, floods. My Chinese brother and sister had died of an unknown sickness. Adultery, perhaps only a mistake during good times, became a crime when the village needed food.

The round moon cakes and round doorways, the round 39 tables of graduated size that fit one roundness inside another, round windows and rice bowls—these talismen had lost their power to warn this family of the law: a family must be whole, faithfully keeping the descent line by having sons to feed the old and the dead, who in turn look after the family. The villagers came to show my aunt and her lover-in-hiding a broken house. The villagers were speeding up the circling of events because she was too shortsighted to see that her infidelity had already harmed the village, that waves of consequences would return unpredictably, sometimes in disguise, as now, to hurt her. This roundness had to be made coin-sized so that she would see its circumference: punish her at the birth of her baby. Awaken her to the inexorable. People who refused fatalism because they could invent small resources insisted on culpability. Deny accidents and wrest fault from the stars.

After the villagers left, their lanterns now scattering in 40 various directions toward home, the family broke their silence and cursed her. "Aiaa, we're going to die. Death is coming. Death is coming. Look what you've done. You've killed us. Ghost! Dead ghost! Ghost! You've never been born." She ran out into the fields, far enough from the house so that she could no longer hear their voices, and pressed herself against the earth, her own land no more. When she felt the birth coming, she thought that she had been hurt. Her body seized together. "They've hurt me too much," she thought. "This is gall, and it will kill me." Her forehead and knees against the earth, her body convulsed and then released her onto her back. The black well of sky and stars went out and out and out forever;

her body and her complexity seemed to disappear. She was one of the stars, a bright dot in blackness, without home, without a companion, in eternal cold and silence. An agoraphobia rose in her, speeding higher and higher, bigger and bigger; she would not be able to contain it; there would be no end to fear.

Flayed, unprotected against space, she felt pain return, focusing her body. This pain chilled her—a cold, steady kind of surface pain. Inside, spasmodically, the other pain, the pain of the child, heated her. For hours she lay on the ground, alternately body and space. Sometimes a vision of normal comfort obliterated reality: she saw the family in the evening gambling at the dinner table, the young people massaging their elders' backs. She saw them congratulating one another, high joy on the mornings the rice shoots came up. When these pictures burst, the stars drew yet further apart. Black space opened. 41

She got to her feet to fight better and remembered that old-fashioned women gave birth in their pigsties to fool the jealous, pain-dealing gods, who do not snatch piglets. Before the next spasms could stop her, she ran to the pigsty, each step a rushing out into emptiness. She climbed over the fence and knelt in the dirt. It was good to have a fence enclosing her, a tribal person alone. 42

Laboring, this woman who had carried her child as a foreign growth that sickened her every day, expelled it at last. She reached down to touch the hot, wet, moving mass, surely smaller than anything human, and could feel that it was human after all—fingers, toes, nails, nose. She pulled it up on to her belly, and it lay curled there, butt in the air, feet precisely tucked one under the other. She opened her loose shirt and buttoned the child inside. After resting, it squirmed and thrashed and she pushed it up to her breast. It turned its head this way and that until it found her nipple. There, it made little snuffling noises. She clenched her teeth at its preciousness, lovely as a young calf, a piglet, a little dog. 43

She may have gone to the pigsty as a last act of respon- 44

71

sibility: she would protect this child as she had protected its father. It would look after her soul, leaving supplies on her grave. But how would this tiny child without family find her grave when there would be no marker for her anywhere, neither in the earth nor the family hall? No one would give her a family hall name. She had taken the child with her into the wastes. At its birth the two of them had felt the same raw pain of separation, a wound that only the family pressing tight could close. A child with no descent line would not soften her life but only trail after her, ghost-like, begging her to give it purpose. At dawn the villagers on their way to the fields would stand around the fence and look.

Full of milk, the little ghost slept. When it awoke, she 45 hardened her breasts against the milk that crying loosens. Toward morning she picked up the baby and walked to the well.

Carrying the baby to the well shows loving. Otherwise 46 abandon it. Turn its face into the mud. Mothers who love their children take them along. It was probably a girl; there is some hope of forgiveness for boys.

"Don't tell anyone you had an aunt. Your father does 47 not want to hear her name. She has never been born." I have believed that sex was unspeakable and words so strong and fathers so frail that "aunt" would do my father mysterious harm. I have thought that my family, having settled among immigrants who had also been their neighbors in the ancestral land, needed to clean their name, and a wrong word would incite the kinspeople even here. But there is more to this silence: they want me to participate in her punishment. And I have.

In the twenty years since I heard this story I have not 48 asked for details nor said my aunt's name; I do not know it. People who can comfort the dead can also chase after them to hurt them further—a reverse ancestor worship. The real punishment was not the raid swiftly inflicted by the villagers, but the family's deliberately forgetting her.

Her betrayal so maddened them, they saw to it that she would suffer forever, even after death. Always hungry, always needing, she would have to beg food from other ghosts, snatch and steal it from those whose living descendants give them gifts. She would have to fight the ghosts massed at crossroads for the buns a few thoughtful citizens leave to decoy her away from village and home so that the ancestral spirits could feast unharassed. At peace, they could act like gods, not ghosts, their descent lines providing them with paper suits and dresses, spirit money, paper houses, paper automobiles, chicken, meat, and rice into eternity—essences delivered up in smoke and flames, steam and incense rising from each rice bowl. In an attempt to make the Chinese care for people outside the family, Chairman Mao encourages us now to give our paper replicas to the spirits of outstanding soldiers and workers, no matter whose ancestors they may be. My aunt remains forever hungry. Goods are not distributed evenly among the dead.

My aunt haunts me—her ghost drawn to me because now, after fifty years of neglect, I alone devote pages of paper to her, though not origamied into houses and clothes. I do not think she always means me well. I am telling on her, and she was a spite suicide, drowning herself in the drinking water. The Chinese are always very frightened of the drowned one, whose weeping ghost, wet hair hanging and skin bloated, waits silently by the water to pull down a substitute.

————— ♦ —————

For Study and Discussion

QUESTIONS ABOUT PURPOSE

1. What occasion prompts Kingston's mother to tell her daughter the story about the forgotten aunt? Why is it a story "to grow up on"?

2. Why does Kingston's need for "ancestral help" explain her purpose in devoting so many "pages of paper" to her "forerunner"?

3. In the process of trying to interpret the meaning of her aunt's story, what other purposes does Kingston accomplish? For example, what does she reveal about the difficulties of life in the village and life among the barbarians?

QUESTIONS ABOUT AUDIENCE

1. What preconceptions about life in China might a modern American audience bring to this essay? To what extent are those preconceptions confirmed by the mother's story?

2. Who does Kingston imagine as the audience for her essay—first-generation Chinese immigrants like her parents, second-generation Chinese-Americans like herself, or more general (non-Chinese) readers? To which audience does she direct her comments in the middle of her essay? Explain your answer.

3. How do Kingston's comments in the last two paragraphs suggest that she may have imagined her aunt as the reader of her essay?

QUESTIONS ABOUT STRATEGIES

1. How would you characterize the pace of the opening story in Kingston's essay? How does the first sentence establish that pace? How does the mother's refusal to retell the story provide Kingston with a reason for employing a different pace for her speculation about her aunt?

2. What are the various conflicts in the mother's story? What additional conflicts does Kingston see in the story? To what extent are those conflicts present in her own life? For example, how does the aunt's "curse" resemble Kingston's sense that she has "hexed" herself?

3. How does Kingston vary her point of view in this essay? In which of the various re-creations of her aunt's story is she a detached observer? a sympathetic witness? In each case, why does Kingston's choice of point of view seem appropriate to the scene she is re-creating?

QUESTIONS FOR DISCUSSION

1. What is the Chinese attitude toward traditions? How does storytelling help perpetuate those traditions? In what sense does Kingston's storytelling fulfill the Chinese expectation that "women were to maintain the past against the flood"?
2. What is the Chinese attitude toward waste? Why do the Chinese view a private life, romantic love, and, especially, adultery as extravagances?
3. How do you explain Kingston's assertion that "the real punishment was not the raid swiftly inflicted by the villagers, but the family's deliberately forgetting her"?

My Furthest-Back Person—
"The African"

ALEX HALEY

───────── ◆ ─────────

*Alex Haley was born in 1921 in Ithaca, New York,
and attended Elizabeth City Teacher's College (North
Carolina) before enlisting in the United States Coast
Guard. During his twenty years in the service (1939–
1959), he worked as a staff journalist, learning the
skills he would need when he retired to pursue a
career as a writer. In his first book,* The Autobiography of Malcolm X *(1965), Haley helps another man
tell his life story. In his second book,* Roots *(1976),
Haley tells the story of his own family history. The
televised version of that story became one of our
nation's most discussed public events. "My Furthest-
Back Person—'The African,'" written for* The New
York Times Magazine, *is Haley's account of how he
tracked down the story that eventually became* Roots:
The Saga of an American Family.

My Grandma Cynthia Murray Palmer lived in Henning, 1
Tenn. (pop. 500), about 50 miles north of Memphis. Each
summer as I grew up there, we would be visited by several women relatives who were mostly around Grandma's
age, such as my Great Aunt Liz Murray who taught in
Oklahoma, and Great Aunt Till Merriwether from Jackson, Tenn., or their considerably younger niece, Cousin
Georgia Anderson from Kansas City, Kan., and some
others. Always after the supper dishes had been washed,
they would go out to take seats and talk in the rocking

chairs on the front porch, and I would scrunch down, listening, behind Grandma's squeaky chair, with the dusk deepening into night and the lightning bugs flickering on and off above the now shadowy honeysuckles. Most often they talked about our family—the story had been passed down for generations—until the whistling blur of lights of the southbound Panama Limited train *whooshing* through Henning at 9:05 P.M. signaled our bedtime.

So much of their talking of people, places and events I 2 didn't understand: For instance, what was an "Ol' Massa," an "Ol' Missus" or a "plantation"? But early I gathered that white folks had done lots of bad things to our folks, though I couldn't figure out why. I guessed that all that they talked about had happened a long time ago, as now or then Grandma or another, speaking of someone in the past, would excitedly thrust a finger toward me, exclaiming, "Wasn't big as *this* young'un!" And it would astound me that anyone as old and grey-haired as they could relate to my age. But in time my head began both a recording and picturing of the more graphic scenes they would describe, just as I also visualized David killing Goliath with his slingshot, Old Pharaoh's army drowning, Noah and his ark, Jesus feeding that big multitude with nothing but five loaves and two fishes, and other wonders that I heard in my Sunday school lessons at our New Hope Methodist Church.

The furthest-back person Grandma and the others 3 talked of—always in tones of awe, I noticed—they would call "The African." They said that some ship brought him to a place that they pronounced " 'Naplis." They said that then some "Mas' John Waller" bought him for his plantation in "Spotsylvania County, Va." This African kept on escaping, the fourth time trying to kill the "hateful po' cracker" slave-catcher, who gave him the punishment choice of castration or of losing one foot. This African took a foot being chopped off with an ax against a tree stump, they said, and he was about to die. But his life was saved by "Mas' John's" brother—"Mas' William

Waller," a doctor, who was so furious about what had happened that he bought the African for himself and gave him the name "Toby."

Crippling about, working in "Mas' William's" house 4
and yard, the African in time met and mated with "the big house cook named Bell," and there was born a girl named Kizzy. As she grew up her African daddy often showed her different kinds of things, telling her what they were in his native tongue. Pointing at a banjo, for example, the African uttered, *"ko"*; or pointing at a river near the plantation, he would say, *"Kamby Bolong."* Many of his strange words started with a *"k"* sound, and the little, growing Kizzy learned gradually that they identified different things.

When addressed by other slaves as "Toby," the mas- 5
ter's name for him, the African said angrily that his name was *"Kin-tay."* And as he gradually learned English, he told young Kizzy some things about himself—for instance, that he was not far from his village, chopping wood to make himself a drum, when four men had surprised, overwhelmed, and kidnaped him.

So Kizzy's head held much about her African daddy 6
when at age 16 she was sold away onto a much smaller plantation in North Carolina. Her new "Mas' Tom Lea" fathered her first child, a boy she named George. And Kizzy told her boy all about his African grandfather. George grew up to be such a gamecock fighter that he was called "Chicken George," and people would come from all over and "bet big money" on his cockfights. He mated with Matilda, another of Lea's slaves; they had seven children, and he told them the stories and strange sounds of their African great-grandfather. And one of those children, Tom, became a blacksmith who was bought away by a "Mas' Murray" for his tobacco plantation in Alamance County, N.C.

Tom mated there with Irene, a weaver on the planta- 7
tion. She also bore seven children, and Tom now told them all about their African great-great-grandfather, the

faithfully passed-down knowledge of his sounds and stories having become by now the family's prideful treasure.

The youngest of that second set of seven children was 8 a girl, Cynthia, who became my maternal Grandma (which today I can only see as fated). Anyway, all of this is how I was growing up in Henning at Grandma's, listening from behind her rocking chair as she and the other visiting old women talked of that African (never then comprehended as *my* great-great-great-great-grandfather) who said his name was *"Kin-tay,"* and said *"ko"* for banjo, *"Kamby Bolong"* for river, and a jumble of other *"k"*-beginning sounds that Grandma privately muttered, most often while making beds or cooking, and who also said that near his village he was kidnaped while chopping wood to make himself a drum.

The story had become nearly as fixed in my head as 9 in Grandma's by the time Dad and Mamma moved me and my two younger brothers, George and Julius, away from Henning to be with them at the small black agricultural and mechanical college in Normal, Ala., where Dad taught.

To compress my next 25 years: When I was 17 Dad 10 let me enlist as a mess boy in the U.S. Coast Guard. I became a ship's cook out in the South Pacific during World War II, and at night down by my bunk I began trying to write sea adventure stories, mailing them off to magazines and collecting rejection slips for eight years before some editors began purchasing and publishing occasional stories. By 1949 the Coast Guard had made me its first "journalist"; finally with 20 years' service, I retired at the age of 37, determined to make a full time career of writing. I wrote mostly magazine articles; my first book was "The Autobiography of Malcolm X."

Then one Saturday in 1965 I happened to be walk- 11 ing past the National Archives building in Washington. Across the interim years I had thought of Grandma's old stories—otherwise I can't think what diverted me up the Archives' steps. And when a main reading room desk

79

attendant asked if he could help me, I wouldn't have dreamed of admitting to him some curiosity hanging on from boyhood about my slave forebears. I kind of bumbled that I was interested in census records of Alamance County, North Carolina, just after the Civil War.

The microfilm rolls were delivered, and I turned them 12 through the machine with a building sense of intrigue, viewing in different census takers' penmanship an endless parade of names. After about a dozen microfilmed rolls, I was beginning to tire, when in utter astonishment I looked upon the names of Grandma's parents: Tom Murray, Irene Murray . . . older sisters of Grandma's as well— every one of them a name that I'd heard countless times on her front porch.

It wasn't that I hadn't believed Grandma. You just 13 *didn't* not believe my Grandma. It was simply so uncanny actually seeing those names in print and in official U.S. Government records.

During the next several months I was back in Wash- 14 ington whenever possible, in the Archives, the Library of Congress, the Daughters of the American Revolution Library. (Whenever black attendants understood the idea of my search, documents I requested reached me with miraculous speed.) In one source or another during 1966 I was able to document at least the highlights of the cherished family story. I would have given anything to have told Grandma, but, sadly, in 1949 she had gone. So I went and told the only survivor of those Henning front-porch storytellers: Cousin Georgia Anderson, now in her 80's in Kansas City, Kan. Wrinkled, bent, not well herself, she was so overjoyed, repeating to me the old stories and sounds; they were like Henning echoes: "Yeah, boy, that African say his name was 'Kin-tay'; he say the banjo was 'ko,' and river 'Kamby Bolong,' an' he was off choppin' some wood to make his drum when they grabbed 'im!" Cousin Georgia grew so excited we had to stop her, calm her down, "You go 'head, boy! Your grandma an' all of 'em—they up there watching what you do!"

That week I flew to London on a magazine assignment. 15
Since by now I was steeped in the old, in the past, scarcely
a tour guide missed me—I was awed at so many historical
places and treasures I'd heard of and read of. I came upon
the Rosetta stone in the British Museum, marveling anew
at how Jean Champollion, the French archeologist, had
miraculously deciphered its ancient demotic and hiero-
glyphic texts . . .

The thrill of that just kept hanging around in my head. 16
I was on a jet returning to New York when a thought hit
me. Those strange, unknown-tongue sounds, always part
of our family's old story . . . they were obviously bits of
our original African *"Kin-tay's"* native tongue. What specific tongue? Could I somehow find out?

Back in New York, I began making visits to the United 17
Nations Headquarters lobby; it wasn't hard to spot Africans. I'd stop any I could, asking if my bits of phonetic
sounds held any meaning for them. A couple of dozen
Africans quickly looked at me, listened, and took off—
understandably dubious about some Tennesseean's accent
alleging "African" sounds.

My research assistant, George Sims (we grew up to- 18
gether in Henning), brought me some names of ranking
scholars of African linguistics. One was particularly intriguing: a Belgian- and English-educated Dr. Jan Vansina;
he had spent his early career living in West African villages, studying and tape-recording countless oral histories
that were narrated by certain very old African men; he
had written a standard textbook, "The Oral Tradition."

So I flew to the University of Wisconsin to see Dr. 19
Vansina. In his living room I told him every bit of the
family story in the fullest detail that I could remember it.
Then, intensely, he queried me about the story's relay
across the generations, about the gibberish of *"k"* sounds
Grandma had fiercely muttered to herself while doing
her housework, with my brothers and me giggling beyond
her hearing at what we had dubbed "Grandma's noises."

Dr. Vansina, his manner very serious, finally said, 20

81

"These sounds your family has kept sound very probably of the tongue called 'Mandinka.' "

I'd never heard of any "Mandinka." Grandma just told   21
of the African saying "ko" for banjo, or "Kamby Bolong" for a Virginia river.

Among Mandinka stringed instruments, Dr. Vansina   22
said, one of the oldest was the "kora."

"Bolong," he said was clearly Mandinka for "river."   23
Preceded by "Kamby," it very likely meant "Gambia River."

Dr. Vansina telephoned an eminent Africanist col-   24
league, Dr. Philip Curtin. He said that the phonetic "Kin-tay" was correctly spelled "Kinte," a very old clan that had originated in Old Mali. The Kinte men tradition-ally were blacksmiths, and the women were potters and weavers.

I knew I must get to the Gambia River.   25

The first native Gambian I could locate in the U.S. was   26
named Ebou Manga, then a junior attending Hamilton College in upstate Clinton, N.Y. He and I flew to Da-kar, Senegal, then took a smaller plane to Yundum Air-port, and rode a van to Gambia's capital, Bathurst. Ebou and his father assembled eight Gambia government offi-cials. I told them Grandma's stories, every detail I could remember, as they listened intently, then reacted. " 'Kamby Bolong' of course is Gambia River!" I heard. "But more clue is your forefather's saying his name was 'Kinte.' " Then they told me something I would never even have fantasized—that in places in the back country lived very old men, commonly called griots, who could tell centuries of the histories of certain very old family clans. As for Kintes, they pointed out to me on a map some family villages, Kinte-Kundah, and Kinte-Kundah Janneh-Ya, for instance.

The Gambian officials said they would try to help me.   27
I returned to New York dazed. It is embarrassing to me now, but despite Grandma's stories, I'd never been con-cerned much with Africa, and I had the routine images

of African people living mostly in exotic jungles. But a compulsion now laid hold of me to learn all I could, and I began devouring books about Africa, especially about the slave trade. Then one Thursday's mail contained a letter from one of the Gambian officials, inviting me to return there.

Monday I was back in Bathurst. It galvanized me when   28
the officials said that a *griot* had been located who told the *Kinte* clan history—his name was Kebba Kanga Fofana. To reach him, I discovered, required a modified safari: renting a launch to get upriver, two land vehicles to carry supplies by a roundabout land route, and employing finally 14 people, including three interpreters and four musicians, since a *griot* would not speak the revered clan histories without background music.

The boat Baddibu vibrated upriver, with me acutely   29
tense: Were these Africans maybe viewing me as but another of the pith-helmets? After about two hours, we put in at James Island, for me to see the ruins of the once British-operated James Fort. Here two centuries of slave ships had loaded thousands of cargoes of Gambian tribespeople. The crumbling stones, the deeply oxidized swivel cannon, even some remnant links of chain seemed all but impossible to believe. Then we continued upriver to the left-bank village of Albreda, and there put ashore to continue on foot to Juffure, village of the *griot*. Once more we stopped, for me to see *toubob kolong*, "the white man's well," now almost filled in, in a swampy area with abundant, tall, saw-toothed grass. It was dug two centuries ago to "17 men's height deep" to insure survival drinking water for long-driven, famishing coffles of slaves.

Walking on, I kept wishing that Grandma could hear   30
how her stories had led me to the *"Kamby Bolong."* (Our surviving storyteller Cousin Georgia died in a Kansas City hospital during this same morning, I would learn later.) Finally, Juffure village's playing children, sighting us, flashed an alert. The 70-odd people came rushing from their circular, thatch-roofed, mud-walled huts, with goats

bounding up and about, and parrots squawking from up in the palms. I sensed him in advance somehow, the small man amid them, wearing a pillbox cap and an off-white robe—the *griot.* Then the interpreters went to him, as the villagers thronged around me.

And it hit me like a gale wind: every one of them, the whole crowd, was *jet black.* An enormous sense of guilt swept me—a sense of being some kind of hybrid . . . a sense of being impure among the pure. It was an awful sensation.　31

The old *griot* stepped away from my interpreters and the crowd quickly swarmed around him—all of them buzzing. An interpreter named A. B. C. Salla came to me; he whispered: "Why they stare at you so, they have never seen here a black American." And that hit me: I was symbolizing for them twenty-five millions of us they had never seen. What did they think of me—of us?　32

Then abruptly the old *griot* was briskly walking toward me. His eyes boring into mine, he spoke in Mandinka, as if instinctively I should understand—and A. B. C. Salla translated:　33

"Yes . . . we have been told by the forefathers . . . that many of us from this place are in exile . . . in that place called America . . . and in other places."　34

I suppose I physically wavered, and they thought it was the heat; rustling whispers went through the crowd, and a man brought me a low stool. Now the whispering hushed—the musicians had softly begun playing *kora* and *balafon,* and a canvas sling lawn seat was taken by the *griot,* Kebba Kanga Fofana, aged 75 "rains" (one rainy season each year). He seemed to gather himself into a physical rigidity, and he began speaking the *Kinte* clan's ancestral oral history; it came rolling from his mouth across the next hours . . . 17th- and 18th-century *Kinte* lineage details, predominantly what men took wives; the children they "begot," in the order of their births; those children's mates and children.　35

Events frequently were dated by some proximate singu-　36

lar physical occurrence. It was as if some ancient scroll were printed indelibly within the *griot's* brain. Each few sentences or so, he would pause for an interpreter's translation to me. I distill here the essence:

The *Kinte* clan began in Old Mali, the men generally 37 blacksmiths "... who conquered fire," and the women potters and weavers. One large branch of the clan moved to Mauretania from where one son of the clan, Kairaba Kunta Kinte, a Moslem Marabout holy man, entered Gambia. He lived first in the village of Pakali N'Ding; he moved next to Jiffarong village; "... and then he came here, into our own village of Juffure."

In Juffure, Kairaba Kunta Kinte took his first wife, "... a 38 Mandinka maiden, whose name was Sireng. By her, he begot two sons, whose names were Janneh and Saloum. Then he got a second wife, Yaisa. By her, he begot a son, Omoro."

The three sons became men in Juffure. Janneh and 39 Saloum went off and founded a new village, Kinte-Kundah Janneh-Ya. "And then Omoro, the youngest son, when he had 30 rains, took as a wife a maiden, Binta Kebba.

"And by her, he begot four sons—Kunta, Lamin, Su- 40 wadu, and Madi ..."

Sometimes, a "begotten," after his naming, would be 41 accompanied by some later-occurring detail, perhaps as "... in time of big water (flood), he slew a water buffalo." Having named those four sons, now the *griot* stated such a detail.

"About the time the king's soldiers came, the eldest of 42 these four sons, Kunta, when he had about 16 rains, went away from this village, to chop wood to make a drum ... and he was never seen again ..."

Goose-pimples the size of lemons seemed to pop all 43 over me. In my knapsack were my cumulative notebooks, the first of them including how in my boyhood, my Grandma, Cousin Georgia and the others told of the African *"Kin-tay"* who always said he was kidnaped near his village—while chopping wood to make a drum ...

I showed the interpreter, he showed and told the *griot*, 44
who excitedly told the people; they grew very agitated.
Abruptly then they formed a human ring, encircling me,
dancing and chanting. Perhaps a dozen of the women
carrying their infant babies rushed in toward me, thrust-
ing the infants into my arms—conveying, I would later
learn, "the laying on of hands . . . through this flesh which
is us, we are you, and you are us." The men hurried me
into their mosque, their Arabic praying later being translated outside: "Thanks be to Allah for returning the long
lost from among us." Direct descendants of Kunta Kinte's
blood brothers were hastened, some of them from nearby
villages, for a family portrait to be taken with me, surrounded by actual ancestral sixth cousins. More symbolic
acts filled the remaining day.

When they would let me leave, for some reason I 45
wanted to go away over the African land. Dazed, silent
in the bumping Land Rover, I heard the cutting staccato
of talking drums. Then when we sighted the next village,
its people came thronging to meet us. They were all—
little naked ones to wizened elders—waving, beaming,
amid a cacophony of crying out; and then my ears identified their words: *"Meester Kinte! Meester Kinte!"*

Let me tell you something: I am a man. But I remem- 46
ber the sob surging up from my feet, flinging up my hands
before my face and bawling as I had not done since I was
a baby . . . the jet-black Africans were jostling, staring . . .
I didn't care, with the feelings surging. If you really knew
the odyssey of us millions of black Americans, if you really
knew how we came in the seeds of our forefathers, captured, driven, beaten, inspected, bought, branded, chained
in foul ships, if you really knew, you needed weeping . . .

Back home, I knew that what I must write, really, was 47
our black saga, where any individual's past is the essence
of the millions'. Now flat broke, I went to some editors I
knew, describing the Gambian miracle, and my desire to
pursue the research; Doubleday contracted to publish, and

Reader's Digest to condense the projected book; then I
had advances to travel further.

What ship brought Kinte to Grandma's " 'Naplis" (An- 48
napolis, Md., obviously)? The old *griot*'s time reference
to "king's soldiers" sent me flying to London. Feverish
searching at last identified, in British Parliament records,
"Colonel O'Hare's Forces," dispatched in mid-1767 to protect the then British-held James Fort whose ruins I'd visited. So Kunta Kinte was down in some ship probably
sailing later that summer from the Gambia River to
Annapolis.

Now I feel it was fated that I had taught myself to 49
write in the U.S. Coast Guard. For the sea dramas I had
concentrated on had given me years of experience searching among yellowing old U.S. maritime records. So now
in English 18th Century marine records I finally tracked
ships reporting themselves in and out to the Commandant
of the Gambia River's James Fort. And then early one
afternoon I found that a Lord Ligonier under a Captain
Thomas Davies had sailed on the Sabbath of July 5, 1767.
Her cargo: 3,265 elephants' teeth, 3,700 pounds of beeswax,
800 pounds of cotton, 32 ounces of Gambian gold, and 140
slaves; her destination: "Annapolis."

That night I recrossed the Atlantic. In the Library of 50
Congress the Lord Ligonier's arrival was one brief line in
"Shipping In The Port Of Annapolis—1748–1775." I located the author, Vaughan W. Brown, in his Baltimore
brokerage office. He drove to Historic Annapolis, the
city's historical society, and found me further documentation of her arrival on Sept. 29, 1767. (Exactly two centuries
later, Sept. 29, 1967, standing, staring seaward from an
Annapolis pier, again I knew tears.) More help came in
the Maryland Hall of Records. Archivist Phebe Jacobsen
found the Lord Ligonier's arriving customs declaration
listing, "98 Negroes"—so in her 86-day crossing, 42 Gam-
bians had died, one among the survivors being 16-year-
old Kunta Kinte. Then the microfilmed Oct. 1, 1767,

Maryland Gazette contained, on page two, an announce-
ment to prospective buyers from the ship's agents, Daniel
of St. Thos. Jenifer and John Ridout (the Governor's secretary): "from the River GAMBIA, in AFRICA . . . a cargo of
choice, healthy SLAVES . . ."

———— ♦ ————

For Study and Discussion

QUESTIONS ABOUT PURPOSE

1. Is Haley's primary purpose to tell the story of his fam-
    ily or to tell the story of how he uncovered the story
    of his family? Explain your answer.
2. What relationship does Haley see between his story
    and the history of black Americans?
3. What is the purpose of storytelling in the Haley family?

QUESTIONS ABOUT AUDIENCE

1. How are the reader and young Haley in similar posi-
    tions at the beginning of the essay?
2. How would a reader who had seen the television series
    Roots have an advantage in these early sections of the
    narrative?
3. Haley says that the *griot's* stories "came rolling from
    his mouth across the next hours." Why does Haley de-
    cide not to retell all these stories for his readers?

QUESTIONS ABOUT STRATEGIES

1. How does Haley distinguish between the sequence of
    events in his search and the sequence of events in the
    Haley family history?

2. In the centuries of the family saga there are many stories worth telling. Haley says he can mention only the highlights. How does this statement explain his pacing of paragraphs 10 and 11–13?
3. Haley manages to maintain a historically objective point of view for most of the essay. Where does he express a more personal point of view?

QUESTIONS FOR DISCUSSION

1. What does Haley's essay reveal about the relationship between scholarly procedures and sheer luck?
2. What is the relationship between the past (the events that happened) and history (a story about those events)?
3. In what ways might the history of your family portray in miniature the history of a town, region, or country?

Narration as a Writing Strategy

POINTS TO CONSIDER

1. What is the point of your narrative? Why do you want to tell it? Do you want to *tell* what happened, *explain* why something happened, or *argue* that what happened should be interpreted in one way? Summarize the essence of your essay and the point it makes by filling in the blanks of the following statement: "I want to tell you about _____ in order to demonstrate _____."

2. How likely is it that your audience has already read similar stories or had similar experiences? How much will you have to tell your audience to set up the major conflict of the essay? Will your readers want you to explain the meaning of the events or will an account of the events be self-explanatory? If an explanation is necessary, will your readers need an explanation as the events occur or will they expect an interpretive summary in the conclusion?

3. What is the principal conflict in your narrative? How does that conflict begin, develop, conclude? Which events in your narrative can be summarized and which must be developed into scenes? How many individual scenes can you develop and still maintain the essential unity of your essay? What is your attitude toward the events in your narrative? Should you treat the material objectively, humorously, passionately?

PREWRITING EXERCISES

1. List, in timetable fashion, the sequence of events that produced a moment of happiness or tragedy. When did the sequence actually begin? How long did it take to develop? How long did it take to be resolved? Did you *know* you were experiencing happiness or tragedy *dur-*

ing the moment it was happening? As you chart the sequence, try to determine the relationship between duration and significance. Are the events that last the longest necessarily the most important? If you were to use your timetable as an outline for an essay, which events would you describe in the most detail?

2. Select one of the smaller moments within the longer event you charted in exercise #1 and chart it. Record every detail, every feeling, every reaction as though you were viewing the moment in slow motion. A good test for this exercise would be to chart an event that lasted only ten or fifteen seconds. How long did Jean Shepherd's moment of truth last?

3. Outline one event—a trip to the store, a school election, an afternoon in the park—according to different chronological patterns. Begin in the middle and return to the beginning before finishing the story. Begin at the end and try to work back to the beginning. You may even wish to move back and forth between two significant time periods, as White does in his essay. The purpose of this experiment is to discover which presentation of the events most successfully emphasizes the principal conflict in your narrative. If the end of the story is *the* important scene, then it should be placed in the most emphatic position—the end. If the end is important only because certain events caused it, then perhaps the *end* could go at the beginning and those events could be the focus of your narrative.

4. Experiment with the pacing of events in an action-filled experience (participating in an athletic contest) or an actionless experience (resting in a tranquil environment). First try to match pace to action—fast-paced summaries for fast-paced action, slow-paced scenes for slow-paced action. Then consider the effect of mismatching pace and action. What happens to the focus of your narrative when an action-filled scene is paced slowly or an actionless scene is paced quickly?

5. Think about the same story from different points of view. How would an enemy, friend, or unknown bystander record your moment of victory or defeat? How

does changing the position of the narrator—participating in the action, observing the action, trying to remember the action—change the story? Test the various possibilities by (1) outlining the action of the plot for several classmates, (2) assigning them separate identities, and then (3) encouraging them to create different interpretations of the same story.

TOPICS FOR WRITING IN CLASS

1. Select a proverb such as "The early bird gets the worm" and then narrate a personal experience that either illustrates or refutes the ideas in the old saying. You may want to use a whimsical parody of such proverbs ("He who laughs, lasts"; "Too much of something is simply wonderful") or create your own theory of human behavior and illustrate it with a narrative.

2. Recount one of the stories you were told "to grow up on." You may want to follow Kingston's model by telling the complete story first, quickly and dramatically, and then speculating on what the story means and how it connects to your life. Or you may want to pace the story throughout the narrative, pausing on occasion to consider why the people acted as they did and why your family storyteller selected you as an appropriate audience.

3. Report an experience in which you had to give orders to other people. You may wish to begin by summarizing several experiences when you had to take orders. What objections did you have to these orders and the leader who gave them? What promises did you make to yourself about how you would act if you were ever a leader? Now that you are a leader what new promises have you made? Select a scene to narrate that will reveal how the change in position influenced a change in your attitude.

TOPICS FOR WRITING OUT OF CLASS

1. Explain how an incident in your life caused you to question or defend the values of your family. Like Kingston, you will need to summarize what those values were (perhaps even establish how they were formed) before you narrate the experience that prompted you to re-evaluate them.

2. Compose a narrative about the first time you perceived that unintentional error could have tragic consequences. You may select an event you witnessed (somebody else's error) or an event you participated in (your error). You may also wish to pause during the narration to speculate on the chain of cause and effect (If only X hadn't done Y, then Z wouldn't have happened) or conclude by weighing the wisdom that "has blood on it" (Now I realize the importance of careful judgment).

3. Chronicle a significant event in the life of your family that occurred during a major crisis in the life of the nation—the Depression, World War II, Civil Rights Movement, Vietnam. Consider how the personal experience of your family was *similar to* or *different from* the public experience of the country. Select a story that allows you to examine the reactions of your family to one issue—unemployment, racial prejudice, military induction—in some detail.

◆

DESCRIPTION

◆

DEFINITION

A descriptive essay is a word-picture of a person, place, or thing. To *describe* means to make a copy or trace a figure. Like painters and photographers, writers of descriptive essays create pictures of interesting subjects (an old woman, a small town, a discarded basball mitt) by focusing on their most characteristic and vivid details (a gnarled hand, a tree-lined street, a broken strap). Painters and photographers display their pictures as completed products:

all the subject is seen all at once. Writers reveal their pictures in stages: the subject is seen developing one word at a time. These words are selected to appeal to the senses and are arranged so that the reader experiences the subject as it grows into a mental picture.

PURPOSE

Description is used either as a device to support other forms of writing or as a dominant writing strategy. For example, description is used in narration to establish the scene of a story, in exposition to develop the steps in an analysis, and in persuasion to clarify the evidence of an argument. The amount of description in such forms of writing may range from a few sentences to several long sections, depending on the author's purpose and the needs of the audience. In the selections that follow, description is the dominant strategy and is used to produce pictures of subjects as specific as a grizzly bear and as general as a culture.

There are two kinds of description, each directed by its own purpose. OBJECTIVE, or technical, description provides factual information about the object. For example, a writer composing an encyclopedia entry on volcanoes would describe their typical characteristics—formation, eruption, destruction. SUBJECTIVE, or impressionistic, description expresses the psychological impact of the subject on the writer. In an impressionistic depiction of a volcano, a writer would reveal how the sights and sounds of one specific volcano (the fiery flow of its lava, the hissing explosion of its escaping steam) inspired a certain emotional reaction (fear of the volcano's destructive power, astonishment at its eerie beauty). On some occasions, as in the descriptions of the eruption of Mount St. Helens in Washington state, writers will use both technical and impressionistic details to strengthen and enrich their portraits.

AUDIENCE

Writers of descriptive essays must consider how much *and* what kind of descriptive detail their audience needs. Both considerations depend upon how much their audience already knows about the subject. If the subject is unusual (volcanoes), then readers will need a lot of information, much of it technical, simply to understand the unfamiliar sights documented in the essay. If the subject is familiar (a lawn sprinkler), then readers will need fewer technical details but more impressionistic observations if they are to *see* those ordinary sights they presume they already understand.

Establishing the right mixture of descriptive detail depends to some extent on a writer's anticipation of an audience's expectations. A writer describing Mount St. Helens assumes that readers will want an efficient, matter-of-fact characterization of volcanoes and some sense of what it *feels* like to see one erupting. A writer describing a lawn sprinkler assumes that readers probably have few expectations. Most people know what a lawn sprinkler looks and feels like. In such a situation, a writer is free to use strategies that will create a new vision of a subject (for example, portraying the lawn sprinkler as marking the languid pulse of summer).

STRATEGIES

The *four* strategies for writing a descriptive essay are (1) appeal to the senses, (2) identify special features, (3) select vivid details, and (4) arrange details in a pattern. Because description makes a direct APPEAL TO THE SENSES, writers must first consider what information each of the five senses adds to the understanding of a subject. John McPhee depends on sight to identify the dimension, color, and movements of the grizzly bear, but his subject really comes to life when he illustrates how the bear (which has extraordinarily poor vision) senses the world—standing on its hind legs to sniff what it cannot see or walking over a tree to scratch its belly.

The information communicated by each sense helps identify a subject's SPECIAL FEATURES. Every object, person, or place possesses unique characteristics that writers must consider in planning a descriptive essay. John McPhee recognizes the *special* features of his subject when he maintains a respectful distance from the grizzly bear. His strategy is to rely on anecdotes about other bears to complete his portrait. Patricia Hampl is able to characterize her grandmother by describing her special ability to toss around old clichés and overused routines to encourage her family to eat. In addition to considering a subject's special features, writers must also determine how special conditions such as time, weather, events, and the mood of the observer influence the way a subject is perceived. For example, Carol Bly suggests that her view of farm work changes significantly during each hour of the day.

The third strategy employed in a descriptive essay is the SELECTION OF DETAILS. Without exact and evocative details a description is vague, fuzzy, unintelligible—like a distant billboard seen without your glasses. But the mere addition of details will not bring a subject into sharp focus. Details must be *selected* carefully so that they contribute to the writer's sense of audience and purpose. Patricia Hampl assumes that most of her readers are familiar with large family meals, but her detailed description of the wily strategies of her Napoleonic grandmother makes a commonplace occasion seem like an epic ordeal. N. Scott Momaday, on the other hand, assumes that his readers have little familiarity with the bleak landscapes of the Kiowa Indians. His selection of details not only provides a unified portrait of this world but also illustrates how the Kiowas transformed the landmarks of their lifeless landscape into the legends of their culture.

After the appropriate details have been selected, they must be ARRANGED IN A PATTERN. The simplest pattern is organized by the logic of the eye and may take two forms. In the first, the writer is a *fixed observer*, describing the details of a scene as they would be seen in a framed picture —from side to side, top to bottom, or center to periphery. In the second, the writer enters the scene and becomes a *moving observer*, noting details as they are encountered— moving toward a tree, by a house, and over a bridge. Momaday employs the first technique when he describes his grandmother at prayer and the second when he re-traces the epic journey of his people from the mountains to the plains.

A more complex arrangement of details is organized by the logic of the imagination and may also take two forms. In the first, the writer compares the details of one scene with the details of another to form a *metaphor* or *framed image*. Momaday provides a vivid example of this technique when he repeats the Kiowas' myth of origin: the people envisioned their journey from the sunless forest to the open prairie as "entering the world through a hollow log." In the second form, the writer arranges the details of a scene so that they reveal the *dominant impression* they made on the observer. George Orwell uses this tech-nique to record his reaction to the poor of Marrakech: "The people have brown faces—besides, there are so many of them. Are they really the same flesh as yourself? Do they even have names? Or are they merely a kind of un-differentiated brown stuff, about as individual as bees or coral insects?"

By studying the essays that follow, you will discover the strategies writers use to accomplish what novelist Joseph Conrad identified as the purpose of his writing: "My task which I am trying to achieve is, by the power of the written word, to make you hear, to make you feel—it is, before all, to make you *see*. That—and no more, and it is everything."

Grizzly

JOHN McPHEE

◆

John McPhee was born in 1931 in Princeton, New
Jersey, received his undergraduate education at Princeton University, and studied at Cambridge University.
His first job was as a television writer for "Robert
Montgomery Presents," but he soon switched to journalism and became an assistant editor for Time, then
a staff writer for The New Yorker. His books, which
cover an intriguing range of subjects, include Oranges
(1967), an historical, geographical, botanical, and an-
ecdotal study of the fruit; Levels of the Game (1969),
an analysis of tennis; The Curve of Binding Energy
(1974), an examination of the world's nuclear-materials
safeguard problems; and The Place de la Concord
Suisse (1984), a character sketch of the Swiss Army.
In all his work McPhee displays an uncanny ability to
make the unfamiliar or complex subject lucid—indeed,
almost familiar. "Grizzly," taken from McPhee's book
about Alaska, Coming into the Country (1976), describes the writer's encounter with the bear that rules
the Arctic terrain.

We passed first through stands of fireweed, and then over   1
ground that was wine-red with the leaves of bearberries.
There were curlewberries, too, which put a deep-purple
stain on the hand. We kicked at some wolf scat, old as
winter. It was woolly and white and filled with the hair
of a snowshoe hare. Nearby was a rich inventory of caribou pellets and, in increasing quantity as we moved down-
hill, blueberries—an outspreading acreage of blueberries.
Fedeler stopped walking. He touched my arm. He had in
an instant become even more alert than he usually was,

and obviously apprehensive. His gaze followed straight on down our intended course. What he saw there I saw now. It appeared to me to be a hill of fur. "Big boar grizzly," Fedeler said in a near-whisper. The bear was about a hundred steps away, in the blueberries, grazing. The head was down, the hump high. The immensity of muscle seemed to vibrate slowly—to expand and contract, with the grazing. Not berries alone but whole bushes were going into the bear. He was big for a barren-ground grizzly. The brown bears of Arctic Alaska (or grizzlies; they are no longer thought to be different) do not grow to the size they will reach on more ample diets elsewhere. The barren-ground grizzly will rarely grow larger than six hundred pounds.

"What if he got too close?" I said.   2

Fedeler said, "We'd be in real trouble."   3

"You can't outrun them," Hession said.   4

A grizzly, no slower than a racing horse, is about half   5
again as fast as the fastest human being. Watching the great mound of weight in the blueberries, with a fifty-five-inch waist and a neck more than thirty inches around, I had difficulty imagining that he could move with such speed, but I believed it, and was without impulse to test the proposition. Fortunately, a slight southerly wind was coming up the Salmon valley. On its way to us, it passed the bear. The wind was relieving, coming into our faces, for had it been moving the other way the bear would not have been placidly grazing. There is an old adage that when a pine needle drops in the forest the eagle will see it fall; the deer will hear it when it hits the ground; the bear will smell it. If the boar grizzly were to catch our scent, he might stand on his hind legs, the better to try to see. Although he could hear well and had an extraordinary sense of smell, his eyesight was not much better than what was required to see a blueberry inches away. For this reason, a grizzly stands and squints, attempting to bring the middle distance into focus, and the gesture is often misunderstood as a sign of anger and forthcoming

attack. If the bear were getting ready to attack, he would be on four feet, head low, ears cocked, the hair above his hump muscle standing on end. As if that message were not clear enough, he would also chop his jaws. His teeth would make a sound that would carry like the ringing of an axe.

One could predict, but not with certainty, what a 6 grizzly would do. Odds were very great that one touch of man scent would cause him to stop his activity, pause in a moment of absorbed and alert curiosity, and then move, at a not undignified pace, in a direction other than the one from which the scent was coming. That is what would happen almost every time, but there was, to be sure, no guarantee. The forest Eskimos fear and revere the grizzly. They know that certain individual bears not only will fail to avoid a person who comes into their country but will approach and even stalk the trespasser. It is potentially inaccurate to extrapolate the behavior of any one bear from the behavior of most, since they are both intelligent and independent and will do what they choose to do according to mood, experience, whim. A grizzly that has ever been wounded by a bullet will not forget it, and will probably know that it was a human being who sent the bullet. At sight of a human, such a bear will be likely to charge. Grizzlies hide food sometimes—a caribou calf, say, under a pile of scraped-up moss—and a person the bear might otherwise ignore might suddenly not be ignored if the person were inadvertently to step into the line between the food cache and the bear. A sow grizzly with cubs, of course, will charge anything that suggests danger to the cubs, even if the cubs are nearly as big as she is. They stay with their mother two and a half years.

If a wolf kills a caribou, and a grizzly comes along while 7 the wolf is feeding on the kill, the wolf puts its tail between its legs and hurries away. A black bear will run from a grizzly, too. Grizzlies sometimes kill and eat black bears. The grizzly takes what he happens upon. He is an opportunistic eater. The predominance of the grizzly in his terrain is challenged by nothing but men and ravens. To frustrate ravens from stealing his food, he will lie down and sleep on top of a carcass, occasionally swatting the birds as if they were big black flies. He prefers a vegetable diet. He can pulp a moosehead with a single blow, but he is not lusting always to kill, and when he moves through his country he can be something munificent, going into copses of willow among unfleeing moose and their calves, touching nothing, letting it all breathe as before. He may, though, get the head of a cow moose between his legs and rake her flanks with the five-inch knives that protrude from the ends of his paws. Opportunistic. He removes and eats her entrails. He likes porcupines, too, and when one turns and presents to him a pygal bouquet of quills, he will leap into the air, land on the other side, chuck the fretful porpentine beneath the chin, flip it over, and, with a swift ventral incision, neatly remove its body from its skin, leaving something like a sea urchin behind him on the ground. He is nothing if not athletic. Before he dens, or just after he emerges, if his mountains are covered with snow he will climb to the brink of some impossible schuss, sit down on his butt, and shove off. Thirty-two, sixty-four, ninety-six feet per second, he plummets down the mountainside, spray snow flying to either side, as he approaches collision with boulders and trees. Just short of catastrophe, still going at bonecrushing speed, he flips to his feet and walks sedately onward as if his ride had not occurred.

His population density is thin on the Arctic barren ground. He needs for his forage at least fifty and perhaps a hundred square miles that are all his own—sixty-four thousand acres, his home range. Within it, he will move, typically, eight miles a summer day, doing his travelling through the twilight hours of the dead of night. To scratch his belly he walks over a tree—where forest exists. The tree bends beneath him as he passes. He forages in the morning, generally; and he rests a great deal, particularly after he eats. He rests fourteen hours a day. If he becomes

8

hot in the sun, he lies down in a pool in the river. He sleeps on the tundra—restlessly tossing and turning, forever changing position. What he could be worrying about I cannot imagine.

His fur blends so well into the tundra colors that sometimes it is hard to see him. Fortunately, we could see well enough the one in front of us, or we would have walked right to him. He caused a considerable revision of our travel plans. Not wholly prepared to follow the advice of Andy Russell, I asked Fedeler what one should do if a bear were to charge. He said, "Take off your pack and throw it into the bear's path, then crawl away, and hope the pack will distract the bear. But there is no good thing to do, really. It's just not a situation to be in."

————— ◆ —————

For Study and Discussion

QUESTIONS ABOUT PURPOSE

1. What kind of description of the grizzly does McPhee want to give? Objective? Subjective? Both? Why?
2. What is McPhee's purpose in focusing on one specific bear? What does he add to his description by his discussions of the general category of bears?
3. What does McPhee attempt to accomplish by describing how the bear impressed him?

QUESTIONS ABOUT AUDIENCE

1. What does McPhee assume his readers know about grizzlies?
2. Does the opening of the essay make the reader interested in the descriptive information that follows? If so, in what ways?

3. How does McPhee's comparison of the grizzly to other animals help his readers?

QUESTIONS ABOUT STRATEGIES

1. McPhee only *sees* the bear. How does his description of the bear's senses add dimension to his portrait?
2. What special features of his subject require McPhee to be a fixed observer?
3. How does McPhee arrange his descriptive detail to demonstrate that the grizzly is the predominant beast in its terrain?

QUESTIONS FOR DISCUSSION

1. Why does McPhee characterize the grizzly as an "opportunistic eater"?
2. How does McPhee's discussion of the bear's intelligence and independence modify that characterization?
3. What does McPhee's account of the bear sliding down the hill or tossing in its sleep add to this portrait?

The Potent Center

PATRICIA HAMPL

♦

Patricia Hampl was born in 1946 in St. Paul, Minnesota, and educated at the University of Minnesota, where she now teaches writing. Always deeply involved in the concerns of her literary community, Hampl wrote poetry, much of it about her beloved St. Paul. Woman Before an Aquarium, *her first volume of poems, was published by the University of Pittsburgh Press in 1978; a second volume,* Resort, *was published by Houghton Mifflin in 1983. Hampl has long been fascinated by the powers of memory, beauty, and community. These are the themes of* A Romantic Education *(1981), a much-acclaimed memoir that was awarded the Houghton Mifflin Literary Fellowship. Writing in a diversity of forms, Hampl continues to evoke "the roots and mystery of place"; her works in progress include a novel and an opera libretto. "The Potent Center," excerpted from* A Romantic Education, *is at once a comic and nostalgic sketch of the elaborate ordeal of eating Sunday dinner at her Czech grandmother's house.*

Food was the potent center of my grandmother's life. 1
Maybe the immense amount of time it took to prepare meals during most of her life accounted for her passion. Or it may have been her years of work in various kitchens on the hill and later, in the house of Justice Butler: after all, she was a professional. Much later, when she was dead and I went to Prague, I came to feel the motto I knew her by best—*Come eat*—was not, after all, a personal statement, but a racial one, the *cri de coeur* of Middle Europe.

Often, on Sundays, the entire family gathered for din- 2
ner at her house. Dinner was at 1 P.M. My grandmother
would have preferred the meal to be at the old time of
noon, but her children had moved their own Sunday dinner hour to the more fashionable (it was felt) 4 o'clock, so
she compromised. Sunday breakfast was something my
mother liked to do in a big way, so we arrived at my grandmother's hardly out of the reverie of waffles and orange
rolls, before we were propped like rag dolls in front of a
pork roast and sauerkraut, dumplings, hot buttered carrots,
rye bread and rollikey, pickles and olives, apple pie and ice
cream. And coffee.

Coffee was a food in that house, not a drink. I always 3
begged for some because the magical man on the Hills
Brothers can with his turban and long robe scattered with
stars and his gold slippers with pointed toes, looked deeply
happy as he drank from his bowl. The bowl itself reminded me of soup, Campbell's chicken noodle soup, my
favorite food. The distinct adultness of coffee and the
robed man with his deep-drinking pleasure made it clear
why the grownups lingered so long at the table. The
uncles smoked cigars then, and the aunts said, "Oh, those
cigars."

My grandmother, when she served dinner, was a vir- 4
tuoso hanging on the edge of her own ecstatic performance. She seemed dissatisfied, almost querulous until she
had corralled everybody into their chairs around the table,
which she tried to do the minute they got into the house.
No cocktails, no hors d'oeuvres (pronounced, by some of
the family, "horse's ovaries"), just business. She was a
little power crazed: she had us and, by God, we were going
to eat. She went about it like a goose breeder forcing
pellets down the gullets of those dumb birds.

She flew between her chair and the kitchen, always 5
finding more this, extra that. She'd given you the *wrong*
chicken breast the first time around; now she'd found the
right one: eat it too, eat it fast, because after the chicken
comes the rhubarb pie. Rhubarb pie with a thick slice of

cheddar cheese that it was imperative every single person eat.

We had to eat fast because something was always out there in the kitchen panting and charging the gate, champing at the bit, some mound of rice or a Jell-O fruit salad or vegetable casserole or pie was out there, waiting to be let loose into the dining room. 6

She had the usual trite routines: the wheedlings, the silent pout ("What! You don't like my brussels sprouts? I thought you liked *my* brussels sprouts," versus your wife's/sister's/mother's. "I made that pie just for you," etc., etc.) But it was the way she tossed around the old clichés and the overused routines, mixing them up and dealing them out shamelessly, without irony, that made her a pro. She tended to peck at her own dinner. Her plate, piled with food, was a kind of stage prop, a mere bending to convention. She liked to eat, she was even a greedy little stuffer, but not on these occasions. She was a woman possessed by an idea, given over wholly to some phantasmagoria of food, a mirage of stuffing, a world where the endless chicken and the infinite lemon pie were united at last at the shore of the oceanic soup plate that her children and her children's children alone could drain . . . if only they would try. 7

She was there to bolster morale, to lead the troops, to give the sharp command should we falter on the way. The futility of saying no was supreme, and no one ever tried it. How could a son-in-law, already weakened near the point of imbecility by the once, twice, thrice charge to the barricades of pork and mashed potato, be expected to gather his feeble wit long enough to ignore the final call of his old commander when she sounded the alarm: "Pie, Fred?" 8

Just when it seemed as if the food-crazed world she had created was going to burst, that she had whipped and frothed us like a sack of boiled potatoes under her masher, just then she pulled it all together in one easeful stroke like the pro she was. 9

She stood in the kitchen doorway, her little round 10

Napoleonic self sheathed in a cotton flowered pinafore apron, the table draped in its white lace cloth but spotted now with gravy and beet juice, the troops mumbling indistinctly as they waited at their posts for they knew not what. We looked up at her stupidly, weakly. She said nonchalantly, "Anyone want another piece of pie?" No, no more pie, somebody said. The rest of the rabble grunted along with him. She stood there with the coffeepot and laughed and said, "Good! Because there *isn't* any more pie."

No more pie. We'd eaten it all, we'd put away everything in that kitchen. We were exhausted and she, gambler hostess that she was (but it was her house she was playing), knew she could offer what didn't exist, knew us, knew what she'd wrought. There was a sense of her having won, won something. There were no divisions among us now, no adults, no children. Power left the second and third generations and returned to the source, the grandmother who reduced us to mutters by her art.

That wasn't the end of it. At 5 p.m. there was "lunch" —sandwiches and beer; the sandwiches were made from the leftovers (mysteriously renewable resources, those roasts). And at about 8 p.m. we were at the table again for coffee cake and coffee, the little man in his turban and his coffee ecstasy and his pointed shoes set on the kitchen table as my grandmother scooped out the coffee and dumped it into a big enamel pot with a crushed eggshell. By then everyone was alive and laughing again, the torpor gone. My grandfather had been inviting the men, one by one, into the kitchen during the afternoon where he silently (the austere version of memory—but he must have talked, must have said *something*) handed them jiggers of whiskey, and watched them put the shot down in one swallow. Then he handed them a beer, which they took out in the living room. I gathered that the *little* drink in the tiny glass shaped like a beer mug was some sort of antidote for the *big* drink of beer. He sat on the chair in the kitchen with a bottle of beer on the floor next to him and played his concertina, allowing society to form itself around him—while he lived he was the center—but not seeking it, not going into the living room. And not talking. He held to his music and the kindly, medicinal administration of whiskey.

By evening, it seemed we could eat endlessly, as if we'd   13 had some successful inoculation at dinner and could handle anything. I stayed in the kitchen after they all reformed in the dining room at the table for coffee cake. I could hear them, but the little man in his starry yellow robe was on the table in the kitchen and I put my head down on the oil cloth very near the curled and delighted tips of his pointed shoes, and I slept. Whatever laughter there was, there was. But something sweet and starry was in the kitchen and I lay down beside it, my stomach full, warm, so safe I'll live the rest of my life off the fat of that vast family security.

———— ◆ ————

For Study and Discussion

QUESTIONS ABOUT PURPOSE

1. What is the primary purpose of Hampl's essay—to describe a scene (Sunday dinner) or to describe a character (her grandmother)? How does the first sentence of the essay suggest that the scene and the character are inseparable?

2. Why does Hampl's characterization of her grandmother as a "pro" enhance the description of this "ecstatic performance"?

3. In addition to describing her grandmother's Sunday performance, what else does Hampl describe in this essay? Consider, for example, the mood and meaning of her last paragraph.

QUESTIONS ABOUT AUDIENCE

1. To what extent does Hampl assume that her readers are familiar with family meals similar to the one she describes? Explain your answer.
2. What assumptions does Hampl make about her audience when she alludes to Campbell's soup and Hills Brothers coffee?
3. How does Hampl's description of her grandmother's "usual trite routines" help readers gain a new vision of something that may seem familiar?

QUESTIONS ABOUT STRATEGIES

1. How does Hampl's selection of details evoke the sights, smells, and sounds of the Sunday dinner? For example, how does she evoke the deep-drinking pleasure of coffee?
2. How do Hampl's military comparisons—her grandmother as "Napoleonic" commander, her family as "the troops," and the dining room table as their "posts" —help create a dominant impression of the meal?
3. How does Hampl use her grandfather's performance in the kitchen to vary the mood of her essay?

QUESTIONS FOR DISCUSSION

1. Hampl describes her grandmother as a woman "possessed by an idea, given over wholly to some phantasmagoria of food, a mirage of stuffing. . . ." What does this description suggest about the way many people view the purpose of food in their lives?
2. What does this essay reveal about the relationship between family power and the preparation and consumption of food?
3. Why, in your opinion, does food so often figure intensely in a person's memories?

Getting Tired

CAROL BLY

♦

*Carol Bly was born in 1930 in Duluth, Minnesota,
and educated at Wellesley College and the University
of Minnesota. For twenty-three years she lived on a
farm near Madison, Minnesota, raising four children
and writing stories and essays. Always interested in
rural community development, Bly has worked as a
humanities consultant for the National Farmer's Union
and the Land Stewardship Project. She currently
teaches writing at Hamline University and the University of Minnesota Summer Arts Program. Her
stories have appeared in the* American Review, The
New Yorker, *and* Houghton Mifflin's Best American
Short Stories 1983. *Her essays have appeared in many
regional magazines; some of the best of them were
collected in* Letters from the Country *(1981), a provocative and loving look at the American landscape
from the perspective of a small town. In "Getting
Tired" Bly describes the gigantic machinery and exhausting routines required for cornpicking and plowing.*

The men have left a gigantic 6600 combine a few yards   1
from our grove, at the edge of the stubble. For days it was
working around the farm; we heard it on the east, later on
the west, and finally we could see it grinding back and
forth over the windrows on the south. But now it has been
simply squatting at the field's edge, huge, tremendously
still, very professional, slightly dangerous.

We all have the correct feelings about this new com-   2
bine: this isn't the good old farming where man and soil
are dusted together all day; this isn't farming a poor man

112

can afford, either, and therefore it further threatens his hold on the American "family farm" operation. We have been sneering at this machine for days, as its transistor radio, amplified well over the engine roar, has been grinding up our silence, spreading a kind of shrill ghetto evening all over the farm.

But now it is parked, and after a while I walk over to it 3 and climb up its neat little John Deere-green ladder on the left. Entering the big cab up there is like coming up into a large ship's bridge on visitors' day—heady stuff to see the inside workings of a huge operation like the Queen Elizabeth II. On the other hand I feel left out, being only a dumbfounded passenger. The combine cab has huge windows flaring wider at the top; they lean forward over the ground, and the driver sits so high behind the glass in its rubber moldings it is like a movie-set spaceship. He has obviously come to dominate the field, whether he farms it or not.

The value of the 66 is that it can do anything, and to 4 change it from a combine into a cornpicker takes one man about half an hour, whereas most machine conversions on farms take several men a half day. It frees its owners from a lot of monkeying.

Monkeying, in city life, is what little boys do to clocks 5 so they never run again. In farming it has two quite different meanings. The first is small side projects. You monkey with poultry, unless you're a major egg handler. Or you monkey with ducks or geese. If you have a very small milk herd, and finally decide that prices plus state regulations don't make your few Holsteins worthwhile, you "quit monkeying with them." There is a hidden dignity in this word: it precludes mention of money. It lets the wife of a very marginal farmer have a conversation with a woman who may be helping her husband run fifteen hundred acres. "How you coming with those geese?" "Oh, we've been real disgusted. We're thinking of quitting monkeying with them." It saves her having to say, "We lost our shirts on those darn geese."

The other meaning of monkeying is wrestling with and   6
maintaining machinery, such as changing heads from
combining to cornpicking. Farmers who cornpick the old
way, in which the corn isn't shelled automatically during
picking in the field but must be elevated to the top of a
pile by belt and then shelled, put up with some monkeying.

Still, cornpicking and plowing is a marvelous time of   7
the year on farms; one of the best autumns I've had recently had a few days of fieldwork in it. We were outside
all day, from six in the morning to eight at night—coming
in only for noon dinner. We ate our lunches on a messy
truck flatbed. (For city people who don't know it: *lunch*
isn't a noon meal; it is what you eat out of a black lunch
pail at 9 A.M and 3 P.M. If you offer a farmer a cup of coffee at 3:30 P.M. he or she is likely to say, "No thanks, I've
already had lunch.") There were four of us hired to help
—a couple to plow, Celia (a skilled farmhand who worked
steady for our boss), and me. Lunch was always two sandwiches of white commercial bread with luncheon meat, and
one very generous piece of cake-mix cake carefully wrapped
in Saran Wrap. (I never found anyone around here self-
conscious about using Saran Wrap when the Dow Chemical Company was also making napalm.)

It was very pleasant on the flatbed, squinting out over   8
the yellow picked cornstalks—each time we stopped for
lunch, a larger part of the field had been plowed black.
We fell into the easy psychic habit of farmworkers: admiration of the boss. "Ja, I see he's buying one of those
big 4010s," someone would say. We always perked up at
inside information like that. Or "Ja," as the woman hired
steady told us, "he's going to plow the home fields first this
time, instead of the other way round." We temporary
help were impressed by that, too. Then, with real flair,
she brushed a crumb of luncheon meat off her jeans, the
way you would make sure to flick a gnat off spotless tennis
whites. It is the true feminine touch to brush a crumb off

pants that are encrusted with Minnesota Profile A heavy loam, many swipes of SAE 40 oil, and grain dust.

All those days, we never tired of exchanging informa- 9 tion on how *he* was making out, what *he* was buying, whom *he* was going to let drive the new tractor, and so on. There is always something to talk about with the other hands, because farming is genuinely absorbing. It has the best quality of work: nothing else seems real. And everyone doing it, even the cheapest helpers like me, can see the layout of the whole—from spring work, to cultivating, to small grain harvest, to cornpicking, to fall plowing.

The second day I was promoted from elevating corn- 10 cobs at the corn pile to actual plowing. Hour after hour I sat up there on the old Alice, as she was called (an Allis-Chalmers WC that looked rusted from the Flood). You have to sit twisted part way around, checking that the plowshares are scouring clean, turning over and dropping the dead crop and soil, not clogging. For the first two hours I was very political. I thought about what would be good for American farming—stronger marketing organizations, or maybe a law like the Norwegian Odal law, preventing the breaking up of small farms or selling them to business interests. Then the sun got high, and each time I reached the headlands area at the field's end I dumped off something else, now my cap, next my jacket, finally my sweater.

Since the headlands are the last to be plowed, they 11 serve as a field road until the very end. There are usually things parked there—a pickup or a corn trailer—and things dumped—my warmer clothing, our afternoon lunch pails, a broken furrow wheel someone picked up.

By noon I'd dropped all political interest, and was 12 thinking only: how unlike this all is to Keats's picture of autumn, a "season of mists and mellow fruitfulness." This gigantic expanse of horizon, with everywhere the easy growl of tractors, was simply teeming with extrovert energy. It wouldn't calm down for another week, when whoever was lowest on the totem pole would be sent out to check a field for dropped parts or to drive away the last machines left around.

The worst hours for all common labor are the hours after noon dinner. Nothing is inspiring then. That is when people wonder how they ever got stuck in the line of work they've chosen for life. Or they wonder where the cool Indian smoke of secrets and messages began to vanish from their marriage. Instead of plugging along like a cheerful beast working for me, the Allis now smelled particularly gassy. To stay awake I froze my eyes onto an indented circle in the hood around the gas cap. Someone had apparently knocked the screw cap fitting down into the hood, so there was a moat around it. In this moat some overflow gas leapt in tiny waves. Sometimes the gas cap was a castle, this was the moat; sometimes it was a nuclear-fission plant, this was the horrible hot-water waste. Sometimes it was just the gas cap on the old Alice with the spilt gas bouncing on the hot metal. 13

Row after row. I was stupefied. But then around 2:30 the shadows appeared again, and the light, which had been dazing and white, grew fragile. The whole prairie began to gather itself for the cool evening. All of a sudden it was wonderful to be plowing again, and when I came to the field end, the filthy jackets and the busted furrow wheel were just benign mistakes: that is, if it chose to, the jacket could be a church robe, and the old wheel could be something with some pride to it, like a helm. And I felt the same about myself: instead of being someone with a half interest in literature and a half interest in farming doing a half-decent job plowing, I could have been someone desperately needed in Washington or Zurich. I drank my three o'clock coffee joyously, and traded the other plowman a Super-Valu cake-mix lemon cake slice for a Holsum baloney sandwich because it had garlic in it. 14

By seven at night we had been plowing with headlights for an hour. I tried to make up games to keep going, 15

116

on my second wind, on my third wind, but labor is labor after the whole day of it; the mind refuses to think of ancestors. It refuses to pretend the stalks marching up to the right wheel in the spooky light are men-at-arms, or to imagine a new generation coming along. It doesn't care. Now the Republicans could have announced a local meeting in which they would propose a new farm program whereby every farmer owning less than five hundred acres must take half price for his crop, and every farmer owning more than a thousand acres shall receive triple price for his crop, and I was so tired I wouldn't have shown up to protest.

A million hours later we sit around in a daze at the dining-room table, and nobody says anything. In low, courteous mutters we ask for the macaroni hotdish down this way, please. Then we get up in ones and twos and go home. Now the farm help are all so tired we *are* a little like the various things left out on the headlands—some tools, a jacket, someone's thermos top—used up for that day. Thoughts won't even stick to us any more. 16

Such tiredness must be part of farmers' wanting huge machinery like the Deere 6600. That tiredness that feels so good to the occasional laborer and the athlete is disturbing to a man destined to it eight months of every year. But there is a more hidden psychology in the issue of enclosed combines versus open tractors. It is this: one gets too many impressions on the open tractor. A thousand impressions enter as you work up and down the rows: nature's beauty or nature's stubbornness, politics, exhaustion, but mainly the feeling that all this repetition—last year's cornpicking, this year's cornpicking, next year's cornpicking—is taking up your lifetime. The mere repetition reveals your eventual death. 17

When you sit inside a modern combine, on the other hand, you are so isolated from field, sky, all the real world, that the brain is dulled. You are not sensitized to your own mortality. You aren't sensitive to anything at all. 18

This must be a common choice of our mechanical era: 19
to hide from life inside our machinery. If we can hide
from life in there, some idiotic part of the psyche reasons,
we can hide from death in there as well.

---- ♦ ----

For Study and Discussion

QUESTIONS ABOUT PURPOSE

1. In what ways does Bly's title, "Getting Tired," convey
   the primary purpose of her essay? For example, is
   Bly's purpose simply to describe the fatigue of the
   farmworker? Explain your answer.
2. Why does Bly open and close her essay with a description of a gigantic combine? Does her attitude toward
   and understanding of this machine change during the
   essay? Explain your answer.
3. Bly extends her description beyond sensory details into
   an argument about the value of the small family farm.
   Why does she do so?

QUESTIONS ABOUT AUDIENCE

1. How does Bly's definition of the word *monkeying* reveal her assumptions about the probable identity of
   her readers?
2. What kind of technical information does she provide
   for those readers so that they understand the work she
   is describing?
3. How does she use impressionistic detail to enable her
   readers to experience routines with which they may
   be unfamiliar?

QUESTIONS ABOUT STRATEGIES

1. How does Bly use the lunch on the flatbed truck and the conversation about the activities of the boss to create scenes that appeal to the senses?
2. How does she select and arrange details to describe the various attitudes she has toward her work during the day? For example, how does she use the gas cap to convey her feelings during the "worst hours" of the day?
3. How does Bly describe the Deere 6600? What aspects of the machine remind her of an ocean liner, a space ship, a ghetto?

QUESTIONS FOR DISCUSSION

1. In what ways does this essay contradict the myths about the beauty and benefits of farm life? For example, why does Bly suggest that her picture of the autumn harvest is unlike the one found in John Keats's ode "To Autumn"?
2. What does Bly suggest is the ultimate effect of fatigue on one's mind and will? How does she illustrate this effect with her comment about the meeting of the local Republican party?
3. What does this essay reveal about the relationship between people and machines? According to Bly, how do we use machines to hide from life and death?

The Way to Rainy Mountain

N. SCOTT MOMADAY

————— ◆ —————

N. Scott Momaday, a Kiowa Indian, was born in Law-
ton, Oklahoma, in 1934 and was educated at the
University of New Mexico and Stanford University. Although he has taught English and comparative literature at several universities, most recently at Stanford
University, his vital interests are American Indian art,
history, and culture. His books include House Made
of Dawn (1968), winner of the Pulitzer Prize for fiction, and The Way to Rainy Mountain (1969), a
collection of Kiowa Indian folk tales. In the autobiographical narrative that introduces these tales,
Momaday evokes the landscapes, the legends, and the
people that created the Kiowa culture.

A single knoll rises out of the plain in Oklahoma, north   1
and west of the Wichita Range. For my people, the Kiowas, it is an old landmark, and they gave it the name
Rainy Mountain. The hardest weather in the world is
there. Winter brings blizzards, hot tornadic winds arise in
the spring, and in summer the prairie is an anvil's edge.
The grass turns brittle and brown, and it cracks beneath
your feet. There are green belts along the rivers and
creeks, linear groves of hickory and pecan, willow and
witch hazel. At a distance in July or August the steaming
foliage seems almost to writhe in fire. Great green and yellow grasshoppers are everywhere in the tall grass, popping

up like corn to sting the flesh, and tortoises crawl about on the red earth, going nowhere in the plenty of time. Loneliness is an aspect of the land. All things in the plain are isolate; there is no confusion of objects in the eye, but *one* hill or *one* tree or *one* man. To look upon that landscape in the early morning, with the sun at your back, is to lose the sense of proportion. Your imagination comes to life, and this, you think, is where Creation was begun.

I returned to Rainy Mountain in July. My grandmother had died in the spring, and I wanted to be at her grave. She had lived to be very old and at last infirm. Her only living daughter was with her when she died, and I was told that in death her face was that of a child.

I like to think of her as a child. When she was born, the Kiowas were living the last great moment of their history. For more than a hundred years they had controlled the open range from the Smoky Hill River to the Red, from the headwaters of the Canadian to the fork of the Arkansas and Cimarron. In alliance with the Comanches, they had ruled the whole of the southern Plains. War was their sacred business, and they were among the finest horsemen the world has ever known. But warfare for the Kiowas was preeminently a matter of disposition rather than of survival, and they never understood the grim, unrelenting advance of the U.S. Cavalry. When at last, divided and ill-provisioned, they were driven onto the Staked Plains in the cold rains of autumn, they fell into panic. In Palo Duro Canyon they abandoned their crucial stores to pillage and had nothing then but their lives. In order to save themselves, they surrendered to the soldiers at Fort Sill and were imprisoned in the old stone corral that now stands as a military museum. My grandmother was spared the humiliation of those high gray walls by eight or ten years, but she must have known from birth the affliction of defeat, the dark brooding of old warriors.

Her name was Aho, and she belonged to the last culture to evolve in North America. Her forebears came down from the high country in western Montana nearly

121

three centuries ago. They were a mountain people, a mysterious tribe of hunters whose language has never been positively classified in any major group. In the late seventeenth century they began a long migration to the south and east. It was a journey toward the dawn, and it led to a golden age. Along the way the Kiowas were befriended by the Crows, who gave them the culture and religion of the Plains. They acquired horses, and their ancient nomadic spirit was suddenly free of the ground. They acquired Tai-me, the sacred Sun Dance doll, from that moment the object and symbol of their worship, and so shared in the divinity of the sun. Not least, they acquired the sense of destiny, therefore courage and pride. When they entered upon the southern Plains they had been transformed. No longer were they slaves to the simple necessity of survival; they were a lordly and dangerous society of fighters and thieves, hunters and priests of the sun. According to their origin myth, they entered the world through a hollow log. From one point of view, their migration was the fruit of an old prophecy, for indeed they emerged from a sunless world.

Although my grandmother lived out her long life in 5 the shadow of Rainy Mountain, the immense landscape of the continental interior lay like memory in her blood. She could tell of the Crows, whom she had never seen, and of the Black Hills, where she had never been. I wanted to see in reality what she had seen more perfectly in the mind's eye, and traveled fifteen hundred miles to begin my pilgrimage.

Yellowstone, it seemed to me, was the top of the world, 6 a region of deep lakes and dark timber, canyons and waterfalls. But, beautiful as it is, one might have the sense of confinement there. The skyline in all directions is close at hand, the high wall of the woods and deep cleavages of shade. There is a perfect freedom in the mountains, but it belongs to the eagle and the elk, the badger and the bear. The Kiowas reckoned their stature by the distance they see, and they were bent and blind in the wilderness.

Descending eastward, the highland meadows are a stair-   7
way to the plain. In July the inland slope of the Rockies is
luxuriant with flax and the buckwheat, stonecrop and lark-
spur. The earth unfolds and the limit of the land recedes.
Clusters of trees, and animals grazing far in the distance,
cause the vision to reach away and wonder to build upon
the mind. The sun follows alonger course in the day, and
the sky is immense beyond all comparison. The great billowing clouds that sail upon it are shadows that move
upon the grain like water, dividing light. Farther down, in
the land of the Crows and Blackfeet, the plain is yellow.
Sweet clover takes hold of the hills and bends upon itself
to cover and seal the soil. There the Kiowas paused on
their way; they had come to the place where they must
change their lives. The sun is at home on the plains. Precisely there does it have the certain character of a god.
When the Kiowas came to the land of the Crows, they
could see the dark lees of the hills at dawn across the Big-
horn River, the profusion of light on the grain shelves, the
oldest deity ranging after the solstices. Not yet would they
veer southward to the caldron of the land that lay below;
they must wean their blood from the northern winter and
hold the mountains a while longer in their view. They
bore Tai-me in procession to the east.

A dark mist lay over the Black Hills, and the land was   8
like iron. At the top of a ridge I caught sight of Devil's
Tower upthrust against the gray sky as if in the birth of
time the core of the earth had broken through its crust and
the motion of the world was begun. There are things in
nature that engender an awful quiet in the heart of man;
Devil's Tower is one of them. Two centuries ago, because
they could not do otherwise, the Kiowas made a legend at
the base of the rock. My grandmother said:
Eight children were there at play, seven sisters and their
brother. Suddenly the boy was struck dumb; he trembled
and began to run upon his hands and feet. His fingers
became claws, and his body was covered with fur. Di-
rectly there was a bear where the boy had been. The sis-

123

ters were terrified; they ran, and the bear after them. They came to the stump of a great tree, and the tree spoke to them. It bade them climb upon it, and as they did so it began to rise into the air. The bear came to kill them, but they were just beyond its reach. It reared against the tree and scored the bark all around with its claws. The seven sisters were borne into the sky, and they became the stars of the Big Dipper.

From that moment, and so long as the legend lives, the Kiowas have kinsmen in the night sky. Whatever they were in the mountains, they could be no more. However tenuous their well-being, however much they had suffered and would suffer again, they had found a way out of the wilderness.

My grandmother had a reverence for the sun, a holy regard that now is all but gone out of mankind. There was a wariness in her, and an ancient awe. She was a Christian in her later years, but she had come a long way about, and she never forgot her birthright. As a child she had been to the Sun Dances; she had taken part in those annual rites, and by them she had learned the restoration of her people in the presence of Tai-me. She was about seven when the last Kiowa Sun Dance was held in 1887 on the Washita River above Rainy Mountain Creek. The buffalo were gone. In order to consummate the ancient sacrifice—to impale the head of a buffalo bull upon the medicine tree—a delegation of old men journeyed into Texas, there to beg and barter for an animal from the Goodnight herd. She was ten when the Kiowas came together for the last time as a living Sun Dance culture. They could find no buffalo; they had to hang an old hide from the sacred tree. Before the dance could begin, a company of soldiers rode out from Fort Sill under orders to disperse the tribe. Forbidden without cause the essential act of their faith, having seen the wild herds slaughtered and left to rot upon the ground, the Kiowas backed away forever from the medicine tree. That was July 20, 1890, at the great bend of the Washita. My grandmother was there.

8

Without bitterness, and for as long as she lived, she bore a vision of deicide.

Now that I can have her only in memory, I see my [10] grandmother in the several postures that were peculiar to her: standing at the wood stove on a winter morning and turning meat in a great iron skillet; sitting at the south window, bent above her beadwork, and afterwards, when her vision failed, looking down for a long time into the fold of her hands; going out upon a cane, very slowly as she did when the weight of age came upon her; praying. I remember her most often at prayer. She made long, rambling prayers out of suffering and hope, having seen many things. I was never sure that I had the right to hear, so exclusive were they of all mere custom and company. The last time I saw her she prayed standing by the side of her bed at night, naked to the waist, the light of a kerosene lamp moving upon her dark skin. Her long, black hair, always drawn and braided in the day, lay upon her shoulders and against her breasts like a shawl. I do not speak Kiowa, and I never understood her prayers, but there was something inherently sad in the sound, some merest hesitation upon the syllables of sorrow. She began in a high and descending pitch, exhausting her breath to silence; then again and again—and always the same intensity of effort, of something that is, and is not, like urgency in the human voice. Transported so in the dancing light among the shadows of her room, she seemed beyond the reach of time. But that was illusion; I think I knew then that I should not see her again.

---- ◆ ----

For Study and Discussion

QUESTIONS ABOUT PURPOSE

1. How does Momaday's title provide an explanation of his purpose?

2. What connection does he establish among his three subjects—the land, the people, and their culture?

3. What is Momaday's reason for returning to his grandmother's house?

QUESTIONS ABOUT AUDIENCE

1. What audience does Momaday presume he is addressing throughout the essay? How do you know?

2. Why is the historical information (for example, paragraph 9) necessary for that audience?

3. How does Momaday use the legend of Devil's Tower to help his readers *see* the way the Kiowas see?

QUESTIONS ABOUT STRATEGIES

1. How many sensory details does Momaday cite in his opening paragraph? What special effect do they create?

2. How does Momaday arrange the details in paragraphs 5, 6, and 7?

3. Momaday remembers his grandmother in several significant poses. What does each one of these "pictures" tell us about her?

QUESTIONS FOR DISCUSSION

1. How does the Kiowas' belief that they could measure "their stature by the distance they could see" explain their history?

2. What does this essay reveal about the importance of oral traditions?

3. What significance does Momaday attach to the fact that he does not speak Kiowa?

Marrakech

GEORGE ORWELL

——————— ◆ ———————

*George Orwell (a pen name for Eric Blair, 1903–1950)
was born in Motihari, Bengal, where his father was
employed with the Bengal civil service. He was brought
to England at an early age for schooling (Eton), but
rather than completing his education at the university
he served with the Indian imperial police in Burma
(1922–1927). He wrote about these experiences in his
first novel,* Burmese Days. *Later he returned to Europe
and worked at various jobs (*Down and Out in Paris
and London, *1933) before fighting on the Republican
side of the Spanish Civil War (*Homage to Catalonia,
*1938). Orwell's attitudes toward war and government
are reflected in his most famous books,* Animal Farm
(1945) and Nineteen Eighty-Four *(1949). In "Marrakech" (from* Such, Such Were the Joys, *1945), Orwell
describes the people most European visitors to Northern Africa fail to "see."*

As the corpse went past the flies left the restaurant table   1
in a cloud and rushed after it, but they came back a few
minutes later.

The little crowd of mourners—all men and boys, no   2
women—threaded their way across the market-place between the piles of pomegranates and the taxis and the
camels, wailing a short chant over and over again. What
really appeals to the flies is that the corpses here are never
put into coffins, they are merely wrapped in a piece of
rag and carried on a rough wooden bier on the shoulders
of four friends. When the friends get to the burying-

ground they hack an oblong hole a foot or two deep, dump the body in it and fling over it a little of the dried-up, lumpy earth, which is like broken brick. No gravestone, no name, no identifying mark of any kind. The burying-ground is merely a huge waste of hummocky earth, like a derelict building-lot. After a month or two no one can even be certain where his own relatives are buried.

When you walk through a town like this—two hundred 3 dred thousand inhabitants, of whom at least twenty thousand own literally nothing except the rags they stand up in—when you see how the people live, and still more how easily they die, it is always difficult to believe that you are walking among human beings. All colonial empires are in reality founded upon that fact. The people have brown faces—besides, there are so many of them! Are they really the same flesh as yourself? Do they even have names? Or are they merely a kind of undifferentiated brown stuff, about as individual as bees or coral insects? They rise out of the earth, they sweat and starve for a few years, and then they sink back into the nameless mounds of the graveyard and nobody notices that they are gone. And even the graves themselves soon fade back into the soil. Sometimes, out for a walk, as you break your way through the prickly pear, you notice that it is rather bumpy underfoot, and only a certain regularity in the bumps tells you that you are walking over skeletons.

I was feeding one of the gazelles in the public 4 gardens.

Gazelles are almost the only animals that look good to 5 eat when they are still alive, in fact, one can hardly look at their hindquarters without thinking of mint sauce. The gazelle I was feeding seemed to know that this thought was in my mind, for though it took the piece of bread I was holding out it obviously did not like me. It nibbled rapidly at the bread, then lowered its head and tried to butt me, then took another nibble and then butted again. Probably its idea was that if it could drive me away the bread would somehow remain hanging in mid-air.

An Arab navvy working on the path nearby lowered 6
his heavy hoe and sidled slowly towards us. He looked
from the gazelle to the bread and from the bread to the
gazelle, with a sort of quiet amazement, as though he had
never seen anything quite like this before. Finally he said
shyly in French:

"I could eat some of that bread." 7

I tore off a piece and he stowed it gratefully in some 8
secret place under his rags. This man is an employee of
the Municipality.

When you go through the Jewish quarters you gather 9
some idea of what the medieval ghettoes were probably
like. Under their Moorish rulers the Jews were only allowed to own land in certain restricted areas, and after
centuries of this kind of treatment they have ceased to
bother about overcrowding. Many of the streets are a good
deal less than six feet wide, the houses are completely
windowless, and sore-eyed children cluster everywhere in
unbelievable numbers, like clouds of flies. Down the cen-
tre of the street there is generally running a little river of
urine.

In the bazaar huge families of Jews, all dressed in the 10
long black robe and little black skull-cap, are working in
dark fly-infested booths that look like caves. A carpenter
sits crosslegged at a prehistoric lathe, turning chair-legs
at lightning speed. He works the lathe with a bow in his
right hand and guides the chisel with his left foot, and
thanks to a lifetime of sitting in this position his left leg
is warped out of shape. At his side his grandson, aged six,
is already starting on the simpler parts of the job.

I was just passing the coppersmiths' booths when some- 11
body noticed that I was lighting a cigarette. Instantly,
from the dark holes all round, there was a frenzied rush
of Jews, many of them old grandfathers with flowing
grey beards, all clamouring for a cigarette. Even a blind
man somewhere at the back of one of the booths heard
a rumour of cigarettes and came crawling out, groping
in the air with his hand. In about a minute I had used

up the whole packet. None of these people, I suppose, works less than twelve hours a day, and every one of them looks on a cigarette as a more or less impossible luxury.

As the Jews live in self-contained communities they 12 follow the same trades as the Arabs, except for agriculture. Fruit-sellers, potters, silversmiths, blacksmiths, butchers, leatherworkers, tailors, water-carriers, beggars, porters—whichever way you look you see nothing but Jews. As a matter of fact there are thirteen thousand of them, all living in the space of a few acres. A good job Hitler wasn't here. Perhaps he was on his way, however. You hear the usual dark rumours about the Jews, not only from the Arabs but from the poorer Europeans.

"Yes, mon vieux, they took my job away from me and 13 gave it to a Jew. The Jews! They're the real rulers of this country, you know. They've got all the money. They control the banks, finance—everything."

"But," I said, "isn't it a fact that the average Jew is 14 a labourer working for about a penny an hour?"

"Ah, that's only for show! They're all moneylenders 15 really. They're cunning, the Jews."

In just the same way, a couple of hundred years ago, 16 poor old women used to be burned for witchcraft when they could not even work enough magic to get themselves a square meal.

All people who work with their hands are partly in- 17 visible, and the more important the work they do, the less visible they are. Still, a white skin is always fairly conspicuous. In northern Europe, when you see a labourer ploughing a field, you probably give him a second glance. In a hot country, anywhere south of Gibraltar or east of Suez, the chances are that you don't even see him. I have noticed this again and again. In a tropical landscape one's eye takes in everything except the human beings. It takes in the dried-up soil, the prickly pear, the palm tree and the distant mountain, but it always misses the peasant hoeing at his patch. He is the same colour as the earth, and a great deal less interesting to look at.

It is only because of this that the starved countries of Asia and Africa are accepted as tourist resorts. No one would think of running cheap trips to the Distressed Areas. But where the human beings have brown skins their poverty is simply not noticed. What does Morocco mean to a Frenchman? An orange-grove or a job in Government service. Or to an Englishman? Camels, castles, palm trees, Foreign Legionnaires, brass trays, and bandits. One could probably live there for years without noticing that for nine-tenths of the people the reality of life is an endless, back-breaking struggle to wring a little food out of an eroded soil.

Most of Morocco is so desolate that no wild animal bigger than a hare can live on it. Huge areas which were once covered with forest have turned into a treeless waste where the soil is exactly like broken-up brick. Nevertheless a good deal of it is cultivated, with frightful labour. Everything is done by hand. Long lines of women, bent double like inverted capital L's, work their way slowly across the fields, tearing up the prickly weeds with their hands, and the peasant gathering lucerne for fodder pulls it up stalk by stalk instead of reaping it, thus saving an inch or two on each stalk. The plough is a wretched wooden thing, so frail that one can easily carry it on one's shoulder, and fitted underneath with a rough iron spike which stirs the soil to a depth of about four inches. This is as much as the strength of the animals is equal to. It is usual to plough with a cow and a donkey yoked together. Two donkeys would not be quite strong enough, but on the other hand two cows would cost a little more to feed. The peasants possess no harrows, they merely plough the soil several times over in different directions, finally leaving it in rough furrows, after which the whole field has to be shaped with hoes into small oblong patches to conserve water. Except for a day or two after the rare rainstorms there is never enough water. Along the edges

18

19

of the fields channels are hacked out to a depth of thirty or forty feet to get at the tiny trickles which run through the subsoil.

Every afternoon a file of very old women passes down the road outside my house, each carrying a load of firewood. All of them are mummified with age and the sun, and all of them are tiny. It seems to be generally the case in primitive communities that the women, when they get beyond a certain age, shrink to the size of children. One day a poor old creature who could not have been more than four feet tall crept past me under a vast load of wood. I stopped her and put a five-sou piece (a little more than a farthing) into her hand. She answered with a shrill wail, almost a scream, which was partly gratitude but mainly surprise. I suppose that from her point of view, by taking any notice of her, I seemed almost to be violating a law of nature. She accepted her status as an old woman, that is to say as a beast of burden. When a family is travelling it is quite usual to see a father and a grown-up son riding ahead on donkeys, and an old woman following on foot, carrying the baggage.

But what is strange about these people is their invisibility. For several weeks, always at about the same time of day, the file of old women had hobbled past the house with their firewood, and though they had registered themselves on my eyeballs I cannot truly say that I had seen them. Firewood was passing—that was how I saw it. It was only that one day I happened to be walking behind them, and the curious up-and-down motion of a load of wood drew my attention to the human being beneath it. Then for the first time I noticed the poor old earth-coloured bodies, bodies reduced to bones and leathery skin, bent double under the crushing weight. Yet I suppose I had not been five minutes on Moroccan soil before I noticed the overloading of the donkeys and was infuriated by it. There is no question that the donkeys are damnably treated. The Moroccan donkey is hardly bigger than a St. Bernard dog, it carries a load which in the British

Army would be considered too much for a fifteen-hands mule, and very often its pack-saddle is not taken off its back for weeks together. But what is peculiarly pitiful is that it is the most willing creature on earth, it follows its master like a dog and does not need either bridle or halter. After a dozen years of devoted work it suddenly drops dead, whereupon its master tips it into the ditch and the village dogs have torn its guts out before it is cold.

This kind of thing makes one's blood boil, whereas— 22 on the whole—the plight of the human beings does not. I am not commenting, merely pointing to a fact. People with brown skins are next door to invisible. Anyone can be sorry for the donkey with its galled back, but it is generally owing to some kind of accident if one even notices the old woman under her load of sticks.

———— ◆ ————

For Study and Discussion

QUESTIONS ABOUT PURPOSE

1. To what extent is Orwell's title appropriate? Does he describe Marrakech?
2. How is Orwell's description of the poor related to his explanation of the Europeans' failure to *see* them?
3. Why is Orwell's own statement of purpose—"I am not commenting, merely pointing to a fact"—*not* an accurate assessment of his intentions in this essay?

QUESTIONS ABOUT AUDIENCE

1. Who is the audience for Orwell's essay? How does he involve them in his description? See paragraphs 3 and 9.

2. How does paragraph 18 suggest that Orwell may be thinking about a specific audience for his essay?

3. What response does Orwell anticipate his readers will have to his essay? Do you *see* the woman under the load of sticks?

QUESTIONS ABOUT STRATEGIES

1. How does Orwell select and arrange details in paragraphs 1–3? How do the irregular bumps underfoot provide an appropriate conclusion to this section?

2. What difference does Orwell see between the positions of fixed and moving observer? How do paragraphs 20–23 illustrate this difference?

3. Locate all the references in which Orwell compares the poor to animals. What evidence does he offer that the poor see themselves as animals?

QUESTIONS FOR DISCUSSION

1. Are "people who work with their hands partly invisible"? To whom? Why?

2. What does Orwell mean when he says that all colonial empires are founded on the "fact" that the poor are not human beings? What other organizations are founded on such "facts"?

3. What evidence can you cite to support or refute Orwell's assertion that our attitudes and values determine what we see?

─────── ◆ ───────

Description as a Writing Strategy

1. Is the *primary* purpose of your descriptive essay to present factual information about your subject or to evoke the sensations of experiencing it? What kinds of detail will you have to exclude if you elect to write either an objective or subjective description? What kinds of technical detail will strengthen your subjective portrait? What kinds of impressionistic detail will enrich your objective description?

2. If your subject is unfamiliar to your readers, what kinds of information must you provide so that they will understand what they are seeing? If it is familiar, what new angle can you develop so that they will see something they have failed to notice? What kind of directions do you need to give your readers so that they see your subject the way you want them to see it?

3. What are the special features of your subject that you must consider—size, accessibility, complexity? What do each of your five senses reveal about your subject? How can you select and arrange vivid details to make your readers sense your subject? Which details reveal the most about the unique character of your subject or your purpose in writing about it?

PREWRITING EXERCISES

1. Select a potential subject for a meditation exercise (for example, a special dinner). Close your eyes and then, by working your way systematically through the five senses, try to remember each feature of the meal. How did the food *look* on the table—color, shape, arrangement? How did it *feel* to be seated at the table—the

135

feel of your clothes, chair, silverware? What were the distinctive smells and tastes of each dish? What sounds did people make—serving the meal, eating it, talking about it?

2. Using a large drawing pad, map a place that has had some significance in your life (for example, a childhood neighborhood). First try to establish the boundaries of the map and its significant physical landmarks. Then use various organizing systems—games, travel routes, seasons—to generate more detailed information. Write a brief explanation beside every feature you draw—for example, "short-cut to school."

3. Examine several photographs of the same person. Try to determine the subject's distinctive physical features and characteristic ways of dressing and behaving. How would you photograph your subject? Consider various possibilities—candid, posed, at rest, in action. If you were to pose your subject, what setting would you select, what attire would you recommend, what props would you use, who else (if anyone) would be included in the picture? You may wish to experiment with some of these poses by sighting your subject through your own camera.

4. Examine a stationary object such as a statue from several positions. First, circle the statue, establishing a different fixed position at several points. Next, move toward, by, and away from the statue. Vary the means of movement—walking, riding a bicycle, driving a car. Finally, observe the statue from several unusual perspectives—from underneath the bushes or atop a distant building; in the middle of the night or in the middle of a rainstorm.

5. Select a number of subjects and then construct an analogy chart. List in one column the distinctive features of the subjects. In the opposite column, write down whatever analogy (or resemblance) comes to mind. Some of the analogies may seem obvious (the three buildings looked like stacked cereal boxes); others may seem bizarre (the two lovers were entangled like a plate of spaghetti).

TOPICS FOR WRITING IN CLASS

1. Write about an unusual machine (helicopter) or animal (thoroughbred racehorse) that you encountered for the first time. You may wish to contrast the descriptive information you obtained through books, television, or rumor with your actual experience of *seeing* the subject firsthand.

2. Describe the appearance and behavior of *one* member of your family or a friend during some significant activity. You may focus on a significant but commonplace activity such as preparing the evening meal or writing the monthly checks. Or you may select a special occasion such as a wedding or graduation ceremony.

3. Describe your favorite summer place—a back porch, a swimming pool, a baseball diamond, a campsite. Try to evoke both the special features of this landscape—its physical detail and identifying activities—*and* the special feelings they prompted in you.

TOPICS FOR WRITING OUT OF CLASS

1. Describe the best-known monument in your town or neighborhood. You may interpret the word *monument* literally (a statuesque general astride a prancing iron horse) or figuratively (the tallest building or silliest sign). In addition to describing its physical features, research the person, cause, or enterprise identified with the monument. Who designed it, when was it built, why was it built, what local legends have accumulated about it?

2. Portray a landscape that impressed you as the scariest or most serene place you ever saw. You may wish to begin by describing the images of fear or bliss that appear in the media (horror movies, travel magazines) to establish your criteria. But your purpose is to describe an actual place—to portray a special landscape and account for your special psychological response to it.

3. Write an essay in which you demonstrate how habits or values shape perception. Like Bly, you may want to describe how fatigue changes people's observation of little things. Or, like Orwell, you may want to describe how presumptions or prejudice prevent people from seeing big things. This essay could be written for a specific audience and purpose—to convince the town council that they should not demolish an old building. It could also be written for a more general audience and purpose—to help readers see the textures of experience that surround them.

PROCESS ANALYSIS

DEFINITION

A *process* is an operation that moves through a series of steps to bring about a desired result. Almost anything, from the simple act of getting out of bed in the morning to the most complex transactions of the stock exchange, can be considered a process. For purposes of clarity, processes are often classified by the principal functions in their operation: natural (the birth of a baby) or mechanical (the ignition of a car engine); physical (dancing) or mental (writing). *Analysis* is the division of something into parts in order to understand the whole. For example, English teachers analyze the lines of a poem, doctors analyze the symptoms of a patient, and politicians analyze the opinions of individuals and groups within the electorate. A *process analysis* essay (1) divides a process into its individual steps, (2) explains the movement of the process (step by step) from beginning to end, and (3) interprets the function of each step as it relates to the other steps in the sequence and to the production of the desired result.

PURPOSE

The two major purposes of a process analysis essay are to GIVE DIRECTIONS and to PROVIDE INFORMATION. Sometimes these purposes are difficult to separate from one another because giving directions about how to do a task (hit a baseball) also requires providing information on how the whole process works (the rules of the game—the strike zone, walks, hits, baserunning, outs, scoring). But usually the two purposes can be seen as distinct because they accomplish different objectives. Giving directions enables readers to perform a task (change a tire). Providing information satisfies readers' curiosity about a task although they may never have the inclination or opportunity to perform it (pilot a spaceship).

Process analysis essays are often written for two other purposes: to demonstrate that (1) an apparently difficult process is really simple, or that (2) an apparently simple process is quite complicated. In the first case, the purpose may be to prove how a complex process may be simplified by using one specific method (cooking a six-course dinner with a microwave oven). In the second case, the purpose may be to explain how a carefully calculated plan makes a process appear simple (the preparations for an informal television interview).

AUDIENCE

The process analysis essay requires a thoughtful assessment of audience. First, writers must decide whether they are writing *to* an audience (giving directions) or writing *for* an audience (providing information). Writing *to* an audience permits writers to address readers who are already interested in a subject: "If *you* want to plant a productive garden, *you* must follow these seven steps." Writing *for* an audience allows writers to speak from a detached perspective but requires them to capture the interest of general readers: "Although many Americans are concerned about nuclear power, few understand how a nuclear power plant works."

Second, writers must determine the probable knowledge gap between themselves and their audience. To analyze a process effectively, writers should research it thoroughly or have firsthand knowledge of its operation. Indeed, writing about a procedure suggests a degree of expertise. If writers anticipate that most of their audience possesses similar expertise, then they can make certain assumptions about their presentation. A judge explaining courtroom procedure to a group of law students assumes that he does not have to define the special meaning of the word *brief*. On the other hand, if the intended audience has little (or only general) knowledge of a process, writers can assume nothing. A French chef writing a cookbook for a group of occasional cooks will have to explain the use of certain tools and define many terms. If writers presume their readers are experts when they are are not, they will confuse or annoy them. If they presume their readers need to be told everything when they don't, then they will bore or antagonize them.

STRATEGIES

The most effective strategy for writing a process analysis is to organize the essay according to the following *five* steps: overview, special terms, sequence of steps, examples, and results. The first two steps prepare readers to understand the process, the next two illustrate the process in action, and the last one explains the effectiveness of the outcome.

Most writers begin by providing an OVERVIEW of the whole process. Such an overview includes (1) defining the objective of the process, (2) identifying (and numbering) the steps in the sequence, (3) grouping some small steps into larger organizational units, and (4) calling attention to those steps or units that will receive the most emphasis. In "Insert Flap 'A' and Throw Away" S. J. Perelman's comic difficulties with the Self-Running 10-Inch Scale-Model Delivery-Truck Kit Powered by Magic Motor occur because the "writer" of the instructions has failed to provide an intelligible overview of the assembly process. By contrast, the writers of "Riveters" begin by explaining that riveters work in teams of four, that each team member has a special name and function, and that there are precise methods for achieving and measuring a team's success.

Every process has it own SPECIAL TERMS to describe tools, tasks, and methods. These terms must be defined if the process is to be understood. Some writers define special terms at the beginning so that readers will understand the terms when they are used later in the essay. Other writers define terms throughout the essay, pausing to explain their special meaning the first time they are introduced into the analysis. The authors of "Riveters" combine these strategies by listing the major terms at the beginning of the essay (heater, catcher, bucker-up, gunman) and then defining them in more detail when their functions in the process become the subject of analysis.

A process analysis essay must provide a clear and careful presentation of the SEQUENCE OF STEPS. Such a presentation interprets the reasons for each step and often includes the following advice: (1) *Do Not Omit Any Step.* A sequence is a sequence because all steps depend upon one another. Omitting a step can produce disastrous results, as S. J. Perelman learns when he dismisses those instructions he does not understand. (2) *Do Not Reverse Steps.* A sequence is a sequence because each step must be performed according to a necessary and logical pattern. If the riveters wait to align the holes in the girders until after they get the red-hot rivet, it will be too late to complete their job. (3) *Suspend Certain Steps.* Occasionally, a whole series of steps must be suspended, and another process completed, before the sequence can resume. Bob Evans warns the would-be "swing-dancer" that he will have to stop in the middle of learning dance routines in order to be outfitted by the wardrobe mistress. (4) *Do Not Overlook Steps Within Steps.* Every sequence has a series of smaller steps buried within each step. Malcolm Cowley outlines the four stages of writing a story but suggests that there are other, hidden stages. (5) *Avoid Certain Steps.* It is often tempting to insert steps that are not listed but that appear "logical." Richard Selzer suggests that following such an impulse in the operating room can produce tragic results.

Four kinds of EXAMPLES may be used to explain the steps in a sequence: (1) *Pictures.* Graphs, charts, and blueprints are often used to illustrate the operation of a process. Such pictures should certainly be drawn more carefully than those mentioned in "Insert Flap 'A' and Throw Away." (2) *Anecdotes.* Personal experience can be used to clarify or simplify the analysis of a process. Malcolm Cowley analyzes the writing process by citing the personal experiences of a wide range of professional writers. (3) *Variants.* Alternative steps can be mentioned to demonstrate flexibility in a process. For example, each writer that Cowley cites seems to work within the four-stage process in a different way. (4) *Comparisons.* Comparisons can be introduced to help readers see that a complex process is really similar to a process they already know. Richard Selzer employs this strategy when he suggests that the work of a surgeon is similar to the work of a priest, a poet, or a traveler in a dangerous country.

Although the process analysis essay emphasizes the process, it also tries to assess the RESULTS the process produces. That assessment is usually stated in two questions: How do I know it's done? and How do I know it's good? Answering these questions is no simple task. For example, Malcolm Cowley suggests that many writers revise endlessly, and Richard Selzer realizes that a successful surgery may still result in the death of his patient.

Insert Flap "A" and Throw Away

S. J. PERELMAN

———— ◆ ————

S(idney) J(oseph) Perelman (1904–1980) was born in Brooklyn, New York, and educated at Brown University. He began his career as a writer-cartoonist with College Humor *magazine but soon moved to* The New Yorker, *where his contributions established his claim to the title of funniest man in America. Most of the material he wrote for* The New Yorker *was collected in over thirty books, including* Crazy Like a Fox *(1944),* Swiss Family Perelman *(1950), and* Vinegar Puss *(1975). Perelman's humor also found its way to Hollywood. Three of his most famous screenplays are "Monkey Business" (1931) and "Horse Feathers" (1932) for the Marx Brothers and "Around the World in Eighty Days" (1956), for which he won an Oscar. In the following selection, taken from* The Most of S. J. Perelman *(1962), Perelman explains how assembling mechanical gadgets can induce a nervous breakdown.*

One stifling summer afternoon last August, in the attic 1
of a tiny stone house in Pennsylvania, I made a most
interesting discovery: the shortest, cheapest method of
inducing a nervous breakdown ever perfected. In this technique (eventually adopted by the psychology department
of Duke University, which will adopt anything), the subject is placed in a sharply sloping attic heated to 340°F.
and given a mothproof closet known as the Jiffy-Cloz to
assemble. The Jiffy-Cloz, procurable at any department

store or neighborhood insane asylum, consists of half a dozen gigantic sheets of red cardboard, two plywood doors, a clothes rack, and a packet of staples. With these is included a set of instructions mimeographed in pale-violet ink, fruity with phrases like "Pass Section F through Slot AA, taking care not to fold tabs behind washers (see Fig. 9)." The cardboard is so processed that as the subject struggles convulsively to force the staple through, it suddenly buckles, plunging the staple deep into his thumb. He thereupon springs up with a dolorous cry and smites his knob (Section K) on the rafters (RR). As a final demonic touch, the Jiffy-Cloz people cunningly omit four of the staples necessary to finish the job, so that after indescribable purgatory, the best the subject can possibly achieve is a sleazy, capricious structure which would reduce any self-respecting moth to helpless laughter. The cumulative frustration, the tropical heat, and the soft, ghostly chuckling of the moths are calculated to unseat the strongest mentality.

In a period of rapid technological change, however, it 2 was inevitable that a method as cumbersome as the Jiffy-Cloz would be superseded. It was superseded at exactly nine-thirty Christmas morning by a device called the Self-Running 10-Inch Scale-Model Delivery-Truck Kit Powered by Magic Motor, costing twenty-nine cents. About nine on that particular morning, I was spread-eagled on my bed, indulging in my favorite sport of mouth-breathing, when a cork fired from a child's air gun mysteriously lodged in my throat. The pellet proved awkward for a while, but I finally ejected it by flailing the little marksman (and his sister, for good measure) until their welkins rang, and sauntered in to breakfast. Before I could choke down a healing fruit juice, my consort, a tall, regal creature indistinguishable from Cornelia, the Mother of the Gracchi, except that her foot was entangled in a roller skate, swept in. She extended a large, unmistakable box covered with diagrams.

"Now don't start making excuses," she whined. "It's 3

146

just a simple cardboard toy. The directions are on the
back—"

"Look, dear," I interrupted, rising hurriedly and pull-   4
ing on my overcoat, "it clean slipped my mind. I'm supposed to take a lesson in crosshatching at Zim's School
of Cartooning today."

"On Christmas?" she asked suspiciously.   5

"Yes, it's the only time they could fit me in," I coun-   6
tered glibly. "This is the big week for crosshatching, you
know, between Christmas and New Year's."

"Do you think you ought to go in your pajamas?" she   7
asked.

"Oh, that's O.K.," I smiled. "We often work in our   8
pajamas up at Zim's. Well, goodbye now. If I'm not home
by Thursday, you'll find a cold snack in the safe-deposit
box." My subterfuge, unluckily, went for naught, and in
a trice I was sprawled on the nursery floor, surrounded
by two lambkins and ninety-eight segments of the Self-
Running 10-Inch Scale-Model Delivery-Truck Construction Kit.

The theory of the kit was simplicity itself, easily intel-   9
ligible to Kettering of General Motors, Professor Millikan,
or any first-rate physicist. Taking as my starting point
the only sentence I could comprehend, "Fold down on all
lines marked 'fold down'; fold up on all lines marked 'fold
up,' " I set the children to work and myself folded up
with an album of views of Chili Williams. In a few moments, my skin was suffused with a delightful tingling
sensation and I was ready for the second phase, lightly
referred to in the directions as "Preparing the Spring Motor Unit." As nearly as I could determine after twenty
minutes of mumbling, the Magic Motor ("No Electricity—
No Batteries—Nothing to Wind—Motor Never Wears
Out") was an accordion-pleated affair operating by torsion,
attached to the axles. "It is necessary," said the text, "to
cut a slight notch in each of the axles with a knife (see
Fig. C). To find the exact place to cut this notch, lay
one of the axles over diagram at bottom of page."

"Well, *now* we're getting someplace!" I boomed, with 10 a false gusto that deceived nobody. "Here, Buster, run in and get Daddy a knife."

"I dowanna," quavered the boy, backing away. "You 11 always cut yourself at this stage." I gave the wee fellow an indulgent pat on the head that flattened it slightly, to teach him civility, and commandeered a long, serrated bread knife from the kitchen. "Now watch me closely, children," I ordered. "We place the axle on the diagram as in Fig. C, applying a strong downward pressure on the knife handle at all times." The axle must have been a factory second, because an instant later I was in the bathroom grinding my teeth in agony and attempting to stanch the flow of blood. Ultimately, I succeeded in contriving a rough bandage and slipped back into the nursery without awakening the children's suspicions. An agreeable surprise awaited me. Displaying a mechanical aptitude clearly inherited from their sire, the rascals had put together the chassis of the delivery truck.

"Very good indeed," I complimented (naturally, one 12 has to exaggerate praise to develop a child's self-confidence). "Let's see—what's the next step? Ah, yes. 'Lock into box shape by inserting tabs, C, D, E, F, G, H, J, K, and L into slots C, D, E, F, G, H, J, K, and L. Ends of front axle should be pushed through holes A and B.' " While marshaling the indicated parts in their proper order, I emphasized to my rapt listeners the necessity of patience and perseverance. "Haste makes waste, you know," I reminded them. "Rome wasn't built in a day. Remember, your daddy isn't always going to be here to show you."

"Where *are* you going to be?" they demanded. 13

"In the movies, if I can arrange it," I snarled. Poising 14 tabs C, D, E, F, G, H, J, K, and L in one hand and the corresponding slots in the other, I essayed a union of the two, but in vain. The moment I made one set fast and tackled another, tab and slot would part company, thumbing their noses at me. Although the children were too immature to understand, I saw in a flash where the trouble lay. Some idiotic employee at the factory had punched out the wrong design, probably out of sheer spite. So that was his game, eh? I set my lips in a grim line and, throwing one hundred and fifty-seven pounds of fighting fat into the effort, pounded the component parts into a homogeneous mass.

"There," I said with a gasp, "that's close enough. Now then, who wants candy? One, two, three—everybody off to the candy store!" 15

"We wanna finish the delivery truck!" they wailed. "Mummy, he won't let us finish the delivery truck!" Threats, cajolery, bribes were of no avail. In their jungle code, a twenty-nine-cent gewgaw bulked larger than a parent's love. Realizing that I was dealing with a pair of monomaniacs, I determined to show them who was master and wildly began locking the cardboard units helter-skelter, without any regard for the directions. When sections refused to fit, I gouged them with my nails and forced them together, cackling shrilly. The side panels collapsed; with a bestial oath, I drove a safety pin through them and lashed them to the roof. I used paper clips, bobby pins, anything I could lay my hands on. My fingers fairly flew and my breath whistled in my throat. "You want a delivery truck, do you?" I panted. "All right, I'll show you!" As merciful blackness closed in, I was on my hands and knees, bunting the infernal thing along with my nose and whinnying, "Roll, confound you, roll!" 16

"Absolute quiet," a carefully modulated voice was saying, "and fifteen of the white tablets every four hours." I opened my eyes carefully in the darkened room. Dimly I picked out a knifelike character actor in pince-nez lenses and a morning coat folding a stethoscope into his bag. "Yes," he added thoughtfully, "if we play our cards right, this ought to be a long, expensive recovery." From far away, I could hear my wife's voice bravely trying to control her anxiety. 17

"What if he becomes restless, Doctor?" 18

149

"Get him a detective story," returned the leech. "Or 19 better still, a nice, soothing picture puzzle—something he can do with his hands."

———— ♦ ————

For Study and Discussion

QUESTIONS ABOUT PURPOSE

1. What process is Perelman analyzing in this essay?
2. Why does Perelman use both the Jiffy-Cloz and the toy truck to illustrate that process?
3. What does Perelman demonstrate about writing and reading directions?

QUESTIONS ABOUT AUDIENCE

1. Does Perelman assume that he and his readers share a common experience? What do you think it is?
2. What assumptions does Perelman make about the mechanical aptitude of men, women, and children?
3. What reaction does Perelman anticipate from his readers when he charges that "some idiotic employee at the factory had punched out the wrong design"?

QUESTIONS ABOUT STRATEGIES

1. Which of the five steps for organizing a process analysis does Perelman include in his account of the assembly of the toy truck? Which of the five warnings does he ignore?
2. Perelman the writer is illustrating a different process from the one Perelman the character illustrates. How does the boy's statement, "You always cut yourself at this stage," call attention to the two separate processes?

3. How does Perelman demonstrate that the process has produced the desired result? Why is the doctor's advice ironic?

QUESTIONS FOR DISCUSSION

1. What seems to be the cause of Perelman's impatience with mechanical devices and the technology that produces them? How would you characterize those people who seem able to cope with technology?

2. Perelman (the character) assumes that a "civilized man" has more important things to do than assemble a child's toy. How would you describe the activities he prefers?

3. How does Perelman's parody of the direction-following process help establish the features of a successful process analysis?

Riveters

THE EDITORS OF
FORTUNE MAGAZINE

───────── ◆ ─────────

*Fortune magazine was born in February 1930, just
three months after the Great Crash of 1929. Throughout its fifty-year history the magazine has established
a standard of excellence for writing about American
business. Fortune's early staff was loaded with poets
because publisher Henry Luce believed it was "easier
to turn poets into business journalists than to turn
bookkeepers into writers." The long list of distinguished authors who contributed to the magazine includes James Agee, Archibald MacLeish, and William
H. Whyte, Jr. Photographers Margaret Bourke-White
and Walker Evans and artist Saul Steinberg also contributed memorable work. Published in the October
1930 issue, "Riveters" explains the work of the men
who were at that moment erecting skyscrapers such
as the Empire State Building.*

The most curious fact about a riveter's skill is that he is
not one man but four: "heater," "catcher," "bucker-up,"
and "gun-man." The gang is the unit. Riveters are hired
and fired as gangs, work in gangs, and learn in gangs. If
one member of a gang is absent on a given morning, the
entire gang is replaced. A gang may continue to exist after
its original members have all succumbed to slippery girders or the business end of a pneumatic hammer or to a
foreman's zeal or merely to the temptations of life on
earth. And the skill of the gang will continue with it.
Men overlap each other in service and teach each other

what they know. The difference between a gang which can drive 525 inch-and-an-eighth rivets in a working day and a gang which can drive 250 is a difference of co-ordination and smoothness. You can learn how not to make mistakes and how not to waste time. You learn how to heat a rivet and how not to overheat it, how to throw it accurately but not too hard, how to drive it and when to stop driving it, and precisely how much you can drink in a cold wind or a July sun without losing your sense of the width and balance of a wooden plank. And all these things, or most of them, an older hand can tell you.

Eagle's Gang, a veteran of the Forty Wall Street job, is 2 reputed in the trade to be one of the best gangs in the city. The gang takes its name from its heater and organizer, E. Eagle, a native of Baltimore. It is the belief of timekeepers, foremen, and the leaders of other gangs that Mr. Eagle is a man of property in his home town and indulges in the sport of riveting for mysterious reasons. There are also myths about the gun-man and the bucker-up, brothers named Bowers from some South Carolina town. They are said never to speak. Even in a profession where no man is able to speak, their silence stands out. The catcher is George Smith, a New Yorker. There are no stories about George.

The actual process of riveting is simple enough—in 3 description. Rivets are carried to the job by the rivet boy, a riveter's apprentice whose ambition it is to replace one of the members of the gang—which one, he leaves to luck. The rivets are dumped into a keg beside a small coke furnace. The furnace stands on a platform of loose boards roped to steel girders which may or may not have been riveted. If they have not been riveted there will be a certain amount of play in the temporary bolts. The furnace is tended by the heater or passer. He wears heavy clothes and gloves to protect him from the flying sparks and intense heat of his work, and he holds a pair of tongs about a foot-and-a-half long in his right hand. When a rivet is needed, he whirls the furnace blower until the coke is white-hot, picks up a rivet with his tongs, and drives it into the coals. His skill as a heater appears in his knowledge of the exact time necessary to heat the steel. If he overheats it, it will flake, and the flakes will permit the rivet to turn in its hole. And a rivet which gives in its hole is condemned by the inspectors.

When the heater judges that his rivet is right, he turns 4
to face the catcher, who may be above or below him or fifty or sixty or eighty feet away on the same floor level with the naked girders between. There is no means of handing the rivet over. It must be thrown. And it must be accurately thrown. And if the floor beams of the floor above have been laid so that a flat trajectory is essential, it must be thrown with considerable force. The catcher is therefore armed with a smallish, battered tin can, called a cup, with which to catch the red-hot steel. Various patented cups have been put upon the market from time to time but they have made little headway. Catchers prefer the ancient can.

The catcher's position is not exactly one which a sports- 5
man catching rivets for pleasure would choose. He stands upon a narrow platform of loose planks laid over needle beams and roped to a girder near the connection upon which the gang is at work. There are live coils of pneumatic tubing for the rivet gun around his feet. If he moves more than a step or two in any direction, he is gone, and if he loses his balance backward he is apt to end up at street level without time to walk. And the object is to catch a red-hot iron rivet weighing anywhere from a quarter of a pound to a pound and a half and capable, if he lets it pass, of drilling an automobile radiator or a man's skull 500 feet below as neatly as a shank of shrapnel. Why more rivets do not fall is the great mystery of skyscraper construction. The only reasonable explanation offered to date is the reply of an erector's foreman who was asked what would happen if a catcher on the Forty Wall Street job let a rivet go by him around lunch hour. "Well," said the foreman, "he's not supposed to."

There is practically no exchange of words among riveters. Not only are they averse to conversation, which would be reasonable enough in view of the effect they have on the conversation of others, but they are averse to speech in any form. The catcher faces the heater. He holds his tin can up. The heater swings his tongs, releasing one handle. The red iron arcs through the air in one of those parabolas so much admired by the stenographers in the neighboring windows. And the tin can clanks.

Meantime the gun-man and the bucker-up have prepared the connection—aligning the two holes, if necessary, with a drift pin driven by a sledge or by a pneumatic hammer—and removed the temporary bolts. They, too, stand on loose-roped boards with the column or the beam between them. When the rivet strikes the catcher's can, he picks it out with a pair of tongs held in his right hand, knocks it sharply against the steel to shake off the glowing flakes, and rams it into the hole, an operation which is responsible for his alternative title of sticker. Once the rivet is in place, the bucker-up braces himself with his dolly bar, a short heavy bar of steel, against the capped end of the rivet. On outside wall work he is sometimes obliged to hold on by one elbow with his weight out over the street and the jar of the riveting shaking his precarious balance. And the gun-man lifts his pneumatic hammer to the rivet's other end.

The gun-man's work is the hardest work, physically, done by the gang. The hammers in use for steel construction work are supposed to weigh around thirty pounds and actually weigh about thirty-five. They must not only be held against the rivet end, but held there with the gun-man's entire strength, and for a period of forty to sixty seconds. (A rivet driven too long will develop a collar inside the new head.) And the concussion to the ears and to the arms during that period is very great. The whole platform shakes and the vibration can be felt down the column thirty stories below. It is common practice for the catcher to push with the gun-man and for the gun-man and the bucker-up to pass the gun back and forth between them when the angle is difficult. Also on a heavy rivet job the catcher and the bucker-up may relieve the gun-man at the gun.

The weight of the guns is one cause, though indirect, 9 of accidents. The rivet set, which is the actual hammer at the point of the gun, is held in place, when the gun leaves the factory, by clips. Since the clips increase the weight of the hammer, it is good riveting practice to knock them off against the nearest column and replace them with a hank of wire. But wire has a way of breaking, and when it breaks there is nothing to keep the rivet set and the pneumatic piston itself from taking the bucker-up or the catcher on the belt and knocking him into the next block.

Riveters work ordinarily eight hours a day at a wage 10 of $15.40 a day. They are not employed in bad or slippery weather, and they are not usually on the regular pay roll of the erectors, but go from job to job following foremen whom they like. There is no great future for a riveter. A good gun-man may become an assistant foreman, a pusher, whose duty it is to keep the various gangs at work. But pushers are used for such work only on very large jobs.

It would perhaps be more accurate to say that a riv- 11 eter's future is not bright at all. The rates charged for compensation insurance are generally accepted as the best barometer of risk. Starrett Brothers & Eken fix, in their insurance department, a rate of $23.45 per $100 of pay for erecting and painting steel frame structures. Rates of other companies run to $30 per $100 of pay. The only higher rate is for wrecking work. The next lower rate ($15.08) is for building raising. Masonry is $6.07 and carpentry $4.39. Figures on industrial accidents published by the U.S. Department of Labor bear the same connotation. In one year the frequency of accidents, per 1,000,000 hours' exposure, was 228.9 for fabricators and erectors as against 54 for general building.

There was an adage at one time current to the effect 12

that it cost a life to a floor to build a skyscraper. The computation may have originated with a famous downtown building of fifteen years ago in which, with the steel at the fifth floor five deaths had already occurred. (The Travelers Insurance Company, called in to take over the insurance in that case, made a study of the conditions of the job, recommended certain changes, enforced its own supervision, and saw the remaining thirty-two stories built with but one more fatality.) Or the saying may have arisen and may have been true in the days of ten-story skyscrapers. But to apply it, like the architect's 6 per cent fee, to seventy-story buildings would be pure extravagance. Nevertheless a bloodless building is still a marvel. Five Hundred Fifth Avenue, which has had no deaths to date, is used as an object lesson for builders by the insurance companies, and the Chrysler Building, which was built with the loss of one life, was awarded a certificate of merit by the Building Trades Employers' Association. Four men were killed on the Manhattan Company job, and five were reported to have been killed on the Empire State by the middle of July. In general, deaths run from three to eight on sizable buildings. These figures, in the opinion of the Travelers Company, are excessive. The Travelers would allow a buiding two at the most.

Such accidents are of course expensive, but injuries [13] short of death are more costly. Liability of $875,000 for deaths was incurred in the building trades in the New York district in the last six months of 1928, and $3,145,586 for deaths and injuries. The total of both for the same period in 1929 was $3,885,881.

The safety campaign in the construction industry is [14] blocked by various causes of which the novelty of skyscraper construction and the prevalence of shoestring construction projects are two of the most obvious. More important than either, however, is the attitude of construction workmen. Their trade inures them to danger and they are, as a class, as willing to take risks for others as for themselves. A riveter who has seen three or four hundred red-hot rivets a day kept off the heads of the members of the Stock Exchange by an old tin can gets used to the idea. In a recent accident case a man had been injured in the street by the fall of a hammer in use on a building half a block away. No possible wind velocity would account for the drift. The only explanation was that the hammer had been thrown from one man to another. And had missed.

------ ♦ ------

For Study and Discussion

QUESTIONS ABOUT PURPOSE

1. What are the two main divisions of this essay? What is the purpose of each division—to give directions or to provide information?

2. What do the writers want to demonstrate about the work of the riveters? Does their analysis make the work appear more or less complex? Explain your answer.

3. In its fifty-year history *Fortune* magazine has published articles about all kinds of work. What common purpose do you suppose these articles share?

QUESTIONS ABOUT AUDIENCE

1. How do you know that the intended readers of this essay are probably the people who look at (or work in) skyscrapers rather than the people who build them?

2. What "identity" do the writers assign to their readers when they say "all these things, or most of them, an older hand can tell you"? Who is the "older hand"?

3. The writers seem to assign a different identity to their readers in the last five paragraphs of the essay. How would you characterize that identity?

QUESTIONS ABOUT STRATEGIES

1. How do the writers organize their presentation of the riveting process? Which steps receive the most emphasis? Which steps must be suspended while others are completed?
2. Make a list of the special tasks, tools, and methods defined in this essay. How do the special skills required of each man help define his job?
3. Identify all the warnings included in the process. How does the adage about one life a floor help dramatize the consequences of error?

QUESTIONS FOR DISCUSSION

1. How does the following sentence make use of concrete words and sensory images: "A riveter who has seen three or four hundred red-hot rivets a day kept off the heads of the members of the Stock Exchange by an old tin can gets used to the idea." Identify and discuss other instances where the writers have used particularly vivid descriptive detail.
2. If there is "no great future" for a riveter, why does he continue working at his job? In what ways does this analysis help you understand the appeal of his job?
3. Based on your reading of this essay, what specific recommendations could you make to improve safety on the job?

How to Get a Job as a "Swing Dancer" in a Hit Broadway Show

BOB EVANS

——————— ◆ ———————

Robert A. Evans was born in Westwood, New Jersey, in 1922. Upon graduation from high school he went immediately into show business. He danced in fourteen Broadway musicals, among them the original New York companies of "Guys and Dolls," "Pajama Game," "Damn Yankees," "Music Man," and "Subways Are For Sleeping." In addition to conducting his own dance classes, Evans played drums for choreographer Peter Gennaro's classes for three years, an experience that led him to write two books on Latin American rhythms. At present he is employed with New York's public television station (WNET) as an associate director. In the following essay, first published in Harper's *in 1964, Evans draws upon his experience with the New York theater to explain the ordeals of a "swing dancer."*

After a musical has opened in New York and has had the rare privilege of getting unanimous raves from the critics, everyone from the producers, writers, and directors right on down to the chorus relaxes to bask in the sunlight of critical acceptance, public support, and financial gain. 1

The dancers, especially, enjoy the hit in a strange sort of way. They immediately go back to the strenuous activity of daily jazz and ballet classes, masochistically stretching and twisting in order to stay in shape for auditions when this show eventually closes. After the stren- 2 uous activity of daytime classes, the theatre often becomes a place to rest up and recuperate for tomorrow's classes. Out come the magazines, books, knitting, and small change for poker games, and even possibly TV with the sound turned way down; the whole thing takes on the atmosphere of a USO.

At this point the management, in the flush of success, decides that it can afford an extra dancer to cover the possibility that dancers will be out sick from time to time. Now, as a rule, dancers are never sick during the rehearsal and out-of-town tryout periods unless they have fallen out of a window or been run over, but once the show is back in New York for a long run, illness becomes really fashionable. This extra dancer is known in the trade as a "swing dancer." It takes a good dancer to fill the job because it requires the ability to dance every position in every number and adjust to a variety of partners. Also, it means no cocktails before coming to work nights.

The management informs Equity, the theatrical union, to notify its members of an audition, but they are not told the nature of the job so that the turnout will be full strength. The inference is that the audition will be for the much-treasured straight replacement in the show, but word usually leaks out anyway that it's for the swing job. Regardless of that, everyone goes for the simple reason that everyone needs a job.

There are usually seventy-five to a hundred eager perspirants for this one position, stretching, kicking, and limbering up all over the stage. (Actually, both a boy and a girl are hired to cover all the dancers' steps and positions.) The step chosen for the audition is always the hardest one in the show. This movement is probably done only once in a number for, say, two measures, but at the audition the dancers get the dubious privilege of doing it over and over again all afternoon in a cold and dim theatre. After anywhere from three to five grueling hours of elimination, interspersed with occasional lineups to see who is still standing (similar in method to the longshoremen's shape-up), a dancer is picked and told the job is his. He accepts, of course, because all that torture has convinced him how lucky he was to be picked out of all those other good dancers who were also tearing themselves limb from limb to get the job.

The dancers with whom the swing boy will be work- 6 ing can be divided into roughly two groups. Group one becomes entrenched like wood ticks on a hunting dog for a long run in the show. To qualify for this group you must eventually bring some or all of the following items to the theatre: coffee, tea, sugar, powdered milk, spoons, knives and forks, glasses and cups, hot plates, coffee pots, extra umbrellas and rubbers, aspirin, toothpaste and brush, mouthwash, all shaving things, books, magazines, foam-rubber cushions, plus any other creature comforts that the theatre lacks. Often these dressing rooms wind up being more comfortable and convenient than apartments. When the show closes it usually takes two or three trips with a couple of suitcases to clean the dressing table off.

Group two is made up of the "I can't wait to get the 7 hell out of this show" type who has been bored with the show practically from the first day of rehearsal. Since these individuals consider their talents wasted and/or ignored, they don't "dig in" so they won't have too much to cart away when they make a hasty exit out of the present hit into a brand-new flop. They shave at home and bring coffee in containers. Their dressing room table is bare save for makeup and possibly a few essentials such as framed photos of themselves and perhaps the *New York Times* crossword puzzle so that they don't have to talk to anybody in the dressing room. Downstairs in the "recreation area," which is really the basement of the theatre, Group one has taken all the chairs and the well-lit areas. At the same time Group two is going around driving everyone to distraction with anarchy and insurrection. This is the grim, battle-scarred atmosphere that the swing boy walks into.

Your first evening you report to the theatre in your 8

best suit, which you hope is still in style, as you will no doubt go out front to watch the show. While you wait backstage, the girl dancers smile at you sweetly and say good evening, for no one except the stage manager stands around backstage with a suit on and so they think you must be someone important from the front office. When they find out you're just the extra dancer they all relax again and lose themselves in reveries of self-appreciation.

Under normal conditions it would be a lot of fun to go out front and watch a Broadway show free, but right now the only thing on your mind is to find out how hard the dancing is and hope that there aren't any acrobatic tricks or lifts you can't do. Everything else in the show, including the principals and the plot, is unimportant. All that counts is eight dancing boys and their partners, to watch all at once. If the first act is loaded with hard dances, you think maybe you can just quietly disappear during the intermission and never be heard from again. If the dancing hasn't scared you away, you go up to the dressing room after the curtain where everyone will ask you how you liked the show. What is really meant by this is "How was I?" and you should have some compliments ready because each dancer is sure that he is as exciting on stage as Jack the Ripper would be at the Annual Streetwalkers' Picnic. It's always a good idea to get as many people as you can on your side in the beginning, because you'll need them later on when your popularity wanes.

The next night you are introduced to the wardrobe mistress, the threat of the threads. She didn't especially like you even before she met you. Nothing personal, of course, but the swing boy creates a new problem for her. He must have costumes to cover every dance possibility, and the management has suggested that she whip up a complete wardrobe out of the stuff discarded from numbers and finales out of town. Since the management doesn't expect to see a bill for new costumes up at the office it doesn't get one, because the wardrobe mistress wants to be sure the firm considers her for their new show next year. All in all, this puts quite a strain on her as she usually hasn't any dancers' costumes left over, but there always seem to be plenty of overly large singers' costumes which are destined to make the new boy look like the comedy relief in the show. Everything is basted; they're afraid to cut material since the swing boy may not work out and the next one may be taller or something.

From rehearsal days to the time the show opens in 11 New York there have been so many changes in the numbers that the dance captain is often as confused as the swing boy because he hasn't had a chance to see what the other dancers have been doing behind his back for three months. Naturally, you learn the dance captain's part first until he can find out what the rest of the dancers have been up to. The best way for him to find out is to call a rehearsal, the purpose of which is supposed to be for you to learn all the parts, but actually the dance captain is so busy asking everybody one by one, "Now exactly what movement are you doing on this count?" that you never get to do any of the parts. But you've got an ace in the hole. You have gone to the five-and-ten and bought yourself a jumbo-size notebook and you are diligently writing down every movement and/or count, or at least you had better be doing it because these notes may be your only contact with reality and may save your life when the time comes . . . providing you can dope out what you have written down.

After a few weeks of watching and a whole notebook 12 full of counts, half of which are all wrong, the inevitable happens. When you arrive at the theatre one evening, a half-hour early to be on the safe side, before you even sign in, you're hit with the news that you're on tonight. Naturally the boy who is out is the one you haven't been watching and you haven't the vaguest idea what he does or where he goes in the numbers. Eighty pages of counts and positions, and not one page for the sick dancer, who is out because he wants to catch a television show he danced on that was taped during the past summer. Incidentally, when some of the more considerate dancers feel they are going to be out, say for a matinee, they give you a hint by coughing and trying to look ill the night before so that you can watch them on stage and not be caught the next evening with your notes down.

It's very exciting for the whole cast when the swing boy is going on for the first time. It gives them something to look forward to that evening. The rest of the dancers arrive and tell you that everything is going to be fine and that you will be just great, which is about as honest as an income-tax return. After putting on a very bad makeup, with one eyebrow penciled in thicker than the other, you rush down to the basement to get into your basted singer's costume because you're going to rehearse three lifts with one girl or one lift with three girls—it really doesn't matter anymore since it's already too late to learn anything. The first girl says something like this, which is supposed to be reassuring but which really makes you feel helpless: 13

"Don't worry about a thing, honey; all you have to do is just grab me and I'll do all the rest." 14

You're dispensable, right off the bat! After three minutes of practicing five lifts, or five minutes of practicing three lifts, you stand there with a possible double hernia while the girls leave with such reassuring phrases as, "It'll be great." "Don't be afraid, you won't drop me, only please be careful of that right thumb you sprained in rehearsal . . . it's still very sore." "Good luck, honey" (with a kiss thrown back). As soon as they reach the dressing room, the first one rolls her eyes and says, "Boy, what a night this is going to be!" The other one says, "Yeah, well, I'm glad my folks saw the show last week." The third one says, "Oh, boy, are my ribs going to be sore tomorrow." 15

I guess we don't have to go into the details of the 16

performance because it happens just the way everyone expected, only worse. It doesn't seem to work out like that classic Ruby Keeler movie where you're brilliant going on for the first time and everyone just loves you for saving the show. What happens is this: When you aren't counting out loud, you're looking for the girl you're supposed to be lifting right this second, who looks entirely different with her stage makeup on. You can't find anybody because all the girls are dressed alike except for different lace work at the hem of their costumes which you probably couldn't see even if you weren't nervous, so you run to a girl singer instead of your partner and try to lift her. The leading man, who is singing stage center right in the way of all the dancers, hasn't seen you at all up until this minute, and he muffs a lyric trying to figure out who the new singer is and why he's dancing in the number in the first place. If you don't kick the leading lady, who is in the way also, you will at least muss up her intricate hour-and-a-half hairdo as you go flying past. All during this your basted singer's costume is coming apart at the seams. At the blackout at the end of the number, someone luckily pulls you back out of the way of the fast-falling, one-and-a-half-ton curtain, but you get smashed anyway by an avalanche of stagehands rushing onstage to clear the set in the dark.

Back in the dressing room, the hollow consolation of the other dancers ring all around you: "That was great for the first time. Nobody could have done better." "The audience doesn't know what's going on in the dance numbers anyway. They'd never catch all those little goofs you were making. Maybe the only one they really did see was when your shoe flew off into the orchestra pit after you cartwheeled the wrong way into the desk." "I guess I shouldn't have told you the choreographer was out front watching. It didn't make you nervous, did it? He probably wasn't even watching you." 17

After the show, the swing boy either goes home to sulk in front of the television set with a beer, or else he goes all 18 out and gets potted at some bar. So the next time you see a dancer at a bar loaded and babbling incoherently, please be tolerant. It is just possible that he is a swing boy and he really isn't celebrating anything.

———— ♦ ————

For Study and Discussion

QUESTIONS ABOUT PURPOSE

1. To what extent is the title of this essay misleading? What other processes does Evans describe in addition to how to get a job?
2. How do the contrasting scenes described in the first three and concluding paragraphs help explain the major purpose of this essay?
3. What do paragraphs 6 and 7 contribute to the purpose of this essay?

QUESTIONS ABOUT AUDIENCE

1. How would you characterize the audience Evans addresses in the first seven paragraphs?
2. The anticipated audience for this essay seems to change in paragraph 8. What detail signals that change?
3. The audience seems to change a second time in paragraph 18. Who is the "you" in this concluding paragraph?

QUESTIONS ABOUT STRATEGIES

1. What kinds of information does Evans provide in his overview section? Why is this information necessary to analyze the job of the swing dancer?

2. How does Evans illustrate the sequence of steps that the swing dancer must follow to prepare himself for a performance? What steps give him the most difficulty?

3. Where and how does Evans quote dialogue from the other dancers? What do they think of the swing dancer?

QUESTIONS FOR DISCUSSION

1. What does the example from the classic Ruby Keeler movie suggest about the way many people view jobs in show business?

2. How does this essay establish the difference between practice and performance?

3. What other kinds of work are designed to look like play?

How Writers Work

MALCOLM COWLEY

◆

*Malcolm Cowley was born in 1898 in Belsano, Penn-
sylvania, and educated at Harvard University. He
interrupted his studies to drive an ambulance during
World War I. After the war he completed his education but soon returned to Europe to live among the
American expatriates in Paris. In the 1930s he worked
as a literary editor for* The New Republic, *and since
1948 he has served as a literary consultant for* The
Viking Press. *Cowley is best known for* Exile's Return
*(1934), an autobiographical history of those writers of
his generation who produced their great work during
the 1920s. But perhaps his greatest achievement as
an editor and critic was his "discovery" and presentation of the writings of William Faulkner in* The Portable
Faulkner *(1946), a book that almost singlehandedly
established Faulkner's reputation as one of America's
greatest novelists. In 1958 Cowley collected and introduced the first series of interviews with modern authors,* The Paris Review Interviews. *His other interpretations of modern literary history include* The
Literary Situation *(1954) and* A Second Flowering
*(1973). In 1980 he published an autobiographical ac-
count of the aging process,* The View from Eighty. *In
"How Writers Work" (excerpted from his introduction to* The Paris Review Interviews), *Cowley analyzes
the four stages that writers work through—with considerable stylistic variation—in composing stories.*

There would seem to be four stages in the composition of   1
a story. First comes the germ of the story, then a period
of more or less conscious meditation, then the first draft,
and finally the revision, which may be simply "pencil
work," as John O'Hara calls it—that is, minor changes in

169

wording—or may lead to writing several drafts and what amounts to a new work.

The germ of a story is something seen or heard, or 2 heard about, or suddenly remembered; it may be a remark casually dropped at the dinner table (as in the case of Henry James's story, *The Spoils of Poynton*), or again it may be the look on a stranger's face. Almost always it is a new and simple element introduced into an existing situation or mood; something that expresses the mood in one sharp detail; something that serves as a focal point for a hitherto disorganized mass of remembered material in the author's mind. James describes it as "the precious particle . . . the stray suggestion, the wandering word, the vague echo, at a touch of which the novelist's imagination winces as at the prick of some sharp point," and he adds that "its virtue is all in its needle-like quality, the power to penetrate as finely as possible."

In the case of one story by the late Joyce Cary, the 3 "precious particle" was the wrinkles on a young woman's forehead. He had seen her on the little boat that goes around Manhattan Island, "a girl of about thirty," he says, "wearing a shabby skirt. She was enjoying herself. A nice expression, with a wrinkled forehead, a good many wrinkles. I said to my friend, 'I could write about that girl . . .'" but then he forgot her. Three weeks later, in San Francisco, Cary woke up at four in the morning with a story in his head—a purely English story with an English heroine. When he came to revise the story he kept wondering, "Why all these wrinkles? That's the third time they come in. And I suddenly realized," he says, "that my English heroine was the girl on the Manhattan boat. Somehow she had gone down into my subconscious, and came up again with a full-sized story."

The woman with the wrinkled forehead could hardly 4 have served as the germ of anything by Frank O'Connor, for his imagination is auditive, not visual. "If you're the sort of person," he says, "that meets a girl in the street and instantly notices the color of her eyes and of her hair and the sort of dress she's wearing, then you're not in the least like me. . . . I have terribly sensitive hearing and I'm terribly aware of voices." Often his stories develop from a remark he has overheard. That may also be the case with Dorothy Parker, who says, "I haven't got a visual mind. I hear things." Faulkner does have a visual mind, and he says that *The Sound and the Fury* "began with a mental picture. I didn't realize at the time it was symbolical. The picture was of the muddy seat of a little girl's drawers in a pear tree, where she could see through a window where her grandmother's funeral was taking place and report what was happening to her brothers on the ground below. By the time I explained who they were and what they were doing and how her pants got muddy, I realized it would be impossible to get all of it into a short story and it would have to be a book." At other times the precious particle is something the author has read—preferably a book of memoirs or history or travel, one that lies outside his own field of writing. Robert Penn Warren says, "I always remember the date, the place, the room, the road, when I first was struck. For instance, *World Enough and Time.* Katherine Anne Porter and I were both in the Library of Congress as fellows. We were in the same pew, had offices next to each other. She came in one day with an old pamphlet, the trial of Beauchamp for killing Colonel Sharp. She said, 'Well, Red, you better read this.' There it was. I read it in five minutes. But I was six years making the book. Any book I write starts with a flash, but takes a long time to shape up."

The book or story shapes up—assumes its own specific form, that is—during a process of meditation that is the second stage in composition. Angus Wilson calls it "the gestatory period" and says that it is "very important to me. That's when I'm persuading myself of the truth of what I want to say, and I don't think I could persuade my readers unless I'd persuaded myself first." The period may last for years, as with Warren's novels (and most of Henry James's), or it may last exactly two days, as in the extraordinary case

5

171

of Georges Simenon. "As soon as I have the beginning," Simenon explains, "I can't bear it very long. . . . And two days later I begin writing." The meditation may be, or seem to be, wholly conscious. The writer asks himself questions—"What should the characters do at this point? How can I build to a climax?"—and answers them in various fashions before choosing the final answers. Or most of the process, including all the early steps, may be carried on without the writer's volition. He wakes before daybreak with the whole story in his head, as Joyce Cary did in San Francisco, and hastily writes it down. Or again—and I think most frequently—the meditation is a mixture of conscious and unconscious elements, as if a cry from the depths of sleep were being heard and revised by the waking mind.

Often the meditation continues while the writer is engaged in other occupations: gardening, driving his wife to town (as Walter Mitty did), or going out to dinner. "I never quite know when I'm not writing," says James Thurber. "Sometimes my wife comes up to me at a dinner party and says, 'Dammit, Thurber, stop writing.' She usually catches me in the middle of a paragraph. Or my daughter will look up from the dinner table and ask, 'Is he sick?' 'No,' my wife says, 'he's writing.' I have to do it that way on account of my eyes." When Thurber had better vision he used to do his meditating at the typewriter, as many other writers do. Nelson Algren, for example, finds his plots simply by writing page after page, night after night. "I always figured," he says, "the only way I could finish a book and get a plot was just to keep making it longer and longer until something happens." 6

The first draft of a story is often written at top speed; probably that is the best way to write it. Dorothy Canfield Fisher . . . once compared the writing of a first draft with skiing down a steep slope that she wasn't sure she was clever enough to manage. "Sitting at my desk one morning," she says, "I 'pushed off' and with a tingle of not altogether pleasurable excitement and alarm, felt myself 'going.' I 'went' almost as precipitately as skis go down a long 7

172

white slope, scribbling as rapidly as my pencil could go, indicating whole words with a dash and a jiggle, filling page after page with scrawls." Frank O'Connor explains the need for haste in his own case. "Get black on white," he says, "used to be Maupassant's advice—that's what I always do. I don't give a hoot what the writing's like, I write any sort of rubbish which will cover the main outlines of the story, then I can begin to see it." There are other writers, however, who work ahead laboriously, revising as they go. William Styron says, "I seem to have some neurotic need to perfect each paragraph—each sentence, even —as I go along." Dorothy Parker reports that it takes her six months to do a story: "I think it out and then write it sentence by sentence—no first draft. I can't write five words but that I change seven."

O'Connor doesn't start changing words until the first draft is finished, but then he rewrites, so he says, "endlessly, endlessly, endlessly." There is no stage of composition at which these authors differ more from one another than in this final stage of preparing a manuscript for the printer. Even that isn't a final stage for O'Connor. "I keep on rewriting," he says, "and after it's published, and then after it's published in book form, I usually rewrite it again. I've rewritten versions of most of my early stories, and one of these days, God help, I'll publish these as well." Françoise Sagan, on the other hand, spends "very little" time in revision. Simenon spends exactly three days in revising each of his short novels. Most of that time is devoted to tracking down and crossing out the literary touches—"adjectives, adverbs, and every word which is there just to make an effect. Every sentence which is there just for the sentence. You know, you have a beautiful sentence—cut it." Joyce Cary was another deletionist. Many of the passages he crossed out of his first drafts were those dealing explicitly with ideas. "I work over the whole book," he says, "and cut out anything that does not belong to the emotional development, the texture of feeling." Thurber revises his stories by rewriting them from the beginning,

8

173

time and again. "A story I've been working on," he says, "... was rewritten fifteen complete times. There must have been close to two hundred and forty thousand words in all the manuscripts put together, and I must have spent two thousand hours working at it. Yet the finished story can't be more than twenty thousand words." That would make it about the longest piece of fiction he has written. Men like Thurber and O'Connor, who rewrite "endlessly, endlessly," find it hard to face the interminable prospect of writing a full-length novel.

For short-story writers the four stages of composition 9 are usually distinct, and there may even be a fifth, or rather a first, stage. Before seizing upon the germ of a story, the writer may find himself in a state of "generally intensified emotional sensitivity ... when events that usually pass unnoticed suddenly move you deeply, when a sunset lifts you to exaltation, when a squeaking door throws you into a fit of exasperation, when a clear look of trust in a child's eyes moves you to tears." I am quoting again from Dorothy Canfield Fisher, who "cannot conceive," she says, "of any creative fiction written from any other beginning." There is not much doubt, in any case, that the germ is precious largely because it serves to crystallize a prior state of feeling. Then comes the brooding or meditation, then the rapidly written first draft, then the slow revision; for the story writer everything is likely to happen in more or less its proper order. For the novelist, however, the stages are often confused. The meditation may have to be repeated for each new episode. The revision of one chapter may precede or follow the first draft of the next.

That is not the only difference between writing a short 10 story and writing a novel.... I was confirmed in an old belief that the two forms are separate and that mere length is not their distinguishing feature. A long short story— say of forty thousand words—is not the same as a novel of forty thousand words, nor is it likely to be written by the same person.... The division that goes deepest is not between older and younger writers, or men and women writers, or French and English writers; it is the division between those who think in terms of the short story and those who are essentially novelists.

Truman Capote might stand for those who think in [11] terms of the short story, since he tells us that his "more unswerving ambitions still revolve around this form." A moment later he says, "I invariably have the illusion that the whole play of a story, its start and middle and finish, occur in my mind simultaneously—that I'm seeing it in one flash." He likes to know the end of a story before writing the first word of it. Indeed, he doesn't start writing until he has brooded over the story long enough to exhaust his emotional response to the material. "I seem to remember reading," he says, "that Dickens, as he wrote, choked with laughter over his own humor and dripped tears all over the page when one of his characters died. My own theory is that the writer should have considered his wit and dried his tears long, long before setting out to evoke similar reactions of the reader." The reactions of the reader, not of the writer, are Capote's principal concern.

For contrast take . . . Simenon, who is a true novelist [12] even if his separate works, written and revised in about two weeks, are not much longer than some short stories. Each of them starts in the same fashion. "It is almost a geometrical problem," he says. "I have such a man, such a woman, in such surroundings. What can happen to them to oblige them to go to their limit? That's the question. It will be sometimes a very simple incident, anything which will change their lives. Then I write my novel chapter by chapter." Before setting to work Simenon has scrawled a few notes on a big manila envelope. The interviewer asks whether these are an outline of the action. "No, no," Simenon answers. ". . . On the envelope I put only the names of the characters, their ages, their families. I know nothing whatever about the events which will occur later. Otherwise"—and I can't help putting the statement in italics—"*it would not be interesting to me.*"

Unlike Capote, who says that he is physically incapable [13]

175

of writing anything he doesn't think will be paid for
(though I take it that payment is, for him, merely a necessary token of public admiration), Simenon would "certainly," he says, continue writing novels if they were
never published. But he wouldn't bother to write them if
he knew what the end of each novel would be, for then *it
would not be interesting.* He discovers his fable not in one
flash, but chapter by chapter, as if he were telling a continued story to himself. "On the eve of the first day," he
says, "I know what will happen in the first chapter. Then
day after day, chapter after chapter, I find what comes
later. After I have started a novel I write a chapter each
day, without ever missing a day. Because it is a strain, I
have to keep pace with the novel. If, for example, I am ill
for forty-eight hours I have to throw away the previous
chapters. And I never return to that novel." Like Dickens
he lets himself be moved, even shattered, by what he is
writing. "All the day," he says, "I am one of my characters"—always the one who is driven to his limit. "I feel
what he feels. . . . And it's almost unbearable after five or
six days. That is one of the reasons why my novels are so
short; after eleven days I can't—it's impossible. I have
to— It's physical. I am too tired."

Nobody else writes in quite the same fashion as Sime- 14
non. He carries a certain attitude toward fiction to the
furthest point that it can be carried by anyone who writes
books to be published and read. But the attitude in itself is
not unusual, and in fact it is shared to some extent by all
the true novelists who explain their methods in this book.
Not one of them starts by making a scene-by-scene outline,
as Henry James did before writing each of his later novels.
James had discovered what he called the "divine principle
of the Scenario" after writing several unsuccessful plays,
and in essence the principle, or method, seems to be drama-
tistic rather than novelistic. The dramatist, like the short-
story writer, has to know where he is going and how he
will get there, scene by scene, whereas all the novelists
interviewed by *The Paris Review* are accustomed to mak-

ing voyages of exploration with only the roughest of maps. Mauriac says, "There is a point of departure, and there are some characters. It often happens that the first characters don't go any further and, on the other hand, vaguer, more inconsistent characters show new possibilities as the story goes on and assume a place we hadn't foreseen." Françoise Sagan says that she has to start writing to have ideas. In the beginning she has "a character, or a few characters, and perhaps an idea for a few of the scenes up to the middle of the book, but it all changes in the writing. For me writing is a question of finding a certain rhythm." (One thinks of Simenon and his feeling that he has to keep pace with the novel.) "My work," says Moravia, ". . . is not prepared beforehand in any way. I might add, too, that when I'm not working I don't think of my work at all." Forster does lay plans for his work, but they are subject to change. "The novelist," he says, "should, I think, always settle when he starts what is going to happen, what his major event is to be. He may alter this event as he approaches it, indeed he probably will, indeed he probably had better, or the novel becomes tied up and tight. But the sense of a solid mass ahead, a mountain round or over which or through which the story must go, is most valuable and, for the novels I've tried to write, essential. . . . When I began *A Passage to India* I knew that something important happened in the Malabar Caves, and that it would have a central place in the novel —but I didn't know what it would be."

Most novelists, one might generalize on this evidence,   15 are like the chiefs of exploring expeditions. They know who their companions are (and keep learning more about them); they know what sort of territory they will have to traverse on the following day or week; they know the general object of the expedition, the mountain they are trying to reach, the river of which they are trying to discover the source. But they don't know exactly what their route will be, or what adventures they will meet along the way, or how their companions will act when pushed to the limit.

They don't even know whether the continent they are trying to map exists in space or only within themselves. "I think that if a man has the urge to be an artist," Simenon muses, "it is because he needs to find himself. Every writer tries to find himself through his characters, through all his writing." He is speaking for the novelist in particular. Short-story writers come back from their briefer explorations to brood over the meaning of their discoveries; then they perfect the stories for an audience. The short story is an *exposition*; the novel is often and perhaps at its best an *inquisition* into the unknown depths of the novelist's mind.

◆

For Study and Discussion

QUESTIONS ABOUT PURPOSE

1. Is Cowley's primary purpose to give directions or to provide information? Explain your answer.
2. What complexities does Cowley reveal in what appears at first to be a simple, four-stage process?
3. To what extent does Cowley's analysis reveal that there are no common features in the work habits of professional writers? Explain your answer.

QUESTIONS ABOUT AUDIENCE

1. This essay is an excerpt from Cowley's introduction to a collection of interviews with the writers he mentions in his analysis. What kind of assumptions does Cowley make about the readers reading his introduction?
2. In reading Cowley's essay, what disadvantages do you face because those interviews are not available in this text?

3. How does Cowley anticipate the needs of his readers? Even those readers who have access to the interviews may not know the work or reputations of all the writers who are included. How does Cowley characterize each writer so that his readers recognize a type if not an individual writer?

QUESTIONS ABOUT STRATEGIES

1. Where does Cowley establish an overview of the writing process? Where does he introduce each stage as he moves through his analysis of the process?
2. Most of Cowley's analysis is based on the testimony of individual writers. How does he use these anecdotes to illustrate variations within the process?
3. How does Cowley use the comparison between a writer and an explorer to suggest the ways in which a complex intellectual process may be similar to a more familiar physical process?

QUESTIONS FOR DISCUSSION

1. Does this essay confirm the popular supposition that writers are spontaneous and unpredictable—that they work by impulse rather than by a systematic process? Explain your answer.
2. What does this essay suggest about the way any individual must learn to adapt a process to his or her own personality and habits?
3. What do Cowley's comments about Dorothy Canfield Fisher's description of "intensified emotional intensity" and Truman Capote's admission that he is "physically incapable of writing anything he doesn't think will be paid for" reveal about some of the hidden steps in any process?

The Knife

RICHARD SELZER

◆

*Richard Selzer was born in Troy, New York, in 1928,
and educated at Union College and Albany Medical
College. In 1960, after his internship and postdoctoral
study, Selzer established a private practice in general
surgery and became an associate professor of surgery
in the Yale University medical school. His articles
on various aspects of medicine have appeared in magazines such as* Harper's, Esquire, Redbook, *and* Made-
moiselle, *and his books include a volume of short
stories,* Rituals of Surgery *(1974); a collection of essays
on the life of a doctor,* Mortal Lessons *(1977); and*
Letters to a Young Doctor *(1983). In "The Knife,"
reprinted from* Mortal Lessons, *Selzer uses a language
of poetic intensity to describe the steps of the surgical process.*

One holds the knife as one holds the bow of a cello or a   1
tulip—by the stem. Not palmed nor gripped nor grasped,
but lightly, with the tips of the fingers. The knife is not
for pressing. It is for drawing across the field of skin. Like
a slender fish, it waits, at the ready, then, go! It darts, followed by a fine wake of red. The flesh parts, falling away
to yellow globules of fat. Even now, after so many times,
I still marvel at its power—cold, gleaming, silent. More,
I am still struck with a kind of dread that it is I in
whose hand the blade travels, that my hand is its vehicle, that yet again this terrible steel-bellied thing and

I have conspired for a most unnatural purpose, the laying open of the body of a human being.

A stillness settles in my heart and is carried to my hand. It is the quietude of resolve layered over fear. And it is this resolve that lowers us, my knife and me, deeper and deeper into the person beneath. It is an entry into the body that is nothing like a caress; still, it is among the gentlest of acts. Then stroke and stroke again, and we are joined by other instruments, hemostats and forceps, until the wound blooms with strange flowers whose looped handles fall to the sides in steely array.   2

There is sound, the tight click of clamps fixing teeth into severed blood vessels, the snuffle and gargle of the suction machine clearing the field of blood for the next stroke, the litany of monosyllables with which one prays his way down and in: *clamp, sponge, suture, tie, cut.* And there is color. The green of the cloth, the white of the sponges, the red and yellow of the body. Beneath the fat lies the fascia, the tough fibrous sheet encasing the muscles. It must be sliced and the red beef of the muscles separated. Now there are retractors to hold apart the wound. Hands move together, part, weave. We are fully engaged, like children absorbed in a game or the craftsmen of some place like Damascus.   3

Deeper still. The peritoneum, pink and gleaming and membranous, bulges into the wound. It is grasped with forceps, and opened. For the first time we can see into the cavity of the abdomen. Such a primitive place. One expects to find drawings of buffalo on the walls. The sense of trespassing is keener now, heightened by the world's light illuminating the organs, their secret colors revealed—maroon and salmon and yellow. The vista is sweetly vulnerable at this moment, a kind of welcoming. An arc of the liver shines high and on the right, like a dark sun. It laps over the pink sweep of the stomach, from whose lower border the gauzy omentum is draped, and through which veil one sees, sinuous, slow as just-fed snakes, the indolent coils of the intestine.   4

You turn aside to wash your gloves. It is a ritual cleansing. One enters this temple doubly washed. Here is man as microcosm, representing in all his parts the earth, perhaps the universe.   5

I must confess that the priestliness of my profession has ever been impressed on me. In the beginning there are vows, taken with all solemnity. Then there is the endless harsh novitiate of training, much fatigue, much sacrifice. At last one emerges as celebrant, standing close to the truth lying curtained in the Ark of the body. Not surplice and cassock but mask and gown are your regalia. You hold no chalice, but a knife. There is no wine, no wafer. There are only the facts of blood and flesh.   6

And if the surgeon is like a poet, then the scars you have made on countless bodies are like verses into the fashioning of which you have poured your soul. I think that if years later I were to see the trace from an old incision of mine, I should know it at once, as one recognizes his pet expressions.   7

But mostly you are a traveler in a dangerous country, advancing into the moist and jungly cleft your hands have made. Eyes and ears are shuttered from the land you left behind; mind empties itself of all other thought. You are the root of groping fingers. It is a fine hour for the fingers, their sense of touch so enhanced. The blind must know this feeling. Oh, there is risk everywhere. One goes lightly. The spleen. No! No! Do not touch the spleen that lurks below the left leaf of the diaphragm, a manta ray in a coral cave, its bloody tongue protruding. One poke and it might rupture, exploding with sudden hemorrhage. The filmy omentum must not be torn, the intestine scraped or denuded. The hand finds the liver, palms it, fingers running along its sharp lower edge, admiring. Here are the twin mounds of the kidneys, the apron of the omentum hanging in front of the intestinal coils. One lifts it aside and the fingers dip among the loops, searching, mapping territory, establishing boundaries. Deeper still, and the womb is touched, then held like a small muscular   8 bottle—the womb and its earlike appendages, the ovaries. How they do nestle in the cup of a man's hand, their power all dormant. They are frailty itself.

There is a hush in the room. Speech stops. The hands 9 of the others, assistants and nurses, are still. Only the voice of the patient's respiration remains. It is the rhythm of a quiet sea, the sound of waiting. Then you speak, slowly, the terse entries of a Himalayan climber reporting back.

"The stomach is okay. Greater curvature clean. No 10 sign of ulcer. Pylorus, duodenum fine. Now comes the gallbladder. No stones. Right kidney, left, all right. Liver . . . uh-oh."

Your speech lowers to a whisper, falters, stops for a 11 long, long moment, then picks up again at the end of a sigh that comes through your mask like a last exhalation.

"Three big hard ones in the left lobe, one on the right. 12 Metastatic deposits. Bad, bad. Where's the primary? Got to be coming from somewhere."

The arm shifts direction and the fingers drop lower and 13 lower into the pelvis—the body impaled now upon the arm of the surgeon to the hilt of the elbow.

"Here it is." 14

The voice goes flat, all business now. 15

"Tumor in the sigmoid colon, wrapped all around it, 16 pretty tight. We'll take out a sleeve of the bowel. No colostomy. Not that, anyway. But, God, there's a lot of it down there. Here, you take a feel."

You step back from the table, and lean into a sterile 17 basin of water, resting on stiff arms, while the others locate the cancer. . . .

What is it, then, this thing, the knife, whose shape is 18 virtually the same as it was three thousand years ago, but now with its head grown detachable? Before steel, it was bronze. Before bronze, stone—then back into unremembered time. Did man invent it or did the knife precede him here, hidden under ages of vegetation and hoofprints, lying in wait to be discovered, picked up, used?

The scalpel is in two parts, the handle and the blade. 19 Joined, it is six inches from tip to tip. At one end of the handle is a narrow notched prong upon which the blade is slid, then snapped into place. Without the blade, the handle has a blind, decapitated look. It is helpless as a trussed maniac. But slide on the blade, click it home, and the knife springs instantly to life. It is headed now, edgy, leaping to mount the fingers for the gallop to its feast.

Now is the moment from which you have turned aside, 20 from which you have averted your gaze, yet toward which you have been hastened. Now the scalpel sings along the flesh again, its brute run unimpeded by germs or other frictions. It is a slick slide home, a barracuda spurt, a rip of embedded talon. One listens, and almost hears the whine—nasal, high, delivered through that gleaming metallic snout. The flesh splits with its own kind of moan. It is like the penetration of rape.

The breasts of women are cut off, arms and legs sliced 21 to the bone to make ready for the saw, eyes freed from sockets, intestines lopped. The hand of the surgeon rebels. Tension boils through his pores, like sweat. The flesh of the patient retaliates with hemorrhage, and the blood chases the knife wherever it is withdrawn.

Within the belly a tumor squats, toadish, fungoid. A 22 gray mother and her brood. The only thing it does not do is croak. It too is hacked from its bed as the carnivore knife lips the blood, turning in it in a kind of ecstasy of plenty, a gluttony after the long fast. It is just for this that the knife was created, tempered, heated, its violence beaten into paper-thin force.

At last a little thread is passed into the wound and 23 tied. The monstrous booming fury is stilled by a tiny thread. The tempest is silenced. The operation is over. On the table, the knife lies spent, on its side, the bloody meal smear-dried upon its flanks. The knife rests.

And waits. 24

◆

For Study and Discussion

QUESTIONS ABOUT PURPOSE

1. How do you know that Selzer does not intend to give directions on how to perform surgery?
2. Selzer calls surgery "unnatural," but he also calls it "among the gentlest of arts." How do both interpretations help clarify his purpose in writing this essay?
3. What is Selzer's purpose in discussing the principal tool of his trade—the knife? Look particularly at paragraphs 19–24.

QUESTIONS ABOUT AUDIENCE

1. The surgeon may be *the* expert in our culture. What effect does Selzer anticipate when he admits to his readers that his "quietude of resolve [is] layered over fear"?
2. What assumptions does Selzer make about the knowledge of his audience? What assumptions does he make about their apprehension—their preference not to be told *everything?*
3. Although Selzer does not expect his readers to retrace his steps, he does seem to address them directly on several occasions. To whom is he speaking when he says, "No! No! Do not touch the spleen . . ."?

QUESTIONS ABOUT STRATEGIES

1. Which of the principal steps in the surgical procedure does Selzer describe? How does he use color to mark transition from step to step?
2. Make a list of the special terms in this essay. How many does Selzer define?

3. More than any writer in this section, Selzer uses comparisons to illustrate the process he is analyzing. What characteristics do most of these comparisons have in common?

QUESTIONS FOR DISCUSSION

1. Surgeons are known for their skilled hands. What is Selzer's attitude toward the subject of hands? Analyze his many references to them throughout this essay.
2. How does Selzer present the drama of the operating room? What is the relationship of the surgeon to the other members of the surgical team?
3. What kinds of dreadful mysteries are usually associated with surgery? Does Selzer's analysis make the process seem any less terrifying?

Process Analysis as a Writing Strategy

POINTS TO CONSIDER

1. Is your primary purpose to give directions, step by step, on how to do something, or to provide information, in general outline, on how something works? What is your *secondary* purpose? Have you discovered an easier, quicker, more efficient method for performing a process? Have you uncovered the complicated procedure that must be followed if the process is to look effortless? Your primary purpose determines how and to whom you will present the process. Your secondary purpose determines what you want to prove about the process.

2. Who is the audience for your essay—readers who expect to retrace the steps you are analyzing or readers who have a general curiosity about the operations of a process? Speak to the first group directly: "Do this. Don't do that." Address the second group from a more detached perspective but try to capture their interest: "Most people have heard about this, but few know how it really works." And finally, be sure to anticipate the expertise of your readers. Don't confuse them by omitting information they need. Don't antagonize them by "talking down" to them about something they already know.

3. Have you presented the process in a clear, organized, and logical sequence? Have you provided an overview of the sequence so that your readers understand the purpose and major divisions of the process before they read your detailed analysis of individual steps? Have you provided definitions of special terms? Do you interpret the steps in the sequence by giving reasons, providing warnings, and citing examples? Have you discussed the results of the process?

PREWRITING EXERCISES

1. Outline the steps you use to complete a common process (for example, washing your hair, shaving your beard, ironing a shirt). Group the steps into major divisions, make a list of special tools, and include any personal techniques you have developed to improve the process. Exchange outlines with other members of the class and discuss interesting variations. How often do you wash your hair? Do you use an electric shaver or a straight razor? Do you iron the back first or the sleeves first?

2. Examine a set of directions for performing a simple mechanical procedure (affixing a parking permit to your windshield, refilling a stapler, making a long distance telephone call). Do the directions follow the five-step strategy? When you follow the instructions, do you get the desired result? How would you improve the directions?

3. Research the proper steps in a process unknown to you. Research is also a process, so your first task is to find out where you find out about the process. Who knows the procedure for changing your major, registering to vote, getting your car repaired after an accident? Once you have researched the process, "walk" through it step by step. What steps have you overlooked? What advice would you give to someone who wants to know the best procedure?

4. Examine the charts, graphs, and illustrations in the textbooks of several different subjects—history, engineering, chemistry. Textbooks often use such "pictorials" to clarify a process such as photosynthesis or mass production. After you have studied various pictorial techniques, draw a chart of a particularly complicated process. Illustrate the major divisions, the step-by-step movement, and the results of the process.

5. Select a process in which you consider yourself an expert, such as building a brick wall. Assign yourself the task of explaining this process to a group of novices. (You may even want to identify a specific audience—

for example, fourth-grade students.) Identify another process your audience already knows, such as making a sandwich. Now construct a series of comparisons between the simpler process and the more complicated process you intend to explain to them.

TOPICS FOR WRITING IN CLASS

1. Give directions on how to use your favorite tool. There are, of course, standard methods for using every tool, but because this tool is your personal favorite you should supply "insider's" instructions—those methods that have made the tool work effectively for you.

2. Provide information on the tasks you (and your fellow workers) used to complete a job successfully. Most jobs—stocking groceries, making hamburgers, selling shoes—require workers to follow established procedures. In addition to explaining these procedures, you may wish to mention those instances where your failure to follow procedures produced surprising results.

3. Describe your experience discovering the sequence of steps in a new process. The focus of your essay should be the process of research—*how* you found out where to go, who to talk to, and what to do—rather than the process you are researching. Write about one of the examples suggested in Prewriting Exercise #3 or select your own.

TOPICS FOR WRITING OUT OF CLASS

1. Analyze a *physical* process you perform particularly well, such as hitting a golf ball, making an omelet, or whittling a wooden figure. In addition to outlining the basic steps, you may want to mention your own personal experience, or the experience of professionals, to clarify the process. Be sure to include special tips that make the process operate smoothly and appear effortless.

189

2. Analyze the steps in a complicated *mental* process, such as studying for a test, writing an essay, or selecting a major. Remember, although a mental process usually contains more individual steps than a physical process, those steps are often difficult to isolate because they must be performed simultaneously. Cowley's essay on the writing process provides an effective analysis of a mental process.

3. Analyze a process that confuses, intimidates, or terrifies most people. Selzer's essay on the surgical process is obviously a good model for this assignment. Your purpose is to clarify (or demystify) the process. An effective strategy for accomplishing this purpose may be personal experience: "I did this and survived to tell the tale. So can you."

COMPARISON AND CONTRAST

To *compare* means to look for similarities. To *contrast* means to look for differences. Although the two words have opposite meanings, they are usually considered part of the same process—making comparisons. In a given situation, similarities or differences may be more evident, but each always implies the existence of the other (like *and* unlike). Comparisons are made at all levels of experience, from the most trivial (this sweater versus that sweater) to the most important (this job versus that job), and often lead to some kind of choice (chocolate or vanilla,

Republican or Democrat). The *comparison and contrast* essay organizes this basic intellectual process into a systematic plan for analyzing and evaluating the points of similarity and difference between two or more things.

PURPOSE

The two forms of the comparison and contrast essay have different purposes. The STRICT comparison explores the relationship between things in the same class. The FANCIFUL comparison establishes a relationship between things in different classes.

The *strict* comparison compares only those things that share significant points of similarity—actors with actors, musicians with musicians, but *not* actors with musicians. One purpose of such a comparison is to provide similar information about both subjects (the ingredients in two brands of breakfast cereal). Another purpose is to demonstrate that similar things (two students in the same class) are really different *or* different things (two teachers of different subjects) are really similar. A final purpose for this side-by-side comparison is to present a conclusion (which of two basketball players at the same position is superior) or to recommend a choice (which of two cars in the same price range is the best buy).

The *fanciful* comparison creates an imaginative relationship between dissimilar things for some specific occasion. More a special device than a dominant writing strategy, the fanciful comparison is often used to introduce a complex idea by noting its similarity to something simple and concrete (the human heart works like a pump). It is also used to add complexity and dimension to the two things being compared (the astronauts landing on the moon were like Columbus discovering the new world). Unlike the strict comparison, the fanciful comparison is not used to present conclusions or recommend choices.

Instead, it restricts its purpose to discovering hidden and striking resemblances between two unlikely subjects.

AUDIENCE

Writers of comparison and contrast essays must anticipate the *expertise* and *expectations* of their readers. As they assess the probable knowledge of their audience, writers must decide whether (1) both items in the comparison are known, (2) neither item is known, or (3) one item is known. If both items are known (two television programs), writers can shorten the demonstration of similarity and concentrate on the reasons for making the comparison. If neither item is known (two Eastern religions), writers will have to discuss each according to general concepts familiar to their audience. If only one of the items is known (American Congress and British Parliament), then writers should remind their readers of the familiar before introducing them to the unknown.

As they assess the expectations of their audience, writers should remember that comparisons are made according to the principle of equality. Readers expect the analysis of one part to be matched with an analysis of its counterpart. This does not mean that writers must devote identical space to similarities and differences. Most essays emphasize one or the other. It does mean, however, that writers should design their essays to fulfill their readers' desire for order and balance.

STRATEGIES

The two basic strategies for organizing a comparison and contrast essay are the SUBJECT-BY-SUBJECT (or divided) pattern and the POINT-BY-POINT (or alternating) pattern. As its name suggests, the subject-by-subject strategy presents all the information about one subject before considering information on the second subject. Mark Twain uses this method in "Two Views of the River" when he describes the Mississippi River viewed first from the poetic perspective of an apprentice and then from the practical perspective of a pilot.

The point-by-point pattern, on the other hand, presents the information about each subject according to points of similarity. At each point, information about the first subject is followed by information about the second subject. If Mark Twain's essay were *reorganized* to conform to this pattern, it would describe one aspect of the river (the color of the water) from the poetic and then from the practical perspective. The essay would follow this procedure with each successive point.

Although both strategies provide useful methods for making comparisons, each has strengths and weaknesses that must be considered in planning an essay. The principal strength of the *divided pattern* is that it presents each subject as a unified whole. It is particularly effective in short essays, such as Twain's, where the writer wants to focus attention on the two subjects and where the reader can remember the number and sequence of the points being analyzed. Its chief weakness is that it can expand into two separate essays. When the essay is long, the two subjects complex, and the points of comparison many, the divided pattern becomes difficult for both writer and reader to manage.

The principal strength of the *alternating pattern* is that it presents the two subjects side by side according to their points of comparison. It is particularly effective in longer essays, such as John Leggett's "Ross and Tom," where the writer wants to demonstrate many complex points of comparison and where the reader needs help seeing how points are supposed to match up. Its chief weakness is that it can reduce analysis to list making. If the essay is short, the subjects simple, and the points of comparison few (or in need of little extended development), the alternating pattern becomes a mechanical exercise for both writer and reader.

Writers often make the best of both worlds by COM-BINING STRATEGIES. They begin an essay in the divided pattern in order to establish a coherent view of the first subject. But when they move on to the second subject, they shift to the alternating pattern in order to demonstrate the many connections between the two subjects. For example, Barry Lopez's comparison of ravens and crows and Ada Louise Huxtable's comparison of people who live with clutter and people who live without it illustrate these strategies working in combination.

To ensure the effectiveness of their analyses the writers of comparison-contrast essays follow *three* rules: (1) *Balance Parts,* (2) *Include Reminders,* and (3) *Supply Reasons.* Murray Ross designs his analysis of football, baseball, and myth so that each part is balanced by its counterpart. These pairs are equal in number and arranged in parallel patterns that move from the simple to the complex (place, structure, time, style, values). Ross also includes transitional phrases and sentences to remind his readers that certain information in one part of his analysis connects with information in the other part ("Baseball is part of a comic tradition which insists that its participants be humans, while football, in the heroic mode, asks that its players be more than that"). And finally, Ross tells his readers, on several occasions, *why* he is comparing football, baseball, and myth ("Whatever can be said, mythically, about these games would seem to apply directly and particularly to our culture").

Two Views of the River

MARK TWAIN

◆

Mark Twain (a pen name for Samuel Clemens, 1835–
1910) was born in Florida, Missouri, and grew up in
the river town of Hannibal, Missouri, where he
watched the comings and goings of the steamboats
he would eventually pilot. Twain spent his young
adult life working as a printer, a pilot on the Missis-
sippi, and a frontier journalist. After the Civil War, he
began a career as a humorist and storyteller, writing
such classics as The Adventures of Tom Sawyer
(1876), Life on the Mississippi *(1883),* The Adventures
of Huckleberry Finn *(1885), and* A Connecticut Yankee
in King Arthur's Court *(1889). His place in American*
writing was characterized best by editor William Dean
Howells, who called Twain the "Lincoln of our liter-
ature." In "Two Views of the River," taken from Life
on the Mississippi, *Twain compares the way he saw*
the river as an innocent apprentice to the way he saw
it as an experienced pilot.

Now when I had mastered the language of this water, and   1
had come to know every trifling feature that bordered the
great river as familiarly as I knew the letters of the alpha-
bet, I had made a valuable acquisition. But I had lost
something, too. I had lost something which could never
be restored to me while I lived. All the grace, the beauty,
the poetry, had gone out of the majestic river! I still keep
in mind a certain wonderful sunset which I witnessed
when steamboating was new to me. A broad expanse of
the river was turned to blood; in the middle distance the

red hue brightened into gold, through which a solitary log came floating black and conspicuous; in one place a long, slanting mark lay sparkling upon the water; in another the surface was broken by boiling, tumbling rings, that were as many-tinted as an opal; where the ruddy flush was faintest, was a smooth spot that was covered with graceful circles and radiating lines, ever so delicately traced; the shore on our left was densely wooded, and the somber shadow that fell from this forest was broken in one place by a long, ruffled trail that shone like silver; and high above the forest wall a clean-stemmed dead tree waved a single leafy bough that glowed like a flame in the un-obstructed splendor that was flowing from the sun. There were graceful curves, reflected images, woody heights, soft distances; and over the whole scene, far and near, the dis-solving lights drifted steadily, enriching it every passing moment with new marvels of coloring.

I stood like one bewitched. I drank it in, in a speechless rapture. The world was new to me, and I had never seen anything like this at home. But as I have said, a day came when I began to cease from noting the glories and the charms which the moon and the sun and the twilight wrought upon the river's face; another day came when I ceased altogether to note them. Then, if that sunset scene had been repeated, I should have looked upon it without rapture, and should have commented upon it, inwardly, after this fashion: "This sun means that we are going to have wind to-morrow; that floating log means that the river is rising, small thanks to it; that slanting mark on the water refers to a bluff reef which is going to kill somebody's steamboat one of these nights, if it keeps on stretching out like that; those tumbling 'boils' show a dissolving bar and a changing channel there; the lines and circles in the slick water over yonder are a warning that that troublesome place is shoaling up dangerously; that silver streak in the shadow of the forest is the 'break' from a new snag, and he has located himself in the very best place he could have found to fish for steamboats; that tall dead tree, with a

2

single living branch, is not going to last long, and then how is a body ever going to get through this blind place at night without the friendly old landmark?"

No, the romance and beauty were all gone from the river. All the value any feature of it had for me now was the amount of usefulness it could furnish toward compassing the safe piloting of a steamboat. Since those days, I have pitied doctors from my heart. What does the lovely flush in a beauty's cheek mean to a doctor but a "break" that ripples above some deadly disease? Are not all her visible charms sown thick with what are to him the signs and symbols of hidden decay? Does he ever see her beauty at all, or doesn't he simply view her professionally, and comment upon her unwholesome condition all to himself? And doesn't he sometimes wonder whether he has gained most or lost most by learning his trade?

——— ◆ ———

For Study and Discussion

QUESTIONS ABOUT PURPOSE

1. What does Twain think he has gained and lost by learning the river?
2. Why does Twain *divide* the two views of the river rather than *alternate* them beneath several headings?
3. What similarities does Twain see between the pilot and the doctor?

QUESTIONS ABOUT AUDIENCE

1. How does Twain establish his credentials as an expert on both points of view for his audience?
2. Does he anticipate that his readers share the poetic or practical view of the river? Explain your answer.

3. How does he expect his readers to answer the questions he raises in paragraph 3?

QUESTIONS ABOUT STRATEGIES

1. How does Twain's choice of words distinguish between the poetic and practical views of the river?
2. What sequence does Twain use to arrange his points of comparison?
3. Where does Twain use transitional phrases and sentences to match up the parts of his comparison?

QUESTIONS FOR DISCUSSION

1. Do you think the appreciation of beauty depends upon a blissful innocence of danger? Explain.
2. Does knowledge destroy one's ability to appreciate beauty? Explain.
3. Besides the pilot and the doctor, can you identify other professions where people lose as much as they gain by learning their trade?

Ross and Tom

JOHN LEGGETT

———————— ♦ ————————

*John Leggett was born in 1917 in New York City and
educated at Yale University. He served as an officer
in the Pacific Fleet during World War II and later
became a publicity director and editor for Houghton
Mifflin in Boston, Massachusetts, the company that
published both Ross Lockridge and Thomas Heggen.
After 1960 Leggett worked as an editor at Harper
& Row in New York; he is now director of the University of Iowa Writers Workshop. His own books
include* Wilder Stone *(1960),* The Gloucester Branch
(1964), Who Took the Gold Away *(1969),* Ross and
Tom: Two American Tragedies *(1974), and* Gulliver
House *(1979), a novel about a publishing house. In
the following selection (the introduction to* Ross and
Tom*) Leggett compares and contrasts two authors
whose sudden fame ended in disillusionment and
early death.*

Taking my life is inconceivable to me. I shall lose it soon
enough. To abandon even one of my allotted minutes
might be to miss some important or funny thing, perhaps
even the point.

Also—and there is a connection—I am ambitious. I
have been bred to "getting ahead," to the belief that if
I fall behind, shame and starvation will catch me, but if I
achieve some thing I will be looked after, admired and
loved in perpetuity. Long ago I accepted these as the rules
of the game. I only quarrel with them when the score is
running against me.

Sometime during World War II I decided to have my 3
achievement as a writer. It took me five years and a fat
swatch of rejection slips to find out how hard that was
and, in frustration, to take a job with a book publisher.

Thus it was in Houghton Mifflin's warren overlooking 4
Boston Common that I learned about a dark side of achievement—how, a few years earlier, two young novelists, just
my age and no more promising in background, had been
published so successfully that their first books made them
rich and famous. Then, at the peak of their acclaim, they
died.

The first, Ross Lockridge, took his own life, locking his 5
new garage doors behind his new Kaiser and asphyxiating
himself. The second, Thomas Heggen, drowned in his
bathwater—an accident, it was claimed, but it was the
accident of a desperate man.

Tom and Ross were similar in that neither had any 6
previous notoriety and they came from obscure, middle-
class, Midwest backgrounds. Yet as men they could not
have been more different.

Ross was an oak of prudence and industry. He rarely 7
drank and he never smoked. He excelled at everything he
did. He had married his hometown sweetheart, was proudly
faithful to her and produced four fine children. After a
sampling of success on both coasts he had gone home to
the Indiana of his parents and childhood friends.

Tom Heggen had a taste for low life. He had been di- 8
vorced, had no children and shared bachelor quarters in
New York with an ex-actor and screenwriter, Dorothy
Parker's estranged husband, Alan Campbell. Tom was a
drinker and a pill addict. He turned up regularly at the
fashionable restaurant "21," usually bringing along a new
girl, a dancer or an actress.

After the success of their first novels, neither Ross nor 9
Tom had been able to start a new book. At the time of
their deaths neither had written anything in months.

What had happened to them? There were grumblings 10
that some villainy of Houghton Mifflin's had done Ross

Lockridge in, that in publishing his huge novel, *Raintree County*, the firm had exploited him, somehow threatened both his income and his privacy. (There had been a quarrel and Ross had made unpleasant accusations.)

Could it have been fatigue—had the two novelists written themselves out, found they had nothing more to say? Or was it disappointment: had the finished book—or in Heggen's case the dramatic version of *Mister Roberts* which was then playing on Broadway—fallen short of some original notion of perfection? There are always spoilers. *Raintree County*'s first reviews had called it a masterpiece and compared its author to Thomas Wolfe, but these were followed by some contemptuous ones, and there had been a denouncement by a Jesuit priest which struck at Ross's own self-doubts.

Still, none of these sounded as likely an explanation as that of the bitch-goddess herself—the writer spoiled by success, his need to write smothered in a surfeit of reward. Clearly there is something disillusioning in attainment. Many writers (such as J. D. Salinger and James Gould Cozzens, among others) drift into unproductivity after a big, popular success, just as the very productive ones such as Henry James are often those who pursue, yet never quite attain, an enthusiastic public embrace.

There is still another area for conjecture. Suppose that Tom Heggen's and Ross Lockridge's final act was not one of surrender at all, but defiance. Perhaps success had brought them to some promontory from which they could see the whole of their path and from there they had made this appalling comment about it. What could so disillusion them about that view? I needed to know. If they were rejecting their own incentives, they were, so far as I knew, rejecting mine.

Searching for an entryway to their spirits, I drew a professional comparison. Lockridge was a Vesuvius. When he was at work, twenty or thirty pages spewed from his typewriter each day, some on their way to the wastebasket, others to be revised, endlessly before they were satisfactory, but always expanding. Progress toward a desired shape was by laying on more material.

Heggen was the reverse, a distiller. The molding was 15 a prelude to writing and was done in his head. He would sit by the hour, staring out a window, so that a passerby would think him daydreaming. But then he would turn to his typewriter and strike a flawless passage, each word and inflection so precisely chosen there was no need for revision.

But in spite of this difference in the way they worked, 16 Ross and Tom appeared to be equally single-minded about writing, each compelled to it with a force that dwarfed the other elements of his life. Thus the common experience preceding their deaths, of wanting to write again and not being able to, is significant. The being able to—the energy —is the essential part of incentive and I had the impression they had lost that, knew they had lost it and knew that without it they were useless men.

What *is* a writer's incentive? That he has a gift for 17 expression in words can be taken for granted; but I suspect that gift doesn't contribute half so much to motivation as social failure. I know that my own feelings of inadequacy and shyness were first routed when, in the third grade, my piece on tadpoles appeared in the school paper, and I suspect that only a man who doubts the persuasiveness of his tongue and fists would sit alone dirtying good paper when he could be in company.

Wanting to write fiction has even more elaborate roots 18 and these reach not just into a writer's present reveries but back into his childhood. When he is read to, when he is sick and is brought an adventure book with his medicine, a child gets a first set of furnishings for his dream world. When he graduates to adult novels his debt to fiction is increased by a more utilitarian, though still romantic, vision of himself and a way to behave. If he chooses wisely and is lucky in the library he can find dream enough to sustain him for a lifetime.

But the path of a writer is too lonely and discouraging 19

for any kind of propulsion but the hugest. In an essay on Willa Cather, Leon Edel notes that for her novel about an ambitious opera singer, *The Song of the Lark*, she chose the epigraph "It was a wondrous lovely storm that drove me," and that this was not only appropriate for Thea, the heroine, but for the author.

"It was a wondrous, lovely storm that drove Willa [20] Cather," he says, "and what she cared for above all was the storm. With success achieved . . . she felt depressed. She didn't know what to do with success; or rather, she seems to have experienced a despair altogether out of proportion to the actual circumstances of her achievement . . . Success, by the very testimony of the tales she wrote, created for Willa Cather a deep despair and even a wish for death . . ."

Willa Cather's experience of depression in achievement [21] makes a striking parallel with Ross's and Tom's. And I cannot find a better description for the kind of force a novelist wants to contain than "the wondrous lovely storm." It is vague, yet so evocative of the emotion and energy that can bring forth a significant book—wondrous in its mysterious origin and awesome power, lovely because it is not terrifying at all, but blissful, as though it is love itself.

When I first looked into Tom Heggen's and Ross Lock- [22] ridge's lives, seeking some clues to their deaths, I found myself in barren country. Neither had the nature for casual confessions nor the kind of apprenticeships which called for public self-examinations. An even bigger difficulty lay with those who had known them best. They suffered from having been present at, yet unable to prevent, a tragedy. Understandably the families were wary of talking about the darker, human parts of the natures and experiences of the two writers.

Still, inconsequential, even irrelevant details about [23] them intrigued me. Instead of flagging, my interest grew. Occasionally I felt I might be guilty of dancing on their graves, a jig for my own compensating survival. But what most absorbed me was self-discovery.

Ross, Tom and I grew up to the same music, worshiping the same idols, suffering from the same inhibitions. It was remarkably easy for me to slip into their adolescent skins. As an adult and a writer, I could recognize in those highs of self-certainty, in those plunging lows of self-doubt, my own emotional weather. Finally, in each of their natures—one black, reckless; the other a marching band of virtues—I saw two halves of my own.

24

◆

For Study and Discussion

QUESTIONS ABOUT PURPOSE

1. Why is Leggett personally fascinated by the careers of Ross and Tom?
2. What does he hope to discover by comparing the two writers?
3. Why does he include the information on Willa Cather?

QUESTIONS ABOUT AUDIENCE

1. What audience does Leggett assume for this essay—writers, publishers, critics, general readers? How do you know?
2. How much does Leggett think his readers already know about Ross Lockridge and Tom Heggen?
3. What concepts does Leggett use to give his readers a context for the comparison?

QUESTIONS ABOUT STRATEGIES

1. How does Leggett present the major points of similarity between Ross and Tom?
2. How does Leggett's "professional" comparison in paragraphs 14–15 help characterize the difference between the two men?
3. How does Leggett use his own experience (and the experience of other writers) to clarify his purpose and interest his readers?

QUESTIONS FOR DISCUSSION

1. What meanings does Leggett attribute to the phrase "the wondrous lovely storm"? Can you think of activities, other than writing a novel, where the phrase might apply?
2. How do you react to Leggett's theory that suicide can be an act of defiance rather than surrender?
3. What definitions does this essay provide for the following words: *incentive, fame, fulfillment?*

The Raven

BARRY LOPEZ

◆

Barry Lopez was born in 1945 in Port Chester, New York, and educated at the University of Notre Dame and the University of Oregon. For the last ten years he has lived near the Willamette Forest in Oregon and worked as a full-time writer and free-lance photographer. His articles and photographs on various aspects of the natural environment have appeared in National Wildlife, American Forests, Audubon, *and other magazines. His works include* Desert Notes: Reflections in the Eye of the Raven *(1976) and* River Notes: The Dance of the Herons *(1979), the first two books of a trilogy;* Of Wolves and Men *(1978); and* Winter Count, *a collection of short fiction. Lopez is regarded as a superb naturalist who possesses the imagination and voice of a poet. In "The Raven," from* Desert Notes, *he contrasts two birds that the casual observer may see as quite similar.*

I am going to have to start at the other end by telling you 1 this: there are no crows in the desert. What appear to be crows are ravens. You must examine the crow, however, before you can understand the raven. To forget the crow completely, as some have tried to do, would be like trying to understand the one who stayed without talking to the one who left. It is important to make note of who has left the desert.

To begin with, the crow does nothing alone. He can- 2 not abide silence and he is prone to stealing things, twigs and bits of straw, from the nests of his neighbors. It is a game with him. He enjoys tricks. If he cannot make up his mind the crow will take two or three wives, but this is not a game. The crow is very accommodating and he admires compulsiveness.

Crows will live in street trees in the residential areas of great cities. They will walk at night on the roofs of parked cars and peck at the grit; they will scrape the pinpoints of their talons across the steel and, with their necks outthrust, watch for frightened children listening in their beds. 3

Put all this to the raven: he will open his mouth as if to say something. Then he will look the other way and say nothing. Later, when you have forgotten, he will tell you he admires the crow. 4

The raven is larger than the crow and has a beard of black feathers at his throat. He is careful to kill only what he needs. Crows, on the other hand, will search out the great horned owl, kick and punch him awake, and then, for roosting too close to their nests, they will kill him. They will come out of the sky on a fat, hot afternoon and slam into the head of a dozing rabbit and go away laughing. They will tear out a whole row of planted corn and eat only a few kernels. They will defecate on scarecrows and go home and sleep with 200,000 of their friends in an atmosphere of congratulation. Again, it is only a game; this should not be taken to mean that they are evil. 5

There is however this: when too many crows come together on a roost there is a lot of shoving and noise and a white film begins to descend over the crows' eyes and they go blind. They fall from their perches and lie on the ground and starve to death. When confronted with this information, crows will look past you and warn you vacantly that it is easy to be misled. 6

The crow flies like a pigeon. The raven flies like a hawk. He is seen only at a great distance and then not very clearly. This is true of the crow too, but if you are very clever you can trap the crow. The only way to be sure 7 what you have seen is a raven is to follow him until he dies of old age, and then examine the body.

Once there were many crows in the desert. I am told it 8 was like this: you could sit back in the rocks and watch a pack of crows working over the carcass of a coyote. Some would eat, the others would try to squeeze out the vultures. The raven would never be seen. He would be at a distance, alone, perhaps eating a scorpion.

There was, at this time, a small alkaline water hole at 9 the desert's edge. Its waters were bitter. No one but crows would drink there, although they drank sparingly, just one or two sips at a time. One day a raven warned someone about the dangers of drinking the bitter water and was overheard by a crow. When word of this passed among the crows they felt insulted. They jeered and raised insulting gestures to the ravens. They bullied each other into drinking the alkaline water until they had drunk the hole dry and gone blind.

The crows flew into canyon walls and dove straight 10 into the ground at forty miles an hour and broke their necks. The worst of it was their cartwheeling across the desert floor, stiff wings outstretched, beaks agape, white eyes ballooning, surprising rattlesnakes hidden under sage bushes out of the noonday sun. The snakes awoke, struck and held. The wheeling birds strew them across the desert like sprung traps.

When all the crows were finally dead, the desert bac- 11 teria and fungi bored into them, burrowed through bone and muscle, through aqueous humor and feathers until they had reduced the stiff limbs of soft black to blue dust.

After that, there were no more crows in the desert. The 12 few who watched from a distance took it as a sign and moved away.

Finally there is this: one morning four ravens sat at the 13 edge of the desert waiting for the sun to rise. They had been there all night and the dew was like beads of quicksilver on their wings. Their eyes were closed and they were as still as the cracks in the desert floor.

The wind came off the snow-capped peaks to the north 14 and ruffled their breath feathers. Their talons arched in the white earth and they smoothed their wings with sleek, dark bills. At first light their bodies swelled and their eyes flashed purple. When the dew dried on their wings they lifted off from the desert floor and flew away in four directions. Crows would never have had the patience for this.

If you want to know more about the raven: bury your- 15 self in the desert so that you have a commanding view of the high basalt cliffs where he lives. Let only your eyes protrude. Do not blink—the movement will alert the raven to your continued presence. Wait until a generation of ravens has passed away. Of the new generation there will be at least one bird who will find you. He will see your eyes staring up out of the desert floor. The raven is cautious, but he is thorough. He will sense your peaceful intentions. Let him have the first word. Be careful: he will tell you he knows nothing.

If you do not have the time for this, scour the weathered 16 desert shacks for some sign of the raven's body. Look under old mattresses and beneath loose floorboards. Look behind the walls. Sooner or later you will find a severed foot. It will be his and it will be well preserved.

Take it out in the sunlight and examine it closely. 17 Notice that there are three fingers that face forward, and a fourth, the longest and like a thumb, that faces to the rear. The instrument will be black but no longer shiny, the back of it sheathed in armor plate and the underside padded like a wolf's foot.

At the end of each digit you will find a black, curved 18 talon. You will see that the talons are not as sharp as you might have suspected. They are made to grasp and hold fast, not to puncture. They are more like the jaws of a trap than a fistful of ice picks. The subtle difference serves the raven well in the desert. He can weather a storm on

a barren juniper limb; he can pick up and examine the
crow's eye without breaking it.

———— ◆ ————

For Study and Discussion

QUESTIONS ABOUT PURPOSE

1. What is Lopez's primary purpose—to explain the dif-
    ference between the raven and the crow or to demon-
    strate why the raven is superior to the crow? Explain
    your answer.
2. According to Lopez, why did the crow leave the desert?
3. Why is it difficult to "understand the one who stayed
    without talking to the one who left"?

QUESTIONS ABOUT AUDIENCE

1. Throughout the essay Lopez uses direct address, as in
    "you must examine the crow," "if you want to know
    more about the raven." What advantages does this
    give him in establishing a relationship with his readers?
2. In choosing to discuss the crow first, what assump-
    tions does Lopez make about his readers' experience?
3. To what extent does Lopez expect his readers to fol-
    low his instructions in paragraphs 15–18?

QUESTIONS ABOUT STRATEGIES

1. Where does Lopez use the divided pattern? Where does
    he use the alternating pattern? What aspect of his
    subject causes him to combine the two strategies?
2. How does he use the story of the water hole to charac-
    terize the difference between the two birds?

3. How does Lopez use comparisons to other birds—pigeon, hawk, vulture—to distinguish between the raven and the crow?

QUESTIONS FOR DISCUSSION

1. What human qualities does Lopez attribute to the two birds? For example, why does the crow live in the city and the raven live in the desert?
2. How does their manner of killing help distinguish the two birds? In particular, how does Lopez's characterization of the raven's talons help identify its attitude toward its prey?
3. In paragraph 4 Lopez says that the raven admires the crow. What information does he provide in his essay to justify this assertion?

Modern-Life Battle:
Conquering Clutter

ADA LOUISE HUXTABLE

◆

Ada Louise Huxtable was born in 1921 in New York City and was educated at Hunter College and New York University. After teaching at a number of small liberal arts colleges, she worked from 1946 to 1950 as the assistant curator of architecture and design at The Museum of Modern Art. In the 1950s she was awarded Fulbright and Guggenheim fellowships and became a contributing editor to Progressive Architecture. *Beginning in 1963, she worked for over a decade as the architecture critic for* The New York Times. *On occasion she continues to contribute her critical commentary to that newspaper in her column, "Design Notebook." In 1970 she was awarded the first Pulitzer Prize for distinguished criticism, and recently she received the prestigious McArthur Foundation Award. Her most important books include* Pier Luigi Nervi *(1960),* Classic New York *(1964),* Will They Ever Finish Bruckner Boulevard? *(1970), and* Kicked a Building Lately? *(1976). In "Modern-Life Battles: Conquering Clutter," first published in* The New York Times *in 1981, Huxtable compares people who "clutter compulsively" and those who "just as compulsively throw things away."*

There are two kinds of people in the world—those who   1
have a horror of a vacuum and those with a horror of the
things that fill it. Translated into domestic interiors, this
means people who live with, and without, clutter. (Dictionary definition: jumble, confusion, disorder.) The reasons for clutter, the need to be surrounded by things, goes
deep, from security to status. The reasons for banning

213

objects, or living in as selective and austere an environment as possible, range from the esthetic to the neurotic. This is a phenomenon of choice that relates as much to the psychiatrist as to the tastemaker.

Some people clutter compulsively, and others just as compulsively throw things away. Clutter in its highest and most organized form is called collecting. Collecting can be done as the Collyer brothers did it, or it can be done with art and flair. The range is from old newspapers to Fabergé.

This provides a third category, or what might be called calculated clutter, in which the objets d'art, the memorabilia that mark one's milestones and travels, the irresistible and ornamental things that speak to pride, pleasure and temptation, are constrained by decorating devices and hierarchal principles of value. This gives the illusion that one is in control.

Most of us are not in control. My own life is an unending battle against clutter. By that I do not mean to suggest that I am dedicated to any clean-sweep asceticism or arrangements of high art; I am only struggling to keep from drowning in the detritus of everyday existence, or at least to keep it separate from the possessions that are meant to be part of what I choose to believe is a functional-esthetic scheme.

Really living without clutter takes an iron will, plus a certain stoicism about the little comforts of life. I have neither. But my eye requires a modest amount of beauty and serenity that clutter destroys. This involves eternal watchfulness and that oldest and most relentless of the housewife's occupations, picking up. I have a feeling that picking up will go on long after ways have been found to circumvent death and taxes.

I once saw a home in which nothing had ever been picked up. Daily vigilance had been abandoned a long time ago. Although disorder descends on the unwary with the speed of light, this chaos must have taken years to achieve; it was almost a new decorating art form.

The result was not, as one might suppose, the idio- 7
syncratic disorder of a George Price drawing, where things
are hung from pipes and hooks in permanent arrangements
of awesome convenience.

This was an expensive, thoughtful, architect-designed 8
house where everything had simply been left where it
landed. Pots and pans, linens and clothing, toys and uten-
sils were tangled and piled everywhere, as well as all of
those miscellaneous items that go in, and usually out, of
most homes. No bare spot remained on furniture or floor.
And no one who lived there found it at all strange, or
seemed to require any other kind of domestic landscape.
They had no hangups, in any sense of the word.

I know another house that is just as full of things, but 9
the difference is instructive. This is a rambling old house
lived in for many years by a distinguished scholar and his
wife, whose love of the life of the mind and its better
products has only been equaled by their love of life.

In this very personal and knowledgeable eclecticism, 10
every shared intellectual and cultural experience led to the
accumulation of discoveries, mementos and objets de vertu,
kept casually at hand or in unstudied places. Tabletops
and floors are thickets of books and overflow treasures.
There is enormous, overwhelming, profligate clutter. And
everything has meaning, memory and style.

At the opposite extreme is the stripped, instant, homo- 11
geneous style, created whole and new. These houses and
apartments, always well-published, either start with nothing, which is rare, or clear everything out that the owners
have acquired, which must take courage, desperation, or
both. This means jettisoning the personal baggage, and
clutter, of a lifetime.

I confess to very mixed reactions when I see these sleek 12
and shining couples in their sleek and shining rooms, with
every perfect thing in its perfect place. Not the least of my
feelings is envy. Do these fashionable people, elegantly
garbed and posed in front of the lacquered built-ins with
just the right primitive pot and piece of sculpture and the

latest exotic tree, feel a tremendous sense of freedom and release? Have they been liberated by their seamless new look?

More to the point, what have they done with their 13 household lares and penates, the sentimental possessions of their past? Did they give them away? Send them to auction galleries and thrift shops? Go on a trip while the decorator cleared them all out? Take a deduction for their memories? Were they tempted to keep nothing? Do they ever have any regrets?

This, of course, is radical surgery. The rest of us resort 14 to more conventional forms of clutter combat. Houses have, or had, attics and cellars. Old apartments provide generous closets, which one fills with things that are permanently inaccessible and unneeded. In the city, there is stolen space, in elevator and service halls. And there is the ultimate catch-all—the house in the country.

Historically, clutter is a modern phenomenon, born of 15 the industrial revolution. There was a time when goods were limited; and the rich and fashionable were few in number and objects were precious and hard to come by. Clutter is a 19th-century esthetic; it came with the abundance of products combined with the rise of purchasing power, and the shifts in society that required manifestations of status and style.

Victorian parlors were a jungle of elaborate furnishings 16 and ornamental overkill. The reforms of the Arts and Crafts movement in the later 19th century only substituted a more "refined" kind of clutter—art pottery, embroidered mottos, handpainted tiles and porcelains, vases of bullrushes and peacock feathers. There were bewildering "artful" effects borrowed from the studio or atelier.

Clutter only became a bad word in the 20th century. 17 The modern movement decreed a new simplicity—white walls, bare floors, and the most ascetic of furnishings in the most purified of settings. If ornament was crime, clutter was taboo.

Architects built houses and decorators filled them. An- 18

tiques were discovered and every kind of collecting boomed. There were even architects of impeccable modernist credentials—Charles Eames and Alexander Girard—who acquired and arranged vast numbers of toys and treasures. They did so with a discerning eye for the colorful and the primitive that added interest—and clutter—to modern rooms.

Today, clutter is oozing in at a record rate. Architect-collectors like Charles Moore are freewheeling and quixotic in their tastes; high seriousness has been replaced by eclectic whimsy. Nostalgia and fleamarkets coexist on a par with scholarship and accredited antiques. Turning the century on its head, the artifacts of early modernism are being collected by the post-modernist avant-garde. At the commercial level, sophisticated merchandising sells the endless new fashions and products embraced by an affluent consumer society. The vacuum must be filled. And the truth must be told. Our possessions possess us. 19

——— ♦ ———

For Study and Discussion

QUESTIONS ABOUT PURPOSE

1. Is Huxtable's primary purpose to contrast two kinds of people, two attitudes toward possessions, or two assumptions about our ability to control the environment? Explain your answer.

2. What does Huxtable think about the people with no "hang ups" and the people who jettison "the personal baggage" of a lifetime?

3. In the last few paragraphs of her essay, what does Huxtable attempt to demonstrate by her historical analysis of clutter?

QUESTIONS ABOUT AUDIENCE

1. What assumptions does Huxtable make about her readers' attitude toward clutter? For example, why does she discuss people who live with clutter before she discusses people who live without it?

2. How does she use her own experience (see paragraph 4) to establish a relationship with her readers?

3. How does Huxtable's use of a dictionary definition of clutter (see paragraph 1) alert her readers to the ultimate significance of her comparison?

QUESTIONS ABOUT STRATEGIES

1. Where does Huxtable use the divided pattern? How does she combine the divided and alternating patterns?

2. How does she use the description of specific houses to illustrate people's contrasting attitudes toward clutter?

3. How does she express her personal reactions toward each illustration to establish the larger context for her comparison?

QUESTIONS FOR DISCUSSION

1. In her first paragraph, Huxtable suggests that the reasons people live with or without clutter range from esthetic to neurotic. Toward which extreme does your own experience with clutter tend? Why?

2. According to Huxtable, how does our attitude toward clutter reflect our attitude toward the past?

3. In what sense do our possessions define and possess us?

Football Red and Baseball Green

MURRAY ROSS

◆

Murray Ross was born in 1942 in Pasadena, California, just north of the Rose Bowl, which may explain his early love for the spectacle of sport. He was edu-cated at Williams College and the University of Cali-fornia at Berkeley and currently serves as the artistic director of the theater program at the University of Colorado, Colorado Springs. Ross published "Foot-ball Red and Baseball Green" in The Chicago Review *while he was still a graduate student at Berkeley. The essay compares and contrasts the rituals and myths identified with America's two favorite spectator sports.*

The 1970 Superbowl, the final game of the professional   1
football season, drew a larger television audience than
either the moonwalk or Tiny Tim's wedding. This revelation is one way of indicating just how popular spectator
sports are in this country. Americans, or American men
anyway, seem to care about the games they watch as much
as the Elizabethans cared about their plays, and I suspect
for some of the same reasons. There is, in sports, some of
the rudimentary drama found in popular theater: familiar
plots, type characters, heroic and comic action spiced with

new and unpredictable variations. And common to watching both activities is the sense of participation in a shared tradition and in shared fantasies. If it is true that sport exploits these fantasies without significantly transcending them, it seems no less satisfying for all that.

It is my guess that sport spectating involves something more than the vicarious pleasures of identifying with athletic prowess. I suspect that each sport contains a fundamental myth which it elaborates for its fans, and that our pleasure in watching such games derives in part from belonging briefly to the mythic world which the game and its players bring to life. I am especially interested in baseball and football because they are so popular and so uniquely *American*; they began here and unlike basketball they have not been widely exported. Thus whatever can be said, mythically, about these games would seem to apply directly and particularly to our own culture.

Baseball's myth may be the easier to identify since we have a greater historical perspective on the game. It was an instant success during the Industrialization, and most probably it was a reaction to the squalor, the faster pace and the dreariness of the new conditions. Baseball was old fashioned right from the start; it seems conceived in nostalgia, in the resuscitation of the Jeffersonian dream. It established an artificial rural environment, one removed from the toil of an urban life, which spectators could be admitted to and temporarily breathe in. Baseball is a *pastoral* sport, and I think the game can be best understood as this kind of art. For baseball does what all good pastoral does—it creates an atmosphere in which everything exists in harmony.

Consider, for instance, the spatial organization of the game. A kind of controlled openness is created by having everything fan out from home plate, and the crowd sees the game through an arranged perspective that is rarely violated. Visually this means that the game is always seen as a constant, rather calm whole, and that the players and the playing field are viewed in relationship to each other.

Each player has a certain position, a special area to tend, and the game often seems to be as much a dialogue between the fielders and the field as it is a contest between the players themselves: will that ball get through the hole? Can that outfielder run under that fly? As a moral genre pastoral asserts the virtue of communion with nature. As a competitive game, baseball asserts that the team which best relates to the playing field (by hitting the ball in the right places) will be the team which wins.

I suspect baseball's space has a subliminal function too, for topographically it is a sentimental mirror of older America. Most of the game is played between the pitcher and the hitter in the extreme corner of the playing area. This is the busiest, most sophisticated part of the ball park, where something is always happening, and from which all subsequent action depends. From this urban corner we move to a supporting infield, active but a little less crowded, and from there we come to the vast stretches of the outfield. As is traditional in American lore danger increases with distance, and the outfield action is often the most spectacular in the game. The long throw, the double off the wall, the leaping catch—these plays take place in remote territory, and they belong, like most legendary feats, to the frontier.

Having established its landscape, pastoral art operates to eliminate any references to that bigger, more disturbing, more real world it has left behind. All games are to some extent insulated from the outside by having their own rules, but baseball has a circular structure as well which furthers its comfortable feeling of self-sufficiency. By this I mean that every motion of extension is also one of return—a ball hit outside is a *home* run, a full circle. Home—familiar, peaceful, secure—it is the beginning and end of everything. You must go out and you must come back, for only the completed movement is registered.

Time is a serious threat to any form of pastoral. The genre poses a timeless world of perpetual spring, and it

221

does its best to silence the ticking of clocks which remind us that in time the green world fades into winter. One's sense of time is directly related to what happens in it, and baseball is so structured as to stretch out and ritualize whatever action it contains. Dramatic moments are few, and they are almost always isolated by the routine texture of normal play. It is certainly a game of climax and drama, but it is perhaps more a game of repeated and predictable action: the foul balls, the walks, the pitcher fussing around on the mound, the lazy fly ball to centerfield. This is, I think, as it should be, for baseball exists as an alternative to a world of too much action, struggle and change. It is a merciful release from a more grinding and insistent tempo, and its time, as William Carlos Williams suggests, makes a virtue out of idleness simply by providing it:

> The crowd at the ball game
> is moved uniformly
> by a spirit of uselessness
> which delights them . . .

Within this expanded and idle time the baseball fan is 8
at liberty to become a ceremonial participant and a lover of style. Because the action is normalized, how something is done becomes as important as the action itself. Thus baseball's most delicate and detailed aspects are often, to the spectator, the most interesting. The pitcher's windup, the anticipatory crouch of the infielders, the quick waggle of the bat as it poises for the pitch—these subtle minia-ture movements are as meaningful as the home runs and the strikeouts. It somehow matters in baseball that all the tiny rituals are observed: the shortstop must kick the dirt and the umpire must brush the plate with his pocket broom. In a sense baseball is largely a continuous series of small gestures, and I think it characteristic that the game's most treasured moment came when Babe Ruth pointed to the place where he subsequently hit a home run. Baseball is a game where the little things mean a lot, 9

and this, together with its clean serenity, its open space, and its ritualized action is enough to place it in a world of yesterday. Baseball evokes for us a past which may never have been ours, but which we believe was, and certainly that is enough. In the Second World War, supposedly, we fought for "Baseball, Mom and Apple Pie," and considering what baseball means that phrase is a good one. We fought then for the right to believe in a green world of tranquillity and uninterrupted contentment, where the little things would count. But now the possibilities of such a world are more remote, and it seems that while the entertainment of such a dream has an enduring appeal, it is no longer sufficient for our fantasies. I think this may be why baseball is no longer our preeminent national pastime, and why its myth is being replaced by another more appropriate to the new realities (and fantasies) of our time.

Football, especially professional football, is the embodiment of a newer myth, one which in many respects is opposed to baseball's. The fundamental difference is that football is not a pastoral game; it is a heroic one. One way of seeing the difference between the two is by the juxtaposition of Babe Ruth and Jim Brown, both legendary players in their separate genres. Ruth, baseball's most powerful hitter, was a hero maternalized (his name), an epic figure destined for a second immortality as a candy bar. His image was impressive but comfortable and altogether human: round, dressed in a baggy uniform, with a schoolboy's cap and a bat which looked tiny next to him. His spindly legs supported a Santa sized torso, and this comic disproportion would increase when he was in motion. He ran delicately, with quick, very short steps, since he felt that stretching your stride slowed you down. This sort of superstition is typical of baseball players, and typical too is the way in which a personal quirk or mannerism mitigates their awesome skill and makes them poignant and vulnerable.

There was nothing funny about Jim Brown. His 11

muscular and almost perfect physique was emphasized further by the uniform which armored him. Babe Ruth had a tough face, but boyish and innocent; Brown was an expressionless mask under the helmet. In action he seemed invincible, the embodiment of speed and power in an inflated human shape. One can describe Brown accurately only with superlatives, for as a player he was a kind of Superman, undisguised.

Brown and Ruth are caricatures, yet they represent   12
their games. Baseball is part of a comic tradition which insists that its participants be humans, while football, in the heroic mode, asks that its players be more than that. Football converts men into gods, and suggests that magnificence and glory are as desirable as happiness. Football is designed, therefore, to impress its audience rather differently than baseball, as I think comparison will show.

As a pastoral game, baseball attempts to close the gap   13
between the players and the crowd. It creates the illusion, for instance, that with a lot of hard work, a little luck, and possibly some extra talent, the average spectator might well be playing; not watching. For most of us can do a few of the things the ballplayers do: catch a pop-up, field a ground ball, and maybe get a hit once in a while. Chance is allotted a good deal of play in the game. There is no guarantee, for instance, that a good pitch will not be looped over the infield, or that a solidly batted ball will turn into a double play. In addition to all of this, almost every fan feels he can make the manager's decision for him, and not entirely without reason. Baseball's statistics are easily calculated and rather meaningful; and the game itself, though a subtle one, is relatively lucid and comprehensible.

As a heroic game football is not concerned with a   14
shared community of near-equals. It seeks almost the opposite relationship between its spectators and players, one which stresses the distance between them. We are not allowed to identify directly with Jim Brown any more than

we are with Zeus, because to do so would undercut his stature as something more than human. The players do much of the distancing themselves by their own excesses of speed, size and strength. When Bob Brown, the giant all pro tackle says that he could "block King Kong all day," we look at him and believe. But the game itself contributes to the players' heroic isolation. As George Plimpton has graphically illustrated in *Paper Lion*, it is almost impossible to imagine yourself in a professional football game without also considering your imminent humiliation and possible injury. There is scarcely a single play that the average spectator could hope to perform adequately, and there is even a difficulty in really under-standing what is going on. In baseball what happens is what meets the eye, but in football each action is the re-sult of eleven men acting simultaneously against eleven other men, and clearly this is too much for the eye to totally comprehend. Football has become a game of stag-gering complexity, and coaches are now wired in to sev-eral "spotters" during the games so that they too can find out what is happening.

If football is distanced from its fans by its intricacy and 15 its "superhuman" play, it nonetheless remains an intense spectacle. Baseball, as I have implied, dissolves time and urgency in a green expanse, thereby creating a luxurious and peaceful sense of leisure. As is appropriate to a heroic enterprise, football reverses this procedure and converts space into time. The game is ideally played in an oval stadium, not in a "park," and the difference is the elimi-nation of perspective. This makes football a perfect tele-vision game, because even at first hand it offers a flat, perpetually moving foreground (wherever the ball is). The eye in baseball viewing opens up; in football it zeroes in. There is no democratic vista in football, and spectators are not asked to relax, but to concentrate. You are en-couraged to watch the drama, not a medley of ubiquitous gestures, and you are constantly reminded that this event is taking place in time. The third element in baseball is the field; in football this element is the clock. Traditionally heroes do reckon with time, and football players are no exceptions. Time in football is wound up inexorably until it reaches the breaking point in the last minutes of a close game. More often than not it is the clock which emerges as the real enemy, and it is the sense of time running out that regularly produces a pitch of tension uncommon in baseball.

A further reason for football's intensity, surely, is that the game is played like a war. The idea is to win by going through, around or over the opposing team and the battle lines, quite literally, are drawn on every play. Violence is somewhere at the heart of the game, and the combat quality is reflected in football's army language ("blitz," "trap," "zone," "bomb," "trenches," etc.). Coaches often sound like generals when they discuss their strategy. Woody Hayes of Ohio State, for instance, explains his quarterback option play as if it had been conceived in the pentagon: "You know," he says, "the most effective kind of warfare is siege. You have to attack on broad fronts. And that's all the option is—attacking on a broad front. You know General Sherman ran an option right through the South." 16

Football like war is an arena for action, and like war football leaves little room for personal style. It seems to be a game which projects "character" more than personality, and for the most part football heroes, publicly, are a rather similar lot. They tend to become personifications rather than individuals, and, with certain exceptions, they are easily read emblematically as embodiments of heroic qualities such as "strength," "confidence," "perfection," etc.—cliches really, but forceful enough when represented by the play of a Dick Butkus, a Johnny Unitas or a Bart Starr. Perhaps this simplification of personality results in part from the heroes' total identification with their mission, to the extent that they become more character- 17 ized by their work than by what they intrinsically "are." At any rate football does not make allowances for the idiosyncrasies that baseball actually seems to encourage, and as a result there have been few football players as uniquely crazy or human as, say, Casey Stengel or Dizzy Dean.

A further reason for the underdeveloped qualities of 18 football personalities, and one which gets us to the heart of the game's modernity, is that football is very much a game of modern technology. Football's action is largely interaction, and the game's complexity requires that its players mold themselves into a perfectly coordinated unit. Jerry Kramer, the veteran guard and author of *Instant Replay*, writes how Lombardi would work to develop such integration:

> He makes us execute the same plays over and over, a hundred times, two hundred times, until we do every little thing automatically. He works to make the kickoff team perfect, the punt-return team perfect, the field-goal team perfect. He ignores nothing. Technique, technique, technique, over and over and over, until we feel like we're going crazy. But we win.

Mike Garrett, the halfback, gives the player's version: 19

> After a while you train your mind like a computer—put the ideas in, digest it, and the body acts accordingly.

As the quotations imply, pro football is insatiably pre- 20 occupied with the smoothness and precision of play execution, and most coaches believe that the team which makes the fewest mistakes will be the team that wins.

Individual identity thus comes to be associated with the team or unit that one plays for to a much greater extent than in baseball. To use a reductive analogy, it is the difference between *Bonanza* and *Mission Impossible*. Ted Williams is mostly Ted Williams, but Bart Starr is mostly the Green Bay Packers. The latter metaphor is a precise one, since football heroes stand out not because of purely individual acts, but because they epitomize the action and style of the groups they are connected to. Kramer cites the obvious if somewhat self-glorifying historical precedent: "Perhaps," he writes, "we're living in Camelot." Ideally a football team should be what Camelot was supposed to have been, a group of men who function as equal parts of a larger whole, entirely dependent on each other for their total meaning. . . .

Football's collective pattern is only one aspect of the 21 way in which it seems to echo our contemporary environment. The game, like our society, can be thought of as a cluster of people living under great tension in a state of perpetual flux. The potential for sudden disaster or triumph is as great in football as it is in our own age, and although there is something ludicrous in equating interceptions with assassinations and long passes with moonshots, there is also something valid and appealing in the analogies. It seems to me that football does successfully reflect those salient and common conditions which affect us all, and it does so with the end of making us feel better about them and our lot. For one thing, it makes us feel that something can be connected in all this chaos; out of the accumulated pile of bodies something can emerge—a runner breaks into the clear or a pass finds its way to a receiver. To the spectator plays such as these are human and dazzling. They suggest to the audience what it has hoped for (and been told) all along, that technology is still a tool and not a master. Fans get living proof of this every time a long pass is completed; they see at once that it is the result of careful planning, perfect integration and an effective "pattern," but they see too that it is human and that what counts as well is man, his desire, his natural skill and his "grace under pressure." Football metaphysically yokes heroic action and technology together by violence to suggest that they are mutually supportive. It's a doubtful proposition, but given how we live it has its attractions.

Football, like the space program, is a game in the grand manner, yet it is a rather sober sport and often seems to lack that positive, comic vision of which baseball's pastoral is a part. It is a winter game, as those fans who saw the Minnesota Vikings play the Detroit Lions last Thanksgiving were graphically reminded. The two teams played in a blinding snowstorm, and except for the small flags in the corners of the end zones, and a patch of mud wherever the ball was downed, the field was totally obscured. Even through the magnified television lenses the players were difficult to identify; you saw only huge shapes come out of the gloom, thump against each other and fall in a heap. The movement was repeated endlessly and silently in a muffled stadium, interrupted once or twice by a shot of a bare-legged girl who fluttered her pom-poms in the cold. The spectacle was by turns pathetic, compelling and absurd; a kind of theater of oblivion. . . .

A final note. It is interesting that the heroic and pastoral conventions which underlie our most popular sports are almost classically opposed. The contrasts are familiar: city vs. country, aspiration vs. contentment, activity vs. peace and so on. Judging from the rise of professional football we seem to be slowly relinquishing that unfettered rural vision of ourselves that baseball so beautifully mirrors, and we have come to cast ourselves in a genre more reflective of a nation confronted by constant and unavoidable challenges. Right now, like the Elizabethans, we seem to share both heroic and pastoral yearnings, and we reach out to both. Perhaps these divided needs account in part for the enormous attention we as a nation now give to spectator sports. For sport provides one place, at least, where we can have our football and our baseball too.

———— ◆ ————

For Study and Discussion

QUESTIONS ABOUT PURPOSE

1. What connection does Ross establish between games, fans, and myths?
2. Why do you think he chooses to compare baseball and football?
3. Why does he think football is more appropriate to our time?

QUESTIONS ABOUT AUDIENCE

1. What audience does Ross anticipate for his essay? How does he use the first paragraph to identify that audience?
2. What assumptions does Ross make about the knowledge of his readers? For example, why does he present baseball first?
3. What identity does Ross assign to his readers in paragraphs 13 and 14? How does he involve "us" in his analysis?

QUESTIONS ABOUT STRATEGIES

1. How does Ross organize his presentation of the two sports? What does he accomplish by changing strategies?
2. What are the major points of comparison? How are they arranged? How does the comparison of Babe Ruth and Jim Brown support these major points?
3. How does Ross use other comparisons to enrich his essay? What do the colors red and green contribute to his analysis?

QUESTIONS FOR DISCUSSION

1. What personality types does Ross associate with the players of each game? Refine his analysis by suggesting a personality type for each position.

2. What myths are suggested by other sports? For example, how would you characterize the fantasies of basketball and hockey fans?

3. Why do you think Americans are so fascinated with spectator sports? What does Ross mean when he says sports *exploit* our fantasies but do not significantly *transcend* them?

Comparison and Contrast as a Writing Strategy

POINTS TO CONSIDER

1. Is your purpose to explore the relationship between things in the same class (strict comparison) or establish a relationship between things in different classes (fanciful comparison)? What do you want to prove about the two things you are comparing? Are two similar things really different? Are two dissimilar things really alike? Do you want to recommend one item as better than the other or do you merely want to uncover hidden resemblances between them?

2. What do your readers already know about the subjects you are comparing? Do they know both items, neither item, or only one item in the comparison? Adjust your analysis accordingly. If they know both items, don't belabor the obvious. If they don't know either item, provide familiar general principles that will help them interpret the two items. If they know only one item (or know one better than the other), place the familiar item in the first position.

3. Is the subject-by-subject or point-by-point strategy more appropriate to the subject of your comparison? Are there few or many points of comparison? Do you want to present the subjects as complete units or analyze the specific points of comparison? Is there some way you can combine strategies? Which subject should you put first and why? Which points of comparison should you put first and why? Have you balanced each part with its counterpart, included transitional links between the two parts, and provided reasons for comparing them?

PREWRITING EXERCISES

1. List *all* the points of *similarity* you can discover between two people in the *same* class (for example, two

teachers, two athletes, two singers). Circle those points that you consider important, eliminating the minor points or grouping them under larger headings. Select five major points and arrange them in a sequence that seems logical (simple to complex, least dramatic to most dramatic). Outline this sequence according to each strategy (divided and alternating). Exchange outlines with other members of the class and discuss which pattern presents your points best and why.

2. Follow a similar procedure to uncover *differences* between two things usually thought to be quite similar (two products in the same category, two members of the same family, two suburbs in the same city). The purpose of this exercise is to determine whether a side-by-side comparison transforms slight differences into significant differences.

3. Compile a list of advantages and disadvantages for two things in the same class (two cars, two restaurants, two points of view on a controversial political issue). Balance the trade-offs (a big car has more passenger room, but consumes more gasoline). Recommend one thing as superior to the other (Murray's makes better hamburgers than Harry's). Pass this list to other members of the class. Do they agree with your conclusion about which item is superior? What trade-offs have you overlooked? (Voting to reduce government spending could mean voting to reduce expenditures for environmental protection programs.)

4. Make a list of the five most important heroes in American history. Compare your list with similar lists from your classmates, teachers, parents, grandparents, and various members of your community (doctor, minister, mechanic, barber, bartender). What differences do you see in the lists? How do you account for the differences —age, sex, profession, personality? What similarities surprised you?

5. Explore the world of advertising (billboards, magazine ads, television commercials) for examples of fanciful comparisons. Select the five most dramatic examples you can discover and make a point-by-point list of the

comparisons. Be sure to consider both the verbal and the visual, the stated and the unstated, the intentional and unintentional connections between the two items. Exchange lists with members of your class. Which ads are the most effective, the most outrageous? Why?

TOPICS FOR WRITING IN CLASS

1. Select a special place you knew a number of years ago —a backyard, a park, a neighborhood in a town or city. Then write a comparison in which you present two views of the same place: the way it used to be *and* the way it is now. What details have changed? What details have remained the same?

2. Compare and contrast two people who share many common experiences or characteristics—parents, brothers or sisters, roommates. Consider similarities of dress, behavior, and value first. Then designate those quirks and habits that distinguish the two people as individuals.

3. Compare a sport your readers know well (baseball or football) to a sport your readers may know little about (cricket or rugby). Begin with the points of similarity before moving on to the differences in setting, rules, and game strategy.

TOPICS FOR WRITING OUT OF CLASS

1. Use a comparison between two simple attitudes to argue some larger point about contemporary life. Huxtable's essay is a good model for this assignment because she begins with a simple comparison—people's attitude toward clutter—and then constructs an argument about possessions, the past, and the attempt to impose order and meaning on life.

2. Write an essay that compares the way two magazines or newspapers cover the same news story. A productive comparison would be between an American magazine

and an English magazine. Other productive comparisons would result from examining magazines that address different audiences for different purposes—for example, *The National Review* and *The New Republic.*

3. Compare and contrast the arguments on both sides of a controversial issue such as nuclear disarmament or abortion. Such issues produce controversy because there are legitimate arguments on each side. Your comparison may reveal that the two sides actually share some common ground. On the other hand, you may conclude that the two sides are so different that some third party will be required to resolve the deadlock.

---◆---

DIVISION AND
CLASSIFICATION

---◆---

Division and classification are mental processes that often operate in tandem. To *divide* is to separate something (a college, a city) into sections (departments, neighborhoods). To *classify* is to place examples of a subject (restaurants, jobs) into a system of categories (restaurants: moderate, expensive, very expensive; jobs: unskilled, semi-skilled, and skilled). Division moves downward from a single concept to its subunits; classification moves upward from specific examples to groups that share some common characteristic. Television news programs, for example, can be

237

divided into news, features, editorials, sports, and weather, whereas the editorial commentator on the six o'clock news can be grouped with his or her counterparts and then classified according to categories such as style, knowledge, and trustworthiness. Although the two procedures can operate separately, they usually work together in the composing of a classification essay, first to discover and then to demonstrate the relationship among the subdivisions of a subject.

PURPOSE

The chief purpose of a classification essay is to *explain*. It can be used to explain either an established method for organizing information, such as the Library of Congress system for cataloging books, or a new plan for arranging data, such as the Internal Revenue Service's latest schedule for itemizing tax deductions. At one level, the purpose of such explanations is simply to outline the various parts of the system. At a more significant level, the purpose is to define, analyze, and justify the system's organizing principle.

The classification essay can also be used to *entertain* or *persuade*. A writer who concocts an elaborate scheme for classifying fools writes partly to explain the system, but the purpose of classifying is probably to amuse rather than to inform. On the other hand, a writer who explains the organization of a new or controversial plan, such as the metric system, will probably have to persuade readers that the new system is superior to the old one.

AUDIENCE

As with all writing assignments, the classification essay requires a careful assessment of the knowledge and needs of the anticipated audience. If the subject is new (social patterns in a primitive society) or the system of classification specialized (the botanist's procedure for identifying plants), then readers will need precise definitions and ample illustrations for each subcategory. If the subject and the system for classifying it are familiar to most readers (the movies' G, PG, R, and X rating code), then they will not need such an extensive demonstration. In this situation writers usually outline the system to remind readers of common reference points but then move on to analyze the effectiveness of the system with regard to specific examples.

Writers must also consider how their audience may use the classification system explained in their essay. Readers who skim an essay in an airline magazine that classifies rodeo riders may be seeking general information or amusement, but they see the system as self-enclosed—they do not expect to use it in their daily lives. On the other hand, readers who study an essay in a consumer's magazine that classifies stereo equipment may actually want to test the reliability of the system when they shop. In the first case, writers can approach the classifying process informally, dividing the subject into the interesting subcategories and illustrating them with colorful examples. In the second case, writers must be strictly formal, making sure that they divide the subject into all its possible classes and then illustrating them with a wide range of examples.

STRATEGIES

The basic strategy for organizing a classification essay is to *divide the subject* into major categories that show some common trait and then to subdivide those categories into smaller units. Next, the major categories are *arranged in a sequence.* Each of these categories is then *defined*, first by differentiating it from the other categories and second by discussing its most vivid examples. To ensure the success of this strategy, however, writers must be certain that their classification system is *consistent, complete, emphatic,* and *significant.*

When they divide their subject into categories, writers must consistently APPLY THE SAME PRINCIPLE OF SELECTION TO EACH CLASS. This procedure may be difficult to follow if a writer is explaining an established but inconsistent system. Admitting that few things "show as much variety . . . as American candy," Alexander Theroux surveys his subject but uses no single principle of division. For example, his categories include trash candy, log genre, the peanut group, seasonal candies, and candies that "promise more than they ever give." Such inconsistencies can be avoided when writers restrict and control their own classification system. For example, Dorothy Parker classifies short stories by their repetitiveness, Lewis Thomas classifies medical technologies by their cost effectiveness, James Austin classifies chance by the degree of human intervention, and Robert Brustein classifies horror movies by the changing relationship between Scientist and Monster.

After they have divided their subject into separate and consistent categories, writers should MAKE SURE THAT THE DIVISION IS COMPLETE. The simplest kind of division separates a subject into two categories, *A* and *Not-A.* But this division is rarely encouraged because although it informs readers about category *A* (*Good Candy*) it tells them little about that indistinct category of *Not-A* (*All Other Kinds of Candy*). For this reason, writers try to "exhaust" a subject by discovering at least three separate categories to classify and by acknowledging the existence of those examples that cannot be included in the system. Formal classification essays, such as Lewis Thomas's assessment of medical technology, attempt to be definitive. No category or exception may be overlooked. But even informal essays, such as Parker's discussion of the six types of popular fiction or Austin's analysis of the four kinds of chance, strive to achieve a reasonable degree of completeness.

Once the process of division is completed, writers should ARRANGE CATEGORIES AND EXAMPLES IN AN EMPHATIC ORDER. James Austin arranges the four kinds of chance from simple to complex. Lewis Thomas arranges his categories of medical technology from least effective to most effective. And Robert Brustein arranges his three kinds of horror movies in a chronological sequence. In each essay the arrangement of the categories and the discussion of the examples within those categories reinforce the controlling purpose of the classification process—to discover variety in similarity, to distinguish good from bad, to discuss the changes in a form.

Finally, writers should ASSERT THE SIGNIFICANCE OF THEIR CLASSIFICATION SYSTEM. The strength of the classifying procedure is that it allows a subject to be analyzed by any number of systems. The weakness is that it allows a subject to be classified according to all sorts of meaningless categories. American presidents can be classified by campaign themes, administrative competence, or historic decisions. They can also be classified according to height, weight, or shoe size. When a writer such as James Austin or Lewis Thomas classifies a subject according to one particular system, he is asserting that the system is significant, that it tells us something important about the subject. Even when the subject itself seems not particularly profound—candy, popular short stories, horror movies—writers are still obligated to convince their audience that a particular classification system is important if only because it discovers and demonstrates, consistently and completely, the significant subdivisions of the subject.

The Candy Man

ALEXANDER THEROUX

◆

*Alexander Theroux was born in 1939 in Medford,
Massachusetts, and educated at St. Francis College
(Biddeford, Maine) and the University of Virginia.
The "somewhat eccentric" member of a literary family
(his younger brother, Paul, writes novels and travel
literature), Theroux once entered a Trappist monas-
tery, observing two years of silence, before he left to
become a novice in a Franciscan seminary and then
a construction worker in Boston. He lives in an old
farmhouse on Cape Cod, is associated with Phillips
Academy in Andover, Massachusetts, and writes for
such magazines as* Boston, Esquire, The New Yorker,
and Harper's. *His longer writing includes a novel,*
Three Wogs *(1972), and several books for children,*
The Great Wheedle Tragedy *(1975) and* The Schino-
cephalic Waif *(1975). In "The Candy Man," first
published in* Harper's, *Theroux uses his "good taste"
(and displays his extravagant style) to classify the many
delicious subcategories of candy.*

I believe there are few things that show as much variety—   1
that there is so much of—as American candy. The national profusion of mints and munch, pops and drops,
creamfills, cracknels, and chocolate crunch recapitulates
the good and plenty of the Higher Who.

Candy has its connoisseurs and critics both. To some,   2
for instance, it's a subject of endless fascination—those for
whom a root-beer lozenge can taste like a glass of Shakespeare's "brown October" and for whom little pilgrims
made of maple sugar can look like Thracian gold—and to

others, of course, it's merely a wilderness of abominations. You can sample one piece with a glossoepiglottic gurgle of joy or chew down another empty as shade, thin as fraud.

In a matter where tastes touch to such extremes one is 3 compelled to seek through survey what in the inquiry might yield, if not conclusions sociologically diagnostic, then at least a simple truth or two. Which are the best candies? Which are the worst? And why? A sense of fun can feed on queer candy, and there will be no end of argument, needless to say. But, essentially, it's all in the *taste*.

The trash candies—a little lobby, all by itself, of the 4 American Dental Association—we can dismiss right away: candy cigarettes, peanut brittle, peppermint lentils, Life Savers (white only), Necco Wafers (black especially), Christmas candy in general, gumballs, and above all that glaucous excuse for tuck called ribbon candy, which little kids, for some reason, pounce on like a duck on a June bug. I would put in this category all rock candy, general Woolworthiana, and all those little nerks, cupcake sparkles, and decorative sugars like silver buckshot that, though inedible, are actually eaten by the young and indiscriminate, whose teeth turn eerie almost on contact.

In the category of the most abominable tasting, the winner—on both an aesthetic and a gustatory level—must surely be the inscribed Valentine candy heart ("Be Mine," "Hot Stuff," "Love Ya," et cetera). In high competition, no doubt, are bubble-gum cigars, candy corn, marshmallow chicks (bunnies, pumpkins, et cetera), Wacky Wafers (eight absurd-tasting coins in as many flavors), Blow Pops —an owl's pellet of gum inside a choco-pop!—Canada Mints, which taste like petrified Egyptian lime, and, last but not least, those unmasticable beige near-candy peanuts that, insipid as rubber erasers, not only have no bite—the things just give up—but elicit an indescribable antitaste that is best put somewhere between stale marshmallow and dry wall. Every one of these candies, sweating right now in a glass case at your corner store, is to my mind proof positive of original sin. They can be available, I suggest, only for having become favorites of certain indiscriminate fatties at the Food and Drug Administration who must buy them by the bag. But a bat could see they couldn't be a chum of ours if they chuckled.

Now, there are certain special geniuses who can distinguish candies, like wine, by rare deduction: district, commune, vineyard, growth. They know all the wrappers, can tell twinkle from tartness in an instant, and often from sniffing nothing more than the empty cardboard sled of a good candy bar can summon up the scent of the far Moluccas. It is an art, or a skill at least *tending* to art. I won't boast the ability, but allow me, if you will, to be a professor of the fact of it. The connoisseur, let it be said, has no special advantage. Candy can be found everywhere: the airport lounge, the drugstore, the military PX, the student union, the movie house, the company vending machine— old slugs, staler than natron, bonking down into a tray— but the *locus classicus,* of course, is the corner store. 6

The old-fashioned candy store, located on a corner in the American consciousness, is almost obsolete. Its proprietor is always named Sam; for some reason he's always Jewish. Wearing a hat and an apron, he shuffles around on spongy shoes, still tweezers down products from the top shelf with one of those antique metal grapplers, and always keeps the lights off. He has the temperament of a black mamba and makes his best customers, little kids with faces like midway balloons, show him their nickels before they order. But he keeps the fullest glass case of penny candy in the city—spiced baby gums, malted-milk balls, fruit slices, candy fish, aniseed balls, candy pebbles, jelly beans, raspberry stars, bull's-eyes, boiled sweets, the lot. The hit's pretty basic. You point, he scoops a dollop into a little white bag, weighs it, subtracts two, and then asks, "Wot else?" 7

A bright rack nearby holds the bars, brickbats, brand names. Your habit's never fixed when you care about candy. You tend to look for new bars, recent mints, old 8 issues. The log genre, you know, is relatively successful: Bolsters, Butterfingers, Clark Bars, Baby Ruths, O. Henrys, and the Zagnut with its sweet razor blades. Although they've dwindled in size, like the dollar that buys fewer and fewer of them, all have a lushness of weight and good nap and nacre, a chewiness, a thewiness, with tastes in suitable *contre coup* to the bite. You pity their distant cousins, the airy and unmemorable Kit-Kats, Choco'lites, Caravels, and Paydays, johnny-come-latelies with shallow souls and Rice Krispie hearts that taste like budgie food. A submember of American candy, the peanut group, is strong —crunch is often the kiss in a candy romance—and you might favorably settle on several: Snickers, Go Aheads, Mr. Goodbars, Reese's Peanut Butter Cups (of negligible crunch, however), the Crispy, the Crunch, the Munch—a nice trilogy of onomatopoeia—and even the friendly little Creeper, a peanut-butter-filled tortoise great for the one-bite dispatch: Pleep!

Vices, naturally, coexist with virtues. The coconut category, for instance—Mounds, Almond Joys, Waleecos, and their ilk—is toothsome, but can often be tasted in flakes at the folds and rim of your mouth days later. The licorice group, Nibs, Licorice Rolls, Twizzlers, Switzer Twists, and various whips and shoelaces, often smoky to congestion, usually leave a nice smack in the aftertaste. The jawbreaker may last a long time, yes—but who wants it to? Tootsie Pop Drops, Charms, Punch, Starburst Fruit Chews (sic!), base-born products of base beds, are harder than affliction and better used for checker pieces or musket flints or supports to justify a listing bureau.

There are certain candies, however—counter, original, spare, strange—that are gems in both the bite and the taste, not the usual grim marriage of magnesium stearate to lactic acid, but rare confections at democratic prices. Like lesser breeds raising pluperfect cain with the teeth, these are somehow always forgiven; any such list must include: Mary Janes, Tootsie Rolls, Sky Bars, Squirrels, Mint Juleps, the wondrous B-B Bats (a hobbit-sized banana taffy pop

9

10

still to be had for 3¢), and other unforgettable knops and knurls like turtles, chocolate bark, peanut clusters, burnt peanuts, and those genius-inspired pink pillows with the peanut-butter surprise inside for which we're all so grateful. There's an *intelligence* here that's difficult to explain, a sincerity at the essence of each, where solid line plays against stipple and a truth function is solved always to one's understanding and always—*O altitudo!*—to one's taste.

Candy is sold over the counter, won in raffles, awarded on quiz shows, flogged door to door, shipped wholesale in boxes, thrown out at ethnic festivals, and incessantly hawked on television commercials by magic merrymen—clownish pied-pipers in cap-and-bells—who inspirit thousands of kids to come hopping and hurling after them, singing all the way to Cavityville. Why do we eat it? Who gets us started eating it? What sexual or social or semantic preferences are indicated by which pieces? The human palate—tempted perhaps by Nature *herself* in things like slippery elm, spruce gum, sassafras, and various berries—craves sweetness almost everywhere, so much so, in fact, that the flavor of candy commonly denominates American breath-fresheners, throat discs, mouthwash, lipstick, fluoride treatments, toothpaste, cough syrup, breakfast cereals, and even dental floss, fruit salts, and glazes. It's with candy—whether boxed, bottled, or bowed—that we say hello, goodbye, and I'm sorry. There are regional issues, candies that seem at home only in one place and weirdly forbidden in others (you don't eat it at the ballpark, for instance, but on the way there), and of course seasonal candies: Christmas tiffin, Valentine's Day assortments, Thanksgiving mixes, and the diverse quiddities of Easter: spongy chicks, milk-chocolate rabbits, and those monstrositous roc-like eggs twilled with piping on the outside and filled with a huge blob of neosaccharine galvaslab! Tastes change, develop, grow fixed. Your aunt likes mints. Old ladies prefer jars of crystallized ginger. Rednecks wolf

Bolsters, trollops suck lollipops, college girls opt for berries-in-tins. Truck drivers love to click Gobstoppers around the teeth, pubescents crave sticky sweets, the viler the better, and of course great fat teenage boys, their complexions aflame with pimples and acne, aren't fussy and can gorge down a couple of dollars' worth of Milky Ways, $100,000 Bars, and forty-eleven liquid cherries at one go!

The novelty factor can't be discounted. The wrapper 12 often memorizes a candy for you; so capitalism, with its Hollywood brain, has devised for us candies in a hundred shapes and shocks—no, I'm not thinking of the comparatively simple Bit-O-Honey, golden lugs on waxed paper, or Little Nips, wax tonic bottles filled with disgustingly sweet liquid, or even the Pez, those little units that, upon being thumbed, dispense one of the most evil-tasting cacochymicals on earth. Buttons-on-paper—a trash candy—is arguably redeemed by inventiveness of vehicle. But here I'm talking about packaging *curiosa*—the real hype! Flying Saucers, for example, a little plasticene capsule with candy twinkles inside! Big Fake Candy Pens, a goofy fountain pen cartridged with tiny pills that taste like canvatex! Razzles ("First It's a Candy, Then It's a Gum")! Bottle Caps ("The Soda Pop Candy")! Candy Rings, a rosary of cement-tasting beads strung to make up a fake watch, the dial of which can be eaten as a final emetic. Rock Candy on a String, blurbed on the box as effective for throat irritation: "Shakespeare in *Henry IV* mentions its therapeutic value." You believe it, right?

And then there's the pop group: Astro Pops, an 13 umbrella-shaped sugar candy on a stick; Whistle Pops ("The Lollipop with the Built-in Whistle"); and Ring Pops, cherry- or watermelon-flavored gems on a plastic stick—you suck the jewel. So popular are the fizzing Zotz, the trifling Pixie Stix with its powdered sugar to be lapped out of a straw, the Lik-M-Aid Fun Dip, another do-it-yourself stick-licker, and the explosion candies like Space Dust, Volcano Rocks, and Pop Rocks that candy-store merchants have to keep behind the counter to prevent them from getting nobbled. Still, these pale next to the experience of eating just plain old jimmies (or sprinkles or chocolate shot, depending on where you live), which although generally reserved for, and ancillary to, ice cream, can be deliciously munched by the fistful for a real reward. With jimmies, we enter a new category all its own. M&M's, for example: you don't eat them, you mump them.

Other mumping candies might be sugar babies, hostia 14
almonds, bridge mixes, burnt peanuts, and pectin jelly beans. (Jelloids in general lend themselves well to the mump.) I don't think Goobers and Raisinets—dull separately—are worth anything unless both are poured into the pocket, commingled, and mumped by the handful at the movies. (The clicking sound they make is surely one of the few pleasures left in life.) This is a family that can also include Pom Poms, Junior Mints, Milk Duds, Boston Baked Beans, Sixlets ("Candy-coated chocolate-flavored candies" —a nice flourish, that), and the disappointingly banal Jujubes—which reminds me. There are certain candies, Jujubes for instance, that one is just too embarrassed to name out loud (forcing one to point through the candy case and simply grunt), and numbered among these must certainly be Nonpareils, Jujyfruits, Horehound Drops, and Goldenberg's Peanut Chews. You know what I mean. "Give me a *mrmrglpxph* bar." And you point. Interesting, right?

Interesting. The very word is like a bell that tolls me 15
back to more trenchant observations. Take the Sugar Daddy—it curls up like an elf-shoe after a manly bite and upon being sucked could actually be used for flypaper. (The same might be said for the gummier but more exquisite Bonomo's Turkish Taffy.) The Heath bar—interesting again—a knobby little placket that can be drawn down half-clenched teeth with a slucking sound for an instant chocolate rush, whereupon you're left with a lovely ingot of toffee as a sweet surprise. The flaccid Charleston Chew, warm, paradoxically becomes a proud phallus when cold. (Isn't there a metaphysics in the making here?) Who,

until now, has ever given these candies the kind of credit they deserve?

I have my complaints, however, and many of them 16 cross categories. M&M's, for instance, click beautifully but never perspire—it's like eating bits of chrysoprase or sea shingle, you know? Tic Tacs, as well: brittle as gravel and brainless. And while Good 'n' Plenty's are worthy enough mumpers, that little worm of licorice inside somehow puts me off. There is, further, a tactile aspect in candy to be considered. Milk Duds are too nobby and ungeometrical, Junior Mints too relentlessly exact, whereas Reese's Peanut Butter Cups, with their deep-dish delicacy, fascinate me specifically for the strict ribbing around the sides. And then color. The inside of the vapid Three Musketeers bar is the color of wormwood. White bark? Leprosy. Penuche? Death. And then of Hot Tamales, Atom Bombs, cinnamon hearts, and red hots?—swift, slow, sweet, sour, a-dazzle, dim, okay, but personally I think it a matter of breviary that *heat* should have nothing at all to do with candy.

And then Chunkies—tragically, too big for one bite, 17 too little for two. Tootsie Pops are always twiddling off the stick. The damnable tab never works on Hershey Kisses, and it takes a month and two days to open one; even the famous Hershey bar, maddeningly overscored, can never be opened without breaking the bar, and prying is always required to open the ridiculously overglued outer wrapper. (The one with almonds—why?—always slides right out!) And then there are those candies that always promise more than they ever give—the Marathon bar for length, cotton candy for beauty: neither tastes as good as it looks, as no kipper ever tastes as good as it smells; disappointment leads to resentment, and biases form. Jujyfruits—a viscous disaster that is harder than the magnificent British wine-gum (the single greatest candy on earth)—stick in the teeth like tar and have ruined more movies for me than Burt Reynolds, which is frankly going some. And finally Chuckles, father of those respectively descending little clones—spearmint leaves, orange slices, and gum drops—always taste better if dipped in ice water before eating, a want that otherwise keeps sending you to a water fountain for hausts that never seem to end.

You may reasonably charge me, in conclusion, with an 18 insensibility for mistreating a particular kind of candy that you, for one reason or another, cherish, or bear me ill will for passing over another without paying it due acknowledgment. But here it's clearly a question of taste, with reasoning generally subjective. Who, after all, can really explain how tastes develop? Where preferences begin? That they exist is sufficient, and fact, I suppose, becomes its own significance. Which leads me to believe that what Dr. Johnson said of Roman Catholics might less stupidly be said of candies: "In every thing in which they differ from us, they are wrong."

———— ◆ ————

For Study and Discussion

QUESTIONS ABOUT PURPOSE

1. Is Theroux's purpose to explain the various kinds of candy, to argue that some types of candy are better than others, or to entertain his readers by his comic characterization of each type? Explain your answer.

2. How does Theroux's assertion that "essentially, it's all in the *taste*," determine the purpose of his essay? How does he use the quotation from Dr. Johnson in his last paragraph to clarify that purpose?

3. What is Theroux's purpose in listing a specific series of complaints toward the end of his essay? What is the common theme of this criticism?

QUESTIONS ABOUT AUDIENCE

1. How does Theroux's point of view—illustrated by such phrases as "we can dismiss," "they couldn't be a chum of ours," and "why do we eat it?"—help establish his relationship with his readers?

2. What assumptions does Theroux make about his readers when he provides extensive lists of the various kinds of candy? Does he assume that his readers are more likely to be connoisseurs or critics? Explain your answer.

3. How does Theroux anticipate the objections some of his readers may have about his treatment of their favorite candy?

QUESTIONS ABOUT STRATEGIES

1. Make a list of the various categories and subcategories that Theroux mentions in his essay. Does he apply a single principle of selection to divide his subject into its various divisions? Explain your answer.

2. How does Theroux's extensive listing of candies within each category suggest that he has exhausted the category? Can you think of any major category that he has omitted?

3. How does Theroux arrange his various categories? For example, why does he begin with the "trash" candies? Where does he include a discussion of his own favorites?

QUESTIONS FOR DISCUSSION

1. Theroux argues that the human palate craves sweetness. What explanation does he provide to explain this craving?

2. How does Theroux's essay illustrate the old dictum *De gustibus non disputandum est* (It is foolish to argue about matters of taste)?

3. Theroux suggests that our preferences for certain candies "change, develop, grow fixed." He also suggests that our purchase of some kinds of candies causes us embarrassment. What explanation does he provide for this kind of behavior? What kind of explanation can you provide?

The Short Story, Through a Couple of the Ages

DOROTHY PARKER

◆

Dorothy Parker (1893–1967) was born in West End, New Jersey, and was educated at the Blessed Sacrament Convent in New York City. After working briefly for Vogue *and* Vanity Fair, *she became the book reviewer for* The New Yorker *(in its second issue), writing the column "The Constant Reader." In the 1920s she became a charter member of the Algonquin Round Table, an informal literary club that met at the Algonquin Hotel and included such wits as Robert Benchley, George Kaufman, and Alexander Woollcott. Beginning in the 1930s, Parker lived for many years in Hollywood, where she and her husband, Alan Campbell, co-authored numerous screenplays. Her writing includes collections of poems* (Men I'm Not Married To; Women I'm Not Married To, 1922), *short stories* (After Such Pleasures, 1932), *and essays* (The Constant Reader, 1970). *In "The Short Story, Through a Couple of the Ages" (first published in 1927 in* The New Yorker) *Parker classifies popular magazine fiction according to six all-too-familiar plots.*

There was a time, when I still had my strength, that I 1
read nearly all the stories in the more popular magazines.
I did not have to do it; I did it for fun, for I had yet to
discover that there were other and more absorbing diver-
sions that had the advantage of being no strain on the
eyes. But even in those days of my vigor, nearly all the
stories was the best that I could do. I could never go
the full course. From the time I learned to read—which,

I am pretty thoroughly convinced, was when I made my first big mistake—I was always unable to do anything whatever with stories that began in any of these following manners:

(1) "Ho, Felipe, my horse, and *pronto!*" cried *El Sol.* He turned to the quivering girl, and his mocking bow was so low that his *sombrero* swept the flags of the *patio. "Adiós,* then, *señorita,* until *mañana!"* And with a flash of white teeth across the lean young swarthiness of his face, he bounded to the back of his horse and was off, swift as a homing *paloma.*

(2) Everybody in Our Village loved to go by Granny Wilkins' cottage. Maybe it was the lilacs that twinkled a cheery greeting in the dooryard, or maybe it was the brass knocker that twinkled on the white-painted door, or maybe—and I suspect this was the real reason—it was Granny herself, with her crisp white cap, and her wise brown eyes, twinkling away in her dear little old winter apple of a face.

(3) The train chugged off down the long stretch of track, leaving the little new schoolmistress standing alone on the rickety boards that composed the platform of Medicine Bend station. She looked very small indeed, standing there, and really ridiculously young. "I just won't cry!" she said fiercely, swallowing hard. "I won't! Daddy—Daddy would be disappointed in me if I cried. Oh, Daddy—Daddy, I miss you so!"

(4) The country club was ahum, for the final match of the Fourth of July Golf Tournament was in full swing. Many a curious eye lingered on Janet DeLancey, rocking lazily, surrounded as usual by a circle of white-flanneled adorers, for the porch was a-whisper with the rumor that the winner of the match would also be the winner of the hitherto untouched heart of the blond and devastating Janet.

(5) I dunno ez I ought to be settin' here, talkin', when there's the vittles to git fer the men-folks. But, Laws, 'tain't often a body hez a chanct ter talk, up this-a-way.

I wuz tellin' yuh 'bout li'l Mezzie Meigs, ol' Skin-flint Meig's da'ter. She wuz a right peart 'un, Mezzie wuz, and purty!

(6) "For God's sake, don't do it, Kid!" whispered Annie the Wop, twining her slim arms about the Kid's bull-like neck. "Yer promised me yer'd go straight, after the last time. The bulls'll get yer, Kid; they'll send yer up, sure. Aw, Kid, put away yer gat, and let's beat it away somewhere in God's nice, clean country, where yer can raise chickens, like yer always dreamed of doin'." 7

But, with these half-dozen exceptions, I read all the other short stories that separated the Ivory Soap advertisements from the pages devoted to Campbell's Soups. I read about bored and pampered wives who were right on the verge of eloping with slender-fingered, quizzical-eyed artists, but did not. I read of young suburban couples, caught up in the fast set about them, driven to separation by their false, nervous life, and restored to each other by the opportune illness of their baby. I read tales proving that Polack servant-girls have their feelings, too. I read of young men who collected blue jade, and solved mysterious murders, on the side. I read stories of transplanted Russians, of backstage life, of shop-girls' evening hours, of unwanted grandmothers, of heroic collies, of experiments in child-training, of golden-hearted cow-punchers with slow drawls, of the comicalities of adolescent love, of Cape Cod fisherfolk, of Creole belles and beaux, of Greenwich Village, of Michigan Boulevard, of the hard-drinking and easy-kissing younger generation, of baseball players, side-show artists, and professional mediums. I read, in short, more damn tripe than you ever saw in your life. 8

And then I found that I was sluggish upon awakening in the morning, spots appeared before my eyes, and my friends shunned me. I also found that I was reading the same stories over and over, month after month. So I stopped, like that. It is only an old wives' tale that you have to taper off. 9

Recently, though, I took the thing up again. There 10

were rumors about that the American short story had taken a decided turn for the better. Crazed with hope, I got all the more popular and less expensive magazines that I could carry on my shoulders, and sat down for a regular old read. And a regular old read is just what it turned out to be. There they all were—the golden-hearted cow-punchers, the suburban couples, the baseball players, the Creole belles—even dear old Granny Wilkins was twinkling away, in one of them. There were the same old plots, the same old characters, the same old phrases—dear Heaven, even the same old illustrations. So that is why I shot myself.

It is true that in the magazines with quieter covers, with smaller circulations, and with higher purchasing prices, there are good short stories. Their scholarly editors have extended a courteous welcome to the newer writers. And the newer writers are good; they write with feeling and honesty and courage, and they write well. They do not prostitute their talents for money; they do not add words because they are to be paid by the word; scarcely, indeed, do they violate their amateur standing. But here, just as one did in the old days, does one get the feeling of reading the same stories over and over, month after month. There are no golden-hearted cow-punchers, but there are the inevitable mid-western farm families; the laughing Creole belles have given place to the raw tragedies of the Bayou; but the formulae are as rigorous. You must write your story as starkly as it was written just before you did it; if you can out-stark the previous author, you are one up. Sedulous agony has become as monotonous as sedulous sunshine. Save for those occasions when you come upon a Hemingway or an Anderson or a Lardner in your reading, the other stories that meet your eye might all have come from the same pen.

I do not see how Mr. Edward O'Brien stands the strain. Season after season, as inescapable as Christmas, he turns out his collection of what he considers to be the best short stories of their year. To do this, and he does it conscien-

11

12

tiously, he must read and rate every short story in every American magazine of fiction. Me, I should liefer adopt the career of a blood donor.

The Best Short Stories of 1927 is distinguished by the inclusion in it of Ernest Hemingway's superb "The Killers." This is enough to make any book of stories a notable one. There is also Sherwood Anderson's "Another Wife," which seems to me one of his best. But in the other stories I can find only disappointment. They seem to me wholly conventional, in this recent conventionality of anguish. There is no excitement to them; they have all the dogged quiet of too-careful writing. Separate, each one might possibly—oh, possibly—grip you. Grouped together, they string out as flat as Kansas. 13

Their compiler shows himself, in this volume, to be more than ever the unsung hero. In the back of the book, where he lists all the short stories of the year, and grades them, unasked, without a star, with one star, with two stars, or with three stars, according to his notion of their merits, you may gain some idea of what the man has been through. I give you some of the titles of the stories that he has wrestled with: 14

"Vomen Is Easily Veak-Minded"; "Ma Bentley's Christmas Dinner"; "Archibald in Arcady" (there is always one of those, every year); "Fred and Circuses"; "Willie Painter Stays on the Levvel"; "Sylvia Treads among the Goulds"; "Betty Use Your Bean"; "Daddy's Nondetachable Cuffs"; "Ann 'n' Andy"; "Freed 'Em and Weep" (I bet that was a little love); "Jerry Gums the Game"; "Blue Eyes in Trouble"; "Grandflapper" (you can practically write that one for yourself); "She Loops to Conquer"; "Yes, Sir, He's My Maybe"; and "Dot and Will Find Out What It Means to Be Rich," which last sets me wondering into the night just what were the titles that the author threw out as being less adroit. 15

They say Mr. O'Brien makes ample money, on his sales of these stories written by others, and I hope it is true. But no matter how much it is, he deserves more. 16

———— ♦ ————

For Study and Discussion

QUESTIONS ABOUT PURPOSE

1. What does Parker's classification system demonstrate about popular fiction? How does the title of the essay comment on her purpose?

2. What does Parker's statement that "I read nearly all the stories in the more popular magazines . . . for fun" reveal about her motives for creating her classification system?

3. Parker classifies many bad short stories, but she also identifies, indirectly, the qualities of a good short story. What are those qualities?

QUESTIONS ABOUT AUDIENCE

1. This essay was first published in a book review column for *The New Yorker* magazine entitled "The Constant Reader." What assumptions does Parker make about the people who read this column?

2. Does Parker think her audience needs to read the specific stories she mentions in order to understand the types of fiction she classifies? Explain your answer.

3. What kind of relationship does Parker establish with her readers? How do statements such as "so that is why I shot myself" call attention to that relationship?

QUESTIONS ABOUT STRATEGIES

1. What principle of selection does Parker use to classify the six kinds of short stories? What other principles does she use in the essay?

2. How does paragraph 8 contribute to Parker's claim of reasonable completeness?

3. How does Parker arrange the various categories within her essay? How does she distinguish between old and new short story writers?

QUESTIONS FOR DISCUSSION

1. What is Parker's opinion of Mr. Edward O'Brien? Identify some people who have similar jobs.

2. To what extent is Parker's judgment based on her method of analysis? How might reading a single short story, rather than reading a collection of stories, produce a different reaction? How does Parker allow for this possibility?

3. What do the titles in paragraph 15 reveal about the probable content of these stories written over fifty years ago? In what ways are the stories published in today's popular magazines similar to or different from these stories of another age?

Four Kinds of Chance

JAMES H. AUSTIN

◆

*James H. Austin was born in 1925 in Cleveland, Ohio,
and educated at Brown University and Harvard University Medical School. After an internship at Boston
City Hospital and a residency at the Neurological Institute of New York, Austin established a private
practice in neurology, first in Portland, Oregon, and
then in Denver, Colorado. He currently serves as professor and head of the department of neurology at the
University of Colorado Medical School. His major
publication,* Chase, Chance, and Creativity: The
Lucky Art of Novelty *(1978), addresses the issue of
how "chance and creativity interact in biomedical
research." In this essay, published originally in* Saturday Review *in 1974, Austin distinguishes four kinds
of chance by the way humans react to their environment.*

What is chance? Dictionaries define it as something for- 1
tuitous that happens unpredictably without discernible
human intention. Chance is unintentional and capricious,
but we needn't conclude that chance is immune from
human intervention. Indeed, chance plays several distinct
roles when humans react creatively with one another and
with their environment.

We can readily distinguish four varieties of chance if 2
we consider that they each involve a different kind of
motor activity and a special kind of sensory receptivity.

260

The varieties of chance also involve distinctive personality traits and differ in the way one particular individual influences them.

Chance I is the pure blind luck that comes with no effort on our part. If, for example, you are sitting at a bridge table of four, it's "in the cards" for you to receive a hand of all 13 spades, but it will come up only once in every 6.3 trillion deals. You will ultimately draw this lucky hand—with no intervention on your part—but it does involve a longer wait than most of us have time for.

Chance II evokes the kind of luck Charles Kettering had in mind when he said: "Keep on going and the chances are you will stumble on something, perhaps when you are least expecting it. I have never heard of anyone stumbling on something sitting down."

In the sense referred to here, Chance II is not passive, but springs from an energetic, generalized motor activity. A certain basal level of action "stirs up the pot," brings in random ideas that will collide and stick together in fresh combinations, lets chance operate. When someone, *anyone*, does swing into motion and keeps on going, he will increase the number of collisions between events. When a few events are linked together, they can then be exploited to have a fortuitous outcome, but many others, of course, cannot. Kettering was right. Press on. Something will turn up. We may term this the Kettering Principle.

In the two previous examples, a unique role of the individual person was either lacking or minimal. Accordingly, as we move on to Chance III, we see blind luck, but in camouflage. Chance presents the clue, the opportunity exists, but it would be missed except by that one person uniquely equipped to observe it, visualize it conceptually, and fully grasp its significance. Chance III involves a special receptivity and discernment unique to the recipient. Louis Pasteur characterized it for all time when he said: "Chance favors only the prepared mind."

Pasteur himself had it in full measure. But the classic example of his principle occurred in 1928, when Alexan-

261

der Fleming's mind instantly fused at least five elements into a conceptually unified nexus. His mental sequences went something like this: (1) I see that a mold has fallen by accident into my culture dish; (2) the staphylococcal colonies residing near it failed to grow; (3) the mold must have secreted something that killed the bacteria; (4) I recall a similar experience once before; (5) if I could separate this new "something" from the mold, it could be used to kill staphylococci that cause human infections.

Actually, Fleming's mind was exceptionally well prepared for the penicillin mold. Six years earlier, while he was suffering from a cold, his own nasal drippings had found their way into a culture dish, for reasons not made entirely clear. He noted that nearby bacteria were killed, and astutely followed up the lead. His observations led him to discover a bactericidal enzyme present in nasal mucus and tears, called lysozyme. Lysozyme proved too weak to be of medical use, but imagine how receptive Fleming's mind was to the penicillin mold when it later happened on the scene!

One word evokes the quality of the operations involved in the first three kinds of chance. It is *serendipity*. The term describes the facility for encountering unexpected good luck, as the result of: accident (Chance I), general exploratory behavior (Chance II), or sagacity (Chance III). The word itself was coined by the Englishman-of-letters Horace Walpole, in 1754. He used it with reference to the legendary tales of the Three Princes of Serendip (Ceylon), who quite unexpectedly encountered many instances of good fortune on their travels. In today's parlance, we have usually watered down *serendipity* to mean the good luck that comes solely by accident. We think of it as a result, not an ability. We have tended to lose sight of the element of sagacity, by which term Walpole wished to emphasize that some distinctive personal receptivity is involved.

There remains a fourth element in good luck, an unintentional but subtle personal prompting of it. The

English Prime Minister Benjamin Disraeli summed up the principle underlying Chance IV when he noted that "we make our fortunes and we call them fate." Disraeli, a politician of considerable practical experience, appreciated that we each shape our own destiny, at least to some degree. One might restate the principle as follows: *Chance favors the individualized action.*

In Chance IV the kind of luck is peculiar to one person, and like a personal hobby, it takes on a distinctive individual flavor. This form of chance is one-man-made, and it is as personal as a signature. . . . Chance IV has an elusive, almost miragelike, quality. Like a mirage, it is difficult to get a firm grip on, for it tends to recede as we pursue it and advance as we step back. But we still accept a mirage when we see it, because we vaguely understand the basis for the phenomenon. A strongly heated layer of air, less dense than usual, lies next to the earth, and it bends the light rays as they pass through. The resulting image may be magnified as if by a telescopic lens in the atmosphere, and real objects, ordinarily hidden far out of sight over the horizon, are brought forward and revealed to the eye. What happens in a mirage then, and in this form of chance, not only appears farfetched but indeed is farfetched.

About a century ago, a striking example of Chance IV took place in the Spanish cave of Altamira.* There, one day in 1879, Don Marcelino de Sautuola was engaged in his hobby of archaeology, searching Altamira for bones and stones. With him was his daughter, Maria, who had asked him if she could come along to the cave that day. The indulgent father had said she could. Naturally enough, he first looked where he had always found heavy objects before, on the *floor* of the cave. But Maria, unhampered by any such preconceptions, looked not only at the floor but also all around the cave with the open-eyed wonder

11

12

* The cave had first been discovered some years before by an enterprising hunting dog in search of game. Curiously, in 1932 the French cave of Lascaux was discovered by still another dog.

of a child! She looked up, exclaimed, and then he looked up, to see incredible works of art on the cave ceiling! The magnificent colored bison and other animals they saw at Altamira, painted more than 15,000 years ago, might lead one to call it "the Sistine Chapel of Prehistory." Passionately pursuing his interest in archaelogy, de Sautuola, to his surprise, discovered man's first paintings. In quest of science, he happened upon Art.

Yes, a dog did "discover" the cave, and the initial receptivity was his daughter's, but the pivotal reason for the cave paintings' discovery hinged on a long sequence of prior events originating in de Sautuola himself. For when we dig into the background of this amateur excavator, we find he was an exceptional person. Few Spaniards were out probing into caves 100 years ago. The fact that he—not someone else—decided to dig that day in the cave of Altamira was the culmination of his passionate interest in his hobby. Here was a rare man whose avocation had been to educate himself from scratch, as it were, in the science of archaeology and cave exploration. This was no simple passive recognizer of blind luck when it came his way, but a man whose unique interests served as an active creative thrust—someone whose own actions and personality would focus the events that led circuitously but inexorably to the discovery of man's first paintings. 13

Then, too, there is a more subtle manner. How do you give full weight to the personal interests that imbue your child with your own curiosity, that inspire her to ask to join you in your own musty hobby, and that then lead you to agree to her request at the critical moment? For many reasons, at Altamira, more than the special receptivity of Chance III was required—this was a different domain, that of the personality and its actions. 14

A century ago no one had the remotest idea our caveman ancestors were highly creative artists. Weren't their talents rather minor and limited to crude flint chippings? But the paintings at Altamira, like a mirage, would quickly magnify this diminutive view, bring up into full focus a 15 distant, hidden era of man's prehistory, reveal sentient minds and well-developed aesthetic sensibilities to which men of any age might aspire. And like a mirage, the events at Altamira grew out of de Sautuola's heated personal quest and out of the invisible forces of chance we know exist yet cannot touch. Accordingly, one may introduce the term *altamirage* to identify the quality underlying Chance IV. Let us define it as the facility for encountering unexpected good luck as the result of highly individualized action. Altamirage goes well beyond the boundaries of serendipity in its emphasis on the role of personal action in chance.

Chance IV is favored by distinctive, if not eccentric, 16 hobbies, personal life-styles, and modes of behavior peculiar to one individual, usually invested with some passion. The farther apart these personal activities are from the area under investigation, the more novel and unexpected will be the creative product of the encounter.

————— ◆ —————

For Study and Discussion

QUESTIONS ABOUT PURPOSE

1. What limitations does Austin see in the dictionary definitions of the word *chance*?
2. What elements of human behavior and attitude does Austin demonstrate by dividing chance into four varieties?
3. What relationship does Austin discover between the words *luck, serendipity, sagacity,* and *altamirage*?

QUESTIONS ABOUT AUDIENCE

1. How would Austin characterize the general knowledge of his readers? Does he assume they have any special knowledge? Explain your answer.

2. What assumptions does Austin make about his readers when he offers them *the best* example rather than several examples to illustrate each category?

3. How does Austin's attitude toward his audience change during the essay? For example, why does he speak directly to his readers when he explains Chance I but address them more formally in his discussion of other categories?

QUESTIONS ABOUT STRATEGIES

1. How does Austin use the principles of *motor activity* and *sensory receptivity* to establish his categories? How does his use of various quotations—for example, "stir up the pot"—call attention to these principles?

2. How does Austin use transitions and summaries to clarify the differences between the major categories? In particular, see paragraphs 6 and 9.

3. How does Austin arrange his four categories? Why doesn't he give equal treatment to each category?

QUESTIONS FOR DISCUSSION

1. Explain the significant differences between Chance III and Chance IV. What difficulties does Austin encounter between the two categories?

2. What incidents in your personal experience would support Austin's classification system? How many examples can you cite in each category?

3. What do you think is the relationship between *ability* and *result*? For example, what is your opinion of Disraeli's assertion that "we make our fortunes and call them fate"?

The Technology of Medicine

LEWIS THOMAS

◆

Lewis Thomas was born in 1913 in Flushing, New York, and was educated at Princeton University and Harvard University Medical School. He held appointments at numerous research hospitals and medical schools before assuming his present position as president of the Sloan-Kettering Cancer Center in New York City. Thomas's early writing, on the subject of pathology, appeared in scientific journals. In 1971 he began contributing a popular column, "Notes of a Biology Watcher," to the New England Journal of Medicine. *In 1974 his collection of these essays,* The Lives of a Cell: Notes of a Biology Watcher, *won the National Book Award for Arts and Letters. His other books include* The Medusa and the Snail: More Notes of a Biology Watcher *(1979),* The Youngest Science *(1983), and* Late Night Thoughts on Listening to Mahler's Ninth Symphony *(1983). In "The Technology of Medicine," from* The Lives of a Cell, *Thomas classifies "three quite different levels of technology in medicine."*

Technology assessment has become a routine exercise for the scientific enterprises on which the country is obliged to spend vast sums for its needs. Brainy committees are continually evaluating the effectiveness and cost of doing various things in space, defense, energy, transportation, and the like, to give advice about prudent investments for the future.

Somehow medicine, for all the $80-odd billion that it is said to cost the nation, has not yet come in for much of this analytical treatment. It seems taken for granted that the technology of medicine simply exists, take it or leave it, and the only major technologic problem which policy-makers are interested in is how to deliver today's kind of health care, with equity, to all the people.

When, as is bound to happen sooner or later, the ana-   3
lysts get around to the technology of medicine itself, they will have to face the problem of measuring the relative cost and effectiveness of all the things that are done in the management of disease. They make their living at this kind of thing, and I wish them well, but I imagine they will have a bewildering time. For one thing, our methods of managing disease are constantly changing—partly un-der the influence of new bits of information brought in from all corners of biologic science. At the same time, a great many things are done that are not so closely related to science, some not related at all.

In fact, there are three quite different levels of tech-   4
nology in medicine, so unlike each other as to seem al-together different undertakings. Practitioners of medicine and the analysts will be in trouble if they are not kept separate.

1. First of all, there is a large body of what might be   5
termed "nontechnology," impossible to measure in terms of its capacity to alter either the natural course of disease or its eventual outcome. A great deal of money is spent on this. It is valued highly by the professionals as well as the patients. It consists of what is sometimes called "suppor-tive therapy." It tides patients over through diseases that are not, by and large, understood. It is what is meant by the phrases "caring for" and "standing by." It is indis-pensable. It is not, however, a technology in any real sense, since it does not involve measures directed at the underlying mechanism of disease.

It includes the large part of any good doctor's time that   6
is taken up with simply providing reassurance, explaining to patients who fear that they have contracted one or an-other lethal disease that they are, in fact, quite healthy.

It is what physicians used to be engaged in at the bed-   7 side of patients with diphtheria, meningitis, poliomyelitis, lobar pneumonia, and all the rest of the infectious diseases that have since come under control.

It is what physicians must now do for patients with in- 8 tractable cancer, severe rheumatoid arthritis, multiple sclerosis, stroke, and advanced cirrhosis. One can think of at least twenty major diseases that require this kind of supportive medical care because of the absence of an effective technology. I would include a large amount of what is called mental disease, and most varieties of cancer, in this category.

The cost of this nontechnology is very high, and getting 9 higher all the time. It requires not only a great deal of time but also very hard effort and skill on the part of physicians; only the very best of doctors are good at coping with this kind of defeat. It also involves long periods of hospitalization, lots of nursing, lots of involvement of nonmedical professionals in and out of the hospital. It represents, in short, a substantial segment of today's expenditures for health.

2. At the next level up is a kind of technology best 10 termed "halfway technology." This represents the kinds of things that must be done after the fact, in efforts to compensate for the incapacitating effects of certain diseases whose course one is unable to do very much about. It is a technology designed to make up for disease, or to postpone death.

The outstanding examples in recent years are the trans- 11 plantations of hearts, kidneys, livers, and other organs, and the equally spectacular inventions of artificial organs. In the public mind, this kind of technology has come to seem like the equivalent of the high technologies of the physical sciences. The media tend to present each new procedure as though it represented a breakthrough and therapeutic triumph, instead of the makeshift that it really is.

In fact, this level of technology is, by its nature, at the 12 same time highly sophisticated and profoundly primitive. It is the kind of thing that one must continue to do until there is a genuine understanding of the mechanisms involved in disease. In chronic glomerulonephritis, for example, a much clearer insight will be needed into the events leading to the destruction of glomeruli by the immunologic reactants that now appear to govern this disease, before one will know how to intervene intelligently to prevent the process, or turn it around. But when this level of understanding has been reached, the technology of kidney replacement will not be much needed and should no longer pose the huge problem of logistics, cost, and ethics that it poses today.

An extremely complex and costly technology for the management of coronary heart disease has evolved—involving specialized ambulances and hospital units, all kinds of electronic gadgetry, and whole platoons of new professional personnel—to deal with the end results of coronary thrombosis. Almost everything offered today for the treatment of heart disease is at this level of technology, with the transplanted and artificial hearts as ultimate examples. When enough has been learned to know what really goes wrong in heart disease, one ought to be in a position to figure out ways to prevent or reverse the process, and when this happens the current elaborate technology will probably be set to one side. 13

Much of what is done in the treatment of cancer, by surgery, irradiation, and chemotherapy, represents halfway technology, in the sense that these measures are directed at the existence of already established cancer cells, but not at the mechanisms by which cells become neoplastic. 14

It is a characteristic of this kind of technology that it costs an enormous amount of money and requires a continuing expansion of hospital facilities. There is no end to the need for new, highly trained people to run the enterprise. And there is really no way out of this, at the present state of knowledge. If the installation of specialized coronary-care units can result in the extension of life for only a few patients with coronary disease (and there is no question that this technology is effective in a few cases), 15

270

it seems to me an inevitable fact of life that as many of these as can be will be put together, and as much money as can be found will be spent. I do not see that anyone has much choice in this. The only thing that can move medicine away from this level of technology is new information, and the only imaginable source of this information is research.

3. The third type of technology is the kind that is so 16 effective that it seems to attract the least public notice; it has come to be taken for granted. This is the genuinely decisive technology of modern medicine, exemplified best by modern methods for immunization against diphtheria, pertussis, and the childhood virus diseases, and the contemporary use of antibiotics and chemotherapy for bacterial infections. The capacity to deal effectively with syphilis and tuberculosis represents a milestone in human endeavor, even though full use of this potential has not yet been made. And there are, of course, other examples: the treatment of endocrinologic disorders with appropriate hormones, the prevention of hemolytic disease of the newborn, the treatment and prevention of various nutritional disorders, and perhaps just around the corner the management of Parkinsonism and sickle-cell anemia. There are other examples, and everyone will have his favorite candidates for the list, but the truth is that there are nothing like as many as the public has been led to believe.

The point to be made about this kind of technology— 17 the real high technology of medicine—is that it comes as the result of a genuine understanding of disease mechanisms, and when it becomes available, it is relatively inexpensive, and relatively easy to deliver.

Offhand, I cannot think of any important human dis- 18 ease for which medicine possesses the outright capacity to prevent or cure where the cost of the technology is itself a major problem. The price is never as high as the cost of managing the same diseases during the earlier stages of no-technology or halfway technology. If a case of typhoid fever had to be managed today by the best methods of 1935, it would run to a staggering expense. At, say, around fifty days of hospitalization, requiring the most demanding kind of nursing care, with the obsessive concern for details of diet that characterized the therapy of that time, with daily laboratory monitoring, and, on occasion, surgical intervention for abdominal catastrophe, I should think $10,000 would be a conservative estimate for the illness, as contrasted with today's cost of a bottle of chloramphenicol and a day or two of fever. The halfway technology that was evolving for poliomyelitis in the early 1950s, just before the emergence of the basic research that made the vaccine possible, provides another illustration of the point. Do you remember Sister Kenny, and the cost of those institutes for rehabilitation, with all those ceremonially applied hot fomentations, and the debates about whether the affected limbs should be totally immobilized or kept in passive motion as frequently as possible, and the masses of statistically tormented data mobilized to support one view or the other? It is the cost of that kind of technology, and its relative effectiveness, that must be compared with the cost and effectiveness of the vaccine.

Pulmonary tuberculosis had similar episodes in its history. There was a sudden enthusiasm for the surgical removal of infected lung tissue in the early 1950s, and elaborate plans were being made for new and expensive installations for major pulmonary surgery in tuberculosis hospitals, and then INH and streptomycin came along and the hospitals themselves were closed up. [19]

It is when physicians are bogged down by their incomplete technologies, by the innumerable things they are obliged to do in medicine when they lack a clear understanding of disease mechanisms, that the deficiencies of the health-care system are most conspicuous. If I were a policy-maker, interested in saving money for health care over the long haul, I would regard it as an act of high prudence to give high priority to a lot more basic research in biologic science. This is the only way to get the full [20] mileage that biology owes to the science of medicine, even though it seems, as used to be said in the days when the phrase still had some meaning, like asking for the moon.

———— ◆ ————

For Study and Discussion

QUESTIONS ABOUT PURPOSE

1. Is Thomas's primary purpose to explain the various kinds of medical technology or to argue that certain technologies are more useful than others? Explain your answer.
2. Why does Thomas think that policy makers have avoided evaluating the cost and effectiveness of medical technology? When they do decide to undertake such an evaluation, what factors will make their job difficult?
3. What does Thomas demonstrate about the relationship between cost-effective technology and a genuine understanding of the disease mechanism?

QUESTIONS ABOUT AUDIENCE

1. How does Thomas's assertion that policy makers are interested in "how to deliver today's kind of health care, with equity, to all people," suggest that he is aware of his readers' interest in the issue he will discuss?
2. What assumptions does he make about his readers when he suggests that the least effective technologies are treated as breakthroughs while the most effective are taken for granted?
3. To what extent does Thomas assume that his readers are familiar with the diseases he uses to illustrate each

category? How does he provide assistance to his readers when the disease may be unfamiliar? See, for example, his discussion of typhoid fever in paragraph 18.

QUESTIONS ABOUT STRATEGIES

1. How does Thomas's definition of his three categories —nontechnology, halfway technology, and effective technology—clarify the single principle he has used to establish his classification system?
2. How does Thomas's discussion of specific diseases demonstrate that his divisions are complete? What aspect of his system enables him to discuss cancer as an illustration in two categories?
3. How does Thomas arrange his categories? How does this arrangement confirm his thesis that when the real mechanism of a disease is understood, medical technology is "relatively inexpensive, and relatively easy to deliver"?

QUESTIONS FOR DISCUSSION

1. What connotations do we usually associate with the word *technology*? How does Thomas define the word?
2. Why does Thomas believe so strongly in "basic research in biologic science"? Why would an investment in such research save money for "health care in the long haul"?
3. What is Thomas's attitude toward his second category, halfway technology? Why does he call it "at the same time highly sophisticated and profoundly primitive"?

Reflections on Horror Movies

ROBERT BRUSTEIN

◆

Robert Brustein was born in 1927 in New York City and educated at Amherst College, Yale University, and Columbia University. He has held faculty positions in English and theater at Cornell University, Vassar College, Columbia University, and Yale University (where he was dean of the Yale School of Drama). Brustein has also worked as the drama critic for The New Republic *and the culture editor for* The New York Review of Books. *He is currently director of the American Repertory Theater in Cambridge, Massachusetts. His articles have appeared in magazines such as* Harper's, Encounter, Commentary, *and* Partisan Review, *and his books include* The Theatre of Revolt *(1964),* Revolution as Theatre *(1971), and* Critical Moments: Reflections on Theatre & Society *(1980). In the following selection, taken from* The Third Theatre *(1969), Brustein classifies various kinds of horror movies in order to examine popular assumptions about science.*

Although horror movies have recently been enjoying a 1
vogue, they have always been perennial supporting features among Grade B and C fare. The popularity of the form is no doubt partly explained by its ability to engage the spectator's feelings without making any serious demand on his mind. In addition, however, horror movies covertly embody certain underground assumptions about science which reflect popular opinions.

The horror movies I am mainly concerned with I have 2
divided into three major categories: Mad Doctor, Atomic

Beast and Interplanetary Monster. They do not exhaust all the types but they each contain two essential characters, the Scientist and the Monster, towards whom the attitudes of the movies are in a revealing state of change.

The Mad Doctor series is by far the most long lived of   3
the three. It suffered a temporary decline in the Forties when Frankenstein, Dracula, and the Wolfman (along with their countless offspring) were first loaned out as straight men to Abbott and Costello, and then set out to graze in the parched pastures of the cheap all-night movie houses, but it has recently demonstrated its durability in a group of English remakes and a Teen-age Monster craze. These films find their roots in certain European folk myths. Dracula was inspired by an ancient Balkan superstition about vampires, the Werewolf is a Middle European folk myth recorded, among other places, in the Breton *lais* of Marie de France, and even Frankenstein, though out of Mary Shelley by the Gothic tradition, has a medieval prototype in the Golem, a monster the Jews fashioned from clay and earth to free them from oppression. The spirit of these films is still medieval, combining a vulgar religiosity with folk superstitions. Superstition now, however, has been crudely transferred from magic and alchemy to creative science, itself a form of magic to the untutored mind. The devil of the Vampire and Werewolf myths, who turned human beings into baser animals, today has become a scientist, and the metamorphosis is given a technical name—it is a "regression" into an earlier state of evolution. The alchemist and devil-conjuring scholar, Dr. Faustus, gives way to Dr. Frankenstein, the research physician, while the magic circle, the tetragrammaton, and the full moon are replaced by test tubes, complicated electrical apparatus, and Bunsen burners.

Frankenstein, like Faustus, defies God by exploring   4
areas where humans are not meant to trespass. In Mary Shelley's book (it is subtitled *A Modern Prometheus*), Frankenstein is a latter-day Faustus, a superhuman creature whose aspiration embodies the expansiveness of his

age. In the movies, however, Frankenstein loses his heroic quality and becomes a lunatic monomaniac, so obsessed with the value of his work that he no longer cares whether his discovery proves a boon or a curse to mankind. When the mad doctor, his eyes wild and inflamed, bends over his intricate equipment, pouring in a little of this and a little of that, the spectator is confronted with an immoral being whose mental superiority is only a measure of his madness. Like the popular image of the theoretical scientist engaged in basic research ("Basic research," says Charles Wilson, "is science's attempt to prove the grass is green"), he succeeds only in creating something badly which nature has already made well. The Frankenstein monster is a parody of man. Ghastly in appearance, clumsy in movement, criminal in behavior, imbecilic of mind, it is superior only in physical strength and resistance to destruction. The scientist has fashioned it in the face of divine disapproval (the heavens disgorge at its birth)—not to mention the disapproval of friends and frightened townspeople—and it can lead only to trouble.

For Dr. Frankenstein, however, the monster symbolizes the triumph of his intellect over the blind morality of his enemies and it confirms him in the ultimate soundness of his thought ("They thought I was mad, but this proves who is the superior being"). When it becomes clear that his countrymen are unimpressed by his achievement and regard him as a menace to society, the monster becomes the agent of his revenge. As it ravages the countryside and terrorizes the inhabitants, it embodies and expresses the scientist's own lust and violence. It is an extension of his own mad soul, come to life not in a weak and ineffectual body but in a body of formidable physical power. (In a movie like *Dr. Jekyll and Mr. Hyde,* the identity of monster and doctor is even clearer; Mr. Hyde, the monster, is the aggressive and libidinous element in the benevolent Dr. Jekyll's personality.) The rampage of the monster is the rampage of mad, unrestrained science which inevitably turns on the scientist, destroying him too. As the lava

5

bubbles over the sinking head of the monster, the crude moral of the film frees itself from the horror and is asserted. Experimental science (and by extension knowledge itself) is superfluous, dangerous, and unlawful, for in exploring the unknown, it leads man to usurp God's creative power. Each of these films is a victory for obscurantism, flattering the spectator into believing that his intellectual inferiority is a sign that he is loved by God.

The Teen-age Monster films, a very recent phenomenon, amend the assumptions of these horror movies in a startling manner. Their titles—*I Was a Teenage Werewolf, I Was a Teenage Frankenstein, Blood of Dracula,* and *Teenage Monster*—(some wit awaits one called *I Had a Teenage Monkey on My Back*)—suggest a Hollywood prank, but they are deadly serious, mixing the conventions of early horror movies with the ingredients of adolescent culture. The doctor, significantly enough, is no longer a fringe character whose madness can be inferred from the rings around his eyes and his wild hair but a respected member of society, a high-school chemistry teacher (*Blood of Dracula*) or a psychoanalyst (*Teenage Werewolf*) or a visiting lecturer from Britain (*Teenage Frankenstein*). Although he gives the appearance of benevolence—he pretends to help teen-agers with their problems—behind this facade he hides evil experimental designs. The monster, on the other hand, takes on a more fully developed personality. He is a victim who begins inauspiciously as an average, though emotionally troubled, adolescent and ends, through the influence of the doctor, as a voracious animal. The monster as teen-ager becomes the central character in the film and the teen-age audience is expected to identify and sympathize with him.

In *I Was a Teenage Werewolf,* the hero is characterized as brilliant but erratic in his studies and something of a delinquent. At the suggestion of his principal, he agrees to accept therapy from an analyst helping maladjusted students. The analyst gets the boy under his control and, after injecting him with a secret drug, turns him into a werewolf. Against his will he murders a number of his contemporaries. When the doctor refuses to free him from this curse, he kills him and is himself killed by the police. In death, his features relax into the harmless countenance of an adolescent.

The crimes of the adolescent are invariably committed 8 against other youths (the doctor has it in for teen-agers) and are always connected with those staples of juvenile culture, sex and violence. The advertising displays show the male monsters, dressed in leather jackets and blue jeans, bending ambiguously over the diaphanously draped body of a luscious young girl while the female teen-age vampire of *Blood of Dracula,* her nails long and her fangs dripping, is herself half-dressed and lying on top of a struggling male (whether to rape or murder him is not clear). The identification of sex and violence is further underlined by the promotion blurbs: "In her eyes DESIRE! in her veins—the blood of a MONSTER!" (*Blood of Dracula*); "A Teenage Titan on a Lustful Binge that Paralyzed a Town with Fear" (*Teenage Monster*). It is probable that these crimes are performed less reluctantly than is suggested and that the adolescent spectator is more thrilled than appalled by this "lustful binge" which captures the attention of the adult community. The acquisition of power and prestige through delinquent sexual and aggressive activity is a familiar juvenile fantasy (the same distributors exploit it more openly in films like *Reform School Girl* and *Drag-Strip Girl*), one which we can see frequently acted out by delinquents in our city schools. In the Teenage Monster films, however, the hero is absolved of his aggressive and libidinous impulses. Although he both feels and acts on them, he can attribute the responsibility to the mad scientist who controls his behavior. What these films seem to be saying, in their underground manner, is that behind the harmless face of the high-school chemistry teacher and the intellectual countenance of the psychoanalyst lies the warped authority responsible for teen-age violence. The adolescent feels victimized by society—turned into a monster by society—and if he behaves in a delinquent manner, society and not he is to blame. Thus, we can see one direction in which the hostility for experimental research, explicit in the Mad Doctor films, can go—it can be transmuted into hatred of adult authority itself.

Or it can go underground, as in the Atomic Beast 9 movies. The Mad Doctor movies, in exploiting the supernatural, usually locate their action in Europe (often a remote Bavarian village) where wild fens, spectral castles, and ominous graveyards provide the proper eerie background. The Atomic Beast movies depend for their effect on the contemporary and familiar and there is a corresponding change in locale. The monster (or "thing" as it is more often called) appears now in a busy American city —usually Los Angeles to save the producer money—where average men walk about in business suits. The thing terrorizes not only the hero, the heroine, and a few anonymous (and expendable) characters in Tyrolean costumes, but the entire world. Furthermore, it has lost all resemblance to anything human. It appears as a giant ant (*Them!*), a prehistoric animal (*Beast from Twenty Thousand Fathoms*), an outsized grasshopper (*Beginning of the End*) or a monstrous spider (*Tarantula*). Although these films, in their deference to science fiction, seem to smile more benignly on scientific endeavor, they are unconsciously closer to the anti-theoretical biases of the Mad Doctor series than would first appear.

All these films are similarly plotted, so the plot of 10 *Beginning of the End* will serve as an example of the whole genre. The scene opens on a pair of adolescents necking in their car off a desert road. Their attention is caught by a weird clicking sound, the boy looks up in horror, the girl screams, the music stings and the scene fades. In the next scene, we learn that the car has been completely demolished and its occupants have disappeared. The police, totally baffled, are conducting fruitless investigations when word comes that a small town nearby has been destroyed in the same mysterious way. Enter the young scientist hero. Examining the wreckage of the town, he discovers a strange fluid which when analyzed proves to have been manufactured by a giant grasshopper. The police ridicule his conclusions and are instantly attacked by a fleet of these grasshoppers, each fifteen feet high, which wipe out the entire local force and a few state troopers. Interrupting a perfunctory romance with the heroine, the scientist flies to Washington to alert the nation. He describes the potential danger to a group of bored politicians and yawning big brass, but they remain skeptical until word comes that the things have reached Chicago and are crushing buildings and eating the occupants. The scientist is then put in charge of the army and air force. Although the military men want to evacuate the city and drop an atomic bomb on it, the scientist devises a safer method of destroying the creatures and proceeds to do so through exemplary physical courage and superior knowledge of their behavior. The movie ends on a note of foreboding: have the things been completely exterminated?

Externally, there seem to be very significant changes 11 indeed, especially in the character of the scientist. No longer fang-toothed, long-haired, and subject to delirious ravings (Bela Lugosi, John Carradine, Basil Rathbone), the doctor is now a highly admired member of society, muscular, handsome, and heroic (John Agar). He is invariably wiser, more reasonable, and more humane than the boneheaded bureaucrats and trigger-happy brass that compose the members of his "team," and he even has sexual appeal, a quality which Hollywood's eggheads have never enjoyed before. The scientist-hero, however, is not a very convincing intellectual. Although he may use technical, polysyllabic language when discussing his findings, he always yields gracefully to the admonition to "tell us in our own words, Doc" and proves that he can speak as simply as you or I; in the crisis, in fact, he is almost monosyllabic. When the chips are down, he loses his glasses (a symbol of his intellectualism) and begins to look like everyone else. The hero's intellect is part of his costume and makeup, easily shed when heroic action is demanded. That he is always called upon not only to outwit the thing but to wrestle with it as well (in order to save the heroine) indicates that he is in constant danger of tripping over the thin boundary between specialist and average Joe.

The fact remains that there is a new separation between the scientist and the monster. Rather than being an extension of the doctor's evil will, the monster functions completely on its own, creating havoc through its predatory nature. We learn through charts, biological film, and the scientist's patient explanations that ants and grasshoppers are not the harmless little beasties they appear but actually voracious insects who need only the excuse of size to prey upon humanity. The doctor, rather than allying himself with the monster in its rampage against our cities, is in strong opposition to it, and reverses the pattern of the Mad Doctor films by destroying it. 12

And yet, if the individual scientist is absolved of all responsibility for the "thing," science somehow is not. These films suggest an uneasiness about science which, though subtle and unpremeditated, reflects unconscious American attitudes. These attitudes are sharpened when we examine the genesis of the thing for, though it seems to rise out of nowhere, it is invariably caused by a scientific blunder. The giant ants of *Them!*, for example, result from a nuclear explosion which caused a mutation in the species; another fission test has awakened, in *Beast from Twenty Thousand Fathoms*, a dinosaur encrusted in polar icecaps; the spider of *Tarantula* grows in size after having been injected with radioactive isotopes, and escapes during a fight in the lab between two scientists; the grasshoppers of *Beginning of the End* enlarge after crawling into some radioactive dust carelessly left about by a researcher. We are left with a puzzling substatement: science destroys the thing but scientific experimentation has created it. 13

I think we can explain this equivocal attitude when 14

we acknowledge that the thing "which is too horrible to name," which owes its birth to an atomic or nuclear explosion, which begins in a desert or frozen waste and moves from there to cities, and which promises ultimately to destroy the world, is probably a crude symbol for the bomb itself. The scientists we see represented in these films are unlike the Mad Doctors in another more fundamental respect: they are never engaged in basic research. The scientist uses his knowledge in a purely defensive manner, like a specialist working on rocket interception or a physician trying to cure a disease. The isolated theoretician who tinkers curiously in his lab (and who invented the atomic bomb) is never shown, only the practical working scientist who labors to undo the harm. The thing's destructive rampage against cities, like the rampage of the Frankenstein monster, is the result of too much cleverness, and the consequences for all the world are only too apparent.

These consequences are driven home more powerfully 15 in movies like *The Incredible Shrinking Man* and *The Amazing Colossal Man* where the audience gets the opportunity to identify closely with the victims of science's reckless experimentation. The hero of the first movie is an average man who, through contact with fallout while on his honeymoon, begins to shrink away to nothing. As he proceeds to grow smaller, he finds himself in much the same dilemma as the other heroes of the *Atomic Beast* series: he must do battle with (now) gigantic insects in order to survive. Scientists can do nothing to save him— after a while they can't even find him—so as he dwindles into an atomic particle he finally turns to God for whom "there is no zero." The inevitable sequel, *The Amazing Colossal Man*, reverses the dilemma. The hero grows to enormous size through the premature explosion of a plutonium bomb. Size carries with it the luxury of power but the hero cannot enjoy his new stature. He feels like a freak and his body is proceeding to outgrow his brain and heart. Although the scientists labor to help him and even succeed in reducing an elephant to the size of a cat, it is too late; the hero has gone mad, demolished Las Vegas and fallen over Boulder Dam. The victimization of man by theoretical science has become, in these two movies, less of a suggestion and more of a fact.

In the Interplanetary Monster movies, Hollywood han- 16 dles the public's ambivalence towards science in a more obvious way, by splitting the scientist in two. Most of these movies feature both a practical scientist who wishes to destroy the invader and a theoretical scientist who wants to communicate with it. In *The Thing,* for example, we find billeted among a group of more altruistic average-Joe colleagues with crew cuts an academic long-haired scientist of the Dr. Frankenstein type. When the evil thing (a highly evolved vegetable which, by multiplying itself, threatens to take over the world) descends in a flying saucer, this scientist tries to perpetuate its life in order "to find out what it knows." He is violently opposed in this by the others who take the occasion to tell him that such amoral investigation produced the atomic bomb. But he cannot be reasoned with and almost wrecks the entire party. After both he and the thing are destroyed, the others congratulate themselves on remaining safe, though in the dark. In *Forbidden Planet* (a sophisticated thriller inspired in part by Shakespeare's *Tempest*), the good and evil elements in science are represented, as in *Dr. Jekyll and Mr. Hyde,* by the split personality of the scientist. He is urbane and benevolent (Walter Pidgeon plays the role) and is trying to realize an ideal community on the far-off planet he has discovered. Although he has invented a robot (Ariel) who cheerfully performs man's baser tasks, we learn that he is also responsible, though unwittingly, for a terrible invisible force (Caliban) overwhelming in its destructiveness. While he sleeps, the aggressive forces in his libido activate a dynamo he has been tinkering with which gives them enormous power to kill those the doctor unconsciously resents. Thus, Freudian psychology is evoked to endow the scientist with guilt. At the end, he accepts his guilt and sacrifices his life in order to combat the being he has created.

The Interplanetary Monster series sometimes reverses 17 the central situation of most horror films. We often find the monster controlling the scientist and forcing him to do its evil will. In *It Conquered the World* the first film to capitalize on Sputnik and Explorer), the projection of a space satellite proves to be a mistake, for it results in the invasion of America by a monster from Venus. The monster takes control of the scientist who, embittered by the indifference of the masses towards his ideas, mistakenly thinks the monster will free men from stupidity. This muddled egghead finally discovers the true intentions of the monster and destroys it, dying himself in the process. In *The Brain from Planet Arous*, a hideous brain inhabits the mind of a nuclear physicist with the intention of controlling the universe. As the physical incarnation of the monster, the scientist is at the mercy of its will until he can free himself of its influence. The monster's intellect, like the intellect of the Mad Doctor, is invariably superior, signified graphically by its large head and small body (in the last film named it is nothing but Brain). Like the Mad Doctor, its superior intelligence is always accompanied by moral depravity and an unconscionable lust for power. If the monster is to be destroyed at all, this will not be done by matching wits with it but by finding some chink in its armor. The chink quite often is a physical imperfection: in *War of the Worlds*, the invading Martians are stopped, at the height of their victory, by their vulnerability to the disease germs of earth. Before this Achilles heel is discovered, however, the scientist is controlled to do evil, and with the monster and the doctor in collaboration again, even in this qualified sense, the wheel has come full circle.

The terror of most of these films, then, stems from the 18 matching of knowledge with power, always a source of fear for Americans—when Nietzsche's Superman enters comic book culture he loses his intellectual and spiritual qualities and becomes a muscle man. The muscle man, even with X-ray vision, poses no threat to the will, but muscle in collaboration with mind is generally thought to have a profound effect on individual destinies. The tendency to attribute everything that happens in the heavens, from flying saucers to Florida's cold wave, to science and the bomb ("Why don't they stop," said an old lady on the bus behind me the other day, "they don't know what they're doing") accounts for the extreme ways in which the scientist is regarded in our culture: either as a protective savior or as a destructive blunderer. It is little wonder that America exalts the physician (and the football player) and ignores the physicist. These issues, the issues of the great debate over scientific education and basic research, assert themselves crudely through the unwieldy monster and the Mad Doctor. The films suggest that the academic scientist, in exploring new areas, has laid the human race open to devastation either by human or interplanetary enemies—the doctor's madness, then, is merely a suitable way of expressing a conviction that the scientist's idle curiosity has shaken itself loose from prudence or principle. There is obviously a sensitive moral problem involved here, one which needs more articulate treatment than the covert and superstitious way it is handled in horror movies. That the problem is touched there at all is evidence of how profoundly it has stirred the American psyche.

———— ◆ ————

For Study and Discussion

QUESTIONS ABOUT PURPOSE

1. Why does Brustein think horror movies are a subject worthy of examination?
2. What changes in the subject does Brustein discover by dividing it into three major categories?

3. What popular attitudes toward science does Brustein think these films demonstrate?

QUESTIONS ABOUT AUDIENCE

1. What assumptions does Brustein make about the general knowledge of his readers? For example, what does a reader have to know in order to understand paragraph 3?
2. How does Brustein characterize the people who watch horror movies? Does he assume that his readers are horror movie fans? Explain your answer.
3. What does Brustein assume about his audience when he provides extensive plot summaries of individual movies?

QUESTIONS ABOUT STRATEGIES

1. How do the labels Brustein uses to identify his three categories call attention to their distinguishing features? What principle does he apply consistently to each category?
2. What subcategories (or variants) does Brustein discuss under each major category? How does his discussion of these subcategories demonstrate the significance of his classification system?
3. How does Brustein arrange his categories, subcategories, and examples? For example, where does he place the discussion of the changing identity of the scientist? How does this placement emphasize the purpose of his essay?

QUESTIONS FOR DISCUSSION

1. Brustein admits that his three categories "do not exhaust all the types," but it is tempting to test his

system with contemporary horror films. Which films fit, which films do not, and why?

2. Most Americans, Brustein asserts, view the scientists as either "protective savior" or "destructive blunderer." If you were asked to classify American attitudes toward the scientist, what other attitudes would you include?

3. Do most movies "embody the underground assumptions" of their viewers? For example, what assumptions are embodied in westerns or detective movies?

Division and Classification as a Writing Strategy

1. Are you going to explain an established classification system or create an original system? Can you simply (1) outline the major categories in the system, or must you (2) define, analyze, and justify each category and subcategory? Is your purpose to *explain* the organization of a system, *entertain* your readers with an amusing way to classify a subject, or *persuade* your readers that one system is superior to another?

2. Are your readers (1) familiar with your subject and the system you are using to classify it, (2) familiar with the subject, but not your system, or (3) unfamiliar with both subject and system? How will the knowledge of your anticipated audience determine the way you define categories and analyze examples? How will your readers use your classification essay? Will they see it as an interesting discussion of a subject or as a plan for examining aspects of their daily lives?

3. What principle are you using to divide your subject into classes? Is the principle significant? Does it reveal something important about your subject? Have you applied the principle consistently to each category? Have you exhausted the subject or are there significant categories you have overlooked? What plan have you developed for discussing your categories? Does the arrangement of categories and examples within categories emphasize your purpose? Have you defined and illustrated each category? Have you provided transitions and summaries to clarify the relationship among the various subdivisions of the subject?

PREWRITING EXERCISES

1. Explore the Yellow Pages of your telephone directory to discover how one subject can be divided. Restaurants, for example, are often divided by cuisine (Italian, Chinese, Mexican), specialty (hamburgers, pizza, fish), or additional services (tavern, delicatessen, caterer). Select one example and determine how many times it is listed or cross-referenced.

2. Make a list of all the ways you can classify a current popular song. Visit the local record store, read various kinds of music magazines, and outline the established categories used in music award ceremonies such as the Grammies. After considering all the possible systems, classify the song according to *the one* system that tells you most about it. Be prepared to defend your system against the alternatives selected by your classmates.

3. Visit an office at your university (Admissions, Financial Aid, Placement) to determine the various ways students are classified. Select one of these systems, study its objectives and organizing principles, and then make a list of corrections, additional considerations or alternative criteria that would substantially improve the classification process. You may want to refine this exercise by examining the classification system used to award grades in your class.

4. Outline an amusing system for classifying typical student behavior such as walking to class, sleeping in class, or cutting class. Establish a system of labels that will help you distinguish category from category (amblers, pacers, dashers) by calling attention to the principle you are using to divide the subject. Exchange outlines for correction and comment.

5. Test an existing classification system such as those published in *Consumer's Report* by using it to buy something—running shoes, a pocket calculator, a clock-radio. Evaluate the precision with which categories are defined and illustrated. Determine the criteria omitted from the system but important to you.

List the examples which fit into the system, are mis-represented by the system, or are not included in the system. Make an assessment of the usefulness of the system, based on your purchase.

TOPICS FOR WRITING IN CLASS

1. Develop a scheme for classifying the people who appear on television talk shows. The most obvious scheme is to classify people by what they do—sing songs, tell jokes, provide information. But other schemes such as their attire, behavior, or reasons for appearing will probably prove more significant.

2. Classify various kinds of trash. You are free to use the word literally or figuratively. If you interpret the word literally, you will be classifying things people actually throw away. If you interpret the word figuratively, you will be classifying something people consider worthless—gossip columns, romance magazines, game shows.

3. Write an essay that classifies various kinds of bad luck. Follow the pattern Austin uses in his essay on chance by arranging the kinds of bad luck in an ascending order of complexity. You may wish to illustrate your categories by using Murphy's Law—"If anything can go wrong, it will."

TOPICS FOR WRITING OUT OF CLASS

1. Write an article for the student humor magazine in which you set up a system for classifying students, faculty, or administrators. To organize your categories select a principle that seems insignificant—what students eat, how faculty dress, where administrators park —but that yields interesting information about the group being classified.

2. Study the criteria used to evaluate success at a job you are familiar with. Identify categories of workers ac-

cording to their ability or willingness to meet those criteria. Then write an essay in which you classify an imaginary work force for an imaginary supervisor. As you define categories and cite examples, you may want to recommend changes in the criteria that would improve the work situation.

3. Group several movies together for a composite movie review to appear in your local newspaper. You may approach this assignment practically—classifying movies that are currently showing in town. Or you may want to write a more reflective essay—classifying movies by form (western, comedy), star (Redford, Streep), director (Spielberg, Bergman), or some personal standard (the worst, the best). In the first case, you must assume that your readers have not seen the films. In the second case, you must assume that they have seen some, but not all, of the films you are classifying.

♦

DEFINITION

♦

DEFINITION

A definition sets boundaries for and describes the essential nature of something. Definitions give the special qualities that identify a person, place, object, process, or concept and distinguish it from others that may be similar.

There are three principal kinds of definitions. The first is a DICTIONARY or LEXICAL DEFINITION. It defines in a narrow way by specifying the class into which an item fits and then giving the item's distinguishing characteristics. For example: "Poetry is a [class] literary form that is [distinguishing characteristic] written in meter, usually di-

vided into lines, and often rhymed." Sometimes dictionary definitions also include synonyms; for instance, poetry
might also be defined as "verse."

The second major kind of definition is STIPULATIVE
DEFINITION, a way of defining that puts special restrictions
on a common term so that both writer and reader understand precisely how the term will be used in a specific
discussion. For instance, an author might write, "For the
purposes of this paper, I am going to define *argument* as
a unit of discourse in which beliefs are supported by
reasons."

The third major kind of definition is EXTENDED DEFINI-
TION, definition that may vary in length from two or three
paragraphs to an entire essay or even a whole book. An
extended definition expands on and illustrates in detail
a key term or concept in order to give the reader a clear
understanding of a complex or general term or concept.
Alone or in combination with other kinds of writing,
extended definition is a favorite strategy of expository
writers.

PURPOSE

Writers use definitions for several purposes. They define
in order to *identify the special nature* of a place, a person, a group, an institution, or a philosophy. For instance,
a writer might use definition to show how Montessori
schools differ from other preschool programs or to show
how New Orleans differs from other southern cities.

Writers may define to *explain.* They may want their
readers to know more about white-water canoeing or the
women's movement or the Worldwide Church of God.
They might also define to *entertain,* to *persuade,* to *instruct,* or to *establish a standard.* Sometimes writers define
for more than one purpose. A press agent, for example,
might write an extended definition of the Sierra Club

both to explain what the group does and to persuade people to join it.

Writers engaged in everyday writing tasks also define for a number of purposes. For example, people who submit autobiographical statements when applying for a scholarship or admission to a professional school are really defining themselves; they want to give their readers information that will distinguish them from other applicants. Writers also need to define problems they want to solve or goals they want to achieve.

AUDIENCE

Before a writer uses definition as a writing strategy, he or she needs to think about what the audience wants from that definition. Why would the audience read the definition, and what does it expect to learn by doing so? The writer may think of several reasons, but the two major ones are likely to be these.

First, the writer can anticipate that the reader wants to learn what is distinctive, typical, or unusual about the person, thing, or concept being defined, so that it can be readily identified. For example, a reader might want to know the difference between professional and amateur athletes. The writer could define professional athletes by pointing out that they play for money—either a salary or prizes—and are free to endorse commercial products and to negotiate contracts. Anyone seeing a billboard on which a football player advertises rental cars would then know that player is a professional.

Second, a writer can anticipate that a reader often wants a definition that sets limits and establishes the basis for a discussion or argument. For instance, the writer who wants to argue that the traditional American small town no longer exists in many parts of the country must begin by defining a traditional American small town.

The person who writes a definition essay should also

remember that readers probably have a specific reason for reading it and do not want to be led off in an unexpected direction. For example, the person who is reading to find out what Existentialism is probably does not want the definition turned into an attack against the premises of that philosophy. So the writer who is defining strictly to clarify or enlighten must be careful not to let bias creep into the definition; the writer who is defining to amuse or persuade need not be so careful.

STRATEGIES

Writers have a variety of defining strategies at their command, strategies that they can use singly or in combination. Probably the favorite defining strategy of all writers is GIVING EXAMPLES. At its most elementary level, giving examples involves pointing at a representative object. Writers use the same technique, but on a more sophisticated level, when they give illustrations that will help the reader visualize specific examples of the term they are defining.

Every writer in this section of the book uses the technique of giving examples, but Joan Didion depends on it most heavily. Perhaps because she is a novelist, she chooses dramatic personal incidents to convey to her reader a feeling that she believes cannot be adequately expressed by adjectives alone.

Writers also define by ANALYZING QUALITIES in order to show what is distinctive about their topic. Tom Wolfe uses this as his chief strategy in "The Right Stuff," identifying and illustrating the particular qualities that a successful fighter pilot must have: nerve, stamina, staying power, and arrogance. He supplements his analysis with examples. Closely related to analyzing qualities is the strategy of ATTRIBUTING CHARACTERISTICS. In writing about water, Elizabeth Janeway points out that two of its quintessential characteristics are fluid strength and eternal changeability.

Another common strategy for defining is DRAWING ANALOGIES. John Ciardi likens the intelligent pursuit of happiness to playing a game by the rules. He also uses the strategy of DEFINING NEGATIVELY, that is, saying what something is *not*. He claims that real happiness does not consist of possessing material things.

Finally, writers define by GIVING FUNCTIONS. Judy Syfers builds her essay "I Want a Wife" almost entirely on this strategy. She shows that one of the important ways in which we define people is by the roles they play and the jobs they do.

Although they commonly employ one or more of these techniques as their principal strategies for defining, writers can also use the methods illustrated in earlier sections of this book. They can define by comparison and contrast; notice how John Leggett defines the personalities of two authors by comparing and contrasting them in "Ross and Tom." They can define by description; that is essentially what Patricia Hampl is doing in "The Potent Center." It is even possible to define a job by process analysis, as the editors of *Fortune* do in "Riveters."

As you read each essay in this section, watch for the techniques of definition each author is using. Which techniques seem most useful to you? And as you read, think about how you could use your own experience and observations to construct an extended definition. You have an abundance of material available to you. At the end of this section you will find suggestions for ways that you might use that material in writing assignments involving definition.

Water

ELIZABETH JANEWAY

♦

Elizabeth Janeway was born in 1913 in Brooklyn, New York, and was educated at Barnard College. She began her career as a fiction writer, publishing numerous short stories and novels, including Daisy Kenyon *(1945),* The Question of Gregory *(1949), and* Accident *(1964). Over the past two decades Janeway has turned her attention increasingly to literary and social criticism. She is the author of four important books on the women's movement:* Man's World, Woman's Place: A Study in Social Mythology *(1971);* Between Myth and Morning: Women Awakening *(1974);* Powers of the Weak *(1980); and* Cross Sections: From a Decade of Change *(1984). In "Water," one of a series of essays she wrote in 1963 for* House and Garden *magazine, Janeway attempts to define the symbolic significance of this most basic natural substance.*

Water is a universal symbol. Tamed and trickling out of   1
the tap, softened and fluoridated, warmed in the boiler by
fires burning million-year-old oil, it is still not quite a commodity. Even for city dwellers some dim memory stirs
from time to time of those ancient eons when water or the
lack of it ruled everything—the sites of habitation, the
paths through the wilderness, the limits of hunting
grounds, famine and abundance, life and death. It can still

shatter human hopes and plans. Thirty years ago, the top soil in the plain states rose into the sky and blew away. Men had ploughed grazing land, counting on rain to bind the soil where the tough grass roots had been cut, and the rain did not come. A migration as great as that of the Mongols poured out of the Dust Bowl toward California. Steinbeck, in *The Grapes of Wrath,* recorded what happened to one bit of flotsam on one stream of this Diaspora. Today, I read in the papers, the Russians are ploughing the virgin Siberian lands as, in the last century, we ploughed the Dakotas. But the stubborn old gods of rivers and rains have not yet submitted to Marxist-Leninist discipline. Disappointing harvests are reported.

Water. "It has caused more wars in the Middle East," 2 writes Freya Stark in one of her brilliant travel books, "than even religion." In the Middle East, that is quite a feat. But there are historians who trace the breakdown of the ancient civilizations along the Tigris, the Euphrates and the Indus to wars and raiding parties which breached dams and ruined irrigation and drainage systems. Whether the cities fell first and the aqueducts and irrigation ditches silted up through neglect, or whether they were deliberately destroyed to strangle the cities, they have never been rebuilt. Let us not imagine, in our smug pride of modernity, that engineers have yet become more powerful than statesmen, for even today, there is desert where once there was fertile land. Civilization takes water for granted, but that is civilization's mistake.

It's not a mistake, though, that will ever be made by 3 those who live past the limits of "city water." Amidst all the denouncing of suburbia, let us give it credit for this: suburban dwellers must face some of the old facts of life, of living and of weather. In the country, water comes out of a well—save for that blessed, lucky trickle which flows to a favored few from a gravity-fed spring (and that is a trickle which, in August, may dwindle disastrously). Civilization, of course, has changed the Old Oaken Bucket into an electric motor pumping so many gallons a minute to a cistern from an artesian well, but it has not changed the nature of the emotions that go with procuring this water, only bunched them together into patches of intensity with stretches of complacence in between. But when the power goes out in a storm, so does the water supply.

Where we used to live, seventy miles from New York, the power had a habit of failing before the telephone lines went. Why this should be, I don't know. But the prudence of the telephone company in locating its poles and stringing its wires allowed messages to get through from neighbor to neighbor before the telephone lines went down and silence followed darkness. Thus, a spreading rash of calls would ripple out from the center of casualty: "We've lost our power. If you still have yours, fill the bathtubs quick." Then the householder (or his wife, if he was a commuter who spent his days in an ivory tower in the city) would go into action and fill tubs and buckets and pots and pans against the drought to come. After one ice storm, the water famine lasted for a week in some parts of the township, and luckier folk invited their neighbors in for baths.

From time to time, as families grew in size or new houses went up with their demanding machines for washing clothes and dishes, new wells had to be dug. Then the drillers would come with their rig and thump away at the ancient granite beneath our green countryside, and the owners would groan and shake a little, too, at the dollars that each hour of thumping represented. There was water, the drillers would report encouragingly, but not yet quite enough, three gallons a minute, five gallons a minute— would they never find the level that would deliver the necessary eight gallons a minute? On and on they went, like persevering, unsuccessful disciples of Moses, smiting the rock. Once a friend of ours, in despair after weeks of fruitless pounding, called in a water dowser. Our friend is the founder of one of the oldest and most respected public opinion polls. It seemed quaintly appropriate to think of an old man with a hazel twig in his hands questioning every foot of the poll taker's land on its water content. At last he said, "Dig here," and they dug, and found water. Of course, it was simply luck—whatever that means.

Water. It is a universal symbol, I wrote, but a symbol of what? Of birth and beginnings, as the scientists, the first chapter of Genesis and Dr. Freud all tell us? Life began in the sea, say the biochemists, when lightning discharges awoke, in the thin soup of almost life, some monstrous protein molecules which married each other: this is our most modern mythology. An older story tells us that the Spirit of God moved on the face of the waters even before His command created Light: which might, after all, be simply a more majestic way of describing the same event. As for Freud, when he had rummaged through enough people's heads and stitched thousands of fragments of dreams together, he came to the cautious conclusion that "to dream of being in water or passing through a stream often symbolized the act of birth." Which is a nice, pedantic, and quite useless conclusion, for it leaves us with another set of waters unexplained. What shall we make of "the bitter, salt, estranging sea," or the rivers of Styx and of Lethe, which are the rivers of death? 6

We must think again. Water can symbolize birth, as it can symbolize death, but essentially its meaning is greater and simpler, and includes both. At the deepest level, water stands as the symbol of Change. Indeed, when St. John, in the Revelations, wished to describe the eternal landscape that would follow upon the Day of Judgment, he said, "There was no more sea." Changeless eternity could go no further. 7

Water is the present tense. It flows. It will not take a shape of its own, but will fill indifferently any jug or pitcher or cup, and then flow out and on, indifferent still, forgetful and uninfluenced. Its strength is the strength of movement. Even "still waters" must "run deep." If they do not, we distrust them and have made a pejorative word 8

for such unnatural behavior—"stagnant," or standing. In
New Mexico, the Indians believe that water can die.
Mary Austin records the legend:

> At midnight drink no water
> For I have heard said
> That on the stroke of midnight
> All water goes dead.

Water is always now. It demands the present participle 9
for its description—gushing, flowing, pouring, sprinkling.
As every gardener knows, last week's soaking and next
week's rain might as well not exist, unless we manage to
string them together by constructing tanks and cisterns
and reservoirs. Thirst is immediate. Water cannot be an
event, it must be a presence. To make it so must be a
primary concern of any stable society, great or small.

Modern man is astonishingly modest about his achieve- 10
ments. I am not at all sure that this is a healthy state of
mind. Might we not be more confident of our ability to
deal with our future problems if we took a bit more pride
in our successful solutions to problems of the past? Mod-
esty is all very well for individuals, but civic pride can give
a community a sense of wholeness and of its obligations
to its citizens. We have somehow lost the knack of celebrating deeds of greatness today, and are apt to go off to
the beach on the Fourth of July, each family by itself, instead of taking a little time to remember our heroes and
refresh our pride.

I would like to see more holidays, and as one of them I 11
would like to propose a Festival of the Waters. It might
well be held on St. Swithin's Day. I imagine pilgrimages
to the Tennessee Valley, to Grand Coulee and to Boulder
Dam. I think of holiday tours along the St. Lawrence Sea-
way, with river steamers full of bands and picnickers toast-
ing all that good sense, engineering training and peace
between nations have wrought there. The irrigated valleys
of California could show off their wealth.

Above all, each city should offer thanks to its sanitary 12 engineers, who might appear with an accompanying guard of master plumbers—for even the grimmest nature may sweeten a little once it feels itself appreciated. The Mayor might read out the proud statistics citing the number of years since typhoid or cholera claimed a victim within his purlieus; and if the statistics should by any chance not be proud, how quick the Mayor and the Department of Sanitation would be to improve them! And each year the ceremony would be crowned by the dedication of some new Wonder of Water: a handsome public pool, or a fountain with a bit of green about it, shining and leaping in the center of the city where passers-by could refresh their eyes. Or a boat basin. Or a new wing on the aquarium. Or—

But you see what I mean. Water is a universal symbol 13 because it is a universal need. As we live now, it is beyond the power of the individual, in the vast majority of cases, to satisfy this need on his own. Only men working together can build reservoirs and aqueducts and dams and hydroelectric stations and sewage conversion plants and, soon no doubt, great structures to desalt the sea and make the desert blossom like the corn tassel and the alfalfa.

Our Festival of Waters, then, would be a holiday to cele- 14 brate the things that men working together can achieve. What could be more appropriate? For as we all know, the just and the unjust both get wet when it rains and thirsty when it does not. Too often, in the past, the just and the unjust have preferred to disagree and to create deserts rather than settle down and share out their water rights. But now our engineering knowledge is growing with the world's population, and with its need for water. Might not, for once, new skills combine with new needs? Might not the just and the unjust decide to work together, literally for dear life? And might not these projects to control the fluid strength and the eternal changeability of water teach us something about controlling the fluid strength and eternal changeability of human nature?

◆

For Study and Discussion

QUESTIONS ABOUT PURPOSE

1. What does Elizabeth Janeway's discussion of the historical importance of water demonstrate about its unique value in our lives?
2. Janeway begins her essay with a number of facts about water. What are they, and why does she introduce them?
3. Why does Janeway assert that "water is the present tense"?

QUESTIONS ABOUT AUDIENCE

1. This essay was first published in *House and Garden*, a magazine whose readers are interested in interior decoration, art, travel, and cultural events. What do you think Janeway assumed about those readers' attitudes toward and range of experiences with water?
2. What assumptions does Janeway make about her readers when she refers to *Mongols*, the *rivers of Styx and Lethe, Steinbeck*, and *Freud*?
3. How does Janeway's argument for a Festival of Waters attempt to alter her readers' perception of the substance she is defining?

QUESTIONS ABOUT STRATEGIES

1. In paragraphs 4 and 5 Janeway moves from writing about water in broad historic terms to writing about her own experience with water when she lived in the suburbs. What does this shift in focus accomplish?
2. How does her description of water in paragraphs 8 and 9 establish its unique characteristics?

3. How does Janeway use the examples of reservoirs, aqueducts, dams, hydroelectric stations, and sewage conversion plants to make her point that "water is a universal symbol because it is a universal need"?

QUESTIONS FOR DISCUSSION

1. Why is water "still not a commodity"? What happens when people believe that it *is* a commodity—something that can be bought, sold, owned?
2. To what extent is Janeway's faith in our engineering knowledge justified? What might prevent the "just and the unjust" from working together?
3. Why, in your opinion, does Janeway think water should be viewed as a symbol of change?

What Is Happiness?

JOHN CIARDI

——————— ◆ ———————

*John Ciardi was born in Boston, Massachusetts, in
1916 and educated at Tufts University and the University of Michigan. He has taught writing at several
universities (among them Harvard and Rutgers), directed the Bread Loaf Writers Conference in Vermont,
and served as poetry editor for* Saturday Review. *His
own writing includes numerous volumes of poetry,
such as* Homeward to America *(1940),* Thirty-Nine
Poems *(1959), and* Person to Person *(1964); several
books for children; an important literature textbook,*
How Does a Poem Mean? *(1960); and a much-praised
verse translation of Dante's* Divine Comedy: The Inferno *(1954),* The Purgatorio *(1961), and* The Paradiso
(1970). In the following essay, first published in
Saturday Review *in 1964, Ciardi defines "happiness"
as an ideal easier to pursue than to produce.*

The right to pursue happiness is issued to Americans with   1
their birth certificates, but no one seems quite sure which
way it ran. It may be we are issued a hunting license but
offered no game. Jonathan Swift seemed to think so when
he attacked the idea of happiness as "the possession of
being well-deceived," the felicity of being "a fool among
knaves." For Swift saw society as Vanity Fair, the land
of false goals.

It is, of course, un-American to think in terms of fools   2
and knaves. We do, however, seem to be dedicated to

the idea of buying our way to happiness. We shall all have made it to Heaven when we possess enough.

And at the same time the forces of American commercialism are hugely dedicated to making us deliberately unhappy. Advertising is one of our major industries, and advertising exists not to satisfy desires but to create them— and to create them faster than any man's budget can satisfy them. For that matter, our whole economy is based on a dedicated insatiability. We are taught that to possess is to be happy, and then we are made to want. We are even told it is our duty to want. It was only a few years ago, to cite a single example, that car dealers across the country were flying banners that read "You Auto Buy Now." They were calling upon Americans, as an act approaching patriotism, to buy at once, with money they did not have, automobiles they did not really need, and which they would be required to grow tired of by the time the next year's models were released.

Or look at any of the women's magazines. There, as Bernard DeVoto once pointed out, advertising begins as poetry in the front pages and ends as pharmacopoeia and therapy in the back pages. The poetry of the front matter is the dream of perfect beauty. This is the baby skin that must be hers. These, the flawless teeth. This, the perfumed breath she must exhale. This, the sixteen-year-old figure she must display at forty, at fifty, at sixty, and forever.

Once past the vaguely uplifting fiction and feature articles, the reader finds the other face of the dream in the back matter. This is the harness into which Mother must strap herself in order to display that perfect figure. These, the chin straps she must sleep in. This is the salve that restores all, this is her laxative, these are the tablets that melt away fat, these are the hormones of perpetual youth, these are the stockings that hide varicose veins.

Obviously no half-sane person can be completely persuaded either by such poetry or by such pharmacopoeia and orthopedics. Yet someone is obviously trying to buy the dream as offered and spending billions every year in the attempt. Clearly the happiness-market is not running out of customers, but what is it trying to buy?

The idea "happiness," to be sure, will not sit still for   7
easy definition: the best one can do is to try to set some extremes to the idea and then work in toward the middle. To think of happiness as acquisitive and competitive will do to set the materialistic extreme. To think of it as the idea one senses in, say, a holy man of India will do to set the spiritual extreme. That holy man's idea of happiness is in needing nothing from outside himself. In wanting nothing, he lacks nothing. He sits immobile, rapt in contemplation, free even of his own body. Or nearly free of it. If devout admirers bring him food he eats it; if not, he starves indifferently. Why be concerned? What is physical is an illusion to him. Contemplation is his joy and he achieves it through a fantastically demanding discipline, the accomplishment of which is itself a joy within him.

Is he a happy man? Perhaps his happiness is only an-   8
other sort of illusion. But who can take it from him? And who will dare say it is more illusory than happiness on the installment plan?

But, perhaps because I am Western, I doubt such cata-   9
tonic happiness, as I doubt the dreams of the happiness-market. What is certain is that his way of happiness would be torture to almost any Western man. Yet these extremes will still serve to frame the area within which all of us must find some sort of balance. Thoreau—a creature of both Eastern and Western thought—had his own firm sense of that balance. His aim was to save on the low levels in order to spend on the high.

Possession for its own sake or in competition with the   10
rest of the neighborhood would have been Thoreau's idea of the low levels. The active discipline of heightening one's perception of what is enduring in nature would have been his idea of the high. What he saved from the low was time and effort he could spend on the high. Tho-

reau certainly disapproved of starvation, but he would put into feeding himself only as much effort as would keep him functioning for more important efforts.

Effort is the gist of it. There is no happiness except 11 as we take on life-engaging difficulties. Short of the impossible, as Yeats put it, the satisfactions we get from a lifetime depend on how high we choose our difficulties. Robert Frost was thinking in something like the same terms when he spoke of "The pleasure of taking pains." The mortal flaw in the advertised version of happiness is in the fact that it purports to be effortless.

We demand difficulty even in our games. We demand 12 it because without difficulty there can be no game. A game is a way of making something hard for the fun of it. The rules of the game are an arbitrary imposition of difficulty. When the spoilsport ruins the fun, he always does so by refusing to play by the rules. It is easier to win at chess if you are free, at your pleasure, to change the wholly arbitrary rules, but the fun is in winning within the rules. No difficulty, no fun.

The buyers and sellers at the happiness-market seem 13 too often to have lost their sense of the pleasure of difficulty. Heaven knows what they are playing, but it seems a dull game. And the Indian holy man seems dull to us, I suppose, because he seems to be refusing to play anything at all. The Western weakness may be in the illusion that happiness can be bought. Perhaps the Eastern weakness is in the idea that there is such a thing as perfect (and therefore static) happiness.

Happiness is never more than partial. There are no 14 pure states of mankind. Whatever else happiness may be, it is neither in having nor in being, but in becoming. What the Founding Fathers declared for us as an inherent right, we should do well to remember, was not happiness but the *pursuit* of happiness. What they might have underlined, could they have foreseen the happiness-market, is the cardinal fact that happiness is in the pursuit itself, in the meaningful pursuit of what is life-engaging and life-revealing, which is to say, in the idea of *becoming.* A nation is not measured by what it possesses or wants to possess, but by what it wants to become.

By all means let the happiness-market sell us minor   15
satisfactions and even minor follies so long as we keep
them in scale and buy them out of spiritual change. I am
no customer for either puritanism or asceticism. But drop
any real spiritual capital at those bazaars, and what you
come home to will be your own poorhouse.

———— ◆ ————

For Study and Discussion

QUESTIONS ABOUT PURPOSE

1. What does Ciardi want to demonstrate about the function of advertising?

2. What two extreme philosophies of the good life does Ciardi criticize?

3. What reservations does Ciardi think we should keep in mind as we pursue happiness?

QUESTIONS ABOUT AUDIENCE

1. Do you think Ciardi is writing primarily for Americans? Why or why not?

2. What kind of people do you think read the *Saturday Review of Literature,* the magazine in which this essay first appeared?

3. Is Ciardi's audience in the 1980s substantially different from what it would have been when the article was first published in 1964?

QUESTIONS ABOUT STRATEGIES

1. Ciardi begins and ends the essay with metaphors. Are they effective? Why or why not?
2. Why does he devote an entire paragraph to Thoreau, the author of *Walden?*
3. How much of the essay is taken up by negative defining? Is the proportion justified?

QUESTIONS FOR DISCUSSION

1. What does Ciardi mean by the "happiness market"? Do you consider his term accurate? Why or why not?
2. What do you interpret Ciardi's own definition of happiness to mean?
3. Do you think Ciardi is saying that there are primary and secondary sources of happiness? If so, what does he think they are?

I Want a Wife

JUDY SYFERS

$\blacklozenge$

Judy Syfers was born in 1937 in San Francisco and was educated at the University of Iowa. She was married in 1960, raised two daughters, and is now divorced, working full time as a secretary in the day and going to school at night in order to "increase [her] income-earning potential." Her essay "I Want A Wife" was first published in Ms. magazine in 1971, and now seems, according to Syfers, "quite prophetic to me in terms of my own life." The essay defines the ironies and anomalies implicit in the word "wife."

I belong to that classification of people known as wives. 1
I am A Wife. And, not altogether incidentally, I am a mother.

Not too long ago a male friend of mine appeared on 2
the scene fresh from a recent divorce. He had one child, who is, of course, with his ex-wife. He is obviously looking for another wife. As I thought about him while I was ironing one evening, it suddenly occurred to me that I, too, would like to have a wife. Why do I want a wife?

I would like to go back to school so that I can become 3

economically independent, support myself, and, if need be, support those dependent upon me. I want a wife who will work and send me to school. And while I am going to school I want a wife to take care of my children. I want a wife to keep track of the children's doctor and dentist appointments. And to keep track of mine, too. I want a wife to make sure my children eat properly and are kept clean. I want a wife who will wash the children's clothes and keep them mended. I want a wife who is a good nurturant attendant to my children, who arranges for their schooling, makes sure that they have an adequate social life with their peers, takes them to the park, the zoo, etc. I want a wife who takes care of the children when they are sick, a wife who arranges to be around when the children need special care, because, of course, I cannot miss classes at school. My wife must arrange to lose time at work and not lose the job. It may mean a small cut in my wife's income from time to time, but I guess I can tolerate that. Needless to say, my wife will arrange and pay for the care of the children while my wife is working.

I want a wife who will take care of *my* physical needs. 4 I want a wife who will keep my house clean. A wife who will pick up after me. I want a wife who will keep my clothes clean, ironed, mended, replaced when need be, and who will see to it that my personal things are kept in their proper place so that I can find what I need the minute I need it. I want a wife who cooks the meals, a wife who is a *good* cook. I want a wife who will plan the menus, do the necessary grocery shopping, prepare the meals, serve them pleasantly, and then do the cleaning up while I do my studying. I want a wife who will care for me when I am sick and sympathize with my pain and loss of time from school. I want a wife to go along when our family takes a vacation so that someone can continue to care for me and my children when I need a rest and change of scene.

I want a wife who will not bother me with rambling 5 complaints about a wife's duties. But I want a wife who will listen to me when I feel the need to explain a rather difficult point I have come across in my course of studies. And I want a wife who will type my papers for me when I have written them.

I want a wife who will take care of the details of my social life. When my wife and I are invited out by my friends, I want a wife who will take care of the babysitting arrangements. When I meet people at school that I like and want to entertain, I want a wife who will have the house clean, will prepare a special meal, serve it to me and my friends, and not interrupt when I talk about the things that interest me and my friends. I want a wife who will have arranged that the children are fed and ready for bed before my guests arrive so that the children do not bother us. I want a wife who takes care of the needs of my guests so that they feel comfortable, who makes sure that they have an ashtray, that they are passed the hors d'oeuvres, that they are offered a second helping of the food, that their wine glasses are replenished when necessary, that their coffee is served to them as they like it. And I want a wife who knows that sometimes I need a night out by myself.

I want a wife who is sensitive to my sexual needs, a wife who makes love passionately and eagerly when I feel like it, a wife who makes sure that I am satisfied. And, of course, I want a wife who will not demand sexual attention when I an not in the mood for it. I want a wife who assumes the complete responsibility for birth control, because I do not want more children. I want a wife who will remain sexually faithful to me so that I do not have to clutter up my intellectual life with jealousies. And I want a wife who understands that *my* sexual needs may entail more than strict adherence to monogamy. I must, after all, be able to relate to people as fully as possible.

If, by chance, I find another person more suitable as a wife than the wife I already have, I want the liberty to replace my present wife with another one. Naturally, I will expect a fresh, new life; my wife will take the children and be solely responsible for them so that I am left free.

When I am through with school and have a job, I want   9
my wife to quit working and remain at home so that my wife can more fully and completely take care of a wife's duties.

My God, who *wouldn't* want a wife?   10

———— ◆ ————

For Study and Discussion

QUESTIONS ABOUT PURPOSE

1. In her definition of the role of a wife, why does Syfers never say, "I want a wife who loves me"?
2. What do you think Syfers wants to demonstrate about the narrator whose statement begins in paragraph 3?
3. Why do you think Syfers lists so many explicit details in her statement of what she wants in a wife?

QUESTIONS ABOUT AUDIENCE

1. How would you describe the regular readers of *Ms.,* the magazine in which this article first appeared?
2. What kind of audience do you think would be most sympathetic to this article? What audience might be angered by it?
3. The article was written over ten years ago. In what significant ways, if any, might the audience who reads it today be different from the original audience?

QUESTIONS ABOUT STRATEGIES

1. Why does Syfers keep repeating the word *wife* instead of occasionally using the pronouns *she* and *her?*

2. Why do you think the author uses the phrases *of course, after all,* and *clutter up* in paragraph 7?

3. By analyzing the categories of duties mentioned in paragraphs 3 through 7, can you detect a pattern of organization in the essay? What is it and why do you think Syfers used it?

QUESTIONS FOR DISCUSSION

1. Some readers might say that parts of Syfers's definition of a wife are stereotyped and no longer true. Other readers would maintain that the definition is still essentially accurate. Which do you believe? In giving your answer, consider the ways in which American society has changed and the ways in which it has remained the same over the past fifteen years.

2. In what way might one say that Syfers's essay really defines husbands as much as it does wives?

3. How closely does Syfers's list of wifely duties correspond to roles filled by most wives that you know?

The Right Stuff

TOM WOLFE

◆

Tom Wolfe was born in 1931 in Richmond, Virginia, and educated at Washington and Lee University and Yale University. After working as a reporter for several newspapers, Wolfe began writing for New York *magazine, where he developed the free-wheeling style he was later to label "the New Journalism." His essays on various aspects of American popular culture have appeared in* Esquire *and* New York *and have been collected in books with memorable titles such as* The Kandy-Kolored Tangerine-Flake Streamline Baby *(1965),* The Electric Kool-Aid Acid Test *(1968),* Radical Chic and Mau-Mauing the Flak Catchers *(1970), and* From Bauhaus to Our House *(1981). Wolfe's interpretation of the origin and growth of the writing style he made famous appears in his introduction to* The New Journalism *(1973). In this selection from* The Right Stuff *(1979) he defines that "ineffable quality" that characterizes America's test pilots and astronauts.*

A young man might go into military flight training believing that he was entering some sort of technical school in which he was simply going to acquire a certain set of skills. Instead, he found himself all at once enclosed in a fraternity. And in this fraternity, even though it was military, men were not rated by their outward rank as ensigns, lieutenants, commanders, or whatever. No, herein the world was divided into those who had it and those who did not. This quality, this *it*, was never named, however, nor was it talked about in any way. [1]

As to just what this ineffable quality was...well, it obviously involved bravery. But it was not bravery in the simple sense of being willing to risk your life. The idea seemed to be that any fool could do that, if that was all that was required, just as any fool could throw away his life in the process. No, the idea here (in the all-enclosing fraternity) seemed to be that a man should have the ability to go up in a hurtling piece of machinery and put his hide on the line and then have the moxie, the reflexes, the experience, the coolness, to pull it back in the last yawning moment—and then to go up again *the next day*, and the next day, and every next day, even if the series should prove infinite—and, ultimately, in its best expression, do so in a cause that means something to thousands, to a people, a nation, to humanity, to God. Nor was there *a test* to show whether or not a pilot had this righteous quality. There was, instead, a seemingly infinite series of tests. A career in flying was like climbing one of those ancient Babylonian pyramids made up of a dizzy progression of steps and ledges, a ziggurat, a pyramid extraordinarily high and steep; and the idea was to prove at every foot of the way up that pyramid that you were one of the elected and anointed ones who had *the right stuff* and could move higher and higher and even—ultimately, God willing, one day—that you might be able to join that special few at the very top, that elite who had the capacity to bring tears to men's eyes, the very Brotherhood of the Right Stuff itself.

None of this was to be mentioned, and yet it was acted out in a way that a young man could not fail to understand. When a new flight (i.e., a class) of trainees arrived at Pensacola, they were brought into an auditorium for a little lecture. An officer would tell them: "Take a look at the man on either side of you." Quite a few actually swiveled their heads this way and that, in the interest of appearing diligent. Then the officer would say: "One of the three of you is not going to make it!"—meaning, not get his wings. That was the opening theme, the *motif* of primary training. We already know that one-third of you do not have the right stuff—it only remains to find out who.

Furthermore, that was the way it turned out. At every 4 level in one's progress up that staggeringly high pyramid, the world was once more divided into those men who had the right stuff to continue the climb and those who had to be *left behind* in the most obvious way. Some were eliminated in the course of the opening classroom work, as either not smart enough or not hardworking enough, and were left behind. Then came the basic flight instruction, in single-engine, propeller-driven trainers, and a few more—even though the military tried to make this stage easy—were washed out and left behind. Then came more demanding levels, one after the other, formation flying, instrument flying, jet training, all-weather flying, gunnery, and at each level more were washed out and left behind. By this point easily a third of the original candidates had been, indeed, eliminated . . . from the ranks of those who might prove to have the right stuff. . . .

Those who remained, those who qualified for carrier 5 duty—and even more so those who later on qualified for *night* carrier duty—began to feel a bit like Gideon's warriors. *So many have been left behind!* The young warriors were now treated to a deathly sweet and quite unmentionable sight. They could gaze at length upon the crushed and wilted pariahs who had washed out. They could inspect those who did not have that righteous stuff.

The military did not have very merciful instincts. 6 Rather than packing up these poor souls and sending them home, the Navy, like the Air Force and the Marines, would try to make use of them in some other role, such as flight controller. So the washout has to keep taking classes with the rest of his group, even though he can no longer touch an airplane. He sits there in the classes staring at sheets of paper with cataracts of sheer human mortification over his eyes while the rest steal looks at him . . . this man reduced to an ant, this untouchable, this poor sonofabitch.

And in what test had he been found wanting? Why, it seemed to be nothing less than *manhood* itself. Naturally, this was never mentioned, either. Yet there it was. *Manliness, manhood, manly courage* ... there was something ancient, primordial, irresistible about the challenge of this stuff, no matter what a sophisticated and rational age one might think he lived in. ...

A fighter pilot soon found he wanted to associate only with other fighter pilots. Who else could understand the nature of the little proposition (right stuff/death) they were all dealing with? And what other subject could compare with it? It was riveting! To talk about it in so many words was forbidden, of course. The very words *death, danger, bravery, fear* were not to be uttered except in the occasional specific instance or for ironic effect. Nevertheless, the subject could be adumbrated in *code* or *by example.* Hence the endless evenings of pilots huddled together talking about flying. On these long and drunken evenings (the bane of their family life) certain theorems would be propounded and demonstrated—and all by *code* and *example.* One theorem was: There are no *accidents* and no fatal flaws in the machines; there are only pilots with the wrong stuff. (I.e., blind Fate can't kill me.) When Bud Jennings crashed and burned in the swamps at Jacksonville, the other pilots in Pete Conrad's squadron said: *How could he have been so stupid?* It turned out that Jennings had gone up in the SNJ with his cockpit canopy opened in a way that was expressly forbidden in the manual, and carbon monoxide had been sucked in from the exhaust, and he passed out and crashed. All agreed that Bud Jennings was a good guy and a good pilot, but his epitaph on the ziggurat was: *How could he have been so stupid?* This seemed shocking at first, but by the time Conrad had reached the end of that bad string at Pax River, he was capable of his own corollary to the theorem: viz., no single factor ever killed a pilot; there was always a chain of mistakes. But what about Ted Whelan, who fell like a rock from 8,100 feet when his parachute failed?

Well, the parachute was merely part of the chain: first, someone should have caught the structural defect that resulted in the hydraulic leak that triggered the emergency; second, Whelan did not check out his seat-parachute rig, and the drogue failed to separate the main parachute from the seat; but even after those two mistakes, Whelan had fifteen or twenty seconds, as he fell, to disengage himself from the seat and open the parachute manually. Why just stare at the scenery coming up to smack you in the face! And everyone nodded. (He failed —but I wouldn't have!) Once the theorem and the corollary were understood, the Navy's statistics about one in every four Navy aviators dying meant nothing. The figures were averages, and averages applied to those with average stuff.

A riveting subject, especially if it were one's own hide that was on the line. Every evening at bases all over America, there were military pilots huddled in officers clubs eagerly cutting the right stuff up in coded slices so they could talk about it. What more compelling topic of conversation was there in the world? In the Air Force there were even pilots who would ask the tower for priority landing clearance so that they could make the beer call on time, at 4 P.M. sharp, at the Officers Club. They would come right out and state the reason. The drunken rambles began at four and sometimes went on for ten or twelve hours. Such conversations! They diced that righteous stuff up into little bits, bowed ironically to it, stumbled blindfolded around it, groped, lurched, belched, staggered, bawled, sang, roared, and feinted at it with self-deprecating humor. Nevertheless!—they never mentioned it by name. No, they used the approved codes, such as: "Like a jerk I got myself into a hell of a corner today." They told of how they "lucked out of it." To get across the extreme peril of his exploit, one would use certain oblique cues. He would say, "I looked over at Robinson"—who would be known to the listeners as a non-com who sometimes rode backseat to read radar—

321

"and he wasn't talking any more, he was just staring at the radar, like this, giving it that *zombie* look. Then I *knew* I was in trouble!" Beautiful! Just right! For it would also be known to the listeners that the non-coms advised one another: "*Never* fly with a lieutenant. *Avoid* captains and majors. Hell, man, do yourself a favor: don't fly with anybody below colonel." Which in turn said: "Those young bucks shoot dice with death!" And yet once in the air the non-com had his own standards. He was determined to remain as outwardly cool as the pilot, so that when the pilot did something that truly petrified him, he would say nothing; instead, he would turn silent, catatonic, like a zombie. Perfect! *Zombie.* There you had it, compressed into a single word all of the foregoing. I'm a hell of a pilot! I shoot dice with death! And now all you fellows know it! And I haven't spoken of that unspoken stuff even once!

———— ♦ ————

For Study and Discussion

QUESTIONS ABOUT PURPOSE

1. What is Wolfe trying to illustrate in his stories about reckless fighter pilots?
2. Wolfe is known primarily as a writer who satirizes our culture. Are there any parts of this essay in which he seems to you to be satirizing fighter pilots or their training?
3. What special qualities does Wolfe define as essential to the lives of fighter pilots?

QUESTIONS ABOUT AUDIENCE

1. Judging by Wolfe's word choice and sentence structure, what assumptions do you think he makes about the educational level of his audience?

2. What groups of readers would be most likely to read Wolfe's book about astronauts, from which this selection was taken? Why do you think they would read it?

3. To what extent do you think Wolfe can anticipate that his audience will be sympathetic toward the pilots he is writing about?

QUESTIONS ABOUT STRATEGIES

1. What is the effect of Wolfe's drawing an analogy between going through flight training and climbing a ziggurat pyramid? How much does the reader have to know about ziggurat pyramids to get the point?

2. What is the effect of the string of verbs Wolfe uses in paragraph 8 in the sentence that begins, "They diced that righteous stuff up into little bits . . ."?

3. How does Wolfe communicate a fighter pilot's image of himself to the reader?

QUESTIONS FOR DISCUSSION

1. In a few words, how would you answer someone who asked you what Wolfe means by his term "the right stuff"?

2. What other occupations or situations can you think of in which a person must go through a series of ordeals and weeding-out procedures in order to prove that he or she has "the right stuff"? Are those procedures similar to the ones Wolfe describes?

3. How American is the tradition of having to prove that one has "the right stuff"? What examples can you give of such traditions existing in other countries and centuries?

Migraines

JOAN DIDION

◆

Joan Didion was born in Sacramento, California, in 1934 and educated at the University of California at Berkeley. She worked first as an associate feature editor for Vogue *and later as a contributing editor for* Saturday Evening Post, National Review, *and* Esquire. *She has written four novels:* Run, River *(1963),* Play It As It Lays *(1970),* A Book of Common Prayer *(1976), and* Democracy *(1984). But it is for her meticulously styled essays, articulating her personal vision of events public and private, that Didion is perhaps best known. Her first collection,* Slouching Towards Bethlehem *(1968), describes the cultural and psychological turmoil of the 1960s; it has been called a "classic" in which each of the essays reflects the feeling that "the center cannot hold." A second collection,* The White Album, *appeared in 1979; and Didion's extended essay about her trip to Central America in 1982,* Salvador, *was published in 1983. In the following essay, taken from* The White Album, *Didion tries to define a medical condition that torments her—migraine headaches.*

Three, four, sometimes five times a month, I spend the 1
day in bed with a migraine headache, insensible to the
world around me. Almost every day of every month, between these attacks, I feel the sudden irrational irritation
and the flush of blood into the cerebral arteries which tell
me that migraine is on its way, and I take certain drugs
to avert its arrival. If I did not take the drugs, I would
be able to function perhaps one day in four. The physiological error called migraine is, in brief, central to the
given of my life. When I was 15, 16, even 25, I used to

think that I could rid myself of this error by simply denying it, character over chemistry. "Do you have headaches *sometimes? frequently? never?*" the application forms would demand. "Check one." Wary of the trap, wanting whatever it was that the successful circumnavigation of that particular form could bring (a job, a scholarship, the respect of mankind and the grace of God), I would check one. "*Sometimes,*" I would lie. That in fact I spent one or two days a week almost unconscious with pain seemed a shameful secret, evidence not merely of some chemical inferiority but of all my bad attitudes, unpleasant tempers, wrongthink.

For I had no brain tumor, no eyestrain, no high blood pressure, nothing wrong with me at all: I simply had migraine headaches, and migraine headaches were, as everyone who did not have them knew, imaginary. I fought migraine then, ignored the warnings it sent, went to school and later to work in spite of it, sat through lectures in Middle English and presentations to advertisers with involuntary tears running down the right side of my face, threw up in washrooms, stumbled home by instinct, emptied ice trays onto my bed and tried to freeze the pain in my right temple, wished only for a neurosurgeon who would do a lobotomy on house call, and cursed my imagination.

It was a long time before I began thinking mechanistically enough to accept migraine for what it was: something with which I would be living, the way some people live with diabetes. Migraine is something more than the fancy of a neurotic imagination. It is an essentially hereditary complex of symptoms, the most frequently noted but by no means the most unpleasant of which is a vascular headache of blinding severity, suffered by a surprising number of women, a fair number of men (Thomas Jefferson had migraine, and so did Ulysses S. Grant, the day he accepted Lee's surrender), and by some unfortunate children as young as two years old. (I had my first when I was eight. It came on during a fire drill at the Columbia

School in Colorado Springs, Colorado. I was taken first home and then to the infirmary at Peterson Field, where my father was stationed. The Air Corps doctor prescribed an enema.) Almost anything can trigger a specific attack of migraine: stress, allergy, fatigue, an abrupt change in barometric pressure, a contretemps over a parking ticket. A flashing light. A fire drill. One inherits, of course, only the predisposition. In other words I spent yesterday in bed with a headache not merely because of my bad attitudes, unpleasant tempers and wrongthink, but because both my grandmothers had migraine, my father has migraine and my mother has migraine.

No one knows precisely what it is that is inherited. 4 The chemistry of migraine, however, seems to have some connection with the nerve hormone named serotonin, which is naturally present in the brain. The amount of serotonin in the blood falls sharply at the onset of migraine, and one migraine drug, methysergide, or Sansert, seems to have some effect on serotonin. Methysergide is a derivative of lysergic acid (in fact Sandoz Pharmaceuticals first synthesized LSD-25 while looking for a migraine cure), and its use is hemmed about with so many contraindications and side effects that most doctors prescribe it only in the most incapacitating cases. Methysergide, when it is prescribed, is taken daily, as a preventive; another preventive which works for some people is old-fashioned ergotamine tartrate, which helps to constrict the swelling blood vessels during the "aura," the period which in most cases precedes the actual headache.

Once an attack is under way, however, no drug touches 5 it. Migraine gives some people mild hallucinations, temporarily blinds others, shows up not only as a headache but as a gastrointestinal disturbance, a painful sensitivity to all sensory stimuli, an abrupt overpowering fatigue, a strokelike aphasia, and a crippling inability to make even the most routine connections. When I am in a migraine aura (for some people the aura lasts fifteen minutes, for others several hours), I will drive through red lights, lose the house keys, spill whatever I am holding, lose the ability to focus my eyes or frame coherent sentences, and generally give the appearance of being on drugs, or drunk. The actual headache, when it comes, brings with it chills, sweating, nausea, a debility that seems to stretch the very limits of endurance. That no one dies of migraine seems, to someone deep into an attack, an ambiguous blessing.

My husband also has migraine, which is unfortunate 6 for him but fortunate for me: perhaps nothing so tends to prolong an attack as the accusing eye of someone who has never had a headache. "Why not take a couple of aspirin," the unafflicted will say from the doorway, or "I'd have a headache, too, spending a beautiful day like this inside with all the shades drawn." All of us who have migraine suffer not only from the attacks themselves but from this common conviction that we are perversely refusing to cure ourselves by taking a couple of aspirin, that we are making ourselves sick, that we "bring it on ourselves." And in the most immediate sense, the sense of why we have a headache this Tuesday and not last Thursday, of course we often do. There certainly is what doctors call a "migraine personality," and that personality tends to be ambitious, inward, intolerant of error, rather rigidly organized, perfectionist. "You don't look like a migraine personality," a doctor once said to me. "Your hair's messy. But I suppose you're a compulsive housekeeper." Actually my house is kept even more negligently than my hair, but the doctor was right nonetheless: perfectionism can also take the form of spending most of a week writing and rewriting and not writing a single paragraph.

But not all perfectionists have migraine, and not all 7 migrainous people have migraine personalities. We do not escape heredity. I have tried in most of the available ways to escape my own migrainous heredity (at one point I learned to give myself two daily injections of histamine with a hypodermic needle, even though the needle so frightened me that I had to close my eyes when I did it), but I still have migraine. And I have learned now to live with it, learned when to expect it, how to outwit it, even how to regard it, when it does come, as more friend than lodger. We have reached a certain understanding, my migraine and I. It never comes when I am in real trouble. Tell me that my house is burned down, my husband has left me, that there is gunfighting in the streets and panic in the banks, and I will not respond by getting a headache. It comes instead when I am fighting not an open but a guerrilla war with my own life, during weeks of small household confusions, lost laundry, unhappy help, canceled appointments, on days when the telephone rings too much and I get no work done and the wind is coming up. On days like that my friend comes uninvited.

And once it comes, now that I am wise in its ways, I no longer fight it. I lie down and let it happen. At first every small apprehension is magnified, every anxiety a pounding terror. Then the pain comes, and I concentrate only on that. Right there is the usefulness of migraine, there in that imposed yoga, the concentration on the pain. For when the pain recedes, ten or twelve hours later, everything goes with it, all the hidden resentments, all the vain anxieties. The migraine has acted as a circuit breaker, and the fuses have emerged intact. There is a pleasant convalescent euphoria. I open the windows and feel the air, eat gratefully, sleep well. I notice the particular nature of a flower in a glass on the stair landing. I count my blessings.

◆

For Study and Discussion

QUESTIONS ABOUT PURPOSE

1. What popular misconceptions about migraine headaches does Didion want to correct?

2. What *emotional* and *physical* responses does she emphasize in her definition?
3. What *intellectual* response does she have toward her own migraines?

QUESTIONS ABOUT AUDIENCE

1. Why might a person who has never had a migraine headache want to read this essay?
2. What could a person who has migraine headaches gain from reading this essay?
3. What experiences might readers have had that would help them to sympathize with Didion's descriptions of migraine headaches?

QUESTIONS ABOUT STRATEGIES

1. What is the effect of Didion's using an "I" narrator in the essay?
2. Why does she switch from "I" in paragraph 4? What is the effect?
3. Analyze how Didion conveys the experience of relief from the headache in the last four sentences of paragraph 8.

QUESTIONS FOR DISCUSSION

1. Trying to define a private experience so that someone else can understand it is a difficult task. Do you think Didion succeeds? If so, why?
2. How does Didion employ the strategies of a creative writer in this essay?
3. If you enjoyed reading this essay, do you think you did so mainly because of the topic or mainly because of Didion's writing style? Or both?

Definition as a Writing Strategy

POINTS TO CONSIDER

1. What is your purpose in writing a definition? Do you want to explain, persuade, entertain, or instruct? Keep your purpose in mind as you write your first draft, and when you finish, reread it with that purpose in mind. Have you given your readers enough information for them to have a clear picture and good understanding of the topic you have defined?

2. Who is your audience and why are they reading your definition? How much do they already know about your topic? What is their vocabulary level and what kinds of references and allusions will they recognize? What strategies for definition are most likely to hold your readers' attention?

3. Is the term you have chosen to define narrow enough so that you can say something significant about it in a thousand words or less? Writers who try to define broad terms like *self-actualization, virtue,* or *truth* in a short paper will almost surely produce a superficial essay.

PREWRITING EXERCISES

1. As you walk around your campus, take notes on how people are dressed. Can you identify a student dress style? A professor's style? Do you recognize certain garments that some groups wear as a way of defining themselves? What kinds of garments define specific groups?

2. Form a group with three or four of your fellow writers and ask one person to serve as recorder. Then, as a group, brainstorm about the essential characteristics of something familiar to all of you—for instance, a good

hamburger, a good place to drink beer, a good country western band, or a good place to ski. See if you can arrive at a common definition of your topic; then discuss how that definition might be used as part of a larger piece of writing.

3. Write without stopping for fifteen minutes, putting down everything you can think of about one topic. For example, write about scuba diving, racquet ball, motorcycles, tending bar, poodles, Arabian horses, TV commercials, or anything else you are interested in. When you finish, decide how much of your material could be used for a definition.

4. Write down the beginning of several sentences in which you compare one thing with another; then read the beginnings over several times to see if some analogies occur to you. One such analogy might be, "To team owners, professional football players are like pieces of equipment." Another might be, "The human body is a complicated machine." Here are some beginnings you might experiment with:

> Driving an eighteen-wheel trailer-tractor truck is like ———.
> Going to college on an athletic scholarship is like
>
> ———.
> Riding the New York subway is like ———.

5. Think of examples of anecdotes, both personal and public, that you could use as illustrations that would help to define these concepts:

a high-stress job	a healthy lifestyle
a funny movie	a champion athlete
a liberated woman	a successful politician
a racist	a dying town

TOPICS FOR WRITING IN CLASS

1. If you have a job or have had one recently, write a definition of your job. Analyze your responsibilities, give examples of what you do on the job, list the

characteristics a person needs to do the job well, and show the purpose of the job for both you and the employer.

2. Write a paragraph defining the audience for which you would write one of the papers suggested under Topics for Writing out of Class. How large would the audience be, how old would they be, what would be the average level of education, what information about the topic could you assume, and what would the audience expect to get from reading your paper?

3. Define your favorite recreation or sport by writing a short paper that answers these questions:

> *What* is it? That is, what is the principal activity involved?
> *Why* do people engage in it? For exercise, entertainment, competition, or what?
> *When* does it happen?
> *Where* does it happen?
> *Who* engages in it?
> *How* is it done? *How much* does it cost?

TOPICS FOR WRITING OUT OF CLASS

1. Write an essay in which you use Judy Syfers's technique of listing functions to define a social role. For example, you might write "I Want a Husband" or "I Want a Mother" and describe all the functions our society seems to expect of a husband or mother. Try to follow Syfers's practice of not using any pronouns or other words that indicate gender. Use description and narration to help your reader visualize the role you are defining.

2. Write an essay that defines a chronic ailment that affects millions of people—for example, arthritis, low blood sugar, diabetes, epilepsy, depression, or alcoholism. Explain *who* has it, *what* its symptoms are, *when* it is most likely to occur, *why* people have it, *how* it affects people, *how* one treats it, and perhaps *how*

people respond to it. If necessary, do some research and talk to people who know about the disease. Use anecdotes and examples to illustrate your points.

3. Study the methods Tom Wolfe uses to define an "ineffable quality," that is, one that cannot be expressed in words. Then write a paper in which you use some of Wolfe's methods to illustrate a hard-to-define quality that you admire. Some possible qualities are:

class	charisma
chutzpah	style
pizzaz	backbone
character	chic
charm	integrity

CAUSE AND EFFECT

DEFINITION

Cause and effect writing (or "causal analysis") is a basic form of exposition that attempts to explain relationships and to answer that most elemental of human questions: "Why?" In all cultures people want to understand the reasons underlying events or behavior; in seeking those reasons people sometimes created myths or superstitions to serve as explanations. In modern times, however, most people attempt to discover and understand causes by means of systematic investigation or reasoning. Such investigations have provided the basis for science and technology and have yielded information that has helped human beings comprehend and control their world. Causal analysis is a primary ingredient in many kinds of writing: scientific, economic, educational, commercial, political—even fictional.

PURPOSE

Of the several purposes that cause and effect writing can serve, the most important is to *inform and educate*. Informative cause and effect writing is important because it helps people to understand their world better, and often they can control events if they understand causes. Much writing about behavior, the environment, natural resources, or the economy is actually written to encourage control.

Another kind of causal analysis is *primarily speculative*. In this kind of writing an author hypothesizes about what factors may be causing certain events or what the consequences of certain actions may be. Writers for newspapers and magazines often use this pattern, picking out a topic of interest, like divorce or inflation, and speculating about why it occurs or what problems it causes. Such writing may be informative or entertaining or both.

A third major purpose of cause and effect writing is to provide *the basis for argument*. Writers point out causal relationships as they try to persuade their readers to approve or disapprove of something. They can argue positively by asserting that certain courses of action will produce good results, or they can argue negatively by claiming that whatever it is they seek to change—an institution, a custom, a law—produces bad results. Much writing about politics, obviously, serves this purpose.

AUDIENCE

Writers can assume that almost everyone is interested in reading about cause and effect because most people are curious about what goes on in the world around them. Because they don't want to think that the world is chaotic and unpredictable, people seek reasons for what they see happening, and they wonder about the connections between the past and the future. Within this large audience, however, several special groups have specific interests that writers of causal analysis need to consider.

One major group of readers are intellectually curious people who want to know how things work and why people behave as they do. They will read explanatory essays about the relationship between air pollutants and skin disease as readily as they will read speculative essays about the causes of voter apathy. These readers are a pleasure to write for because they enjoy expanding their store of information, but the cautious writer knows that this informed audience will be skeptical about oversimplified causal analysis.

Another group who read about cause and effect are those who want to learn how to solve problems and thus gain better control over their lives and their environment. They might be reading to find ways to improve their health through better nutrition, or they might be reading to find out what kinds of child-rearing practices are most likely to promote good parent-child relationships. Authors who write to this audience must remember that these serious-minded readers want responsible answers to their questions. For them, a writer needs to present a rational and well-supported causal analysis.

A third group reads to find out more about cause and effect relationships in the past or in order to learn about investigations that have taken place. This group includes people who read history and biography and articles of social and political analysis; it also includes readers who are interested in explanations of important theories in the physical and behavioral sciences. Writers who write for this audience need to demonstrate their competence in the subjects about which they are writing.

STRATEGIES

Writers may choose among a number of strategies when they write about cause and effect. The simplest one is to describe an action or event and then show what its consequences were. People who write case studies in psychology or social work use this strategy. Marie Winn also uses it in "The Plug-in Drug" when she tells the reader how many hours a week young children spend watching television and then points out the consequences.

Another favorite strategy of authors who write causal analysis is to identify an important problem and examine events or situations that may have caused it. Berton Roueche does this in "The Causes of Alcoholism" when he explains various circumstances that make people become alcoholics.

Conversely, a writer sometimes begins a cause and effect essay by isolating an effect and then looking for plausible explanations of what caused it. E. M. Forster follows this strategy in "My Wood," an essay in which he writes about the changes he noticed in himself after he bought several acres of woods. In writing this kind of essay, the writer must be careful to distinguish between the DIRECT or SIMPLE CAUSE and the INDIRECT and COMPLEX CAUSES. In his essay "Dressing Down" John Brooks examines and then refutes several oversimplified explanations of the jeans phenomenon before offering his own analysis of this curious event in the history of fashion.

Another way to approach cause and effect writing is to focus on two apparently related phenomena and speculate whether there might be a cause and effect connection between them. Such speculation is risky, and the writer who indulges in it should be prepared to back it with a strong and supported argument. Nevertheless, this kind of hypothesizing can be fruitful and enlightening; it is essentially what Ellen Goodman is doing in "The Chem 20 Factor."

There are still other ways to write about cause and

effect; the ones given here are by no means the only strategies that writers can use. In order to be effective and responsible, however, all strategies should meet the following criteria:

First, *the writer should not overstate his or her case.* When writing about complex situations, particularly those that involve people, a writer does best to say, "X will *probably* cause Y" or "A *seems* to be the effect of B" rather than insist that there must be a necessary and direct causal connection between two events. Many plausible cause and effect relationships are difficult to prove conclusively, and the writer who does not claim too much in such instances makes the best impression.

Second, *the writer should not oversimplify cause and effect relationships.* Seldom does an important effect result from a simple and direct cause. For instance, if 15 percent fewer people died of heart attacks in the 1970s than in the 1960s, a researcher should assume that many factors contributed to the decline, not that one element was the cause. Furthermore, most happenings of any significance have more than one effect, and any cause or event may be only one link in a long chain of causes and events. Wise writers qualify their assertions in cause and effect writing with phrases like "a major cause," "one result," and "an immediate effect."

Third, *the careful writer does not mistake coincidence or simple sequence for a necessary cause and effect relationship.* The fact that the crime rate in a state rose the year after the legal drinking age was lowered to eighteen does not mean that there is a direct connection between the two occurrences. An investigator who wanted to prove such a causal relationship would need much more data. The person who jumps to conclusions about cause and effect too quickly often commits the *"false cause"* or *"after this, therefore because of this"* fallacy.

These cautions do not, however, mean that writers should refrain from drawing conclusions about cause and effect until they are absolutely sure of their ground. It is not always possible or wise to wait for complete certainty before writing an analysis of what has happened or a forecast of what may happen. The best any writer can do is to observe carefully and speculate intelligently. That is what the authors of the following essays have done.

The Chem 20 Factor

ELLEN GOODMAN

———— ◆ ————

Ellen Goodman was born in 1941 in Newton, Massa-
chusetts, and educated at Radcliffe College. After
graduation she worked as a researcher and reporter
for Newsweek *magazine, then as a feature writer for*
the Detroit Free Press, *before assuming the position of*
feature writer and columnist for the Boston Globe.
Since 1976 her columns have been syndicated by the
Washington Post Writers Group. In 1980 Goodman
was awarded a Pulitzer Prize in journalism for dis-
tinguished commentary. Many of her columns are
collected in Close to Home *(1979),* At Large *(1980),*
and Turning Points *(1983). In "The Chem 20 Factor,"*
taken from Close to Home, *Goodman argues that the*
atmosphere in one college chemistry course "causes"
the competitive drive in the medical profession.

When I was in college, there was an infamous course 1
known as Chem 20. Organic chemistry was the sieve into
which was poured every premedical student in the university. But only those who came through it with an A
or B could reasonably expect to get into medical school.

Chem 20, therefore, became a psychological laboratory 2
of pre-med anxiety. Every class was a combat mission.
Each grade was a life-or-death matter. It reeked of Olympian anguish and Olympic competitiveness. It taught people whose goal in life was the relief of pain and suffering
that only the fittest, the most single-minded, would
survive.

I remember Chem 20 whenever I read about President 3
Carter's outrage at the medical establishment, or when
someone sardonically points out yet another M.D. plate
on yet another Mercedes Benz, or when the National
Council on Wage and Price Stability points out that the
median income of doctors—$63,000 in 1976—has risen
faster than any other group. In short, at times when other
people talk about the M.D. as a license to make money, I
think of the Chem 20 factor.

I know that we regard doctors as altruistic when they 4
are treating us and avaricious when they are billing us.
But I don't think we can understand the end result—high
fees—unless we understand the process of selection and
even self-selection by which people actually do become
doctors.

On the whole, doctors made a commitment to go into 5
medicine when they were eighteen or nineteen years old,
with the full knowledge that they wouldn't be "practicing" until they were thirty or older. In a "Now Society," they would hold the record among their peers for
delayed gratification. The sort of laid-back, noncompeti-
tive person who wants to "live in the Moment" would
drop out of Chem 20 with an acute case of culture shock
in a week.

It is the dedicated or the narrow-minded (choose one 6
from column A) who go through college competing for
medical school and go through medical school competing
for a good internship and go through internship competing
for a good residency.

Today, residency is not the financial hardship it was 7
when most practicing doctors in this country were young.
The magazine *Hospital Physician* says that the average
doctor in training earns $12,500 to $15,000. But it is still
basically an emotionalized physical-endurance contest.

It is normal for a young doctor to work an eighty- 8
hour week. It is normal to work every other night and
every other weekend. It is normal to be cut off for ten
years from anything approaching a rich personal life. It

is normal to come to regard the world as a hierarchy and a ladder to be climbed. It is, after all, the Chem 20 factor.

While there are thousands of others who work long hours just to keep a toehold in solvency, there is no other professional training that is comparable in terms of sheer stress. So, many of the doctors are sustained through this training by one vision: the Big Payoff. In this society, the Big Payoff is traditionally translated into dollars. 9

The end result of the training process is doctors who are often as addicted to work as patients to morphine. And doctors who have come to genuinely believe that they are "worth" whatever fees they can charge because they "worked for it." 10

I suspect that they are searching—sometimes desperately, and often futilely—for a return on the real investment they have made: their twenties. 11

So, the government may be right when its says that medical fees are spiraling because there is no free-market economy in doctors. The law of supply and demand doesn't work very well in medicine. 12

But this is only half of the story. If they want to see the psychological side, they have to go deeper, further, back to where the system begins—back as far as Chem 20. 13

The course is still being given. Only these days, I hear, there are pre-med students who won't even share their notes. 14

◆

For Study and Discussion

QUESTIONS ABOUT PURPOSE

1. According to Goodman, what lasting effect does taking Chem 20 have on students who complete the course successfully?
2. What sequence of causes and effects is Goodman trying to establish in the essay?

3. What change in attitudes about doctors do you think Goodman wants to bring about in her audience? Does she succeed?

QUESTIONS ABOUT AUDIENCE

1. Do most college freshmen have preconceptions about organic chemistry? What are they?
2. Goodman writes her syndicated column for a general newspaper-reading audience. What kinds of readers in that audience would probably respond favorably to this article?
3. What varied kinds of responses would you expect a young college audience to have after reading this article?

QUESTIONS ABOUT STRATEGIES

1. Why does Goodman use the phrases *combat mission, life-or-death,* and *Olympian* in paragraph 2?
2. What specific examples does Goodman use to trace the stages that a doctor goes through during the years between taking Chem 20 and becoming a highly paid specialist?
3. What techniques does Goodman use to enlist the audience's sympathies for medical students and doctors?

QUESTIONS FOR DISCUSSION

1. How convincing is Goodman's theory about why medical doctors in our society are very well paid?
2. Is there usually a direct correlation between the amount of time and effort professionals invest in their education and the rewards they receive? What examples can you think of?
3. Do you know of any other college course that serves as a screening or testing device for students planning to go into a profession? What is it and how does it act as a screen?

My Wood

E. M. FORSTER

◆

E(dward) M(organ) Forster (1879–1970) was born in London, England, and was educated at King's College, Cambridge. In the early decades of this century he lived and wrote in Greece and Italy. After World War I he moved to India to serve as private secretary to the Maharajah of Dewas State Senior. That experience enabled him to write A Passage to India *(1924), a novel that earned him enough royalties to purchase a small estate in England, where he lived until his death. Forster wrote five other novels—* Where Angels Fear to Tread *(1905),* The Longest Journey *(1907),* A Room With A View *(1908),* Howards End *(1910), and* Maurice *(posthumous)—and several collections of short fiction and literary criticism, the most famous of which is* Aspects of the Novel *(1927). In "My Wood" (from* Abinger Harvest, *1936) he provides a humorous portrait of the "effect of property upon character."*

A few years ago I wrote a book which dealt in part with the difficulties of the English in India. Feeling that they would have had no difficulties in India themselves, the Americans read the book freely. The more they read it the better it made them feel, and a cheque to the author was the result. I bought a wood with the cheque. It is not a large wood—it contains scarcely any trees, and it is intersected, blast it, by a public footpath. Still, it is the first property that I have owned, so it is right that other people should participate in my shame, and should ask themselves, 1 in accents that will vary in horror, this very important question: What is the effect of property upon the character? Don't let's touch economics; the effect of private ownership upon the community as a whole is another question—a more important question, perhaps, but another one. Let's keep to psychology. If you own things, what's their effect on you? What's the effect on me of my wood?

In the first place, it makes me feel heavy. Property does have this effect. Property produces men of weight, and it was a man of weight who failed to get into the Kingdom of Heaven. He was not wicked, that unfortunate millionaire in the parable, he was only stout; he stuck out in front, not to mention behind, and as he wedged himself this way and that in the crystalline entrance and bruised his well-fed flanks, he saw beneath him a comparatively slim camel passing through the eye of a needle and being woven into the robe of God. The Gospels all through couple stoutness and slowness. They point out what is perfectly obvious, yet seldom realized: that if you have a lot of things you cannot move about a lot, that furniture requires dusting, dusters require servants, servants require insurance stamps, and the whole tangle of them makes you think twice before you accept an invitation to dinner or go for a bathe in the Jordan. Sometimes the Gospels proceed further and say with Tolstoy that property is sinful; they approach the difficult ground of asceticism here, where I cannot follow them. But as to the immediate effects of property on people, they just show straightforward logic. It produces men of weight. Men of weight cannot, by definition, move like the lightning from the East unto the West, and the ascent of a fourteen-stone bishop into a pulpit is thus the exact antithesis of the coming of the Son of Man. My wood makes me feel heavy. 2

In the second place, it makes me feel it ought to be larger. 3

The other day I heard a twig snap in it. I was annoyed at first, for I thought that someone was blackberrying, and 4 depreciating the value of the undergrowth. On coming nearer, I saw it was not a man who had trodden on the twig and snapped it, but a bird, and I felt pleased. My bird. The bird was not equally pleased. Ignoring the relation between us, it took fright as soon as it saw the shape of my face, and flew straight over the boundary hedge into a field, the property of Mrs. Henessy, where it sat down with a loud squawk. It had become Mrs. Henessy's bird. Something seemed grossly amiss here, something that would not have occurred had the wood been larger. I could not afford to buy Mrs. Henessy out, I dared not murder her, and limitations of this sort beset me on every side. . . .

In the third place, property makes its owner feel that 5 he ought to do something to it. Yet he isn't sure what. A restlessness comes over him, a vague sense that he has a personality to express—the same sense which, without any vagueness, leads the artist to an act of creation. Sometimes I think I will cut down such trees as remain in the wood, at other times I want to fill up the gaps between them with new trees. Both impulses are pretentious and empty. They are not honest movements towards money-making or beauty. They spring from a foolish desire to express myself and from an inability to enjoy what I have got. Creation, property, enjoyment form a sinister trinity in the human mind. Creation and enjoyment are both very, very good, yet they are often unattainable without a material basis, and at such moments property pushes itself in as a substitute, saying, "Accept me instead—I'm good enough for all three." It is not enough. It is, as Shakespeare said of lust, "The expense of spirit in a waste of shame": it is "Before, a joy proposed; behind, a dream." Yet we don't know how to shun it. It is forced on us by our economic system as the alternative to starvation. It is also forced on us by an internal defect in the soul, by the feeling that in property may lie the germs of self-development and of exquisite or heroic deeds. Our life on earth is, and ought to be, material and carnal. But we have not yet learned to manage our materialism and carnality

properly; they are still entangled with the desire for ownership, where (in the words of Dante) "Possession is one
with loss."

And this brings us to our fourth and final point: the   6
blackberries.

Blackberries are not plentiful in this meagre grove, but   7
they are easily seen from the public footpath which tra-
verses it, and all too easily gathered. Foxgloves, too—people will pull up the foxgloves, and ladies of an educational
tendency even grub for toadstools to show them on the
Monday in class. Other ladies, less educated, roll down
the bracken in the arms of their gentlemen friends. There
is paper, there are tins. Pray, does my wood belong to me
or doesn't it? And, if it does, should I not own it best by
allowing no one else to walk there? There is a wood near
Lyme Regis, also cursed by a public footpath, where the
owner has not hesitated on this point. He had built high
stone walls each side of the path, and has spanned it by
bridges, so that the public circulate like termites while he
gorges on the blackberries unseen. He really does own his
wood, this able chap. And perhaps I shall come to this
in time. I shall wall in and fence out until I really taste
the sweets of property. Enormously stout, endlessly avaricious, pseudo-creative, intensely selfish, I shall weave
upon my forehead the quadruple crown of possession until
those nasty Bolshies come and take it off again and thrust
me aside into the outer darkness.

◆

For Study and Discussion

QUESTIONS ABOUT PURPOSE

1. Why does Forster write about the effects that buying a
    piece of land has on a person's character instead of
    writing about the effects that making money has on a
    person's character? How are the two different?

2. What response do you think Forster wants to encourage among people who are thinking of buying property?

3. Do you get the impression that Forster is apologizing for the effects that owning land has had on him? Why should he apologize?

QUESTIONS ABOUT AUDIENCE

1. What kind of people does Forster seem to think might criticize him for owning property?

2. How would the assumptions and attitudes of American readers in the 1980s probably be similar to those of English readers of the 1920s, when this essay was written? How would they probably be different?

3. How do you think people who own a large amount of property would react to this essay? Would they understand Forster's concerns?

QUESTIONS ABOUT STRATEGIES

1. Using his own experience as a basis, Forster generalizes about the effects on a person of owning property. Do you think he is justified in making his generalizations?

2. How does he use the bird and the blackberries to illustrate how his wood makes him feel possessive?

3. How does he use anecdotes and phrases to give the essay a light-hearted rather than a serious tone?

QUESTIONS FOR DISCUSSION

1. What groups of people have historically claimed that owning private property has undesirable effects?

2. What effects do you think most people expect that owning property will have on them?

3. Is owning things likely to hamper a person's creativity? Why or why not?

Dressing Down

JOHN BROOKS

◆

John Brooks was born in 1920 in New York City and educated at Princeton University. He began his writing career as a contributing editor for Time *magazine but soon became a regular contributor to* The New Yorker. *Brooks's particular skill as a writer resides in his ability to present factual information in an engaging and entertaining style. He has written three novels—*The Big Wheel *(1949),* A Pride of Lions *(1954), and* The Man Who Broke Things *(1958)—but he is at his best reporting on the social and cultural history of American business. His books include* The Seven Fat Years: Chronicles of Wall Street *(1958),* The Fate of the Edsel and Other Business Adventures *(1963), and* Telephone: The First Hundred Years *(1976). His most recent book,* Showing Off in America *(1981), tests sociologist Thorstein Veblen's theories about the American leisure class as they apply to contemporary culture. In "Dressing Down," a chapter from that book, Brooks analyzes the causes and effects of the various stages of the blue jeans phenomenon.*

We come now to the American blue jeans phenomenon, in many ways a pocket summary of the American style of showing off eighty years after Veblen.

Beyond doubt, the jeans phenomenon is a seismic event in the history of dress, and not only in the United States. Indeed, the habit of wearing jeans is—along with the computer, the copying machine, rock music, polio vaccine, and the hydrogen bomb—one of the major contributions of the United States to the postwar world at large.

from *Genoese* and as having originally meant a twilled cotton cloth made in Genoa. The indigo dye that gives blue jeans their characteristic color and tendency to fade is synthetic now, but its prototype, natural dye prepared from the leaves of various plants, has played a rich role in world clothing history, going back to the earliest recorded times.

However, it is unlikely that the hundreds of millions who took up blue jeans in the nineteen-fifties and -sixties were responding to an atavistic urge for denim or for indigo. More plausibly—in the United States, at least—they were to one extent or another making a small, intensely personal, apparently harmless, and surely only partly conscious protest against the sense of powerlessness, impersonality, and regimentation that descended on the country at the time when space vehicles, pesticides, the hydrogen bomb, urban sprawl, and the computer were comparatively new, and when organizations seemed on the way to taking permanent charge of American life, not merely American work, in most places and at nearly all economic levels. We have remarked that impersonality and regimentation infiltrated the clothing styles of the nineteen-fifties. Even schoolchildren—other than those in a few big-city progressive schools, which were regarded in most quarters as somewhere between harmlessly aberrant and downright subversive—were required by parents and school authorities to dress in uniform, often literally. The importance of the requirements, and the anxiety inspired by the possibility of their being defied, is forcefully suggested by the situation in Wisconsin, where for a number of years boys in both public and private schools were prohibited from wearing blue jeans in school, with the sole exception of certifiable members of farm families, who could presumably wear jeans without meaning anything by it.

In a whole galaxy of ways jeans conformed to, and expressed with almost magical precision, the new view of human life that began emerging among young Americans in the late nineteen-fifties and the early nineteen-

8

9

Before the nineteen-fifties, jeans were worn, principally in the West and Southwest of the United States, by children, farmers, manual laborers when on the job, and, of course, cowboys. There were isolated exceptions—for example, artists of both sexes took to blue jeans in and around Santa Fe, New Mexico, in the nineteen-twenties and -thirties; around 1940, the male students at Williams College took them up as a mark of differentiation from the chino-wearing snobs of Yale and Princeton; and in the late forties the female students of Bennington College (not far from Williams) adopted them as a virtual uniform, though only for wear on campus—but it was not until the nineteen-fifties, when James Dean and Marlon Brando wore jeans in movies about youth in revolt against parents and society, when John Wayne wore them in movies about untrammeled heroes in a lawless Old West, and when many schools from coast to coast gave their new symbolism a boost by banning them as inappropriate for classrooms, that jeans acquired the ideological baggage necessary to propel them to national fame.

After that, though, fame came quickly, and it was not long before young Americans—whether to express social dissent, to enjoy comfort, or to emulate their peers—had become so attached to their jeans that some hardly ever took them off. According to a jeans authority, a young man in the North Bronx with a large and indulgent family attained some sort of record by continuously wearing the same pair of jeans, even for bathing and sleeping, for over eight months. Eventually, as all the world knows, the popularity of jeans spread from cowboys and anomic youths to adult Americans of virtually every age and sociopolitical posture, conspicuously including Jimmy Carter when he was a candidate for the presidency. Trucks containing jeans came to rank as one of the three leading targets of hijackers, along with those containing liquor and cigarettes. Estimates of jeans sales in the United States vary wildly, chiefly because the line between jeans and slacks has come to be a fuzzy one. According to the

3

4

most conservative figures, put out by the leading jeans manufacturer, Levi Strauss & Company, of San Francisco, annual sales of jeans of all kinds in the United States by all manufacturers in 1957 stood at around a hundred and fifty million pairs, while for 1977 they came to over five hundred million, or considerably more than two pairs for every man, woman, and child in the country.

Overseas, jeans had to wait slightly longer for their time to come. American Western movies and the example of American servicemen from the West and Southwest stationed abroad who, as soon as the Second World War ended, changed directly from their service uniforms into blue jeans bought at post exchanges started a fad for them among Europeans in the late nineteen-forties. But the fad remained a small one, partly because of the unavailability of jeans in any quantity; in those days, European customers considered jeans ersatz unless they came from the United States, while United States jeans manufacturers were inclined to be satisfied with a reliable domestic market. Being perennially short of denim, the rough, durable, naturally shrink-and-stretch cotton twill of which basic jeans are made, they were reluctant or unable to undertake overseas expansion.

Gradually, though, denim production in the United States increased, and meanwhile demand for American-made jeans became so overwhelming that in parts of Europe a black market for them developed. American jeans manufacturers began exporting their product in a serious way in the early nineteen-sixties. At first, demand was greatest in Germany, France, England, and the Benelux nations; later it spread to Italy, Spain, and Scandinavia, and eventually to Latin America and the Far East. By 1967, jeans authorities estimate, a hundred and ninety million pairs of jeans were being sold annually outside the United States; of these, all but a small fraction were of local manufacture, and not imports from the United States, although American-made jeans were still so avidly

5

6

sought after that some of the local products were bla[ ] counterfeits of the leading American brands, comp[ ] with expertly faked labels. In the late nineteen-sevent[ ] estimated jeans sales outside the United States had doub[ ] in a decade, to three hundred and eighty million pairs, [ ] which perhaps a quarter were now made by America[ ] firms in plants abroad; the markets in Europe, Mexic[ ] Japan, Australia, and other places had come so close to th[ ] saturation point that the fastest-growing jeans market wa[ ] probably Brazil; Princess Anne, of Great Britain, and Princess Caroline, of Monaco, had been photographed wearing jeans, and King Hussein of Jordan was reported to wear them at home in his palace; the counterfeiting of American brands was a huge international undertaking, which the leading American manufacturers combated with world-ranging security operations. In Russia, authentic American Levi's were a black-market item regularly commanding eighty or more dollars per pair. All in all, it is now beyond doubt that in size and scope the rapid global spread of the habit of wearing blue jeans, however it may be explained, is an event without precedent in the history of human attire. But not without explanation in Veblenian theory[ ]

In no sense and in no particular could blue jeans [ ] to be new; in fact, the essence of their popularity [ ] that, in contrast with the characteristic products [ ] ion, they are not new and do not claim to be. [ ] that led the way in sweeping first the Unite[ ] then the world—the straight-leg, cotton-[ ] riveted jeans made by Levi Strauss and c[ ] on sale, with only minor variations fr[ ] style, in 1873. The word *denim* is a [ ] British, of *serge de Nîmes*—the city [ ] France, having been the place wh[ ] tionally produced; the earliest [ ] *Oxford English Dictionary* is [ ] traces the term *jean* back to [ ]

Before the nineteen-fifties, jeans were worn, principally ³ in the West and Southwest of the United States, by children, farmers, manual laborers when on the job, and, of course, cowboys. There were isolated exceptions—for example, artists of both sexes took to blue jeans in and around Santa Fe, New Mexico, in the nineteen-twenties and -thirties; around 1940, the male students at Williams College took them up as a mark of differentiation from the chino-wearing snobs of Yale and Princeton; and in the late forties the female students of Bennington College (not far from Williams) adopted them as a virtual uniform, though only for wear on campus—but it was not until the nineteen-fifties, when James Dean and Marlon Brando wore jeans in movies about youth in revolt against parents and society, when John Wayne wore them in movies about untrammeled heroes in a lawless Old West, and when many schools from coast to coast gave their new symbolism a boost by banning them as inappropriate for classrooms, that jeans acquired the ideological baggage necessary to propel them to national fame.

After that, though, fame came quickly, and it was not ⁴ long before young Americans—whether to express social dissent, to enjoy comfort, or to emulate their peers—had become so attached to their jeans that some hardly ever took them off. According to a jeans authority, a young man in the North Bronx with a large and indulgent family attained some sort of record by continuously wearing the same pair of jeans, even for bathing and sleeping, for over eight months. Eventually, as all the world knows, the popularity of jeans spread from cowboys and anomic youths to adult Americans of virtually every age and sociopolitical posture, conspicuously including Jimmy Carter when he was a candidate for the presidency. Trucks containing jeans came to rank as one of the three leading targets of hijackers, along with those containing liquor and cigarettes. Estimates of jeans sales in the United States vary wildly, chiefly because the line between jeans and slacks has come to be a fuzzy one. According to the most conservative figures, put out by the leading jeans manufacturer, Levi Strauss & Company, of San Francisco, annual sales of jeans of all kinds in the United States by all manufacturers in 1957 stood at around a hundred and fifty million pairs, while for 1977 they came to over five hundred million, or considerably more than two pairs for every man, woman, and child in the country.

Overseas, jeans had to wait slightly longer for their time to come. American Western movies and the example of American servicemen from the West and Southwest stationed abroad who, as soon as the Second World War ended, changed directly from their service uniforms into blue jeans bought at post exchanges started a fad for them among Europeans in the late nineteen-forties. But the fad remained a small one, partly because of the unavailability of jeans in any quantity; in those days, European customers considered jeans ersatz unless they came from the United States, while United States jeans manufacturers were inclined to be satisfied with a reliable domestic market. Being perennially short of denim, the rough, durable, naturally shrink-and-stretch cotton twill of which basic jeans are made, they were reluctant or unable to undertake overseas expansion.

Gradually, though, denim production in the United States increased, and meanwhile demand for American-made jeans became so overwhelming that in parts of Europe a black market for them developed. American jeans manufacturers began exporting their product in a serious way in the early nineteen-sixties. At first, demand was greatest in Germany, France, England, and the Benelux nations; later it spread to Italy, Spain, and Scandinavia, and eventually to Latin America and the Far East. By 1967, jeans authorities estimate, a hundred and ninety million pairs of jeans were being sold annually outside the United States; of these, all but a small fraction were of local manufacture, and not imports from the United States, although American-made jeans were still so avidly sought after that some of the local products were blatant counterfeits of the leading American brands, complete with expertly faked labels. In the late nineteen-seventies, estimated jeans sales outside the United States had doubled in a decade, to three hundred and eighty million pairs, of which perhaps a quarter were now made by American firms in plants abroad; the markets in Europe, Mexico, Japan, Australia, and other places had come so close to the saturation point that the fastest-growing jeans market was probably Brazil; Princess Anne, of Great Britain, and Princess Caroline, of Monaco, had been photographed wearing jeans, and King Hussein of Jordan was reported to wear them at home in his palace; the counterfeiting of American brands was a huge international undertaking, which the leading American manufacturers combated with world-ranging security operations. In Russia, authentic American Levi's were a black-market item regularly commanding eighty or more dollars per pair. All in all, it is now beyond doubt that in size and scope the rapid global spread of the habit of wearing blue jeans, however it may be explained, is an event without precedent in the history of human attire. But not without explanation in Veblenian theory.

In no sense and in no particular could blue jeans claim to be new; in fact, the essence of their popularity may be that, in contrast with the characteristic products of fashion, they are not new and do not claim to be. The brand that led the way in sweeping first the United States and then the world—the straight-leg, cotton-denim, copper-riveted jeans made by Levi Strauss and called Levi's—was on sale, with only minor variations from its present-day style, in 1873. The word *denim* is a corruption, originally British, of *serge de Nîmes*—the city of Nîmes, in southern France, having been the place where the fabric was traditionally produced; the earliest reference to *denim* in the *Oxford English Dictionary* is dated 1695. The same source traces the term *jean* back to 1567, identifying it as deriving from *Genoese* and as having originally meant a twilled cotton cloth made in Genoa. The indigo dye that gives blue jeans their characteristic color and tendency to fade is synthetic now, but its prototype, natural dye prepared from the leaves of various plants, has played a rich role in world clothing history, going back to the earliest recorded times.

However, it is unlikely that the hundreds of millions 8 who took up blue jeans in the nineteen-fifties and -sixties were responding to an atavistic urge for denim or for indigo. More plausibly—in the United States, at least— they were to one extent or another making a small, intensely personal, apparently harmless, and surely only partly conscious protest against the sense of powerlessness, impersonality, and regimentation that descended on the country at the time when space vehicles, pesticides, the hydrogen bomb, urban sprawl, and the computer were comparatively new, and when organizations seemed on the way to taking permanent charge of American life, not merely American work, in most places and at nearly all economic levels. We have remarked that impersonality and regimentation infiltrated the clothing styles of the nineteen-fifties. Even schoolchildren—other than those in a few big-city progressive schools, which were regarded in most quarters as somewhere between harmlessly aberrant and downright subversive—were required by parents and school authorities to dress in uniform, often literally. The importance of the requirements, and the anxiety inspired by the possibility of their being defied, is forcefully suggested by the situation in Wisconsin, where for a number of years boys in both public and private schools were prohibited from wearing blue jeans in school, with the single exception of certifiable members of farm families, who could presumably wear jeans without meaning anything by it.

In a whole galaxy of ways jeans conformed to, and ex- 9 emplified with almost magical precision, the new view of American life that began emerging among young Americans of the late nineteen-fifties and the early nineteen-sixties. Jeans' celebrated durability was a challenge to a society in which planned obsolescence, epitomized by the automobile industry's change of models, had (whether the jeans wearers knew it or not) come to be the mainspring of the national economy. Jeans' association with physical labor confronted the trend of a society in which a constantly larger percentage of the work force was in offices and a smaller percentage in factories and on farms. Jeans' proletarian associations by implication criticized the pretensions of the upwardly mobile at a moment of great national upward mobility, and jeans' air of genuineness similarly criticized the artificiality of a society becoming ever more artificial. Beyond all that, jeans lent themselves naturally to the deeper, more personal feelings of the children of American affluence. It came to be dogma among many of those children that their parents' generation had been and was too rigid in defining sex roles, insisting with a certain hysteria on stereotyped differences between boys and girls in such matters as sports, social activities, and clothing. Where Brooks Brothers and Peck & Peck catered to the stereotypes, blue jeans could be worn with equal comfort, physical and psychic, by both sexes. Finally, jeans had a special propensity for shrinking and stretching as they were washed and worn. (That is, the original jeans had, and the original type still has, but now that the popularity of jeans has long since passed from the realm of connoisseurs to that of a mass public a huge majority of the pairs sold are preshrunk.) This propensity made it possible for a pair, sufficiently conditioned, to end up fitting the wearer with a conformity to his or her anatomical idiosyncrasies that could not be matched by the handiwork of the most expert custom tailor. Natural means accomplished what technical proficiency could not; the jeans wearer, in a world of intractable objects that could not be shaped, at last had an object—if only a pair of pants—that would shape itself to his or her measure, rather than he or she to its.

Over the years after jeans' original flowering in the 10

355

nineteen-fifties their symbolism in the United States evolved. In the late nineteen-sixties, they went through a brief period of identification with hippies, the drug subculture, and opposition to the Vietnam War; in the early nineteen-seventies, as they were taken up more and more by older people, they came to stand to some extent for a search for the Fountain of Youth (youth, it is interesting to note, of a sort very different from what the middle-aged wearers had themselves experienced); and in the late seventies, in a polar reversal of their connotations of twenty years earlier, jeans became an important fashion item, purveyed by Yves Saint-Laurent, Geoffrey Beene, Oscar de la Renta, Calvin Klein, Gloria Vanderbilt, and the like, at prices that would shock a cowboy. Of that more later.

Meanwhile, pundits were having their licks at figuring out what it all meant. The explanations that they came up with were essentially three: that jeans-wearing stood for a new and humanized American consciousness; that it symbolized political and social revolt; and that it reflected the achievement, at long last, of the age-old American dream of classlessness. As follows:

1. Charles Reich in *The Greening of America* (1970) made much of blue jeans as one of the hallmarks—along with rock and folk music, community living, psychedelic drugs, unhomogenized peanut butter, and the expression, "Oh, wow!"—of a new American state of mind that he designated as Consciousness III: adherence to "the sensual beauty of a creative, loving, unrepressed life," which he saw as having arisen "out of the strong soil of the American corporate state."

2. The Canadian philosopher Marshall McLuhan summed up the second hypothesis when he said in 1973, "Jeans represent a ripoff and a rage against the Establishment."

3. The American-dream position was summarized in 1978 by Arthur Asa Berger, a professor at San Francisco

State University. He wrote, "Denim's 'rise' in the world is very much a part of the so-called American Dream, which says that anyone can rise in the world if he has enough will-power and a bit of luck. Denim is one more immigrant...which has made good in America." That is to say, denim is squarely in the American tradition rather than in confrontation with it. And denim's "cultural message" is the encouraging one that "work and play have lost their separate identities and are no longer polar opposites." Moreover, denim has contributed to the breaking down of class distinctions: "The professors look like janitors—and quite often the janitors look like professors." More often than not, "denimization reflects an attempt to escape from one's family and class history"—precisely the possibility that the American dream promised in the first place.

On consideration, none of these explanations will quite do. The trouble with Consciousness III is that it has turned out to have been a fad itself—a pipe dream, the product of a momentary euphoria, inevitably attractive only until the passage of time (and not much time) revealed it as hopelessly romantic and utopian. Between 1970 and 1980, community living, "Oh, wow!" psychedelic drugs, and the sensual beauty of a creative life all lost ground sharply—rock music and unhomogenized peanut butter held firm and closed mixed—while jeans continued to soar in national popularity. It would appear they have something going for them other than conduciveness to love and sensuality. 15

The Establishment ripoff theory will not stand even cursory examination. Jeans merchants contend that while jeans did to some extent represent that early in their glory days in the United States, and probably in Canada, too, they soon ceased doing so; moreover, such connotations were never strongly attached to them in Europe, Australia, or the Far East, and in Latin America were attached to them hardly at all. One can only feel that McLuhan— 16 understandably, since he was apparently called upon to give a comment on the telephone, with no time for reflection —missed a chance to use the worldwide proliferation of jeans-wearing as evidence in support of his celebrated notion, introduced in *Understanding Media* in 1964, of the modern world as a "global village" brought into being chiefly by television. Before jeans—and before television —many villages, nations, and even cultures had often adopted clothing fashions more or less unanimously; the whole world had conspicuously never done so.

The "one more immigrant" position— that jeans-wear- 17
ing is a traditional American phenomenon and not a break with the past at all—is appealing but inadequate. If jeans serve to fulfill specifically American ideals, why are they so popular in Hong Kong, Tenerife, and Patagonia? So far as the jeans fad is concerned, denim, on balance, is far more an American emigrant than immigrant.

Therefore let us summon Veblen from the bullpen— 18
Veblen, who lived when jeans were still work clothes, and who may well have worn Levi's quite innocent of social implications in his nineteenth-century youth on his fa-ther's Wisconsin farm. Putting the jeans phenomenon in a test tube with Veblen's theory of clothing fashion, we immediately find a violent reaction taking place. Right at the start we find, in fact, what appears to be a neat and definitive refutation of the theory. As follows:

Veblen's explanation of fashion	Blue jeans 1965
Must be wastefully expensive	Characteristically inexpensive
Must be inconvenient	Quintessentially convenient
Must be unadaptable to physical work; should hinder any useful exertion	Quintessentially adaptable to work; no hindrance

| Must be uncomfort- able, preferably painful | Quintessentially comfortable* |
| Must be worn free of dirt or wear | Most prized when dirty, worn, and faded |

Here, on its face, seems to be the irrefutable *contra-* [19] Veblen—the evidence that either his theory of fashion had been wrong all along or that it had, with the passage of time, become wrong. But something else was going on under the surface, and not far under. In truth, from its very start the postwar explosion of jeans-wearing was not quite so peaceable-savage as its devotees wanted it to appear. The new jeans wearers of the fifties were seldom entirely simple-hearted. They wanted to put other people down—squares, conservatives, school authorities, defenders of corporations, parents, or a combination of these. Stated another way, they wanted to put down the remnants of Veblen's "leisure class," which over the years had ceased to be a class at all and had become a national majority. And in doing so, of course, they were indulging in that classic Veblenian practice, invidiousness.

As the jeans phenomenon matured, and jeans-wearing [20] gradually changed from an act of revolt to one of conformity, *not* wearing them tended to become, in certain circles, an act of revolt subject to potential censure. To invidiousness was thus added that other Veblenian trait,

---

* However, a signal instance of Levi's as a momentarily uncomfortable garment is enshrined in the corporate history of Levi Strauss & Company. In 1933, Walter Haas, Sr., then president of the company, was camping in the Sierra Nevada near Mt. Whitney when he crouched close to a campfire, causing the crotch rivet of his Levi's—a feature of Levi's right from the beginning—to become uncomfortably hot. Haas mentioned his complaint to some professional wranglers who were in the party, and they earnestly and unanimously declared that they had often had the same trouble. Haas, astonished that no one had ever mentioned the problem to him before, decided then and there that the crotch rivet had to go, and, by vote at the next meeting of the board of directors, it went.

emulation. The introduction in the later nineteen-seventies of designer-name jeans as items of fashion represented the last stage of the transformation. Instead of a symbol of disdain for competitive display, jeans-wearing became competitive display itself. Meanwhile, the industrial situation provided a final twist of irony. Jeans—even "status" jeans designed to sell for twice or three times as much as the original product—happen to be cheaper to produce than other forms of pants, since the cut of the garment requires about one-third fewer labor operations. Here, then, was a high-priced, much-in-demand fashion product that could be produced on the cheap. Small wonder that a flood of quick-buck operators rushed into the business, and jeans-making suddenly became the momentary mecca of the predatory-invidious, Veblenian American entrepreneur.

It is time for a new chart.   21

Veblen's explanation of fashion	*"Status" blue jeans 1980*
Must be wastefully expensive	Wastefully expensive
Must signify invidious comparison to others	Signify invidious comparison
Must be worn in emulation of others	Worn in emulation
Must not be associated with physical work	No longer associated with physical work
Must be worn free of dirt or wear	Most prized now when worn clean and new

In fifteen years, the social overtones of jeans-wear- 22
ing had undergone a polar reversal. Belatedly, Veblen had his revenge. And the broad change in the American style of competitive display since 1900—the change from

straightforward display of money to more complex and sophisticated forms of showing off style, acquired sense of taste, and playful irony, which we have seen exemplified in different ways as regards sports, eating, drinking, class aspirations, office manners, and so on—had found in the jeans phenomenon its symbolic event.

———— ◆ ————

For Study and Discussion

QUESTIONS ABOUT PURPOSE

1. "Dressing Down" is from John Brooks's book *Showing Off in America.* Why does Brooks argue that "dressing down"—wearing casual, everyday clothes—is a form of "showing off"?

2. What is the principal point that Brooks is making about the changing role of jeans in America? What has happened to them that their original manufacturers probably didn't anticipate?

3. In particular, how have the last fifteen years of the jeans phenomenon reflected broad changes in American lifestyle? Why is it "a seismic event in the history of dress"?

QUESTIONS ABOUT AUDIENCE

1. What attitudes and preconceptions do you think average, educated readers would have toward jeans before they read this essay?

2. To what extent does Brooks assume that his readers are part of the revolution in fashion that he is analyzing? In particular, what experiences do college readers have that might make this essay more pertinent for them than it would have been for Brooks's original readers?

3. The information that Brooks provides about jeans in paragraphs 7 and 8 and in the footnote on page 359 is probably new to most readers. How might it affect a reader's perspective on the jeans phenomenon—yours, for example?

QUESTIONS ABOUT STRATEGIES

1. How does Brooks use authorities to provide possible explanations of the complex jeans phenomenon? How does he refute these explanations as oversimplifications?
2. How does Brooks use charts of comparison to illustrate Veblen's theory of dress?
3. How does Brooks use his own analysis to interpret the jeans phenomenon so that it corresponds to Veblen's theory of dress? For example, how does his analysis enable him to revise the first chart into the second chart?

QUESTIONS FOR DISCUSSION

1. Thorstein Veblen's *Theory of the Leisure Class* is the primary authority for much of Brooks's analysis in this essay. To what extent does your understanding of the essay depend on your familiarity with Veblen's theories of dress? To what extent does Brooks reveal the gist of Veblen's theory in his essay?
2. What is Brooks suggesting about the nature of American culture when he asserts that "the habit of wearing jeans is—along with the computer, the copying machine, rock music, polio vaccine, and the hydrogen bomb—one of the major contributions of the United States to the postwar world at large"?
3. How does Brooks account for the popularity of jeans overseas? How do the concepts of invidiousness, emulation, and competitive display (or "showing off") account for the global habit of wearing jeans?

The Plug-In Drug

MARIE WINN

———— ◆ ————

Marie Winn was born in 1937 in Czechoslovakia, educated at Radcliffe and Columbia, and lives with her husband and two sons in New York City. She is the author of ten books for children, as well as many articles for The New York Times Magazine *and* The Village Voice. *In* Children Without Childhood *(1983) she examined the shrinking boundaries between childhood and adulthood. The following essay is the introduction to* The Plug-In Drug: Television, Children and Family *(1977). In it Winn analyzes the effects of extensive television watching on the perception of children.*

Concern about the effects of television on children has centered almost exclusively upon the *contents* of the programs children watch. Social scientists and researchers devise experiments Byzantine in complexity and ingenuity to determine whether watching violent programs makes children behave more aggressively, or conversely, whether watching exemplary programs encourages "prosocial" behavior in children. Studies are conducted to discover whether television commercials make children greedy and materialistic or, as some have suggested, generous and spiritual. Investigators seek to discover whether stereo-types on television affect children's ways of thinking, causing them to become prejudiced, or open-minded, or whatever.

The very nature of the television experience, as op- 2
posed to the contents of the programs, is rarely considered except by apocalyptic thinkers of the McLuhan school who focus on the global consequences of the television experience rather than its effects on individual develop-ment. Perhaps the ever-changing array of sights and sounds coming out of the machine—the wild variety of images meeting the eye and the barrage of human and inhuman sounds reaching the ear—fosters the illusion of a varied experience for the viewer. It is easy to overlook a deceptively simple fact: one is always *watching televi-sion* when one is watching television rather than having any other experience.

Whether the program being watched is "Sesame Street" 3
or "Superman," "The Ascent of Man" or "Popeye," there is a similarity of experience about all television watching. Certain specific physiological mechanisms of the eyes, ears, and brain respond to the stimuli emanating from the television screen regardless of the cognitive content of the programs. It is a one-way transaction that requires the tak-ing in of particular sensory material in a particular way, no matter what the material might be. There is, indeed, no other experience in a child's life that permits quite so much intake while demanding so little outflow.

Preschool children are the single largest television audi- 4
ence in America, spending a greater number of total hours and a greater proportion of their waking day watching tele-vision than any other age group. According to one survey made in 1970, children in the 2–5 age group spend an aver-age of 30.4 hours each week watching television, while children in the 6–11 group spend 25.5 hours watching. The weekly average for adult viewers in 1971 was 23.3 hours. Another survey made in 1971 documented a weekly view-ing time of 34.56 hours for preschool boys and 32.44 hours

for preschool girls. Still other surveys suggest figures up to 54 hours a week for preschool viewers. Even the most conservative estimates indicate that preschool children in America are spending more than a third of their waking hours watching television.

What are the effects upon the vulnerable and developing human organism of spending such a significant proportion of each day engaging in this particular experience? How does the television experience affect a child's language development, for instance? How does it influence his developing imagination, his creativity? How does the availability of television affect the ways parents bring up their children? Are new child-rearing strategies being adopted and old ones discarded because the television set is available to parents for relief? Is the child's perception of reality subtly altered by steady exposure to television unrealities? How does watching television for several hours each day affect the child's abilities to form human relationships? What happens to family life as a result of family members' involvement with television? 5

Though there may never be clear-cut and final answers to these questions, the very fact that they are rarely raised, that the experience *qua* experience is rarely considered, signals the distorted view American parents take of the role of television in their children's lives. 6

THE EXPERTS

The child-care experts and advisers American parents have come to depend on, the Dr. Spocks, the Dr. Ginotts, et al., have ignored the television experience almost completely. In spite of the fact that television viewing takes up more of the average child's waking time than any other single activity, most popular child-care manuals devote only a few paragraphs to television, and even those refer exclusively to the content of the programs children are likely to watch. Among the pages and pages on tensional outlets, fears, anxieties, refusal to eat vegetables, and other 7 matters, parents may find only a few banal warnings to monitor their children's television programs for violence or excessive sex. The most influential of child authorities, Dr. Benjamin Spock, makes no mention of the role of television in the lives of preschool children in his famous guide, and he concludes a half-page section on radio and television programs for older children by suggesting that parents not worry too much about their children's involvement with television, just so long as they get their homework done and get to bed on time. "If the rest of the family is driven mad by having to watch or listen to a child's programs and if they can afford the expense," he advises, "it's worth while to get him a set for his room." . . .

Parents themselves, though often deeply troubled about 8
television and its effects upon their children, center their concern on the subject matter of the programs their children watch, rather than on the television experience itself. Their content-centered approach is epitomized by the activities of an increasingly, important parent-lobbyist organization, Action for Children's Television, known as ACT. This organization, formed in 1968 by a group of Boston mothers, grew out of the common anxieties of the founding parents about television: their children were spending too many hours watching television, the mothers agreed, and the violence that seemed to dominate children's programs was appalling. Moreover, the incessant commercial interruptions were making their children crave a variety of shoddy toys and unwholsome foods. . . .

But is it the specific needs of *children* that are at stake 9
when parents demand better programming? Surely the fact that young children watch so much television reflects the needs of *parents* to find a convenient source of amusement for their children and a moment of quiet for themselves. It seems, then, the need of parents to assuage their gnawing anxieties about the possible effects of hours of quiet, passive television watching that underlies their desire to make those hours less overtly repugnant.

The needs of young children are quite different. The 10

developing child needs opportunities to work out of his basic family relationships, thereby coming to understand himself. The television experience only reduces these opportunities.

The child needs to develop a capacity for self-direction 11 in order to liberate himself from dependency. The television experience helps to perpetuate dependency.

The child needs to acquire fundamental skills in com- 12 munication—to learn to read, write, and express himself flexibly and clearly—in order to function as a social creature. The television experience does not further his verbal development because it does not require any verbal participation on his part, merely passive intake.

The child needs to discover his own strengths and 13 weaknesses in order to find fulfillment as an adult in both work and play. Watching television does not lead him to such discoveries; indeed it only limits his involvement in those real-life activities that might offer his abilities a genuine testing ground.

The young child's need for fantasy is gratified far better 14 by his own make-believe activities than by the adult-made fantasies he is offered on television.

The young child's need for intellectual stimulation is 15 met infinitely better when he can learn by manipulating, touching, *doing*, than by merely watching passively.

And finally, the television experience must be consid- 16 ered in relation to the child's need to develop family skills he will need in order to become a successful parent himself some day. These skills are a product of his present participation in family life, of his everyday experiences as a family member. There is every indication that television has a destructive effect upon family life, diminishing its richness and variety.

Thus it begins to appear that ACT and the concerned 17 parents and educators who support it so hopefully may be misguided in their beliefs and efforts. The television experience is at best irrelevant and at worst detrimental to children's needs. Efforts to make television more attractive to parents and children by improving programming can only lead to the increased reliance of parents upon television as a baby-sitter, and the increased bondage of children to their television sets.

Oddly enough the television industry, though cynical and self-serving in its exploitation of children, often demonstrates a greater understanding of the true needs of children than its most bitter critics. In defending his station's inferior children's programs, a network executive states, "If we were to do *that* [supply quality programs in the afternoon, one of the demands of ACT], a lot of people might say: 'How dare they lock the kids up for another two and a half hours? Let the kids go out and play and let them do their homework. And let them have a learning experience.' I don't think it's incumbent on *us* to provide them with a service that is specific in those terms." 18

It is unlikely that the networks are eschewing good programming for children out of altruism, to avoid tempting kids into watching too much television; junk, after all, is generally cheaper and easier to provide than quality entertainment. Nevertheless, the industry's cool indifference to the quality of children's television fare may be more beneficial for children than the struggle of those who insist that fine children's programs be available at all times. The preponderance of offensive and banal programs may act as a natural check on television viewing since conscientious parents are more likely to limit their children's television inake if only unsavory programs are available.... 19

TELEVISION SAVANTS

Parents may overemphasize the importance of content in considering the effects of television on their children because they assume that the television experience of children is the same as their own. But there is an essential difference between the two: the adult has a vast backlog 20 of real-life experiences; the child does not. As the adult watches television, his own present and past relationships, experiences, dreams, and fantasies come into play, transforming the material he sees, whatever its origins or purpose, into something reflecting his own particular inner needs. The young child's life experiences are limited. He has barely emerged from the preverbal fog of infancy. It is disquieting to consider that hour after hour of television watching constitutes a *primary* activity for him. His subsequent real-life activities will stir memories of television experiences, not, as for the adult watcher, the other way around. To a certain extent the child's early television experiences will serve to dehumanize, to mechanize, to make less *real* the realities and relationships he encounters in life. For him, real events will always carry subtle echoes of the television world.

"I didn't so much *watch* those shows when I was little; 21 I let them wash over me," writes a twenty-year-old who calculates that she has spent 20,000 hours of her life in front of a television set. "Now I study them like a psychiatrist on his own couch, looking hungrily for some clue inside the TV set to explain the person I have become."

Inevitably parents of young children turn their atten- 22 tion to the content of the programs their children watch because they have come to believe that television is an important source of learning. But the television-based learning of the preschool child brings to mind the *idiot savant,* a profoundly retarded person who exhibits some remarkable abilities—one who can, for instance, multiply five-digit numbers in his head or perform other prodigious mathematical feats. The television-educated child can spout words and ideas he does not comprehend and "facts" he doesn't have the experience or knowledge to judge the accuracy of. The small child mimicking television commercials or babbling complex words or sentences learned from television, the young *television savant,* has no more ability to use his television-acquired material for his own human purposes than the defective pseudo-genius has of using his amazing mathematical manipulations.

AN INSIDIOUS NARCOTIC

Because television is so wonderfully available a child 23 amuser and child defuser, capable of rendering a volatile three-year-old harmless at the flick of a switch, parents grow to depend upon it in the course of their daily lives. And as they continue to utilize television day after day, its importance in their children's lives increases. From a simple source of entertainment provided by parents when they need a break from child care, television gradually changes into a powerful and disruptive presence in family life. But despite their increasing resentment of television's intrusions into their family life, and despite their considerable guilt at not being able to control their children's viewing, parents do not take steps to extricate themselves from television's domination. They can no longer cope without it.

In 1948 Jack Gould, the first television critic of *The* 24 *New York Times,* described the impact of the then new medium on American families: "Children's hours on television admittedly are an insidious narcotic for the parent. With the tots fanned out on the floor in front of the receiver, a strange if wonderful quiet seems at hand...."

On first glance it may appear that Gould's pen had 25 slipped. Surely it was the strangely quiet children who were narcotized by the television set, not the parents. But indeed he had penetrated to the heart of the problem before the problem had fully materialized, before anyone dreamed that children would one day spend more of their waking hours watching television than at any other single activity. It is, in fact, the parents for whom television is an irresistible narcotic, not through their own viewing (although frequently this, too, is the case) but at a remove, through their children, fanned out in front of the receiver, strangely quiet. Surely there can be no more insidious a drug than one that you must administer to others in order to achieve an effect for yourself.

———— ◆ ————

For Study and Discussion

QUESTIONS ABOUT PURPOSE

1. What does Winn want concerned parents to think about their children's exposure to television?
2. Would you say that this essay is primarily informative or primarily persuasive? What is the basis for your answer?
3. To what extent are Winn's criticisms directed at the television industry?

QUESTIONS ABOUT AUDIENCE

1. How familiar are you with the experiences Winn describes in her essay? Does your experience make you more or less interested in the topic?
2. How many people do you think would take the trouble to read this essay if they encountered it in the Sunday supplement magazine of their newspaper? Why?
3. Can the audience for this essay change the conditions that Winn condemns? Do you think they will want to after they read the essay?

QUESTIONS ABOUT STRATEGIES

1. What kind of evidence does Winn use to support her claims about the effect of television watching on young children?

The Causes of Alcoholism

BERTON ROUECHÉ

◆

Berton Rouéché was born in 1911 in Kansas City, Missouri, and educated at the University of Missouri. After working for ten years as a reporter for such Midwestern newspapers as the Kansas City Star *and the* St. Louis Post-Dispatch, *Rouéché joined the staff of* The New Yorker, *where his articles earned him awards from the Mystery Writers of America, the National Council of Infant and Child Care, and the American Medical Writers Association. Although Rouéché has published four novels—*Black Weather *(1945),* The Last Enemy *(1956),* Ferral *(1974), and* Fago *(1977)—he is most famous for his books about "medical detection," among them* Eleven Blue Men *(1953),* The Neutral Spirit: A Portrait of Alcohol *(1960),* The Orange Man *(1971), and* The Medical Detectives *(1980). In "The Causes of Alcoholism," reprinted from* The Neutral Spirit, *Rouéché analyzes the many psychobiological and sociological causes of this complex and misunderstood disease.*

The belief that alcoholism stems directly from some personality derangement is the oldest of the explanatory theories still in scientific vogue. It is also the best known, the most popular, and, among the general run of physicians and psychiatrists, the most widely accepted. Among those on active duty in alcohol research, its vogue, however, has waned. This is not to say that they reject it. They merely regard it as incomplete. Alcoholism, in their opinion, is far too dark and prickly to be accounted for so simply. "There is no one cause of alcoholism," Dr. Kant suggests. "It is a psychobiological-sociological problem, which means that certain mental and physical traits have to be present in a certain sociological setting so that alcoholism will develop. Analyzing alcoholics individually, we find a variety of different conflict personalities tending toward this abnormal solution. Even so, the cause of alcoholism in a certain individual is not entirely explained by the conflict situation. We have to consider two distinct problems. In addition to the question why and from what was the individual escaping, we have to find an answer why it took just the form of alcoholism, and not that of some other abnormal reaction."

An eclectic rationale proposed by Dr. Kant and others provides at least a work-horse resolution of these problems. Not everyone, according to this concept, can become an alcoholic. There are certain basic prerequisites. The first of these, and one that tends to be often overlooked, is a normal tolerance for alcohol. Many people cannot drink to drunkenness. Some are physiologically so sensitive to alcohol that a single highball, a bottle of beer, or even a glass of wine will leave them faint and queasy. Others can comfortably tolerate a drink or two but then must stop or risk becoming ill. Moreover, in addition to these constitutional idiosyncratics, there are people who are psychically incapable of drinking. They dislike the effects of alcohol. To them, the feeling of release and relaxation that generally commends its use is unpleasant, and even alarming. They feel exposed, off guard, defenseless. It is sometimes supposed that the alcoholic's excessive thirst for alcohol implies an excessive liking for the taste of drink. The truth is very different. Although many alcoholics, in common with many ordinary drinkers, do like the flavor of whiskey (or gin or rum or brandy or beer or wine), a good many more do not, and there are some who find it gaggingly repellent. To all of these, however, when a drink becomes imperative, a bottle of vanilla extract (or anything containing alcohol) will serve as well as the finest cognac. The alcoholic drinks (as his counterparts the glutton, the gambler, the lecher eat and gamble and wench) not for pleasure but from a compelling psychic need.

A second prerequisite is, of course, the presence of such $_3$ a need. There is no evidence that alcoholism can develop in the absence of some mental or emotional disability. It is only among those so afflicted that the use of alcohol may lead to alcoholism. "The motivations for social drinking are not the motivations for alcoholism," Donald L. Gerard, a consultant in psychiatric research at the Laboratory of Applied Biodynamics, affirms. "Alcoholics do not drink as they do in order to attain 'release of inhibitions.' They drink, just as the opiate addicts take drugs, to get deep, regressive infantile satisfactions, and to establish within themselves a state of psychic well-being." Mary Jane Sherfey, assistant professor of clinical psychiatry at the Cornell University Medical College, has also touched illuminatingly on this sometimes troubled question. Dr. Sherfey assumes, for the purpose of discussion, that there are five general types of drinking habits: total abstaining, moderate or social drinking, heavy social drinking, excessive drinking, and chronic alcoholism. "While it is true," she then points out, "that many alcoholics go through the first four defined conditions to the fifth one of alcoholism, it is not accurate to consider them as 'stages' in the development of chronic alcoholism. These drinking habits exist in everyone, and the majority of people maintain their specific drinking patterns throughout life. There are alcoholics who were never social drinkers. [They passed] from total abstaining almost directly into chronic alcoholism." *

---

* Nevertheless, a progressive pattern in drinking habits has been discerned in the histories of many alcoholics. The stages that characterize its development, as noted by E. M. Jellinek, among others, are: (1) A tendency to consume more drinks, on an accepted drinking occasion, than other members of the group; (2) A tendency to drink more frequently, to take advantage of more accepted drinking occasions, than other members of the group; (3) A tendency to exhibit less behavioral control on accepted drinking occasions than other members of the group; (4) A tendency to experience temporary spells of amnesia during or following drinking parties; (5) A tendency to drink more rapidly, particularly at the start of a drinking occasion, than other

George N. Thompson, associate clinical professor of neurology and psychiatry at the University of Southern California School of Medicine, has followed a somewhat different route to much the same conclusion. "The alcoholic . . . likes to think of himself as a normal individual who has gotten into the vicious habit of drinking but who otherwise has nothing wrong with him," he notes. "In most cases, nothing could be further from the truth. . . . Alcoholism does not result simply from excessive drinking over a long period of years following introduction of the 'habit.' Alcoholism, in fact, is not a habit. It is a result of personality illness. It is a symptom of disease. The alcoholic individual is emotionally sick."

The personality disorders of which alcoholism may be a manifestation are numerous and varied. Their range embraces the total psychopathological spectrum. It is possible, however—and accepted clinical practice—to place all alcoholics in one or another of two widely separated psychiatric categories. A considerable number (perhaps, according to some recent American case studies, thirty-five or forty per cent of the total) are plainly also in the grip of some clearly recognizable disease. Many of them are manic-depressives, some are paranoid schizophrenics or psychopathic personalities, a few are epileptics. A very few are people who have suffered some violent physical injury to the brain. The probable origin of alcoholism is less clear in the other, and larger, group. It is composed of men

4

---

members of the group; (6) A tendency to find more frequent, and increasingly unconventional, occasions for drinking; (7) A tendency to slip out for a surreptitious drink; (8) A tendency to reorder the drinking pattern by eschewing whiskey for gin or drinking only beer or refraining from drinking until after working hours or drinking only at home or only after dinner; (9) An increasing tendency to avoid drinking in company and a preference for drinking alone; (10) A tendency to fancifully rationalize the increasing desire to drink; (11) A tendency to impatiently reject any criticism of the developing drinking pattern, a refusal to discuss the matter; (12) A tendency to start the day with several drinks, to end it in a state of intoxication, to remain intoxicated for several days each week or month.

and women in whom compulsive drinking is the only apparent symptom of abnormality. There appears to be nothing wrong with them that sobriety cannot cure. But close examination usually reveals a personality structure significantly outside the normal range. These people are, for the most part, victims of the sprawling constellation of fears and phobias that is known as psychoneurosis.

Since psychoneurosis thus appears to be the commonest cause of alcoholism, the psychoneurotic is often pictured as the classic alcoholic type. He is certainly equipped for the part. He has (as much as any other emotional cripple) all the conflicts that are necessary to hound a man to drink, and (unlike some of the others) none that drink can't solve. The ubiquitous dread, the rootless fatigue, the tightrope tension, the bogus pains, the hamstringing tics and stammers, the tantrum impatience with frustration, the diffused and unattainable ambitions, the extrasensory perception of slights and criticism, the sexual anesthesia or disgust or impotence—these and a hundred other psychogenic incapacities are peculiarly amenable to alcohol. It is, if not their best, their most immediate remedy. "One thing about alcohol," Charles Orson Gorham remarks in his *Carlotta McBride,* a fictional study of an alcoholic, "it works. It may destroy a man's career, ruin his marriage, turn him into a zombie unconscious in a hallway—but it works. On short term, it works much faster than a psychiatrist or a priest or the love of a husband or a wife. Those things . . . they all take time. They must be developed. . . . But alcohol is always ready to go to work at once. Ten minutes, half an hour, the little formless fears are gone or turned into harmless amusement. But they come back. Oh yes, and they bring reinforcements."

They always come back, and always with reinforcements. And with every proliferation they become harder and harder to quench. Moreover, they tend in time, for reasons still unclear, to establish in the great majority of alcoholics a common character pattern. "Many different types of personalities are capable of becoming addicted to alcohol," Ruth Fox (among others) has noted. "When tested *after* their addiction, they show, however, a surprising similarity of character traits. Some of these are: an extremely low frustration-tolerance, inability to endure anxiety or tension, feelings of isolation, devaluated self-esteem, a tendency to act impulsively, a repetitive 'acting out' of conflicts, often an extreme narcissism and exhibitionism, a tendency toward self-punitive behavior, sometimes somatic preoccupation and hypochondriasis. In addition, there is usually, consciously or unconsciously, marked hostility and rebellion ... and most show strong dependent needs." Nevertheless, despite this similarity of personality and interest there is little genuine camaraderie among alcoholics. They prefer to drink alone, or with their obvious social or intellectual inferiors. For it is only in low company that the alcoholic can both forget his degradation and momentarily soothe himself with delusions of superiority.

A third prerequisite for the development of alcoholism 7 is a suitable social climate. It is not enough that a man be bound and gagged with psychic tensions of the sort that alcohol can loosen; the world is full of trammeled personalities who never take to drink. He must also belong to a culture in which drinking for that purpose is possible. This has always been taken to mean a culture that accepts the use of alcohol. Recent research, however, has severely shaken that temperance-tract assumption. The reverse, it now appears, is closer to the truth. The lowest incidence of alcoholism in the United States occurs among the members of three racial groups whose cultures fully sanction the use of alcohol. These groups are the Jews, the Italians, and the Chinese. The highest incidence occurs among Americans of Irish and Anglo-Saxon origin. In the Irish and Anglo-Saxon cultures (which American culture almost totally reflects), drinking has no certain, well-established, unequivocal role—a moral ambiguity that forces every man to learn for himself (if he can) the perils and pleasures of drink. The trio of minority American cultures are less inertly anarchistic. They leave nothing to do with alcohol to chance.

Although it would be hard to single out three cultures 8 more disparate than the Hebraic, the Latin, and the Chinese, their attitudes toward drink and drinking are remarkably alike. Each group accepts with equanimity the fact that alcohol exists. They agree that it has, as much as bread and meat, a place in human life. They also share an understanding of the place in life it occupies. And they have an equally iron conception of what constitutes its misuse. This is generally held to be not only drinking to the point of drunkenness but any drinking except on those occasions recognized by tradition as seemly—meals (both daily and festive), holiday or family celebrations and (most notably in Jewish culture) religious observances. "The act of drinking is not performed in Jewish culture for the purpose of inducing those changes in emotional state and behavior which are associated with intoxication," Charles R. Snyder, assistant professor of sociology at Yale, establishes in his monograph *Alcohol and the Jews* (Yale Center of Alcohol Studies, 1958). "The Jew does not drink with the aim or idea of getting 'tight' or 'drunk,' to 'feel gay,' or the like. Alcohol is not sought primarily for its psychophysical effects on the human organism. On the contrary . . . the purposes of drinking are of a different kind. [His] drinking is essentially social in character and . . . conformity to the proprieties of the situation is the valued aspect of the entire complex of drinking customs." Moreover, Dr. Snyder adds, "Because of his involvement in a wider pattern of ceremonial and ritual observances, the pious Jew approaches alcoholic beverages with a generalized ritual attitude. . . . A stable attitude toward the drinking of alcoholic beverages is consequently molded which does not leave the outcome of drinking to chance, individual experiment, fear, or ignorance."

Italian culture provides a comparably stable attitude 9 toward drinking. In a complementary monograph, *Alcohol in Italian Culture* (Yale Center of Alcohol Studies, 1958),

Giorgio Lolli, a former medical director of the Connecticut Commission on Alcoholism who is now in private psychiatric practice, and several collaborators define the desirable effects of alcohol as primarily physiological or gastronomic, rather than psychological. "In the eyes of the Italians," they write, "wine is a food. It is a liquid food, as distinguished from solid food, but used in conjunction with the latter and consumed chiefly as a part of their meals.... It should be noted that drinking with meals generally signifies an experience shared by members of a small and mutually controlling group—usually the family unit, where the interplay of male-female and adult-child relationships is of paramount importance. Thus, the shared use of alcoholic beverage—which among the Italians means the shared use of wine—reflects a cohesion or 'sociability' rather than a means to reach it." Chinese culture, like the Hebraic and the Latin, stands opposed to excessive drinking, but in certain circumstances (weddings, banquets, family reunions) it is tolerant of an occasional lapse into drunkenness. Its tolerance is , however, essentially derisive. "The Chinese doesn't drink to get drunk," Milton L. Barnett, assistant professor of anthropology at the University of Wisconsin, points out in a recent sociocultural study. "He drinks so that the other man will get drunk." But, Dr. Barnett continues, "drinking to intoxication is not habitual, dependence on alcohol is uncommon, and alcoholism is a rarity.... Drinking with meals, or at least with some food, is the basic usage, [and] drinking for drinking's sake is frowned upon."

From these and other studies, Albert D. Ullman, associate professor of sociology at Tufts University and a former president of the Professional Association on Alcoholism, concludes, in a comprehensive report to the *Annals of the American Academy of Political and Social Science,* "In any group or society in which the drinking customs, values, and sanctions ... are well-established, known to and agreed upon by all, the rate of alcoholism will be low.... Lack of cultural integration in the sphere of drinking activities and attitudes is directly related to higher rates of alcoholism." To the Jew, the Italian, and the Chinese, alcohol is not, as it often is to less culturally disciplined Americans, a tool. They never duck into a bar because they "need a drink." They never buy a bottle and go home and "drown their sorrows." It never occurs to them that to drink with gusto is a sign (or proof) of masculinity. It also never occurs to them that drinking is "wrong" or "sinful." When they drink, their conscience is clear.

The alcoholic drinks to clear his conscience. The knowledge of his squalid bondage is among the cruelest of the many burdens that alcoholism can impose upon a man, and it is probably the most inevitable. A flood of drinks will usually ease its weight, but it always returns, with sobriety and the hangover. In fact, for many alcoholics the crushing revival of conscience is the quintessence of hangover anguish. "The increasing misery of the hangover is not due to the headache, the nausea, the cold sweats, the chills and fever, or even the shakes," Benjamin Karpman of St. Elizabeth's Hospital suggests in his *The Hangover: A Critical Study in the Psychodynamics of Alcoholism* (Charles C. Thomas, 1957), "but to the emotional pain which accompanies them—the guilt, anxiety, self-accusation, the sense of hopelessness and despair." His patients bear him out. "The emotional pain is by far the most intense," one of them, whose history he records, has testified. "I would say that my hangovers are twenty per cent physical and eighty per cent emotional pain. There is a constant theme which pervades all my hangovers—guilt, remorse, a feeling of complete worthlessness, of being unloved, and, with reason, of moral degeneration; I am the worst person in the world. Generally, this is very intense when I first awake, and it can continue throughout the day and night. I am sure this is the main reason for not being able to face the night without drinking. It is the pain of the feeling about myself that I cannot endure." But more drinks are not always enough to bring release and relief. "A strong sense of guilt would be the prevailing

11

emotion after the night before," another patient quoted by Dr. Karpman has reported. "I couldn't work. Only one thing would be on my mind, to get another drink into me and try and calm my nerves and kill the awful sense of guilt. I would summon enough courage to leave my place . . . and wend my fearful way to the nearest bar. Trembling and shaking on my arrival there, I would order a drink, generally what is termed a boiler-maker—a beer and a shot of whiskey. Several drinks would steady me. Yet there would often still be a sense of guilt, shame, and fear."

Some alcoholics feel that the sense of guilt is too strong to ever be killed. The hangover, in their opinion, never ends. 12

———— ◆ ————

For Study and Discussion

QUESTIONS ABOUT PURPOSE

1. What is the principal belief that Berton Roueché attempts to dispel by his analysis of the causes of alcoholism?
2. What seems to be Roueché's chief forms or area of interest in this essay on a large, complex problem?
3. In this essay Roueché recommends no action, but some recommendations may be implicit. What do you think they are?

QUESTIONS ABOUT AUDIENCE

1. This essay is a chapter in Roueché's book *The Neutral Spirit*. What does Roueché's title suggest to his readers about his attitude toward his subject? How might this title attract readers to his analysis?

2. How much does Roueché assume his readers already know about the subject of alcoholism? To what extent do they subscribe to the popular theories about the disease?

3. How do you think most problem drinkers would react to this essay? Why?

QUESTIONS ABOUT STRATEGIES

1. How does Roueché cite doctors, researchers, and university professors to give authority to his analysis of the complex causes of alcoholism?

2. Why, in your opinion, does Roueché refrain from giving statistics about the percentage of alcoholics in our society or the annual cost of alcoholism?

3. Roueché maintains a neutral and restrained tone in discussing a highly controversial and emotional subject. Why do you think he does so?

QUESTIONS FOR DISCUSSION

1. Many people believe that alcoholism is a serious problem on college campuses. In what ways does Roueché's analysis of the factors that contribute to alcoholism pertain to the drinking problems of some college students?

2. What are some of the common personality traits shared by most alcoholics? Why is it ironic that people with such similar personalities demonstrate "little genuine camaraderie"?

3. Alcoholism is not a new problem in the United States. In fact, a hundred years ago the per capita consumption of alcohol was higher than it is now. From your reading of Roueche's analysis, explain why the problem seems more significant in our time.

◆

Cause and Effect as a Writing Strategy

1. Why are you writing your cause and effect paper? Do you want to explain a process, to argue a point, to make a prediction, or to analyze a situation? Although you may alter your purpose slightly as you write, knowing what you want to do before you begin will help you to set an appropriate tone for your essay. How positive are you that the cause and effect relationship you are explaining is valid? Are you explaining accepted theories or speculating about possible connections? In each case, how will your purpose affect your language? What qualifications may you need to make in writing your paper?

2. Who will read the kind of paper you are writing? Identify an audience and keep it in mind as you write. How much background material will you have to explain to this audience? Will you have to make a detailed analysis of the chain of events you are writing about? What biases for or against your topic might your audience have, and how might those biases affect the way you present that topic? How much specialized language can you use?

3. How much evidence do you need to support the cause and effect claims you are making? Is it possible to *prove* the claim, or should you settle for saying "probably"? Should you use such strategies as *narration*, *description*, or *process analysis* in writing your causal analysis in order to help your readers grasp it more easily? What kind of tone do you want to convey in your writing—serious, whimsical, persuasive? How can you do it?

PREWRITING EXERCISES

1. In ten minutes write down all the *effects* you think might happen from any two of these occurrences:

> moving from a dormitory to an apartment
> swimming a half-mile every day
> taking up white-water canoeing
> declaring yourself a pre-med student
> going on a diet
> selling your car

2. In ten minutes write down all the possible *causes* you can think of for any two of these occurrences:

> enrolling in a course in computer programming
> changing your major
> taking a part-time job
> buying a motorcycle
> getting married
> taking French

3. Examine a weekly news magazine such as *U. S. News and World Report* and decide how many of the articles in the first twenty pages come under the category of causal analysis. Are the articles arguing or explaining? Are they convincing?

4. Make a list showing several causes and effects that could be related to one of these happenings:

> a car stops running
> a student drops a course
> a skater wins an Olympic gold medal
> a building collapses
> a student wins a Rhodes scholarship

5. Forster lists four effects that owning property had on him. List three or four effects that you think these events might have on you:

> owning a $25,000 sports car
> inheriting a farm
> buying a $100,000 Arabian mare
> living in a million-dollar house

TOPICS FOR WRITING IN CLASS

1. If you know what work you plan to do after college, in a paragraph of 100 to 150 words give your reasons for

choosing this work. Think about the indirect or long-range causes for your choice as well as the immediate and direct causes. If you have not yet decided on your profession, discuss your reasons, both direct and indirect, for coming to college.

2. In 150 to 200 words, speculate about the cause and effect relationship that might or might *not* exist between the phenomena described in one of the following pairs of phrases. Think carefully about connections and avoid jumping to conclusions too quickly.

   A. the fast-food   working teen-agers
   industry

   B. more than 50 per-   increase in the divorce
   cent of college   rate
   students are now
   women

   C. increase in mem-   decrease in deaths from
   bership in health   heart attacks
   clubs

   D. decrease in num-   rise in medical costs
   ber of applicants
   admitted to medi-
   cal school

3. Write a short paper in which you describe the effects that one of these experiences has had on you or someone you know:

   being in an automobile accident
   losing a job
   winning a contest
   getting rid of the television set
   buying a new house

TOPICS FOR WRITING OUT OF CLASS

1. The English wit Oscar Wilde once wrote, "There are two tragedies in life: one is not getting what you want and the other is getting it." For an audience of your

fellow students, write a paper describing an occasion on which you succeeded in getting something or doing something that you had wished for very strongly, and the effects turned out to be quite different from what you had anticipated. Use specific examples to illustrate your account.

2. Imagine that your state legislature or the board of governors for your school is considering a proposal that would double your tuition. Write a letter to your legislator or to the president of the board of governors asking him or her to oppose the proposal. In the beginning of your letter show that you understand why such an increase is needed, but then try to show that the bad effects would outweigh the good ones.

3. Write a brochure no longer than 500 words in which you inform an audience of twelve-year-olds about the multiple causes of one of the following problems. Remember to use a vocabulary and writing style suitable for your readers.

> tooth decay
> unhealthy pets
> bicycle accidents
> damaged library books
> boating accidents

PERSUASION
AND ARGUMENT

DEFINITION

Persuasion and argument are varieties of expository writing that readers encounter every day as writers try to convince them to spend money, take action, support a cause, accept an opinion, or consider an idea. The starting point for all these varieties is an *assertion*, a statement of belief or a claim that the writer undertakes to explain and support. At one extreme, both the statement and the support may be highly emotional, depending heavily on biased language and strong appeals to the feelings and instincts; this kind of writing is classified as *persuasion*. At the other extreme, the assertion and support may be strictly rational, depending on logical explanation and appeals to the intelligence; this kind of writing is classified as *argument*. Scientific arguments and grant proposals cluster toward the argument end of the continuum, and advertising and political writing cluster toward the persuasion end.

Seldom, however, does persuasive writing appeal only to the emotions, and seldom does argument rely entirely on reason. Rather, when people write to convince they appeal to both the emotions and the intelligence, but they vary the balance of reason and emotion according to their audience and purpose.

Nor is writing that is primarily rational necessarily better than writing that is primarily emotional. Some occasions for speaking or writing call for appeals to pride and patriotism, for vivid metaphors that reach the senses, and for strong language that will arouse the passions. This kind of writing is called *ceremonial discourse*. The audience already knows and probably agrees with what the speaker is going to say, and they expect not intellectual stimulation but emotional satisfaction and inspiration. Inaugural speeches, graduation addresses, and political speeches usually fit into this ceremonial category, and often they are successful precisely because they are emotional.

Most arguments, however, must be fairly rational if they are to convince critical readers, and those readers are justified in expecting writers to support major assertions with evidence and logic. Generally speaking, people who write effective arguments do what a good trial lawyer does: they present a case persuasively but give strong reasons for believing the assertions they make. And in the final analysis the quality of any piece of argument must be judged not by some absolute standard of rationality, but by how well it fills its intended purpose with the intended audience.

PURPOSE

Although many of us think of controversy when we hear the word *argument,* not all people who write arguments and persuasion are trying to win a dispute. Instead, they may want to persuade people to *support a cause* or *make a commitment.* Political leaders and ministers frequently write for those purposes. Writers may also argue in order *to get people to take action* or *to try to change a situation.* Editorial writers or reformers like Ralph Nader often have those purposes in mind, and so do political activists like labor leaders.

Sometimes writers persuade in order *to change behavior or attitudes.* Someone advocating a new approach to child rearing would have such a purpose, as would a person arguing against racial or sexual prejudice. Other writers argue in order *to refute a theory.* For example, feminist writers continually seek to disprove the belief that women are less talented and creative than men. Writers also use persuasive strategies *to arouse sympathies, to stimulate concern, to win agreement,* and *to provoke anger.* And they may incorporate several of these purposes into one piece of writing.

AUDIENCE

More than any other kind of writing, argument and persuasion require that authors think about their audiences. In order to choose effective rhetorical strategies, a writer must have a clear sense of who may read his or her writing, what kinds of attitudes and biases those persons will bring to the reading, and what the reader expects to get from the essay. Making such an analysis of an audience can be difficult, and sometimes writers have to work by instinct rather than on the basis of good information. Usually, however, a writer can assume that the readers for argumentative and persuasive prose fit into one of the following classes:

1. Readers who already agree with the writer's ideas and are reading or listening mainly for reinforcement or encouragement. These readers do not expect a tightly reasoned and carefully structured argument: rather they want to see their position stated with vigor and conviction.

2. Readers who are interested in the issue the writer is discussing and are inclined to agree with him or her, but who want to know more. Although they are interested in facts and in cause and effect arguments that will help them make a decision, they do not expect a completely rational argument, and they will not object if the writer uses slanted language or emotional examples to strengthen a point.

3. Readers who are neutral on an issue and want explanations and arguments based on evidence and logical reasoning before they make up their minds. For these readers a writer must make a carefully developed and factual argument, although he or she can also reinforce facts with opinions.

4. Readers who are skeptical about an issue and will not take a stand until they hear both sides explained logically and specifically. They want data and documentation from someone who gives the impression that he or she is knowledgeable and capable.

STRATEGIES

Writers who seek to convince readers use a wide range of strategies, but almost all these strategies can be classified in one of three categories of appeal to the reader: emotional appeal, rational appeal, and ethical appeal.

EMOTIONAL or NONLOGICAL STRATEGIES appeal to the emotions, the instincts, the senses, and to personal biases and prejudices. Perhaps the most common of these strategies is *connotative language,* words that trigger favorable or unfavorable reactions from the reader. Words like *slavery, freedom, cowardly,* and *brave* are connotative; so are words that appeal to the senses, such as *slimy, glossy,* or *icy.*

Another nonlogical device for persuading readers is *figurative language,* metaphors, similes, or allusions that engage the emotions and the senses by stimulating the reader to draw comparisons and make associations. The writer who calls uncontrolled growth a "cancer" or calls a contest between unequals a "battle between David and Goliath" is employing figurative language. So is the writer who creates a vivid metaphor that stirs the reader's sympathies.

Writers also use *tone* as a nonlogical persuasive device; that is, they try to convey an attitude in their writing that will predispose readers to accept their arguments. They can establish a friendly tone by using the pronouns *I, you,* and *we.* By using colloquial language and frequent references to their own experiences, they can also create a relaxed tone; and by careful word choice, they can convey an ironic tone, an authoritative tone, or whatever tone suits their purposes.

All the writers in this section of the book use some emotional appeals, but the one who relies on it most heavily is Martin Luther King, Jr., in "I Have a Dream." King draws heavily on metaphor and connotative language to remind his chiefly black listeners of the injustices they have suffered and to inspire them with a vision of a better life. William Styron also plays on his reader's emotions by charging that the tobacco industry is greedy and corrupt.

Rachel Carson uses connotative language and predictions of disaster to add emotional appeal to "The Obligation to Endure," and Marya Mannes complements the statistics and evidence in "Packaged Deception" with personal anecdotes and examples that will make her readers angry. In "An Inquiry into the Persistence of Unwisdom in Government," Barbara Tuchman relies on the connotative term "wooden-headedness" and on her personal insights to enhance her historical argument. Ursula Le Guin strengthens her claim about the value of fantasy by appealing to her readers' nostalgic memories of childhood.

RATIONAL or LOGICAL STRATEGIES appeal to the intelligence and reason and to the reader's common sense. Two major kinds of logical argument are *inductive argument*, in which a writer examines evidence and then draws a conclusion from it, and *deductive argument*, in which a writer makes a generalization and then applies it to a specific case. Writers may also appeal to reason by proving or speculating about cause and effect.

Another logical persuasive device is *comparison*, including *analogy*. A writer can make a point by demonstrating differences and similarities between situations, or by drawing an analogy that explains the unknown by comparing it to the known. Finally, a writer can use the rational methods of *bringing in testimony* (including reports and statistics), *presenting evidence*, and *citing authorities*. All of these involve gathering specific material.

In "The Habit" Styron uses several rational strategies—statistics, cause and effect, testimony, and analogy—to create an argument that resembles a legal argument one might present in court. In "The Obligation to Endure" Carson gathers inductive evidence and cites authorities; she also argues from cause and effect. Mannes builds her argument in "Packaged Deception" around statistics and causal analysis, and Le Guin adds logical appeal to her essay by drawing analogies and speculating about cause and effect. And although Martin Luther King's plea in "I Have a Dream" seems primarily emotional, he too employs historical evidence and appeals to reason.

The third important kind of persuasive strategy is ETHICAL APPEAL, an appeal based on the reputation and credibility of the author. This kind of appeal, which is found in both emotional persuasion and rational argument, convinces because the reader believes that the writer is reliable, sincere, well-informed, and qualified to write on the topic. Readers can be persuaded by ethical appeal either because they recognize and respect the author of an argument, or because the writer does such a good job of selecting and presenting evidence that he or she makes a good impression. Of all the writers in this section, King probably has the strongest ethical appeal because of his reputation and national prestige. William Styron establishes strong ethical appeal in his essay on smoking by acknowledging his own experience in breaking "the habit," and Rachel Carson shows that she is not only a committed environmentalist but also a careful critic who has studied her subject thoroughly.

I Have a Dream

MARTIN LUTHER KING, JR.

◆

*Martin Luther King, Jr. (1929–1968) was born in At-
lanta, Georgia, and educated at Morehouse College,
Crozer Theological Seminary, and Boston University.
Ordained a Baptist minister in his father's church in
1947, King soon became involved in civil rights activities in the South. In 1957 he founded the Southern
Christian Leadership Conference and established him-
self as America's most prominent spokesman for non-
violent racial integration. In 1963 he was named
Time magazine's Man of the Year; in 1964 he was
given the Nobel Prize for Peace; and in 1968 he was
assassinated in Memphis, Tennessee. His writing includes Letter from Birmingham City Jail (1963); Why
We Can't Wait (1964); and Where Do We Go From
Here: Chaos or Community? (1967). "I Have a
Dream" is the famous speech King delivered at the
Lincoln Memorial at the end of the "March on
Washington" in 1963 to commemorate the one-hun-
dredth anniversary of the Emancipation Proclamation.
King argues that realization of the dream of freedom
for all American citizens is long overdue.*

Five score years ago, a great American, in whose symbolic   1
shadow we stand, signed the Emancipation Proclamation.
This momentous decree came as a great beacon light of
hope to millions of Negro slaves who had been seared in
the flames of withering injustice. It came as a joyous
daybreak to end the long night of captivity.

But one hundred years later, we must face the tragic   2
fact that the Negro is still not free. One hundred years
later, the life of the Negro is still sadly crippled by the
manacles of segregation and the chains of discrimination.

One hundred years later, the Negro lives on a lonely island of poverty in the midst of a vast ocean of material prosperity. One hundred years later, the Negro is still languishing in the corners of American society and finds himself an exile in his own land. So we have come here today to dramatize an appalling condition.

In a sense we have come to our nation's Capitol to cash a check. When the architects of our republic wrote the magnificent words of the Constitution and the Declaration of Independence, they were signing a promissory note to which every American was to fall heir. This note was a promise that all men would be guaranteed the unalienable rights of life, liberty, and the pursuit of happiness. 3

It is obvious today that America has defaulted on this promissory note insofar as her citizens of color are concerned. Instead of honoring this sacred obligation, America has given the Negro people a bad check; a check which has come back marked "insufficient funds." But we refuse to believe that the bank of justice is bankrupt. We refuse to believe that there are insufficient funds in the great vaults of opportunity of this nation. So we have come to cash this check—a check that will give us upon demand the riches of freedom and the security of justice. We have also come to this hallowed spot to remind America of the fierce urgency of *now*. This is no time to engage in the luxury of cooling off or to take the tranquilizing drug of gradualism. *Now* is the time to make real the promises of Democracy. *Now* is the time to rise from the dark and desolate valley of segregation to the sunlit path of racial justice. *Now* is the time to open the doors of opportunity to all of God's children. *Now* is the time to lift our nation from the quicksands of racial injustice to the solid rock of brotherhood. 4

It would be fatal for the nation to overlook the urgency of the moment and to underestimate the determination of the Negro. This sweltering summer of the Negro's legitimate discontent will not pass until there is an 5 invigorating autumn of freedom and equality. 1963 is not an end, but a beginning. Those who hope that the Negro needed to blow off steam and will now be content will have a rude awakening if the nation returns to business as usual. There will be neither rest nor tranquility in America until the Negro is granted his citizenship rights. The whirlwinds of revolt will continue to shake the foundations of our nation until the bright day of justice emerges.

But there is something I must say to my people who stand on the warm threshold which leads into the palace of justice. In the process of gaining our rightful place we must not be guilty of wrongful deeds. Let us not seek to satisfy our thirst for freedom by drinking from the cup of bitterness and hatred. We must forever conduct our struggle on the high plane of dignity and discipline. We must not allow our creative protest to degenerate into physical violence. Again and again we must rise to the majestic heights of meeting physical force with soul force. The marvelous new militancy which has engulfed the Negro community must not lead us to a distrust of all white people, for many of our white brothers, as evidenced by their presence here today, have come to realize that their destiny is tied up with our destiny and their freedom is inextricably bound to our freedom. We cannot walk alone.   6

And as we walk, we must make the pledge that we shall march ahead. We cannot turn back. There are those who are asking the devotees of civil rights, "When will you be satisfied?" We can never be satisfied as long as the Negro is the victim of the unspeakable horrors of police brutality. We can never be satisfied as long as our bodies, heavy with the fatigue of travel, cannot gain lodging in the motels of the highways and the hotels of the cities. We cannot be satisfied as long as the Negro's basic mobility is from a smaller ghetto to a larger one. We can never be satisfied as long as a Negro in Mississippi can-   7 not vote and a Negro in New York believes he has nothing for which to vote. No, no, we are not satisfied, and we will not be satisfied until justice rolls down like waters and righteousness like a mighty stream.

I am not unmindful that some of you have come here out of great trials and tribulations. Some of you have come fresh from narrow jail cells. Some of you have come from areas where your quest for freedom left you battered by the storms of persecution and staggered by the winds of police brutality. You have been the veterans of creative suffering. Continue to work with the faith that unearned suffering is redemptive. 8

Go back to Mississippi, go back to Alabama, go back to South Carolina, go back to Georgia, go back to Louisiana, go back to the slums and ghettoes of our northern cities, knowing that somehow this situation can and will be changed. Let us not wallow in the valley of despair. 9

I say to you today, my friends, that in spite of the difficulties and frustrations of the moment I still have a dream. It is a dream deeply rooted in the American dream. 10

I have a dream that one day this nation will rise up and live out the true meaning of its creed: "We hold these truths to be self-evident; that all men are created equal." 11

I have a dream that one day on the red hills of Georgia the sons of former slaves and the sons of former slaveowners will be able to sit down together at the table of brotherhood. 12

I have a dream that the state of Mississippi, a desert state sweltering with the heat of injustice and oppression, will be transformed into an oasis of freedom and justice. 13

I have a dream that my four little children will one day live in a nation where they will not be judged by the color of their skin but by the content of their character. 14

I have a dream today. 15

I have a dream that the state of Alabama, whose governor's lips are presently dripping with the words of interposition and nullification, will be transformed into a 16 situation where little black boys and black girls will be able to join hands with little white boys and white girls and walk together as sisters and brothers.

I have a dream today.   17

I have a dream that one day every valley shall be ex-   18 alted, every hill and mountain shall be made low, the rough places will be made plain, and the crooked places will be made straight, and the glory of the Lord shall be revealed, and all flesh shall see it together.

This is our hope. This is the faith with which I return   19 to the South. With this faith we will be able to hew out of the mountain of despair a stone of hope. With this faith we will be able to transform the jangling discords of our nation into a beautiful symphony of brotherhood. With this fatih we will be able to work together, to pray together, to struggle together, to go to jail together, to stand up for freedom together, knowing that we will be free one day.

This will be the day when all of God's children will   20 be able to sing with new meaning.

> My country, tis of thee
> Sweet land of liberty,
>   Of thee I sing:
> Land where my fathers died,
> Land of the pilgrims' pride,
> From every mountainside
>   Let freedom ring.

And if America is to be a great nation this must be-   21 come true. So let freedom ring from the prodigious hilltops of New Hampshire. Let freedom ring from the mighty mountains of New York. Let freedom ring from the heightening Alleghenies of Pennsylvania!

Let freedom ring from the snowcapped Rockies of   22 Colorado!

Let freedom ring from the curvaceous peaks of Cali-   23 fornia!

But not only that; let freedom ring from Stone Moun- 24
tain of Georgia!

Let freedom ring from Lookout Mountain of Tennessee! 25

Let freedom ring from every hill and molehill of Mis- 26
sissippi. From every mountainside, let freedom ring.

When we let freedom ring, when we let it ring from 27
every village and every hamlet, from every state and every
city, we will be able to speed up that day when all of
God's children, black men and white men, Jews and Gen-
tiles, Protestants and Catholics, will be able to join hands
and sing in the words of the old Negro spiritual, "Free
at last! free at last! thank God almighty, we are free at
last!"

———— ♦ ————

For Study and Discussion

QUESTIONS ABOUT PURPOSE

1. What purpose do you think King has in relating specific injustices in the first eight paragraphs?
2. How does King's purpose seem to change in paragraphs
   10 through 27, when he begins to emphasize the
   phrase "I have a dream"?
3. Why does King use frequent religious and patriotic
   references in the last part of his speech?

QUESTIONS ABOUT AUDIENCE

1. The first audiences for this essay were listeners, not
   readers. How do you think that fact affected the way
   King chose his words and organized his speech?
2. How would you describe King's relationship with his
   audience? What specific phrases or words reveal that
   relationship?

3. What kinds of experiences does King assume that he and the people in his audience have shared?

QUESTIONS ABOUT STRATEGIES

1. Why do you think King makes such extensive use of metaphor in this speech?
2. In what part of the speech does he use historical evidence? Why does he need it for that part?
3. What nonrational persuasive techniques do you recognize in the essay?

QUESTIONS FOR DISCUSSION

1. What other specific situations can you imagine in which the kinds of strategies King uses in this speech might be appropriate?
2. The person who reads this speech in a book is far removed from the original circumstances in which King delivered it. How effective do you think the speech is under these different circumstances?
3. Do you think your knowledge about Martin Luther King, Jr., affects the way you react to this speech now? Describe how and to what extent.

Packaged Deception

MARYA MANNES

♦

*Marya Mannes was born in 1904 in New York City
and was educated by private tutors. She worked first
as a feature editor at* Vogue *and* Glamour *before becoming a staff writer for* The Reporter *and then a
columnist for* McCall's *and* Book Week. *A frequent
guest on radio and television programs, Mannes hosted
her own television show in 1959, "I Speak for Myself." She has contributed articles to* Esquire, Harper's,
and the New York Times Magazine, *and her books
include novels* (Message from a Stranger, *1948), satiri-
cal verse* (Subverse, *1959), an autobiography* (Out of
My Time, *1971), and several collections of essays*
(More in Anger, *1958;* But Will It Sell?, *1964). In
"Packaged Deception," taken from the latter collection, Mannes argues that American manufacturers use
a variety of confusing packages to deceive consumers.*

I am a writer and a housewife. As a writer I sell words   1
and ideas. They are not packaged. The buyer can see
exactly what they are and pay what he thinks they are
worth. As a housewife I buy what is sold to me. It is
packaged. I buy it on faith. That is why, these days, the
word consumer is sometimes spelled s-u-c-k-e-r.

And that is why I stand before you here not as a writer   2
but as a sucker, one of millions who wonder why so much
money drains out of the foodbag and the handbag every
week, and who then forget about it.

Now, I have always believed that the majority of peo- 3
ple were too good to be smart. Ever since we bartered a
beaver pelt for ten eggs, we have assumed that the eggs
were fresh and the pelt was supple, for how else can decent business be transacted? Except for the relation between man and wife, nothing is more intimate than the
relation between the buyer and the seller; and there would
be neither marriage nor commerce if the fundamental
basis of both were not trust. Without trust, a civilized
society cannot endure. When the people who are too
smart to be good fool the people who are too good to be
smart, then society begins to crumble. I think this is what
is happening now, and I believe it must be stopped before
our integrity as Americans is chiseled away as fast as our
dollars are.

What am I talking about? I am talking about certain 4
practices in the market which manage to evade the spirit
of the law while adhering by an eyelash to the letter of
the law. I am talking about what happens when a housewife like myself goes to buy food for her family, and how
she spends her money doing it.

And I am talking about the many small deceptions, 5
most of them deliberate, which make a rational buying
choice—the basis of free enterprise—meaningless. You
can only choose when you know what you are choosing,
and the plain truth is that much of the time we don't.
That great American institution, the supermarkets, those
gleaming palaces of convenience and bounty, have come
to be the greatest exercise in planned confusion since the
bazaars of Samarkand. If you don't believe me, climb into
my pushcart and come around with me, shelf by shelf.

Need some applesauce for the baby? Pick up a few of 6
Brand A's new jars. They look just like the old ones.
They cost the same. But do you know that the new jar
has only seven and a half ounces of applesauce while the
old one had seven and three-quarters ounces? No? You
mean you didn't *look* at that fine print with your glasses?
Now, how about some breakfast food? Well, Brand B's

old box contained six biscuits and weighed six ounces, but when you open the new box which is exactly the same size, you'll find only five ounces of biscuits—a drop in contents of about sixteen per cent. Oh sure, they tell you what's inside the jar or box, but you need a slide rule to figure out the difference. And what housewife with a kid inside the cart and one at her heels can spare the time?

This is confusion number one: to make you think   7 you're getting the same value in the same box at the same price when you're actually getting less. If you complain, the manufacturers say that they're saving you a price raise by reducing the contents. Can you beat it?

Confusion number two is in sizes. Know the differ-   8 ence between Giant and Jumbo? Between two-ounce and a *big* two-ounce? Between a quart and a *full* quart? What's a *tall* 24-inch? What does Extra Long mean? Who's kidding who? And what's the matter with simple sizes, like a pint or two pints or a quart or two quarts? I'll tell you what's the matter. They're too easy to figure. You might know what you were getting. And that goes for the Economy Size too. What economy? If you stop to figure it out, half the time the price per unit remains exactly the same regardless of size, and you save nothing. It just seems economical to us suckers.

Now, let's stop at detergents, where the Giant sizes   9 are. Well, with a box of Brand C, *Giant* means three pounds, five and one-half ounces, but with Brand D, *Giant* means three pounds one and one-fourth ounces; but both boxes look the same size and cost the same price—77 cents. Are the ingredients of the one so superior to the ingredients in the other that four ounces don't matter? And how do you know it, anyway?

Let's move next door to the all-purpose liquid cleaners.   10 With 69 cents you can buy one quart of Brand E, or 1 pint, 12 fluid ounces of Brand F. The shapes are slightly different, but they look the same size. Do you know where the four ounces go? Do you care?

Want some soap pads? Well, you can buy a box of 11
Brand G or a box of Brand H for 13 cents, but unless
you turn the box upside down and use your bifocals, you
won't know that there are only four pads of Brand G compared to five pads of Brand H. Care about one less pad?
Half the time, the quantity of such products is printed in
very small type or in a color that merges in the background. Sometimes it's even printed *underneath* the flap,
and you can't see it until you open it. Do you see it
even then?

Now, you would think that if packages were different 12
sizes, they'd contain different amounts, but that's because
you're congenitally dumb. Brand I, a table salt, is in a
box one inch taller than Brand J, another table salt, but
each has exactly one pound and ten ounces in them.
And how are you to know if the first box is slightly thin-
ner than the second one? Where was your tape measure?

Then there are the simple devices of not really filling 13
the box or bottle. You open up a cereal, say, and you find
an inch or more space on the top—slack-filled, it's called.
Or the liquid in a bottle has an inch or more empty space
above it. And there's the business of using paper to wrap
around crackers or soap and fill the loose space. The
manufacturers will, of course, claim these are necessary
for safe handling and so forth. But we're paying enough
for outer space not to have to pay for inner space,
too.

There's another good gimmick to confuse you: funny 14
shapes of bottles that make any real estimate of contents
impossible.

Then there are all those lovely phrases like the New, 15
the Improved, the Activated, the Super, and so forth.
Don't they give you the impression that you are getting
a better product, justifying a higher price? Well, half the
time you aren't. These words are like the bells the scientists ring to make dogs salivate. You see the word "new"
and you reach for it.

For now, you see, there is no salesman any more to 16

tell you what you are getting. In supermarkets, the *package* is the salesman. The more space he takes up on the shelf (*that's* the reason for Giant and Jumbo, *not* economy), the louder his letters scream at you, the sooner you'll notice him. But while he shouts "Buy me!" he also talks double talk out of the side of his mouth. And while you put *him* in your cart, he picks *your* pocket.

Why? Because you're dumb? Because you're gullible? 17 Because you're careless? Some of us are all of these. But most of us are simply too busy or too tired or too harassed to take a computer, a slide rule, and an M.I.T. graduate to market and figure out what we're buying. And the makers of the goods we buy know this. In fact, they know far more about us than we know about them. They have spent millions of dollars studying us—the consumer. They know what colors and what sizes and what shapes and what words we go for. Compared to them the Big Brother in George Orwell's *1984,* who knows all and sees all, is a piker. The Big Brothers in our society today are not government dictators: they are the sellers and their brainwashing handmaidens, the behavioral scientists. Together, and under the banner of free choice and open competition, they have made us believe that we are getting what we pay for. Their purpose is that innocent goal of free enterprise—to make an extra buck. But when their profit becomes our loss, how innocent is that goal? And what is our loss?

Not much, you may say. An ounce here, a cent there, 18 and what real difference does it make? Most of us have learned to accept the added charges of packaging and advertising and distribution along with the product. But must we pay for deception too?

Just take one figure—baby foods again. Remember the 19 brand where you paid the same price as you used to but got a quarter ounce less food? Well, if your baby ate four jars of this applesauce or carrot puree a day, he would eat twenty-four pounds less food per year—without your knowing it. Do you care? Does it matter?

Maybe it doesn't. We are a spoiled and lazy and waste-   20
ful people; our pay checks were never higher and so what
—that's the way business is done. A little less applesauce,
a few less crackers, a few more pennies here and there:
who cares?

But it isn't a question of applesauce. It's a question   21
of morality. Little deceptions of single consumers can add
up to a mighty deception of a whole people. You may
only lose a penny here and there, but the loss in dollars
sustained daily by American consumers who pay for more
than they get is estimated to be greater than the staggering amount we forfeit to crime and corruption. But it's
not sensational. It doesn't hit the headlines. And who is
going to bring it to your attention? The press which depends on advertising? Television which owes its existence
to products? The makers of the products? As Eliza Doo-
little said in *Pygmalion,* "Not bloody likely!"

Only those whose prime concern is people and not   22
profit can tell us the score: organizations like the Consumers Union and those agencies of government who
regulate the pure and basic world of weights and measures
and law and justice, so that the exchange of goods is a
transaction of trust.

But we, the public, have got to want to know the score.   23
If we don't care, nobody else will care. Dishonest practices, because they succeed, will drive out honest practices,
because they don't. In the end, our condition depends entirely on us. And I think at last we may be beginning to
realize it.

The murmur of rebellion against these widespread de-   24
ceptions and confusions in packaging is swelling daily.
People *are* bringing their slide rules to market, they *are*
taking a good look at what the package says and what
it holds, they *are* beginning to write protests to the manufacturers who manipulate them. But still not enough.

We hear day in and day out of the revolutions that are   25
sweeping the world. I think we are ripe for one here.
And when you hear the testimony that follows in this

chamber, I believe you will think we are ripe for one too —a revolution of the American consumer against the manipulation of his mind and money by practices of packaging and labeling that empty his purse and his market basket while he is looking the other way.

So far the manufacturers guilty of these deceptions 26 are not the majority; yet among them are some of the most respected brand names in the business. They will, of course, deny deliberate deception and produce any number of reasons that they consider both valid and legal for packaging and labeling as they do. But the evidence stands and the confusion mounts.

Ladies and gentlemen—Consumers—we *are* being kid- 27 ded. In the days of McCarthy, Elmer Davis said of those who tried to confuse our thinking, "Don't let them scare you." Today I would like to say of those who try to confuse our buying and our values, "Don't let them kid you."

And I kid you not. 28

——— ◆ ———

For Study and Discussion

QUESTIONS ABOUT PURPOSE

1. What changes in behavior do you think Mannes wants her readers to make in their personal shopping habits? What changes does she want them to seek on a wider scale?

2. What change in the attitudes and practices of the people who run food companies and supermarkets does Mannes want to see?

3. Why does she relate deceptive packaging to "crime" and "corruption" (paragraph 21)?

QUESTIONS ABOUT AUDIENCE

1. This essay was first given as a speech before a Congressional committee and then published in a book. Do you think it would be more effective for listeners or readers? Why?
2. If Mannes were to publish this essay in a magazine, which magazines would be the most suitable? Why?
3. What personal shopping experiences does Mannes count on her readers having had? Is that assumption justified for college readers?

QUESTIONS ABOUT STRATEGIES

1. What effect does Mannes achieve in beginning the essay by talking about herself?
2. What kind of appeal does Mannes use in paragraph 3? What kinds in paragraphs 8, 9, 10, and 11?
3. How would you describe the tone of the paragraphs in which Mannes presents her evidence (paragraphs 6 through 15)? How does she achieve the tone?

QUESTIONS FOR DISCUSSION

1. In paragraphs 6 through 16 Mannes gives examples of how sellers mislead and confuse shoppers through deceptive packaging. Then in paragraph 17, on the basis of this evidence, she compares these sellers to dictators who try to brainwash people and control their behavior. What is your response to this leap from evidence to a conclusion?
2. What response to Mannes's charges do you think food processors and packagers would make?
3. How much responsibility for deceptive packaging do consumers have, and how much influence do you think they could have in getting such practices changed?

Why Are Americans
Afraid of Dragons?

URSULA K. LE GUIN

◆

Ursula Le Guin was born in 1929 in Berkeley, Califor-
nia, and educated at Radcliffe College and Columbia
University. In the 1950s she studied on a Fulbright
Fellowship in Paris; she then worked as a part-time
writing instructor at Mercer University and the Uni-
versity of Idaho before moving to Portland, Oregon,
where she was able to pursue a full-time career as a
writer. She published her first novel, Rocannon's War,
in 1964 and established herself as a leading writer
of science fiction and fantasy. She has contributed
her work to magazines as diverse as The New Yorker
and Fantastic. *Her novels include* The Left Hand of
Darkness *(1969),* The Lathe of Heaven *(1970), and her*
"Earthsea" trilogy, A Wizard of Earthsea *(1968),* The
Tomb of Athean *(1971), and* The Farthest Shore *(1972).*
In "Why Are Americans Afraid of Dragons?", a talk
first given to librarians and then later collected in a
volume of her essays, The Language of the Night:
Essays on Fantasy and Science Fiction *(1979), Le Guin*
presents a "personal defense of the uses of the imagi-
nation," arguing that fantasy is necessary for the kind
of internal exploration that produces whole human
beings.

This was to be a talk about fantasy. But I have not been   1
feeling very fanciful lately, and could not decide what to
say; so I have been going about picking people's brains for
ideas. "What about fantasy? Tell me something about
fantasy." And one friend of mine said, "All right, I'll tell
you something fantastic. Ten years ago, I went to the children's room of the library of such-and-such a city, and

411

asked for *The Hobbit*; and the librarian told me, 'Oh, we keep that only in the adult collection; we don't feel that escapism is good for children.' "

My friend and I had a good laugh and shudder over that, and we agreed that things have changed a great deal in these past ten years. That kind of moralistic censorship of works of fantasy is very uncommon now, in the children's libraries. But the fact that the children's libraries have become oases in the desert doesn't mean that there isn't still a desert. The point of view from which that librarian spoke still exists. She was merely reflecting, in perfect good faith, something that goes very deep in the American character: a moral disapproval of fantasy, a disapproval so intense, and often so aggressive, that I cannot help but see it as arising, fundamentally, from fear. 2

So: Why are Americans afraid of dragons? 3

Before I try to answer my question, let me say that it isn't only Americans who are afraid of dragons. I suspect that almost all very highly technological peoples are more or less antifantasy. There are several national literatures which, like ours, have had no tradition of adult fantasy for the past several hundred years: the French, for instance. But then you have the Germans, who have a good deal; and the English, who have it, and love it, and do it better than anyone else. So this fear of dragons is not merely a Western, or a technological, phenomenon. But I do not want to get into these vast historical questions; I will speak of modern Americans, the only people I know well enough to talk about. 4

In wondering why Americans are afraid of dragons, I began to realize that a great many Americans are not only antifantasy, but altogether antifiction. We tend, as a people, to look upon all works of the imagination either as suspect, or as contemptible. 5

"My wife reads novels. I haven't got the time." 6

"I used to read that science fiction stuff when I was a teenager, but of course I don't now." 7

"Fairy stories are for kids. I live in the real world." 8

Who speaks so? Who is it that dismisses *War and* 9
Peace, The Time Machine, and *A Midsummer Night's Dream* with this perfect self-assurance? It is, I fear, the man in the street—the hardworking, over-thirty American male—the men who run this country.

Such a rejection of the entire art of fiction is related to 10
several American characteristics: our Puritanism, our work ethic, our profit-mindedness, and even our sexual mores.

To read *War and Peace* or *The Lord of the Rings* 11
plainly is not "work"—you do it for pleasure. And if it cannot be justified as "educational" or as "self-improvement," then, in the Puritan value system, it can only be self-indulgence or escapism. For pleasure is not a value, to the Puritan; on the contrary, it is a sin.

Equally, in the businessman's value system, if an act 12
does not bring in an immediate, tangible profit, it has no justification at all. Thus the only person who has an excuse to read Tolstoy or Tolkien is the English teacher, because he gets paid for it. But our businessman might allow himself to read a best-seller now and then: not because it is a good book, but because it is a best-seller—it is a success, it has made money. To the strangely mystical mind of the money-changer, this justifies its existence; and by reading it he may participate, a little, in the power and mana of its success. If this is not magic, by the way, I don't know what is.

The last element, the sexual one, is more complex. 13
I hope I will not be understood as being sexist if I say that, within our culture, I believe that this antifiction attitude is basically a male one. The American boy and man is very commonly forced to define his maleness by rejecting certain traits, certain human gifts and potentialities, which our culture defines as "womanish" or "childish." And one of these traits or potentialities is, in cold sober fact, the absolutely essential human faculty of imagination.

Having got this far, I went quickly to the dictionary. 14

The *Shorter Oxford Dictionary* says: "Imagination. 15
1. The action of imagining, or forming a mental concept

413

of what is not actually present to the senses; 2. The mental consideration of actions or events not yet in existence."

Very well; I certainly can let "absolutely essential human faculty" stand. But I must narrow the definition to fit our present subject. By "imagination," then, I personally mean the free play of the mind, both intellectual and sensory. By "play" I mean recreation, re-creation, the recombination of what is known into what is new. By "free" I mean that the action is done without an immediate object of profit—spontaneously. That does not mean, however, that there may not be a purpose behind the free play of the mind, a goal; and the goal may be a very serious object indeed. Children's imaginative play is clearly a practicing at the acts and emotions of adulthood; a child who did not play would not become mature. As for the free play of an adult mind, its result may be *War and Peace,* or the theory of relativity. 16

To be free, after all, is not to be undisciplined. I should say that the discipline of the imagination may in fact be the essential method or technique of both art and science. It is our Puritanism, insisting that discipline means repression or punishment, which confuses the subject. To discipline something, in the proper sense of the word, does not mean to repress it, but to train it—to encourage it to grow, and act, and be fruitful, whether it is a peach tree or a human mind. 17

I think that a great many American men have been taught just the opposite. They have learned to repress their imagination, to reject it as something childish or effeminate, unprofitable, and probably sinful. 18

They have learned to fear it. But they have never learned to discipline it at all. 19

Now, I doubt that the imagination can be suppressed. If you truly eradicated it in a child, he would grow up to be an eggplant. Like all our evil propensities, the imagination will out. But if it is rejected and despised, it will grow into wild and weedy shapes; it will be deformed. At its best, it will be mere ego-centered daydreaming; at its worst, it 20

will be wishful thinking, which is a very dangerous occupation when it is taken seriously. Where literature is
concerned, in the old, truly Puritan days, the only per-
mitted reading was the Bible. Nowadays, with our secular
Puritanism, the man who refuses to read novels because
it's unmanly to do so, or because they aren't true, will
most likely end up watching bloody detective thrillers on
the television, or reading hack Westerns or sports stories,
or going in for pornography, from *Playboy* on down. It is
his starved imagination, craving nourishment, that forces
him to do so. But he can rationalize such entertainment
by saying that it is realistic—after all, sex exists, and there
are criminals, and there are baseball players, and there
used to be cowboys—and also by saying that it is virile, by
which he means that it doesn't interest most women.

That all these genres are sterile, hopelessly sterile, is a   21
reassurance to him, rather than a defect. If they were
genuinely realistic, which is to say genuinely imagined
and imaginative, he would be afraid of them. Fake real-
ism is the escapist literature of our time. And probably
the ultimate escapist reading is that masterpiece of total
unreality, the daily stock market report.

Now what about our man's wife? She probably wasn't   22
required to squelch her private imagination in order to
play her expected role in life, but she hasn't been trained
to discipline it, either. She is allowed to read novels, and
even fantasies. But, lacking training and encouragement,
her fancy is likely to glom on to very sickly fodder, such
things as soap operas, and "true romances," and nursy
novels, and historico-sentimental novels, and all the rest
of the baloney ground out to replace genuine imaginative
works by the artistic sweatshops of a society that is profoundly distrustful of the uses of the imagination.

What, then, are the uses of the imagination?   23

You see, I think we have a terrible thing here: a hard-   24
working, upright, responsible citizen, a full-grown, educated person, who is afraid of dragons, and afraid of hobbits, and scared to death of fairies. It's funny, but it's also

terrible. Something has gone very wrong. I don't know what to do about it but to try and give an honest answer to that person's question, even though he often asks it in an aggressive and contemptuous tone of voice. "What's the good of it all?" he says. "Dragons and hobbits and little green men—what's the *use* of it?"

The truest answer, unfortunately, he won't even listen 25 to. He won't hear it. The truest answer is, "The use of it is to give you pleasure and delight."

"I haven't got the time," he snaps, swallowing a Maalox 26 pill for his ulcer and rushing off to the golf course.

So we try the next-to-truest answer. It probably won't 27 go down much better, but it must be said: "The use of imaginative fiction is to deepen your understanding of your world, and your fellow men, and your own feelings, and your destiny."

To which I fear he will retort, "Look, I got a raise last 28 year, and I'm giving my family the best of everything, we've got two cars and a color TV. I understand enough of the world!"

And he is right, unanswerably right, if that is what he 29 wants, and all he wants.

The kind of thing you learn from reading about the 30 problems of a hobbit who is trying to drop a magic ring into an imaginary volcano has very little to do with your social status, or material success, or income. Indeed, if there is any relationship, it is a negative one. There is an inverse correlation between fantasy and money. That is a law, known to economists as Le Guin's Law. If you want a striking example of Le Guin's Law, just give a lift to one of those people along the roads who own nothing but a backpack, a guitar, a fine head of hair, a smile, and a thumb. Time and again, you will find that these waifs have read *The Lord of the Rings*—some of them can practically recite it. But now take Aristotle Onassis, or J. Paul Getty: could you believe that those men ever had anything to do, at any age, under any circumstances, with a hobbit?

But, to carry my example a little further, and out of the 31 realm of economics, did you ever notice how very gloomy Mr. Onassis and Mr. Getty and all those billionaires look in their photographs? They have this strange, pinched look, as if they were hungry. As if they were hungry for something, as if they had lost something and were trying to think where it could be, or perhaps what it could be, what it was they've lost.

Could it be their childhood? 32

So I arrive at my personal defense of the uses of the 33 imagination, especially in fiction, and most especially in fairy tale, legend, fantasy, science fiction, and the rest of the lunatic fringe. I believe that maturity is not an out-growing, but a growing up: that an adult is not a dead child, but a child who survived. I believe that all the best faculties of a mature human being exist in the child, and that if these faculties are encouraged in youth they will act well and wisely in the adult, but if they are repressed and denied in the child they will stunt and cripple the adult personality. And finally, I believe that one of the most deeply human, and humane, of these faculties is the power of imagination: so that it is our pleasant duty, as librarians, or teachers, or parents, or writers, or simply as grownups, to encourage that faculty of imagination in our children, to encourage it to grow freely, to flourish like the green bay tree, by giving it the best, absolutely the best and purest, nourishment that it can absorb. And never, under any circumstances, to squelch it, or sneer at it, or imply that it is childish, or unmanly, or untrue.

For fantasy is true, of course. It isn't factual, but it is 34 true. Children know that. Adults know it too, and that is precisely why many of them are afraid of fantasy. They know that its truth challenges, even threatens, all that is false, all that is phony, unnecessary, and trivial in the life they have let themselves be forced into living. They are afraid of dragons, because they are afraid of freedom.

So I believe that we should trust our children. Normal 35 children do not confuse reality and fantasy—they confuse them much less often than we adults do (as a certain great fantasist pointed out in a story called "The Emperor's New Clothes"). Children know perfectly well that unicorns aren't real, but they also know that books about unicorns, if they are good books, are true books. All too often, that's more than Mummy and Daddy know; for, in denying their childhood, the adults have denied half their knowledge, and are left with the sad, sterile little fact: "Unicorns aren't real." And that fact is one that never got anybody anywhere (except in the story "The Unicorn in the Garden," by another great fantasist, in which it is shown that a devotion to the unreality of unicorns may get you straight into the loony bin). It is by such statements as, "Once upon a time there was a dragon," or "In a hole in the ground there lived a hobbit"—it is by such beautiful non-facts that we fantastic human beings may arrive, in our peculiar fashion, at the truth.

—————— ◆ ——————

For Study and Discussion

QUESTIONS ABOUT PURPOSE

1. In what ways does the question in Le Guin's title— Why Are Americans Afraid of Dragons?—embody the central purpose of her essay?

2. What connections does Le Guin establish among fantasy, fiction, and the imagination? What connections does she see among fear, sin, and repression?

3. What changes in attitudes and habits does Le Guin propose for the adult population of this country? How does this proposal relate to the concept of maturity?

QUESTIONS ABOUT AUDIENCE

1. What assumptions does Le Guin make about the attitudes of her original audience (librarians) in her opening story about censorship?

2. What assumptions does she make about the general knowledge of her audience by making allusions to *The Hobbit, War and Peace, The Lord of the Rings,* and "The Unicorn in the Garden"?

3. To what extent does Le Guin anticipate a skeptical response to her argument from a larger group of readers? For example, how does she suppose the normal businessman would respond to her assertions?

QUESTIONS ABOUT STRATEGIES

1. How does Le Guin employ the strategies of definition to demonstrate the value of "the free play of the mind"?

2. How does she set up an imaginary conversation on the "uses" of the imagination to present and resolve various objections to her argument?

3. How do her descriptions of J. Paul Getty and Aristotle Onassis contribute to the effectiveness of her argument? How do they illustrate "Le Guin's Law"?

QUESTIONS FOR DISCUSSION

1. To what extent do you agree with Le Guin's assertion that our rejection of fantasy is related to several American characteristics: "our Puritanism, our work ethic, our profit mindedness, and even our sexual mores"? What does Le Guin suggest about the attitudes of other cultures toward the imagination?

2. Le Guin is a highly respected science fiction writer. How does knowing that fact affect your response to her essay?

3. Do you think Le Guin may be correct about the cultural consequences of Americans' inability to distinguish among escapism, fantasy, and reality? Explain your answer.

The Habit

WILLIAM STYRON

◆

*William Styron was born in 1925 in Newport News,
Virginia, and educated at Duke University. Upon
graduation he came North to work as an associate editor for McGraw-Hill and to study writing at the New
School for Social Research. His first three novels—*
Lie Down in Darkness *(1951),* The Long March *(1957),
and* Set This House on Fire *(1960)—established Styron
as one of the most gifted writers of his generation.
With the publication of* The Confessions of Nat Turner
*(1967), an account of the "only effective, sustained
revolt in the annals of American Negro slavery," he
became one of the most controversial. The novel was
awarded the Pulitzer Prize, but it provoked considerable debate in the racially explosive atmosphere of
the sixties. Styron's other work includes a play,* In the
Clap Stick *(1973), and a widely acclaimed novel,* So-
phie's Choice *(1976). His essays and reviews are collected in* This Quiet Dust and Other Writings *(1982).
"The Habit," reprinted from that volume, first appeared in* The New York Review of Books *on the
occasion of the publication of* The Consumers Union
Report on Smoking *(1963). Styron uses the "inescapable" evidence from that report to construct a persuasive argument for giving up a "mortally corrupting
addiction."*

The lamentable history of the cigarette is that of a mor-   1
tally corrupting addiction having been embraced by millions of people in the spirit of childlike innocence. It is a
history which is also strikingly brief. Cigarettes began to
be manufactured extensively around the turn of the century, but it was not until as recently as 1921 that cigarettes
overtook chewing tobacco, as well as pipes and cigars, in

per capita consumption, and the 1930s were well along before cigarette smoking became the accepted thing for ladies.

The popularity of cigarettes was inevitable and overwhelming. They were not offensive in close quarters, nor messy like pipes and cigars. They were easily portable. They did not look gross and unseemly in a lady's mouth. They were cheap to manufacture, and they were inhalable. Unlike the great majority of pipe and cigar smokers, whose pleasure is predominantly oral and contemplative, most cigarette smokers inhale deep into their lungs with bladelike, rhythmic savagery, inflicting upon themselves in miniature a particularly abrasive form of air pollution. Further, the very fact of inhalation seems to enhance the cigarette's addictive power. Unhappily, few suspected the consequences in terms of health until long after cigarette smoking had gained its colossal momentum. That this type of auto-contamination is a major cause of lung cancer—that it is also a prime causative factor in deaths from coronary artery disease, bronchitis, asthma, emphysema, among other afflictions—was established, and for the first time well publicized, only a decade ago. The effect this knowledge has had upon the public consciousness may be suggested by the fact that sales this year reached the galactic sum of one-half trillion cigarettes —one hundred billion more than in 1953. There is something historically intimidating in the idea that cigarette smoking as a mass diversion and a raging increase in lung cancer have both come about during the lifetime of those who are now no more than fifty years old. It is the very *recentness* of the phenomenon which helps make it so shocking. The hard truth is that human beings have never in such a brief space of time, and in so grand and guileless a multitude, embraced a habit whose unwholesome effects not only would totally outweigh the meager satisfactions but would hasten the deaths of a large proportion of the people who indulged in it. Certainly (and there seems little doubt that the Surgeon General's report will

2

make this clear) only nuclear fallout exceeds cigarette smoking in gravity as a public health problem.

For its lucid presentation of the medical evidence alone, 3 *The Consumers Union Report on Smoking* would be a valuable document. "The conclusion is inescapable," the *Report* begins, "and even spokesmen for the cigarette industry rarely seek to escape it: we are living in the midst of a major lung cancer epidemic. This epidemic hit men first and hardest, but has affected women as well. It cannot be explained away by such factors as improved diagnosis. And there is reason to believe that the worst is yet to come." Yet despite this minatory beginning the tone throughout is one of caution and reasonableness, and the authors—who manage an accomplished prose style rare in such collective undertakings—marshal their facts with such efficiency and persuasion that it is hard to imagine anyone but a fool or a tobacco lobbyist denying the close association between smoking and lung cancer. Yet, of course, not only lung cancer. The *Report* quotes, for instance, data based on an extensive study of smokers and non-smokers among English physicians, where the death rate *from all causes* was found to be doubled among heavy cigarette smokers in the group of men past 65, and quadrupled in the group 35 to 44. And the *Report* adds, with the modest and constructive irony that makes the book, if not exactly a joy, then agreeable to read: "These death rates among smokers are perhaps the least controversial of all the findings to date. For with respect to any particular disease there is always the possibility, however remote, that mistaken diagnosis and other conceivable errors may cast doubt on the statistics. But death is easily diagnosed."

In the end, however, what makes the *Report*'s message 4 supportable to those distracted souls among the millions of American smokers who may wish to kick the habit— or who, having kicked the habit, may wonder if it is not too late—is a kind of muted optimism. For all present evidence seems to indicate that the common cocktail party rationalization ("I've smoked too long to stop now, the damage is done") has no real basis in fact. In research carried out by the American Cancer Society, microscopic studies of the lung tissues of ex-smokers have shown a process in which precancerous cells are dying out instead of flourishing and reproducing as in the tissues of continuing smokers. Here the *Report* states, in regard to a carefully matched group composed in equal numbers of nonsmokers, ex-smokers and smokers: "Metaplastic cells with altered nuclei [i.e., precancerous cells] were found in 1.2 percent of the slides from the lungs of nonsmokers, as compared with 6.0 for ex-smokers—and *93.2 percent* for current smokers."

Certainly such evidence, combined with the fact that ex-smokers have a lung cancer death rate which ranges down to one fifth of that of smokers who continue to smoke, should be of the greatest practical interest to anyone who ponders whether it may be worthwhile abandoning what is, after all, a cheerless, grubby, fumbling addiction. (Only the passion of a convert could provoke these last words. The *Report* was an aid to my stopping a two-pack-a-day habit which commenced in early infancy. Of course, stopping smoking may be in itself a major problem, one of psychological complexity. For myself, after two or three days of great flaccidity of spirit, an aimless oral yearning, aching moments of hunger at the pit of the stomach, and an awful intermittent urge to burst into tears, the problem resolved itself, and in less than a week all craving vanished. Curiously, for the first time in my life, I developed a racking cough, but this, too, disappeared. A sense of smugness, a kind of fatness of soul, is the reward for such a struggle. The intensity of the addiction varies, however, and some people find the ordeal fearfully difficult, if not next to impossible. I do have an urgent suspicion, though, that the greatest barrier to a termination of the habit is the dread of some Faustian upheaval, when in fact that deprivation, while momentarily oppressive, is apt to prove not really cruel at all.)

But if the *Report* is splendidly effective as a caveat, it

may be read for its sociological insights as well. Certainly the history of commerce has few instances of such shameful abdication of responsibility as that displayed by the cigarette industry when in 1952 the "health scare," as it is so winsomely known in the trade, brought about the crisis which will reach a head in this month's report by the Surgeon General. It seems clear that the industry, instead of trying to forestall the inevitable with its lies and evasions, might have acquitted itself with some honor had it made what the *Report* calls the only feasible choices: to have urged caution on smokers, to have given money to independent research organizations, to have avoided propaganda and controversy in favor of unbiased inquiry. At the very least the industry might have soft-pedaled or, indeed, silenced its pitch to young people. But panic and greed dominated the reaction, and during the decade since the smoking–lung cancer link was made public, the official position of the industry has been that, in the matter of lung cancer, the villain is any and everything *but* the cigarette. Even the American Cancer Society is in on the evil plot and, in the words of one industry spokesman, "relies almost wholly upon health scare propaganda to raise millions of dollars from a gullible public."

Meanwhile, $200 million was spent last year on cigarette ballyhoo, and during these last crucial ten years the annual advertising expenditure has increased 134 percent —a vast amount of it, of course, going to entice the very young. One million of these young people, according to the American Public Health Association, will die of smoking-induced lung cancer before they reach the age of seventy years. "Between the time a kid is eighteen and twenty-one, he's going to make the basic decision to smoke or not to smoke," says L. W. Bruff, advertising director of Liggett & Myers. "If he does decide to smoke, we want to get him." I have never met Mr. Bruff, but in my mind's eye I see him, poised like a cormorant above those doomed minnows, and I am amused by the refinement, the weight of conscience, the delicate interplay of intellectual and

7

moral alternatives which go into the making of such a pro-digious thought. As the report demonstrates, however, Mr. Bruff is only typical of the leaders of an industry which last year received a bounty of $7 billion from 63 million American smokers. Perhaps the tragic reality is that neither this estimable report nor that of the Surgeon General can measurably affect, much less really change, such awesome figures.

———————— ◆ ————————

For Study and Discussion

QUESTIONS ABOUT PURPOSE

1. What is Styron's primary purpose in this essay—to explain the findings of *The Consumers Union Report on Smoking,* to demonstrate the ill effects of smoking, or to encourage people to break the habit? Explain your answer.

2. What action do you think Styron would like to promote against the tobacco industry?

3. What is Styron's purpose in beginning his essay with a brief history of cigarettes and the reasons for their popularity?

QUESTIONS ABOUT AUDIENCE

1. The readers of this essay are likely to fall into three groups: nonsmokers, ex-smokers, and smokers. How do you think their responses to the essay will differ?

2. What assumptions does Styron make about his readers when he alludes to "fools" and "tobacco lobbyists" in paragraph 3?

3. In paragraph 4 Styron discusses the report's "muted optimism." To which members of his audience is he

directing this discussion? How do you think they will respond to his argument in this essay?

QUESTIONS ABOUT STRATEGIES

1. How does Styron use his own experience to convince a certain group of his readers that they can break the habit? What does he suggest is the "greatest barrier" to producing this change? (See the last sentence in paragraph 5.)
2. Styron constructs his argument by combining authoritative statistics and strong emotional language. Considering the argument he is making, which strategy seems more effective? Explain your answer.
3. Styron is a major American novelist. What writing techniques does he use here that he might also use in writing a novel?

QUESTIONS FOR DISCUSSION

1. To what extent do you concur with Styron's assertions that "only nuclear fallout exceeds cigarette smoking in gravity as a public health problem"?
2. In addition to the tobacco industry, what other businesses in the history of commerce have displayed a "shameful abdication of responsibility"?
3. This essay was written over twenty years ago. Since that time how have the smoking public and the tobacco industry responded to the charges Styron makes in his argument?

The Obligation to Endure

RACHEL CARSON

◆

Rachel Carson (1907–1964) was born in Springfield, Pennsylvania, and educated at Pennsylvania College for Women and Johns Hopkins University. After graduation she taught for several years in the zoology department of the University of Maryland before accepting a position as aquatic biologist with the United States Bureau of Fisheries (now the Fish and Wildlife Service). She worked at the bureau for over fifteen years, rising to the position of editor-in-chief of publications. Throughout her period of government service Carson wrote about various aspects of her work for both popular audiences (Under the Sea-Wind: A Naturalist's Picture of Ocean Life, 1941) *and scientific audiences* (Fish and Shellfish of the Middle Atlantic Coast, 1945). *With the publication of* The Sea Around Us *(1951), which won the National Book Award, she was able to resign her editorial position and devote full time to her writing. Her books include* The Edge of the Sea *(1955),* Silent Spring *(1962), and* The Sense of Wonder *(1965).* Silent Spring, *certainly Carson's most influential book, was the first major attack on the harmful use of pesticides. Now, more than twenty years later, her argument that the imprudent use of chemicals in the environment threatens our ability to endure seems even more compelling.*

The history of life on earth has been a history of interaction between living things and their surroundings. To a large extent, the physical form and the habits of the earth's vegetation and its animal life have been molded by the environment. Considering the whole span of earthly time, the opposite effect, in which life actually modifies its surroundings, has been relatively slight. Only within the moment of time represented by the present century has one species—man—acquired significant power to alter the nature of his world.

During the past quarter century this power has not only increased to one of disturbing magnitude but it has changed in character. The most alarming of all man's assaults upon the environment is the contamination of air, earth, rivers, and sea with dangerous and even lethal materials. This pollution is for the most part irrecoverable; the chain of evil it initiates not only in the world that must support life but in living tissues is for the most part irreversible. In this now universal contamination of the environment, chemicals are the sinister and little-recognized partners of radiation in changing the very nature of the world—the very nature of its life. Strontium 90, released through nuclear explosions into the air, comes to earth in rain or drifts down as fallout, lodges in soil, enters into the grass or corn or wheat grown there, and in time takes up its abode in the bones of a human being, there to remain until his death. Similarly, chemicals sprayed on croplands or forests or gardens lie long in soil, entering into living organisms, passing from one to another in a chain of poisoning and death. Or they pass mysteriously by underground streams until they emerge and, through the alchemy of air and sunlight, combine into new forms that kill vegetation, sicken cattle, and work unknown harm on those who drink from once pure wells. As Albert Schweitzer has said, "Man can hardly even recognize the devils of his own creation."

It took hundreds of millions of years to produce the life that now inhabits the earth—eons of time in which that developing and evolving and diversifying life reached a state of adjustment and balance with its surroundings. The environment, rigorously shaping and directing the life it supported, contained elements that were hostile as well as supporting. Certain rocks gave out dangerous radiation; even within the light of the sun, from which all life draws its energy, there were short-wave radiations with power to injure. Given time—time not in years but in millennia—life adjusts, and a balance has been reached. For time is the essential ingredient; but in the modern world there is no time.

The rapidity of change and the speed with which new   4
situations are created follow the impetuous and heedless pace of man rather than the deliberate pace of nature. Radiation is no longer merely the background radiation of rocks, the bombardment of cosmic rays, the ultraviolet of the sun that have existed before there was any life on earth; radiation is now the unnatural creation of man's tampering with the atom. The chemicals to which life is asked to make its adjustment are no longer merely the calcium and silica and copper and all the rest of the minerals washed out of the rocks and carried in rivers to the sea; they are the synthetic creations of man's inventive mind, brewed in his laboratories, and having no counterparts in nature.

To adjust to these chemicals would require time on   5
the scale that is nature's; it would require not merely the years of a man's life but the life of generations. And even this, were it by some miracle possible, would be futile, for the new chemicals come from our laboratories in an endless stream; almost five hundred annually find their way into actual use in the United States alone. The figure is staggering and its implications are not easily grasped— 500 new chemicals to which the bodies of men and animals are required somehow to adapt each year, chemicals totally outside the limits of biologic experience.

Among them are many that are used in man's war   6
against nature. Since the mid-1940's over 200 basic chemicals have been created for use in killing insects, weeds, rodents, and other organisms described in the modern vernacular as "pests"; and they are sold under several thousand different brand names.

These sprays, dusts, and aerosols are now applied al-   7
most universally to farms, gardens, forests, and homes—

429

nonselective chemicals that have the power to kill every insect, the "good" and the "bad," to still the song of birds and the leaping of fish in the streams, to coat the leaves with a deadly film, and to linger on in soil—all this though the intended target may be only a few weeds or insects. Can anyone believe it is possible to lay down such a barrage of poisons on the surface of the earth without making it unfit for all life? They should not be called "insecticides," but "biocides."

The whole process of spraying seems caught up in an   8
endless spiral. Since DDT was released for civilian use, a process of escalation has been going on in which ever more toxic materials must be found. This has happened because insects, in a triumphant vindication of Darwin's principle of the survival of the fittest, have evolved super races immune to the particular insecticide used, hence a deadlier one has always to be developed—and then a deadlier one than that. It has happened also because, for reasons to be described later, destructive insects often undergo a "flareback," or resurgence, after spraying in numbers greater than before. Thus the chemical war is never won, and all life is caught in its violent crossfire.

Along with the possibility of the extinction of man-   9
kind by nuclear war, the central problem of our age has therefore become the contamination of man's total environment with such substances of incredible potential for harm—substances that accumulate in the tissues of plants and animals and even penetrate the germ cells to shatter or alter the very material of heredity upon which the shape of the future depends.

Some would-be architects of our future look toward a   10
time when it will be possible to alter the human germ plasm by design. But we may easily be doing so now by inadvertence, for many chemicals, like radiation, bring about gene mutations. It is ironic to think that man might determine his own future by something so seemingly trivial as the choice of an insect spray.

All this has been risked—for what? Future historians   11

may well be amazed by our distorted sense of proportion. How could intelligent beings seek to control a few unwanted species by a method that contaminated the entire environment and brought the threat of disease and death even to their own kind? Yet this is precisely what we have done. We have done it, moreover, for reasons that collapse the moment we examine them. We are told that the enormous and expanding use of pesticides is necessary to maintain farm production. Yet is our real problem not one of *overproduction?* Our farms, despite measures to remove acreages from production and to pay farmers *not* to produce, have yielded such a staggering excess of crops that the American taxpayer in 1962 is paying out more than one billion dollars a year as the total carrying cost of the surplus-food storage program. And is the situation helped when one branch of the Agriculture Department tries to reduce production while another states, as it did in 1958, "It is believed generally that reduction of crop acreages under provisions of the Soil Bank will stimulate interest in use of chemicals to obtain maximum production on the land retained in crops."

All this is not to say there is no insect problem and no 12
need of control. I am saying, rather, that control must be geared to realities, not to mythical situations, and that the methods employed must be such that they do not destroy us along with the insects.

The problem whose attempted solution has brought 13
such a train of disaster in its wake is an accompaniment of our modern way of life. Long before the age of man, insects inhabited the earth—a group of extraordinarily varied and adaptable beings. Over the course of time since man's advent, a small percentage of the more than half a million species of insects have come into conflict with human welfare in two principal ways: as competitors for the food supply and as carriers of human disease.

Disease-carrying insects become important where hu- 14
man beings are crowded together, especially under condi-

tions where sanitation is poor, as in time of natural disaster or war or in situations of extreme poverty and deprivation. Then control of some sort becomes necessary. It is a sobering fact, however, as we shall presently see, that the method of massive chemical control has had only limited success, and also threatens to worsen the very conditions it is intended to curb.

Under primitive agricultural conditions the farmer 15 had few insect problems. These arose with the intensification of agriculture—the devotion of immense acreages to a single crop. Such a system set the stage for explosive increases in specific insect populations. Single-crop farming does not take advantage of the principles by which nature works; it is agriculture as an engineer might conceive it to be. Nature has introduced great variety into the landscape, but man has displayed a passion for simplifying it. Thus he undoes the built-in checks and balances by which nature holds the species within bounds. One important natural check is a limit on the amount of suitable habitat for each species. Obviously then, an insect that lives on wheat can build up its population to much higher levels on a farm devoted to wheat than on one in which wheat is intermingled with other crops to which the insect is not adapted.

The same thing happens in other situations. A genera- 16 tion or more ago, the towns of large areas of the United States lined their streets with the noble elm tree. Now the beauty they hopefully created is threatened with complete destruction as disease sweeps through the elms, carried by a beetle that would have only limited chance to build up large populations and to spread from tree to tree if the elms were only occasional trees in a richly diversified planting.

Another factor in the modern insect problem is one 17 that must be viewed against a background of geologic and human history: the spreading of thousands of different kinds of organisms from their native homes to invade new territories. This worldwide migration has been studied and graphically described by the British ecologist Charles Elton in his recent book *The Ecology of Invasions.* During the Cretaceous Period, some hundred million years ago, flooding seas cut many land bridges between continents and living things found themselves confined in what Elton calls "colossal separate nature reserves." There, isolated from others of their kind, they developed many new species. When some of the land masses were joined again, about 15 million years ago, these species began to move out into new territories—a movement that is not only still in progress but is now receiving considerable assistance from man.

The importation of plants is the primary agent in the 18 modern spread of species, for animals have almost invariably gone along with the plants, quarantine being a comparatively recent and not completely effective innovation. The United States Office of Plant Introduction alone has introduced almost 200,000 species and varieties of plants from all over the world. Nearly half of the 180 or so major insect enemies of plants in the United States are accidental imports from abroad, and most of them have come as hitchhikers on plants.

In new territory, out of reach of the restraining hand of 19 the natural enemies that kept down its numbers in its native land, an invading plant or animal is able to become enormously abundant. Thus it is no accident that our most troublesome insects are introduced species.

These invasions, both the naturally occurring and those 20 dependent on human assistance, are likely to continue indefinitely. Quarantine and massive chemical campaigns are only extremely expensive ways of buying time. We are faced, according to Dr. Elton, "with a life-and-death need not just to find new technological means of suppressing this plant or that animal"; instead we need the basic knowledge of animal populations and their relations to their surroundings that will "promote an even balance and damp down the explosive power of outbreaks and new invasions."

Much of the necessary knowledge is now available but 21 we do not use it. We train ecologists in our universities and even employ them in our governmental agencies but we seldom take their advice. We allow the chemical death rain to fall as though there were no alternative, whereas in fact there are many, and our ingenuity could soon discover many more if given opportunity.

Have we fallen into a mesmerized state that makes us 22 accept as inevitable that which is inferior or detrimental, as though having lost the will or the vision to demand that which is good? Such thinking, in the words of the ecologist Paul Shepard, "idealizes life with only its head out of water, inches above the limits of toleration of the corruption of its own environment ... Why should we tolerate a diet of weak poisons, a home in insipid surroundings, a circle of acquaintances who are not quite our enemies, the noise of motors with just enough relief to prevent insanity? Who would want to live in a world which is just not quite fatal?"

Yet such a world is pressed upon us. The crusade to 23 create a chemically sterile, insect-free world seems to have engendered a fanatic zeal on the part of many specialists and most of the so-called control agencies. On every hand there is evidence that those engaged in spraying operations exercise a ruthless power. "The regulatory entomologists ... function as prosecutor, judge and jury, tax assessor and collector and sheriff to enforce their own orders," said Connecticut entomologist Neely Turner. The most flagrant abuses go unchecked in both state and federal agencies.

It is not my contention that chemical insecticides must 24 never be used. I do contend that we have put poisonous and biologically potent chemicals indiscriminately into the hands of persons largely or wholly ignorant of their potentials for harm. We have subjected enormous numbers of people to contact with these poisons, without their consent and often without their knowledge. If the Bill of Rights contains no guarantee that a citizen shall be secure against lethal poisons distributed either by private individuals or by public officials, it is surely only because our forefathers, despite their considerable wisdom and foresight, could conceive of no such problem.

I contend, furthermore, that we have allowed these chemicals to be used with little or no advance investigation of their effect on soil, water, wildlife, and man himself. Future generations are unlikely to condone our lack of prudent concern for the integrity of the natural world that supports all life.

There is still very limited awareness of the nature of the threat. This is an era of specialists, each of whom sees his own problem and is unaware of or intolerant of the larger frame into which it fits. It is also an era dominated by industry, in which the right to make a dollar at whatever cost is seldom challenged. When the public protests, confronted with some obvious evidence of damaging results of pesticide applications, it is fed little tranquilizing pills of half truth. We urgently need an end to these false assurances, to the sugar coating of unpalatable facts. It is the public that is being asked to assume the risks that the insect controllers calculate. The public must decide whether it wishes to continue on the present road, and it can do so only when in full possession of the facts. In the words of Jean Rostand, "The obligation to endure gives us the right to know."

———— ◆ ————

For Study and Discussion

QUESTIONS ABOUT PURPOSE

1. What is Carson's primary purpose in this essay? How does the essay's title help establish that purpose?
2. How does Carson want us to rearrange our priorities?

3. Although Carson does not demand any specific action, she does recommend several kinds of changes in behavior. Make a list of those recommendations.

QUESTIONS ABOUT AUDIENCE

1. What assumptions does Carson make about the identity of her readers? How does she use the pronoun *we*—as in "we have done it, moreover, for reasons that collapse the moment we examine them"—to identify those readers?
2. If Carson is addressing readers who would have the power to impose strict controls on pesticides, what objections from them would she have to anticipate when she planned her essay? Would the essay be effective with that audience? Why?
3. Although Carson talks about what "we" have done to our environment, she implies that it is another group —a "they"—that has been chiefly responsible for the contamination of our world. What would "they" think of her argument? Has she anticipated their objections? How?

QUESTIONS ABOUT STRATEGIES

1. How does Carson's use of historical perspective at the beginning (and in several other sections) of her essay help establish the rationality of her argument?
2. How does her citation of facts about the creation of new chemicals, the escalation of immunity, and the cost of overproduction lend authority to her case?
3. To what extent does Carson use emotional or ethical appeals in her argument? See, for example, paragraphs 7 and 25.

QUESTIONS FOR DISCUSSION

1. What forces in our country oppose the kind of changes Carson suggests? What is their argument in this controversy?
2. What examples other than nuclear extinction and chemical contamination might be listed as "the devils of our own creation"?
3. What are the educational, political, and economic consequences of Carson's argument? For example, what are the consequences of her assertions in paragraph 21?

An Inquiry into the Persistence of Unwisdom in Government

BARBARA TUCHMAN

◆

*Barbara Tuchman was born in New York City in 1912
and educated at Radcliffe College. She began her career as a journalist, working for* The Nation, *first as a
foreign correspondent (during the Spanish Civil War),
and then as a national correspondent (during World
War II). Her books exhibit a variety of interests—*
Bible and the Sword: England and Palestine from the
Bronze Age to Balfour *(1956);* A Distant Mirror: The
Calamitous Fourteenth Century *(1978)—and two of
them have been awarded the Pulitzer Prize:* The Guns
of August *(1958) and* Stillwell and the American Experiment in China, 1911–1945 *(1972). Tuchman is a
frequent contributor to* Harper's, Atlantic, American
Scholar, *and* Foreign Affairs *magazines, crafting her
essays to meet the demands of both the scholarly
specialist and the general reader. In 1981 she collected
many of these essays in the widely acclaimed* Practicing History. *"An Inquiry into the Persistence of
Unwisdom in Government," first published in* Esquire
*(May 1980), served as the impetus for Tuchman's
most recent book,* The March of Folly: From Troy to
Vietnam *(1984). In this carefully documented historical argument Tuchman demonstrates that those in
charge are often afflicted with "wooden-headedness."*

A problem that strikes one in the study of history, regard-   1
less of period, is why man makes a poorer performance of
government than of almost any other human activity. In
this sphere, wisdom—meaning judgment acting on experience, common sense, available knowledge, and a decent

appreciation of probability—is less operative and more frustrated than it should be. Why do men in high office so often act contrary to the way that reason points and enlightened self-interest suggests? Why does intelligent mental process so often seem to be paralyzed?

Why, to begin at the beginning, did the Trojan authorities drag that suspicious-looking wooden horse inside their gates? Why did successive ministries of George III— that "bundle of imbecility," as Dr. Johnson called them collectively—insist on coercing rather than conciliating the Colonies though strongly advised otherwise by many counselors? Why did Napoleon and Hitler invade Russia? Why did the kaiser's government resume unrestricted submarine warfare in 1917 although explicitly warned that this would bring in the United States and that American belligerency would mean Germany's defeat? Why did Chiang Kai-shek refuse to heed any voice of reform or alarm until he woke up to find that his country had slid from under him? Why did Lyndon Johnson, seconded by the best and the brightest, progressively involve this nation in a war both ruinous and halfhearted and from which nothing but bad for our side resulted? Why does the present Administration continue to avoid introducing effective measures to reduce the wasteful consumption of oil while members of OPEC follow a price policy that must bankrupt their customers? How is it possible that the Central Intelligence Agency, whose function it is to provide, at taxpayers' expense, the information necessary to conduct a realistic foreign policy, could remain unaware that discontent in a country crucial to our interests was boiling up to the point of insurrection and overthrow of the ruler upon whom our policy rested? It has been reported that the CIA was ordered *not* to investigate the opposition to the shah of Iran in order to spare him any indication that we took it seriously, but since this sounds more like the theater of the absurd than like responsible government, I cannot bring myself to believe it.

There was a king of Spain once, Philip III, who is said

to have died of a fever he contracted from sitting too long near a hot brazier, helplessly overheating himself because the functionary whose duty it was to remove the brazier when summoned could not be found. In the late twentieth century, it begins to appear as if mankind may be approaching a similar stage of suicidal incompetence. The Italians have been sitting in Philip III's hot seat for some time. The British trade unions, in a lunatic spectacle, seem periodically bent on dragging their country toward paralysis, apparently under the impression that they are separate from the whole. Taiwan was thrown into a state of shock by the United States' recognition of the People's Republic of China because, according to one report, in the seven years since the Shanghai Communiqué, the Kuomintang rulers of Taiwan had "refused to accept the new trend as a reality."

Wooden-headedness is a factor that plays a remarkably   4
large role in government. Wooden-headedness consists of assessing a situation in terms of preconceived, fixed notions while ignoring or rejecting any contrary signs. It is acting according to wish while not allowing oneself to be confused by the facts.

A classic case was the French war plan of 1914, which   5
concentrated everything on a French offensive to the Rhine, leaving the French left flank from Belgium to the Channel virtually unguarded. The strategy was based on the belief that the Germans would not use reserves in the front line and, without them, could not deploy enough manpower to extend their invasion through the French left. Reports by intelligence agents in 1913 to the effect that the Germans were indeed preparing their reserves for the front line in case of war were resolutely ignored because the governing spirits in France, dreaming only of their own offensive, did not want to believe in any signals that would require them to strengthen their left at the expense of their march to the Rhine. In the event, the Germans could and did extend themselves around the

French left with results that determined a long war and its fearful consequences for our century.

Wooden-headedness is also the refusal to learn from experience, a form in which fourteenth-century rulers were supreme. No matter how often and obviously devaluation of the currency disrupted the economy and angered the people, French monarchs continued to resort to it whenever they were desperate for cash until they provoked insurrection among the bourgeoisie. No matter how often a campaign that depended on living off a hostile country ran into want and even starvation, campaigns for which this fate was inevitable were regularly undertaken. 6

Still another form is identification of self with the state, as currently exhibited by the ayatollah Khomeini. No wooden-headedness is so impenetrable as that of a religious zealot. Because he is connected with a private wire to the Almighty, no idea coming in on a lesser channel can reach him, which leaves him ill equipped to guide his country in its own best interests. 7

Philosophers of government ever since Plato have devoted their thinking to the major issues of ethics, sovereignty, the social contract, the rights of man, the corruption of power, the balance between freedom and order. Few—except Machiavelli, who was concerned with government as it is, not as it should be—bothered with mere folly, although this has been a chronic and pervasive problem. "Know, my son," said a dying Swedish statesman in the seventeenth century, "with how little wisdom the world is governed." More recently, Woodrow Wilson warned, "In public affairs, stupidity is more dangerous than knavery." 8

Stupidity is not related to type of regime; monarchy, oligarchy, and democracy produce it equally. Nor is it peculiar to nation or class. The working class as represented by the Communist governments functions no more rationally or effectively in power than the aristocracy or the 9 bourgeoisie, as has notably been demonstrated in recent history. Mao Tse-tung may be admired for many things, but the Great Leap Forward, with a steel plant in every backyard, and the Cultural Revolution were exercises in unwisdom that greatly damaged China's progress and stability, not to mention the chairman's reputation. The record of the Russian proletariat in power can hardly be called enlightened, although after sixty years of control it must be accorded a kind of brutal success. If the majority of Russians are better off now than before, the cost in cruelty and tyranny has been no less and probably greater than under the czars.

After the French Revolution, the new order was rescued 10 only by Bonaparte's military campaigns, which brought the spoils of foreign wars to fill the treasury, and subsequently by his competence as an executive. He chose officials not on the basis of origin or ideology but on the principle of *"la carrière ouverte aux talents"*—the said talents being intelligence, energy, industry, and obedience. That worked until the day of his own fatal mistake.

I do not wish to give the impression that men in office 11 are incapable of governing wisely and well. Occasionally, the exception appears, rising in heroic size above the rest, a tower visible down the centuries. Greece had her Pericles, who ruled with authority, moderation, sound judgment, and a certain nobility that imposes natural dominion over others. Rome had Caesar, a man of remarkable governing talents, although it must be said that a ruler who arouses opponents to resort to assassination is probably not as smart as he ought to be. Later, under Marcus Aurelius and the other Antonines, Roman citizens enjoyed good government, prosperity, and respect for about a century. Charlemagne was able to impose order upon a mass of contending elements, to foster the arts of civilization no less than those of war, and to earn a prestige supreme in the Middle Ages—probably not equaled in the eyes of contemporaries until the appearance of George Washington.

Possessor of an inner strength and perseverance that 12

442

enabled him to prevail over a sea of obstacles, Washington was one of those critical figures but for whom history might well have taken a different course. He made possible the physical victory of American independence, while around him, in extraordinary fertility, political talent bloomed as if touched by some tropical sun. For all their flaws and quarrels, the Founding Fathers, who established our form of government, were, in the words of Arthur Schlesinger, Sr., "the most remarkable generation of public men in the history of the United States or perhaps of any other nation." It is worth noting the qualities Schlesinger ascribes to them: They were fearless, high-principled, deeply versed in ancient and modern political thought, astute and pragmatic, unafraid of experiment, and—this is significant—"convinced of man's power to improve his condition through the use of intelligence." That was the mark of the Age of Reason that formed them, and though the eighteenth century had a tendency to regard men as more rational than they in fact were, it evoked the best in government from these men.

For our purposes, it would be invaluable if we could   13
know what produced this burst of talent from a base of only two million inhabitants. Schlesinger suggests some contributing factors: wide diffusion of education, challenging economic opportunities, social mobility, training in self-government—all these encouraged citizens to cultivate their political aptitudes to the utmost. Also, he adds, with the Church declining in prestige and with business, science, and art not yet offering competing fields of endeavor, statecraft remained almost the only outlet for men of energy and purpose. Perhaps the need of the moment— the opportunity to create a new political system—is what brought out the best.

Not before or since, I believe, has so much careful and   14
reasonable thinking been invested in the creation of a new political system. In the French, Russian, and Chinese revolutions, too much class hatred and bloodshed were involved to allow for fair results or permanent constitutions.

The American experience was unique, and the system so far has always managed to right itself under pressure. In spite of accelerating incompetence, it still works better than most. We haven't had to discard the system and try another after every crisis, as have Italy and Germany, Spain and France. The founders of the United States are a phenomenon to keep in mind to encourage our estimate of human possibilities, but their example, as a political scientist has pointed out, is "too infrequent to be taken as a basis for normal expectations."

The English are considered to have enjoyed reasonably 15 benign government during the eighteenth and nineteenth centuries, except for their Irish subjects, debtors, child laborers, and other unfortunates in various pockets of oppression. The folly that lost the American colonies reappeared now and then, notably in the treatment of the Irish and the Boers, but a social system can survive a good deal of folly when circumstances are historically favorable or when it is cushioned by large resources, as in the heyday of the British Empire, or absorbed by sheer size, as in this country during our period of expansion. Today there are no more cushions, which makes folly less affordable.

Elsewhere than in government, man has accomplished 16 marvels: invented the means in our time to leave the world and voyage to the moon; in the past, harnessed wind and electricity, raised earthbound stone into soaring cathedrals, woven silk brocades out of the spinnings of a worm, composed the music of Mozart and the dramas of Shakespeare, classified the forms of nature, penetrated the mysteries of genetics. Why is he so much less accomplished in government? What frustrates, in that sphere, the operation of the intellect? Isaac Bashevis Singer, discoursing as a Nobel laureate on mankind, offers the opinion that God had been frugal in bestowing intellect but lavish with passions and emotions. "He gave us," Singer says, "so many emotions and such strong ones that every human being, even if he is an idiot, is a millionaire in emotions."

I think Singer has made a point that applies to our inquiry. What frustrates the workings of intellect is the passions and the emotions: ambition, greed, fear, face-saving, the instinct to dominate, the needs of the ego, the whole bundle of personal vanities and anxieties.

Reason is crushed by these forces. If the Athenians out of pride and overconfidence had not set out to crush Sparta for good but had been content with moderate victory, their ultimate fall might have been averted. If fourteenth-century knights had not been obsessed by the idea of glory and personal prowess, they might have defeated the Turks at Nicopolis with incalculable consequence for all of Eastern Europe. If the English, 200 years ago, had heeded Chatham's knocking on the door of what he called "this sleeping and confounded Ministry" and his urgent advice to repeal the Coercive Acts and withdraw the troops before the "inexpiable drop of blood is shed in an impious war with a people contending in the great cause of publick liberty" or, given a last chance, if they had heeded Edmund Burke's celebrated plea for conciliation and his warning that it would prove impossible to coerce a "fierce people" of their own pedigree, we might still be a united people bridging the Atlantic, with incalculable consequence for the history of the West. It did not happen that way, because king and Parliament felt it imperative to affirm sovereignty over arrogant colonials. The alternative choice, as in Athens and medieval Europe, was close to psychologically impossible.

In the case we know best—the American engagement in Vietnam—fixed notions, preconceptions, wooden-headed thinking, and emotions accumulated into a monumental mistake and classic humiliation. The original idea was that the lesson of the failure to halt fascist aggression during the appeasement era dictated the necessity of halting the so-called aggression by North Vietnam, conceived to be the spearhead of international communism. This was applying the wrong model to the wrong facts, which would have been obvious if our policy makers had taken into

17

18

19

consideration the history of the people on the spot instead of charging forward wearing the blinkers of the cold war.

The reality of Vietnamese nationalism, of which Ho   20
Chi Minh had been the standard-bearer since long before the war, was certainly no secret. Indeed, Franklin Roosevelt had insisted that the French should not be allowed to return after the war, a policy that we instantly abandoned the moment the Japanese were out. Ignoring the Vietnamese demand for self-government, we first assisted the return of the French, and then, when, incredibly, they had been put to rout by the native forces, we took their place, as if Dien Bien Phu had no significance whatever. Policy founded upon error multiplies, never retreats. The pretense that North versus South Vietnam represented foreign aggression was intensified. If Asian specialists with knowledge of the situation suggested a reassessment, they were not persuasive. As a Communist aggressor, Hanoi was presumed to be a threat to the United States, yet the vital national interest at stake, which alone may have justified belligerency, was never clear enough to sustain a declaration of war.

A further, more fundamental error confounded our policy.   21
This was the nature of the client. In war, as any military treatise or any soldier who has seen active service will tell you, it is essential to know the nature—that is, the capabilities *and* intentions—of the enemy and no less so of an ally who is the primary belligerent. We fatally underestimated the one and foolishly overestimated the other. Placing reliance on, or hope in, South Vietnam was an advanced case of wooden-headedness. Improving on the Bourbons, who forgot nothing and learned nothing, our policy makers forgot everything and learned nothing. The oldest lesson in history is the futility and, often, fatality of foreign interference to maintain in power a government unwanted or hated at home. As far back as 500 B.C., Confucius stated, "Without the confidence of the people, no government can stand," and political philosophers have echoed him down through the ages. What else was the

lesson of our vain support of Chiang Kai-shek, within such recent experience? A corrupt or oppressive government may be maintained by despotic means but not for long, as the English occupiers of France learned in the fifteenth century. The human spirit protests and generates a Joan of Arc, for people will not passively endure a government that is in fact unendurable.

The deeper we became involved in Vietnam during the Johnson era, the greater grew the self-deception, the lies, the false body counts, the cheating on Tonkin Gulf, the military mess, domestic dissent, and all those defensive emotions in which, as a result, our leaders became fixed. Their concern for personal ego, public image, and government status determined policy. Johnson was not going to be the first President to preside over defeat; generals could not admit failure nor civilian advisers risk their jobs by giving unpalatable advice. 22

Males, who so far in history have managed government, are obsessed with potency, which is the reason, I suspect, why it is difficult for them to admit error. I have rarely known a man who, with a smile and a shrug, could easily acknowledge being wrong. Why not? *I* can, without any damage to self-respect. I can only suppose the difference is that deep in their psyches, men somehow equate being wrong with being impotent. For a Chief of State, it is almost out of the question, and especially so for Johnson and Nixon, who both seem to me to have had shaky self-images. Johnson's showed in his deliberate coarseness and compulsion to humiliate others in crude physical ways. No self-confident man would have needed to do that. Nixon was a bundle of inferiorities and sense of persecution. I do not pretend to be a psychohistorian, but in pursuit of this inquiry, the psychological factors must be taken into account. Having no special knowledge of Johnson and Nixon, I will not pursue the question other than to say that it was our misfortune during the Vietnam period to have had two Presidents who lacked the self-confidence for a change of course, much less for a grand withdrawal. 23

"Magnanimity in politics," said Edmund Burke, "is not seldom the truest wisdom, and a great Empire and little minds go ill together."

An essential component of that "truest wisdom" is the 24 self-confidence to reassess. Congressman Morris Udall made this point in the first few days after the nuclear accident at Three Mile Island. Cautioning against a hasty decision on the future of nuclear power, he said, "We have to go back and reassess. There is nothing wrong about being optimistic or making a mistake. The thing that is wrong, as in Vietnam, is *persisting* in a mistake when you see you are going down the wrong road and are caught in a bad situation."

The test comes in recognizing when persistence has be- 25 come a fatal error. A prince, says Machiavelli, ought always to be a great asker and a patient hearer of truth about those things of which he has inquired, and he should be angry if he finds that anyone has scruples about telling him the truth. Johnson and Nixon, as far as an outsider can tell, were not great askers; they did not want to hear the truth or to face it. Chiang Kai-shek knew virtually nothing of real conditions in his domain because he lived a headquarters life amid an entourage all of whom were afraid to be messengers of ill report. When, in World War I, a general of the headquarters staff visited for the first time the ghastly landscape of the Somme, he broke into tears, saying, "If I had known we sent men to fight in that, I could not have done it." Evidently he was no great asker either.

Neither, we now know, was the shah of Iran. Like 26 Chiang Kai-shek, he was isolated from actual conditions. He was educated abroad, took his vacations abroad, and toured his country, if at all, by helicopter.

Why is it that the major clients of the United States, 27 a country founded on the principle that government derives its just powers from the consent of the governed, tend to be unpopular autocrats? A certain schizophrenia between our philosophy and our practice afflicts American policy, and this split will always make the policy based on it fall apart. On the day the shah left Iran, an article summarizing his reign said that "except for the generals, he has few friends or allies at home." How useful to us is a ruler without friends or allies at home? He is a kind of luftmensch, no matter how rich or how golden a customer for American business. To attach American foreign policy to a ruler who does not have the acceptance of his countrymen is hardly intelligent. By now, it seems to me, we might have learned that. We must understand conditions —and by conditions, I mean people and history—on the spot. Wise policy can only be made on the basis of *informed,* not automatic, judgments.

When it has become evident to those associated with 28 it that a course of policy is pointed toward disaster, why does no one resign in protest or at least for the peace of his own soul? They never do. In 1917, the German chancellor Bethmann Hollweg pleaded desperately against the proposed resumption of unrestricted submarine warfare, since, by bringing in the United States, it would revive the Allies' resources, their confidence in victory, and their will to endure. When he was overruled by the military, he told a friend who found him sunk in despair that the decision meant *"finis Germaniae."* When the friend said simply, "You should resign," Bethmann said he could not, for that would sow dissension at home and let the world know he believed Germany would fail.

This is always the refuge. The officeholder tells him- 29 self he can do more from within and that he must not reveal division at the top to the public. In fact if there is to be any hope of change in a democratic society, that is exactly what he must do. No one of major influence in Johnson's circle resigned over our Vietnam policy, although several, hoping to play it both ways, hinted their disagreement. Humphrey, waiting for the nod, never challenged the President's policy, although he campaigned afterward as an opponent of the war. Since then, I've always thought the adulation given to him misplaced.

Basically, what keeps officeholders attached to a policy 30 they believe to be wrong is nothing more nor less, I believe, than the lure of office, or Potomac fever. It is the same whether the locus is the Thames or the Rhine or, no doubt, the Nile. When Herbert Lehman ran for a second term as senator from New York after previously serving four terms as governor, his brother asked him why on earth he wanted it. "Arthur," replied the senator, "after you have once ridden behind a motorcycle escort, you are never the same again."

Here is a clue to the question of why our performance 31 in government is worse than in other activities: because government offers power, excites that lust for power, which is subject to emotional drives—to narcissism, fantasies of omnipotence, and other sources of folly. The lust for power, according to Tacitus, "is the most flagrant of all the passions" and cannot really be satisfied except by power over others. Business offers a kind of power but only to the very successful at the very top, and even they, in our day, have to play it down. Fords and Du Ponts, Hearsts and Pultizers nowadays are subdued, and the Rockefeller who most conspicuously wanted power sought it in government. Other activities—in sports, science, the professions, and the creative and performing arts—offer various satisfactions but not the opportunity for power. They may appeal to status seeking and, in the form of celebrity, offer crowd worship and limousines and recognition by headwaiters, but these are the trappings of power, not the essence. Of course, mistakes and stupidities occur in nongovernmental activities too, but since these affect fewer people, they are less noticeable than they are in public affairs. Government remains the paramount field of unwisdom because it is there that men seek power over others— and lose it over themselves.

There are, of course, other factors that lower compe- 32

tence in public affairs, among them the pressure of overwork and overscheduling; bureaucracy, especially big bureaucracy; the contest for votes that gives exaggerated influence to special interests and an absurd tyranny to public opinion polls. Any hope of intelligent government would require that the persons entrusted with high office should formulate and execute policy according to their best judgment and the best knowledge available, not according to every breeze of public opinion. But reelection is on their minds, and that becomes the criterion. Moreover, given schedules broken down into fifteen-minute appointments and staffs numbering in the hundreds and briefing memos of never less than thirty pages, policy makers never have time to *think*. This leaves a rather important vacuum. Meanwhile, bureaucracy rolls on, impervious to any individual or cry for change, like some vast computer that when once penetrated by error goes on pumping it out forever.

Under the circumstances, what are the chances of im- 33 proving the conduct of government? The idea of a class of professionals trained for the task has been around ever since Plato's *Republic*. Something of the sort animates, I imagine, the new Kennedy School of Government at Harvard. According to Plato, the ruling class in a just society should be men apprenticed to the art of ruling, drawn from the rational and the wise. Since he acknowledged that in natural distribution these are few, he believed they would have to be eugenically bred and nurtured. Government, he said, was a special art in which competence, as in any other profession, could be acquired only by study of the discipline and could not be acquired otherwise.

Without reference to Plato, the Mandarins of China 34 were trained, if not bred, for the governing function. They had to pass through years of study and apprenticeship and weeding out by successive examinations, but they do not seem to have developed a form of government much superior to any other, and in the end, they petered out in decadence and incompetence.

In seventeenth-century Europe, after the devastation of 35
the Thirty Years' War, the electors of Brandenburg, soon
to be combined with Prussia, determined to create a strong
state by means of a disciplined army and a trained civil
service. Applicants for the civil positions, drawn from
commoners in order to offset the nobles' control of the
military, had to complete a course of study covering political theory, law and legal philosophy, economics, history, penology, and statutes. Only after passing through
various stages of examination and probationary terms of
office did they receive definitive appointments and tenure
and opportunity for advancement. The higher civil service
was a separate branch, not open to promotion from the
middle and lower levels.

The Prussian system proved so effective that the state 36
was able to survive both military defeat by Napoleon in
1807 and the revolutionary surge of 1848. By then it had
begun to congeal, losing many of its most progressive citizens in emigration to America; nevertheless, Prussian
energies succeeded in 1871 in uniting the German states
in an empire under Prussian hegemony. Its very success
contained the seed of ruin, for it nourished the arrogance
and power hunger that from 1914 through was to bring it
down.

In England, instead of responding in reactionary panic 37
to the thunders from the Continent in 1848, as might have
been expected, the authorities, with commendable enterprise, ordered an investigation of their own government
practices, which were then the virtually private preserve
of the propertied class. The result was a report on the need
for a permanent civil service to be based on training and
specialized skills and designed to provide continuity and
maintenance of the long view as against transient issues
and political passions. Though heavily resisted, the system
was adopted in 1870. It has produced distinguished civil
servants but also Burgess, Maclean, Philby, and the fourth
man. The history of British government in the last 100

years suggests that factors other than the quality of its civil service determine a country's fate.

In the United States, civil service was established chiefly as a barrier to patronage and the pork barrel rather than in search of excellence. By 1937, a presidential commission, finding the system inadequate, urged the development of a "real career service ... requiring personnel of the highest order, competent, highly trained, loyal, skilled in their duties by reason of long experience, and assured of continuity." After much effort and some progress, that goal is still not reached, but even if it were, it would not take care of elected officials and high appointments—that is, of government at the top.

I do not know if the prognosis is hopeful or, given the underlying emotional drives, whether professionalism is the cure. In the Age of Enlightenment, John Locke thought the emotions should be controlled by intellectual judgment and that it was the distinction and glory of man to be able to control them. As witnesses of the twentieth century's record, comparable to the worst in history, we have less confidence in our species. Although professionalism can help, I tend to think that fitness of character is what government chiefly requires. How that can be discovered, encouraged, and brought into office is the problem that besets us.

No society has yet managed to implement Plato's design. Now, with money and image-making manipulating our elective process, the chances are reduced. We are asked to choose by the packaging, yet the candidate seen in a studio-filmed spot, sincerely voicing lines from the TelePrompTer, is not the person who will have to meet the unrelenting problems and crucial decisions of the Oval Office. It might be a good idea if, without violating the First Amendment, we could ban all paid political commercials and require candidates (who accept federal subsidy for their campaigns) to be televised live only.

That is only a start. More profound change must come 41
if we are to bring into office the kind of person our form
of government needs if it is to survive the challenges of
this era. Perhaps rather than educating officials according
to Plato's design, we should concentrate on educating the
electorate—that is, ourselves—to look for, recognize, and
reward character in our representatives and to reject the
ersatz.

---- ♦ ----

For Study and Discussion

QUESTIONS ABOUT PURPOSE

1. In her first paragraph Tuchman clearly states the problem she will address in the essay. In what ways does
   her purpose seem to go beyond this statement?
2. What theory about the relationship of wisdom and
   power is Tuchman attempting to document?
3. What changes does Tuchman propose to correct the
   problem she is analyzing? How optimistic is she that
   these changes will work?

QUESTIONS ABOUT AUDIENCE

1. The readers of *Esquire*, where this essay was originally published, are primarily professional men from
   twenty to fifty years old. In what ways are such readers an appropriate audience for this essay?
2. What assumptions does Tuchman make about her audience's education? In what ways does she assist those
   readers who may not have that education?
3. In what important ways do you think Tuchman would
   have changed this essay if she had been writing it primarily for professional historians?

QUESTIONS ABOUT STRATEGIES

1. How does Tuchman define "wooden-headedness"? How does she arrange her examples to demonstrate its pervasiveness? For example, why does she devote so much attention to Vietnam?
2. How does Tuchman's discussion of good leaders and good systems of government help establish the credibility of her argument?
3. In making her case against wooden-headedness, Tuchman depends heavily upon the "weight of facts," but she also expresses her disgust, frustration, and despair. What part do you think these emotional components play in establishing the effectiveness of her argument?

QUESTIONS FOR DISCUSSION

1. In paragraph 32 Tuchman says that one major cause of bad government may be that men, who are most often in control, have great trouble admitting that they make mistakes, and thus refuse to change disastrous policies. How do you react to that claim? Would having women in charge make a difference? Explain your answer.
2. What examples of wooden-headedness can you think of in current events—local, national, or international?
3. How do you respond to Tuchman's charge that campaign practices in this country promote "the persistence of unwisdom"?

Persuasion and Argument as a Writing Strategy

POINTS TO CONSIDER

1. Why are you writing your essay? Do you want your readers to change in some way, or do you simply want to reinforce an attitude or belief they already hold? How much explanation will you have to give your readers in order to make a convincing argument? Do you want to make a forceful case or will you be satisfied if you can get your readers to consider the points you are making?

2. What category do you think your readers will fall in (see classifications under Audience on pages 367–368)? Given their attitudes, will they probably react best to a primarily emotional or primarily logical appeal? How well do you know your readers? What tone can you take with them? How logical will they expect you to be?

3. How can you establish a strong *ethical appeal* in your paper? What experiences or background do you have that will make your writing sound credible? If your paper is on a complex topic, how can you qualify your assertions so that you won't sound naive or simplistic? What is the best mix of emotion and reason, given your topic and your audience?

PREWRITING EXERCISES

1. In a group of four or six people, divide into two teams and choose a recorder for each side. Each team should brainstorm for ten minutes to think of as many arguments as possible for and against one of the following topics. After ten minutes, each team should take the opposite side of the topic and see how many arguments it can find. At the end of the session, compare notes.

chewing gum	giving children unusual
jogging	names
keeping a gun in	cheating on exams
the house	buying expensive clothes

2. Make two columns on a piece of paper and label one *Favorable* and one *Unfavorable*. Then think of terms you could use to describe one of these topics, putting each one in the appropriate column as you think of it. The terms can be adjectives, slang definitions, or descriptive phrases.

professional football	punk rock music
player	McDonald's hamburgers
professional football	expressways
coach	cats
politician	
housewife	

3. Make two columns on a piece of paper and label one *Positive Associations* and the other one *Negative Associations.* Then think of ten or fifteen animal references writers use in describing people and put each one in the appropriate column.

4. Write down as many kinds of evidence as you can think of that you might use to support one of these assertions:

   A. A college education is a good investment.
   B. Women are still discriminated against in our society.
   C. People's high school experiences leave an indelible impression on them.
   D. Universities should abolish their foreign language requirements.

5. Think of ten people who seem to you to have strong ethical appeal; that is, if you heard them speak on television or saw their names over magazine articles, you would be inclined to agree with them. Try to analyze why they have this kind of appeal.

TOPICS FOR WRITING IN CLASS

1. In one or two paragraphs, analyze how Martin Luther King, Jr., is using metaphors about money as persuasive techniques in this passage:

> In a sense we have come to our nation's Capital to <u>cash a check.</u> When the architects of our republic wrote the magnificent words of the Constitution and the Declaration of Independence, they were signing a <u>promissory note</u> to which every American was to fall heir. This <u>note</u> was a promise that all men would be guaranteed the unalienable rights of life, liberty, and the pursuit of happiness.
>
> It is obvious today that America has <u>defaulted on this promissory note</u> insofar as her citizens of color are concerned. Instead of honoring this sacred obligation, America has given the Negro people <u>a bad check;</u> <u>a check</u> which has come back <u>marked "insufficient funds."</u> We refuse to believe that the <u>bank of justice is bankrupt.</u> We refuse to believe that there are <u>insufficient funds in the great vaults of opportunity.</u> So we have come to <u>cash this check</u>—a <u>check that will give us upon demand the riches of freedom and the security of justice.</u>

2. Imagine that in one hour you will have to appear in court to convince a traffic judge that you should not have your driver's license taken away because you have three speeding tickets and two citations for reckless driving. You are sitting in the waiting room working on your argument. First, write out an analysis of what you think your audience (the judge) would expect from you and what biases and attitudes that judge might have. Then write an analysis of how you would balance emotional, logical, and ethical appeals in your argument. Now write a short—about 250 words—draft for an argument that you think might persuade the judge not to revoke your license.

3. Choose one of the hypothetical situations given below and write a brief biography of the person who would be writing or speaking in the situation. Use your imagination to create experiences and credentials that would build up the writer's or speaker's ethical appeal and make the audience predisposed to agree with him or her. Some details that you might include would be college degrees, books or articles written, professional honors received, public service such as being a senator or a judge, positions held in industry, government, or education, military service, and awards for citizenship.

> *Valerie Nathan*—author of an article on how one gets started writing Gothic romances
>
> *Thomas Miller*—author of a magazine article on scuba diving in the Caribbean
>
> *Elizabeth Conway*—speaker on proposed changes in the method for choosing Vice-Presidential candidates in national elections

TOPICS FOR WRITING OUT OF CLASS

1. For the readers of the student newspaper in your school, write an editorial urging the abolition of one of our holidays that business interests have promoted into a major commercial occasion, for example, Valentine's Day, Mother's Day, or Father's Day. Before you begin, write a short analysis of what points you want to make with your audience and what mixture of emotional and rational appeals would probably work best for your topic.

2. Write a statement for the admissions committee of your state law school or your state medical school. In it argue that admission officers who make decisions chiefly on the basis of the scores the applicants make on the Law Schools Admissions Test or the Medical College Admissions Test are treating minority applicants unfairly. As part of your argument you might invent a story that shows how the circumstances in which many minority applicants live make it difficult

for them to understand some of the test questions. As preparation to write this paper, you could go to the library and check out booklets about preparing for the LSAT and the MCAT; you could also check the *Readers' Guide to Periodical Literature* for articles on scholastic testing.

3. Write an inductive argument on one of the assertions given below. Before you begin to write, decide where you are going to gather your evidence and how many pieces of evidence you need to justify your conclusion. Examine your evidence *first,* and then decide what your conclusion will be. Begin your paper by describing and doing an analysis of your evidence; after that, show how you came to your conclusion.

   1. Television advertisements and programs show (or do not show) men and women in stereotyped roles.
   2. The park system in this city meets (or does not meet) the recreational needs of the people living here.
   3. The salaries and fringe benefits offered young men and women entering the army or navy are (or are not) an adequate incentive for good people to join.

ESSAYS FOR FURTHER READING

The Flow of the River

LOREN EISELEY

———— ♦ ————

Loren Eiseley (1907–1979) was born in Lincoln, Nebraska, and educated at the University of Nebraska and the University of Pennsylvania. He held faculty positions at the University of Kansas, Oberlin College, and the University of Pennsylvania, where he was Franklin Professor of Anthropology and History of Science. He contributed articles to scientific journals, such as American Anthropologist *and* Scientific Monthly, *and popular magazines, such as* Holiday *and* Ladies' Home Journal. *His books include* The Immense Journey *(1957),* Darwin's Century *(1958),* The Mind as Nature *(1962),* The Unexpected Universe *(1969),* The Night Country *(1971), and his autobiography,* All the Strange Hours *(1975). In these books, and in all his writing, Eiseley conveys the scrupulousness of scientific inquiry in beautifully crafted language; his vision is simultaneously that of scientist and poet. In "The Flow of the River," from* The Immense Journey, *he weaves from his own experience an intriguing tale about the magic of water and the mystery of evolution.*

If there is magic on this planet, it is contained in water. 1
Its least stir even, as now in a rain pond on a flat roof
opposite my office, is enough to bring me searching to
the window. A wind ripple may be translating itself into
life. I have a constant feeling that some time I may witness that momentous miracle on a city roof, see life veritably and suddenly boiling out of a heap of rusted pipes and
old television aerials. I marvel at how suddenly a water

beetle has come and is submarining there in a spatter of green algae. Thin vapors, rust, wet tar and sun are an alembic remarkably like the mind; they throw off odorous shadows that threaten to take real shape when no one is looking.

Once in a lifetime, perhaps, one escapes the actual confines of the flesh. Once in a lifetime, if one is lucky, one so merges with sunlight and air and running water that whole eons, the eons that mountains and deserts know, might pass in a single afternoon without discomfort. The mind has sunk away into its beginnings among old roots and the obscure tricklings and movings that stir inanimate things. Like the charmed fairy circle into which a man once stepped, and upon emergence learned that a whole century had passed in a single night, one can never quite define this secret; but it has something to do, I am sure, with common water. Its substance reaches everywhere; it touches the past and prepares the future; it moves under the poles and wanders thinly in the heights of air. It can assume forms of exquisite perfection in a snowflake, or strip the living to a single shining bone cast up by the sea.

Many years ago, in the course of some scientific investigations in a remote western county, I experienced, by chance, precisely the sort of curious absorption by water —the extension of shape by osmosis—at which I have been hinting. You have probably never experienced in yourself the meandering roots of a whole watershed or felt your outstretched fingers touching, by some kind of clairvoyant extension, the brooks of snow-line glaciers at the same time that you were flowing toward the Gulf over the eroded debris of worn-down mountains. A poet, Mac-Knight Black, has spoken of being "limbed . . . with waters gripping pole and pole." He had the idea, all right, and it is obvious that these sensations are not unique, but they are hard to come by; and the sort of extension of the senses that people will accept when they put their ear against a sea shell, they will smile at in the confessions of a bookish professor. What makes it worse is the fact that because of a traumatic experience in childhood, I am not a swimmer, and am inclined to be timid before any large body of water. Perhaps it was just this, in a way, that contributed to my experience.

As it leaves the Rockies and moves downward over the high plains towards the Missouri, the Platte River is a curious stream. In the spring floods, on occasion, it can be a mile-wide roaring torrent of destruction, gulping farms and bridges. Normally, however, it is a rambling, dispersed series of streamlets flowing erratically over great sand and gravel fans that are, in part, the remnants of a mightier Ice Age stream bed. Quicksands and shifting islands haunt its waters. Over it the prairie suns beat mercilessly throughout the summer. The Platte, "a mile wide and an inch deep," is a refuge for any heat-weary pilgrim along its shores. This is particularly true on the high plains before its long march by the cities begins.

The reason that I came upon it when I did, breaking through a willow thicket and stumbling out through ankle-deep water to a dune in the shade, is of no concern to this narrative. On various purposes of science I have ranged over a good bit of that country on foot, and I know the kinds of bones that come gurgling up through the gravel pumps, and the arrowheads of shining chalcedony that occasionally spill out of water-loosened sand. On that day, however, the sight of sky and willows and the weaving net of water murmuring a little in the shallows on its way to the Gulf stirred me, parched as I was with miles of walking, with a new idea: I was going to float. I was going to undergo a tremendous adventure.

The notion came to me, I suppose, by degrees. I had shed my clothes and was floundering pleasantly in a hole among some reeds when a great desire to stretch out and go with this gently insistent water began to pluck at me. Now to this bronzed, bold, modern generation, the struggle I waged with timidity while standing there in knee-deep water can only seem farcical; yet actually for me it was not so. A near-drowning accident in childhood had scarred my reactions; in addition to the fact that I was a nonswimmer, this "inch-deep river" was treacherous with holes and quicksands. Death was not precisely infrequent along its wandering and illusory channels. Like all broad wastes of this kind, where neither water nor land quite prevails, its thickets were lonely and untraversed. A man in trouble would cry out in vain.

I thought of all this, standing quietly in the water, feeling the sand shifting away under my toes. Then I lay back in the floating position that left my face to the sky, and shoved off. The sky wheeled over me. For an instant, as I bobbed into the main channel, I had the sensation of sliding down the vast tilted face of the continent. It was then that I felt the cold needles of the alpine springs at my fingertips, and the warmth of the Gulf pulling me southward. Moving with me, leaving its taste upon my mouth and spouting under me in dancing springs of sand, was the immense body of the continent itself, flowing like the river was flowing, grain by grain, mountain by mountain, down to the sea. I was streaming over ancient sea beds thrust aloft where giant reptiles had once sported; I was wearing down the face of time and trundling cloud-wreathed ranges into oblivion. I touched my margins with the delicacy of a crayfish's antennae, and felt great fishes glide about their work. 7

I drifted by stranded timber cut by beaver in mountain fastnesses; I slid over shallows that had buried the broken axles of prairie schooners and the mired bones of mammoth. I was streaming alive through the hot and working ferment of the sun, or oozing secretively through shady thickets. I *was* water and the unspeakable alchemies that gestate and take shape in water, the slimy jellies that under the enormous magnification of the sun writhe and whip upward as great barbeled fish mouths, or sink indistinctly back into the murk out of which they arose. Turtle and fish and the pinpoint chirpings of individual frogs are all watery projections, concentrations—as man himself 8 is a concentration—of that indescribable and liquid brew which is compounded in varying proportions of salt and sun and time. It has appearances, but at its heart lies water, and as I was finally edged gently against a sand bar and dropped like any log, I tottered as I rose. I knew once more the body's revolt against emergence into the harsh and unsupporting air, its reluctance to break contact with that mother element which still, at this late point in time, shelters and brings into being nine tenths of everything alive.

As for men, those myriad little detached ponds with their own swarming corpuscular life, what were they but a way that water has of going about beyond the reach of rivers? I, too, was a microcosm of pouring rivulets and floating driftwood gnawed by the mysterious animalcules of my own creation. I was three fourths water, rising and subsiding according to the hollow knocking in my veins: a minute pulse like the eternal pulse that lifts Himalayas and which, in the following systole, will carry them away.

Thoreau, peering at the emerald pickerel in Walden Pond, called them "animalized water" in one of his moments of strange insight. If he had been possessed of the geological knowledge so laboriously accumulated since his time, he might have gone further and amusedly detected in the planetary rumblings and eructations which so delighted him in the gross habits of certain frogs, signs of that dark interior stress which has reared sea bottoms up to mountainous heights. He might have developed an acute inner ear for the sound of the surf on Cretaceous beaches where now the wheat of Kansas rolls. In any case, he would have seen, as the long trail of life was unfolded by the fossil hunters, that his animalized water had changed its shapes eon by eon to the beating of the earth's dark millennial heart. In the swamps of the low continents, the amphibians had flourished and had their day; and as the long skyward swing—the isostatic response of the crust—had come about, the era of the cooling grasslands and mammalian life had come into being.

A few winters ago, clothed heavily against the weather, 11
I wandered several miles along one of the tributaries of
that same Platte I had floated down years before. The
land was stark and ice-locked. The rivulets were frozen,
and over the marshlands the willow thickets made such
an array of vertical lines against the snow that tramping
through them produced strange optical illusions and dizzi-
ness. On the edge of a frozen backwater, I stopped and
rubbed my eyes. At my feet a raw prairie wind had swept
the ice clean of snow. A peculiar green object caught my
eye; there was no mistaking it.

Staring up at me with all his barbels spread patheti- 12
cally, frozen solidly in the wind-ruffled ice, was a huge
familiar face. It was one of those catfish of the twisting
channels, those dwellers in the yellow murk, who had
been about me and beneath me on the day of my great
voyage. Whatever sunny dream had kept him paddling
there while the mercury plummeted downward and that
Cheshire smile froze slowly, it would be hard to say. Or
perhaps he was trapped in a blocked channel and had
simply kept swimming until the ice contracted around
him. At any rate, there he would lie till the spring thaw.

At that moment I started to turn away, but something 13
in the bleak, whiskered face reproached me, or perhaps
it was the river calling to her children. I termed it science,
however—a convenient rational phrase I reserve for such
. occasions—and decided that I would cut the fish out of
the ice and take him home. I had no intention of eating
him. I was merely struck by a sudden impulse to test the
survival qualities of high-plains fishes, particularly fishes
of this type who get themselves immured in oxygenless
ponds or in cut-off oxbows buried in winter drifts. I
blocked him out as gently as possible and dropped him,
ice and all, into a collecting can in the car. Then we set
out for home.

Unfortunately, the first stages of what was to prove 14
a remarkable resurrection escaped me. Cold and tired

after a long drive, I deposited the can with its melting water and ice in the basement. The accompanying corpse I anticipated I would either dispose of or dissect on the following day. A hurried glance had revealed no signs of life.

To my astonishment, however, upon descending into 15 the basement several hours later, I heard stirrings in the receptacle and peered in. The ice had melted. A vast pouting mouth ringed with sensitive feelers confronted me, and the creature's gills labored slowly. A thin stream of silver bubbles rose to the surface and popped. A fishy eye gazed up at me protestingly.

"A tank," it said. This was no Walden pickerel. This 16 was a yellow-green, mud-grubbing, evil-tempered inhabitant of floods and droughts and cyclones. It was the selective product of the high continent and the waters that pour across it. It had outlasted prairie blizzards that left cattle standing frozen upright in the drifts.

"I'll get the tank," I said respectfully. 17

He lived with me all that winter, and his departure 18 was totally in keeping with his sturdy, independent character. In the spring a migratory impulse or perhaps sheer boredom struck him. Maybe, in some little lost corner of his brain, he felt, far off, the pouring of the mountain waters through the sandy coverts of the Platte. Anyhow, something called to him, and he went. One night when no one was about, he simply jumped out of his tank. I found him dead on the floor next morning. He had made his gamble like a man—or, I should say, a fish. In the proper place it would not have been a fool's gamble. Fishes in the drying shallows of intermittent prairie streams who feel their confinement and have the impulse to leap while there is yet time may regain the main channel and survive. A million ancestral years had gone into that jump, I thought as I looked at him, a million years of climbing through prairie sunflowers and twining in and out through the pillared legs of drinking mammoth.

"Some of your close relatives have been experimenting 19

with air breathing," I remarked, apropos of nothing, as I gathered him up. "Suppose we meet again up there in the cottonwoods in a million years or so."

I missed him a little as I said it. He had for me the 20 kind of lost archaic glory that comes from the water brotherhood. We were both projections out of that timeless ferment and locked as well in some greater unity that lay incalculably beyond us. In many a fin and reptile foot I have seen myself passing by—some part of myself, that is, some part that lies unrealized in the momentary shape I inhabit. People have occasionally written me harsh letters and castigated me for a lack of faith in man when I have ventured to speak of this matter in print. They distrust, it would seem, all shapes and thoughts but their own. They would bring God into the compass of a shopkeeper's understanding and confine Him to those limits, lest He proceed to some unimaginable and shocking act— create perhaps, as a casual afterthought, a being more beautiful than man. As for me, I believe nature capable of this, and having been part of the flow of the river, I feel no envy—any more than the frog envies the reptile or an ancestral ape should envy man.

Every spring in the wet meadows and ditches I hear 21 a little shrilling chorus which sounds for all the world like an endlessly reiterated "We're here, we're here, we're here." And so they are, as frogs, of course. Confident little fellows. I suspect that to some greater ear than ours, man's optimistic pronouncements about his role and destiny may make a similar little ringing sound that travels a small way out into the night. It is only its nearness that is offensive. From the heights of a mountain, or a marsh at evening, it blends, not too badly, with all the other sleepy voices that, in croaks or chirrups, are saying the same thing.

After a while the skilled listener can distinguish man's 22 noise from the katydid's rhythmic assertion, allow for the offbeat of a rabbit's thumping, pick up the autumnal monotone of crickets, and find in all of them a grave pleasure without admitting any to a place of preëminence in his thoughts. It is when all these voices cease and the waters are still, when along the frozen river nothing cries, screams or howls, that the enormous mindlessness of space settles down upon the soul. Somewhere out in that waste of crushed ice and reflected stars, the black waters may be running, but they appear to be running without life toward a destiny in which the whole of space may be locked in some silvery winter of dispersed radiation.

It is then, when the wind comes straitly across the 23 barren marshes and the snow rises and beats in endless waves against the traveler, that I remember best, by some trick of the imagination, my summer voyage on the river. I remember my green extensions, my catfish nuzzlings and minnow wrigglings, my gelatinous materializations out of the mother ooze. And as I walk on through the white smother, it is the magic of water that leaves me a final sign.

Men talk much of matter and energy, of the struggle 24 for existence that molds the shape of life. These things exist, it is true; but more delicate, elusive, quicker than the fins in water, is that mysterious principle known as "organization," which leaves all other mysteries concerned with life stale and insignificant by comparison. For that without organization life does not persist is obvious. Yet this organization itself is not strictly the product of life, nor of selection. Like some dark and passing shadow within matter, it cups out the eyes' small windows or spaces the notes of a meadow lark's song in the interior of a mottled egg. That principle—I am beginning to suspect—was there before the living in the deeps of water.

The temperature has risen. The little stinging needles 25 have given way to huge flakes floating in like white leaves blown from some great tree in open space. In the car, switching on the lights, I examine one intricate crystal on my sleeve before it melts. No utilitarian philosophy explains a snow crystal, no doctrine of use or disuse. Water has merely leapt out of vapor and thin nothingness in the night sky to array itself in form. There is no logical reason for the existence of a snowflake any more than there is for evolution. It is an apparition from that mysterious shadow world beyond nature, that final world which contains—if anything contains—the explanation of men and catfish and green leaves.

In Search of Our Mothers' Gardens

ALICE WALKER

—————— ◆ ——————

Alice Walker was born in 1944 in Eatonton, Georgia, attended Spelman College, and graduated from Sarah Lawrence College. After college Walker became active in the civil rights movement, helping to register voters in Georgia, teaching in the Head Start program in Mississippi, and working on the staff of the New York City welfare department. In the late sixties she taught at several universities, including Jackson State College and Wellesley College. She now teaches at the University of California at Berkeley. Walker has written a biography for children, Langston Hughes: American Poet *(1973); edited an important literary anthology,* I Love Myself When I'm Laughing . . . and Then Again When I'm Looking Mean and Impressive: A Zora Neale Hurston Reader *(1979); and served as contributing editor to* Ms. *magazine. Her work reveals her interest in the themes of sexism and racism, which are powerfully embodied in her two collections of short stories—*In Love and Trouble *(1973), and* You Can't Keep a Good Woman Down *(1981)—and in her three highly acclaimed novels,* The Third Life of Grace Copeland *(1970),* Meridian *(1976), and, especially,* The Color Purple *(1982). "In Search of Our Mothers' Gardens" (1974), the title essay from her most recent collection of nonfiction (1983), provides Walker with the opportunity to honor the creative legacy left to this generation by generations of anonymous black women.*

I described her own nature and temperament. Told how they needed a larger life for their expression. . . . I pointed out that in lieu of proper channels, her emotions had overflowed into paths that dissipated them. I talked, beautifully I thought, about an art that would be born,

1

an art that would open the way for women the likes of her. I asked her to hope, and build up an inner life against the coming of that day. . . . I sang, with a strange quiver in my voice, a promise song.

Jean Toomer ("Avey," *Cane*)

The poet speaking to a prostitute who falls asleep while he's talking—

When the poet Jean Toomer walked through the South 2 in the early twenties, he discovered a curious thing: black women whose spirituality was so intense, so deep, so *unconscious*, that they were themselves unaware of the richness they held. They stumbled blindly through their lives, creatures so abused and mutilated in body, so dimmed and confused by pain, that they considered themselves unworthy even of hope. In the selfless abstractions their bodies became to the men who used them, they became more than "sexual objects," more even than mere women: they became "Saints." Instead of being perceived as whole persons, their bodies became shrines: what was thought to be their minds became temples suitable for worship. These crazy Saints stared out at the world, wildly, like lunatics—or quietly, like suicides; and the "God" that was in their gaze was as mute as a great stone.

Who were these Saints? These crazy, loony, pitiful 3 women?

Some of them, without a doubt, were our mothers and 4 grandmothers.

In the still heat of the post-Reconstruction South, this 5 is how they seemed to Jean Toomer: exquisite butterflies trapped in an evil honey, toiling away their lives in an era, a century, that did not acknowledge them, except as "the *mule* of the world." They dreamed dreams that no one knew—not even themselves, in any coherent fashion— and saw visions no one could understand. They wandered or sat about the countryside crooning lullabies to ghosts, and drawing the mother of Christ in charcoal on court-house walls.

They forced their minds to desert their bodies and their striving spirits sought to rise, like frail whirlwinds from the hard red clay. And when those frail whirlwinds fell, in scattered particles, upon the ground, no one mourned. Instead, men lit candles to celebrate the emptiness that remained, as people do who enter a beautiful but vacant space to resurrect a God. 6

Our mothers and grandmothers, some of them: moving to music not yet written. And they waited. 7

They waited for a day when the unknown thing that was in them would be made known; but guessed, somehow in their darkness, that on the day of their revelation they would be long dead. Therefore to Toomer they walked, and even ran, in slow motion. For they were going nowhere immediate, and the future was not yet within their grasp. And men took our mothers and grandmothers, "but got no pleasure from it." So complex was their passion and their calm. 8

To Toomer, they lay vacant and fallow as autumn fields, with harvest time never in sight: and he saw them enter loveless marriages, without joy; and become prostitutes, without resistance; and become mothers of children, without fulfillment. 9

For these grandmothers and mothers of ours were not Saints, but Artists; driven to a numb and bleeding madness by the springs of creativity in them for which there was no release. They were Creators, who lived lives of spiritual waste, because they were so rich in spirituality—which is the basis of Art—that the strain of enduring their unused and unwanted talent drove them insane. Throwing away this spirituality was their pathetic attempt to lighten the soul to a weight their work-worn, sexually abused bodies could bear. 10

What did it mean for a black woman to be an artist in 11

our grandmothers' time? In our great-grandmothers' day? It is a question with an answer cruel enough to stop the blood.

Did you have a genius of a great-great-grandmother 12 who died under some ignorant and depraved white overseer's lash? Or was she required to bake biscuits for a lazy backwater tramp, when she cried out in her soul to paint watercolors of sunsets, or the rain falling on the green and peaceful pasturelands? Or was her body broken and forced to bear children (who were more often than not sold away from her)—eight, ten, fifteen, twenty children—when her one joy was the thought of modeling heroic figures of rebellion, in stone or clay?

How was the creativity of the black woman kept alive, 13 year after year and century after century, when for most of the years black people have been in America, it was a punishable crime for a black person to read or write? And the freedom to paint, to sculpt, to expand the mind with action did not exist. Consider, if you can bear to imagine it, what might have been the result if singing, too, had been forbidden by law. Listen to the voices of Bessie Smith, Billie Holiday, Nina Simone, Roberta Flack, and Aretha Franklin, among others, and imagine those voices muzzled for life. Then you may begin to comprehend the lives of our "crazy," "Sainted" mothers and grandmothers. The agony of the lives of women who might have been Poets, Novelists, Essayists, and Short-Story Writers (over a period of centuries), who died with their real gifts stifled within them.

And, if this were the end of the story, we would have 14 cause to cry out in my paraphrase of Okot p'Bitek's great poem:

> O, my clanswomen
> Let us all cry together!
> Come,
> Let us mourn the death of our mother,
> The death of a Queen

The ash that was produced
By a great fire!
O, this homestead is utterly dead
Close the gates
With *lacari* thorns,
For our mother
The creator of the Stool is lost!
And all the young women
Have perished in the wilderness!

But this is not the end of the story, for all the young 15
women—our mothers and grandmothers, *ourselves*—have
not perished in the wilderness. And if we ask ourselves
why, and search for and find the answer, we will know
beyond all efforts to erase it from our minds, just exactly
who, and of what, we black American women are.

One example, perhaps the most pathetic, most mis- 16
understood one, can provide a backdrop for our mothers'
work: Phillis Wheatley, a slave in the 1700s.

Virginia Woolf, in her book *A Room of One's Own,* 17
wrote that in order for a woman to write fiction she must
have two things, certainly: a room of her own (with key
and lock) and enough money to support herself.

What then are we to make of Phillis Wheatley, a slave, 18
who owned not even herself? This sickly, frail black girl
who required a servant of her own at times—her health
was so precarious—and who, had she been white, would
have been easily considered the intellectual superior of
all the women and most of the men in the society of her
day.

Virginia Woolf wrote further, speaking of course not 19
of our Phillis, that "any woman born with a great gift in
the sixteenth century [insert "eighteenth century," insert
"black woman," insert "born or made a slave"] would
certainly have gone crazed, shot herself, or ended her
days in some lonely cottage outside the village, half witch,
half wizard [insert "Saint"], feared and mocked at. For
it needs little skill and psychology to be sure that a highly

gifted girl who had tried to use her gift for poetry would have been so thwarted and hindered by contrary instincts [add "chains, guns, the lash, the ownership of one's body by someone else, submission to an alien religion"], that she must have lost her health and sanity to a certainty."

The key words, as they relate to Phillis, are "contrary 20 instincts." For when we read the poetry of Phillis Wheatley—as when we read the novels of Nella Larsen or the oddly false-sounding autobiography of that freest of all black women writers, Zora Hurston—evidence of "contrary instincts" is everywhere. Her loyalties were completely divided, as was, without question, her mind.

But how could this be otherwise? Captured at seven, 21 a slave of wealthy, doting whites who instilled in her the "savagery" of the Africa they "rescued" her from . . . one wonders if she was even able to remember her homeland as she had known it, or as it really was.

Yet, because she did try to use her gift for poetry in a 22 world that made her a slave, she was "so thwarted and hindered by . . . contrary instincts, that she . . . lost her health. . . ." In the last years of her brief life, burdened not only with the need to express her gift but also with a penniless, friendless "freedom" and several small children for whom she was forced to do strenuous work to feed, she lost her health, certainly. Suffering from malnutrition and neglect and who knows what mental agonies, Phillis Wheatley died.

So torn by "contrary instincts" was black, kidnapped, 23 enslaved Phillis that her description of "the Goddess"— as she poetically called the Liberty she did not have—is ironically, cruelly humorous. And, in fact, has held Phillis up to ridicule for more than a century. It is usually read prior to hanging Phillis's memory as that of a fool. She wrote:

The Goddess comes, she moves divinely fair,
Olive and laurel binds her *golden* hair.

Wherever shines this native of the skies,
Unnumber'd charms and recent graces rise. [My italics]

It is obvious that Phillis, the slave, combed the "God- 24
dess's" hair every morning; prior, perhaps, to bringing in
the milk, or fixing her mistress's lunch. She took her
imagery from the one thing she saw elevated above all
others.

With the benefit of hindsight we ask, "How could she?" 25

But at last, Phillis, we understand. No more snickering 26
when your stiff, struggling, ambivalent lines are forced on
us. We know now that you were not an idiot or a traitor;
only a sickly little black girl, snatched from your home and
country and made a slave; a woman who still struggled to
sing the song that was your gift, although in a land of
barbarians who praised you for your bewildered tongue.
It is not so much what you sang, as that you kept alive,
in so many of our ancestors, *the notion of song.*

Black women are called, in the folklore that so aptly 27
identifies one's status in society, "the *mule* of the world,"
because we have been handed the burdens that everyone
else—*everyone* else—refused to carry. We have also been
called "Matriarchs," "Superwomen," and "Mean and Evil
Bitches." Not to mention "Castraters" and "Sapphire's
Mama." When we have pleaded for understanding, our
character has been distorted; when we have asked for simple caring, we have been handed empty inspirational ap-
pellations, then stuck in the farthest corner. When we
have asked for love, we have been given children. In
short, even our plainer gifts, our labors of fidelity and love,
have been knocked down our throats. To be an artist and
a black woman, even today, lowers our status in many respects, rather than raises it: and yet, artists we will be.

Therefore we must fearlessly pull out of ourselves and 28
look at and identify with our lives the living creativity
some of our great-grandmothers were not allowed to know.

I stress *some* of them because it is well known that the majority of our great-grandmothers knew, even without "knowing" it, the reality of their spirituality, even if they didn't recognize it beyond what happened in the singing at church—and they never had any intention of giving it up.

How they did it—those millions of black women who were not Phillis Wheatley, or Lucy Terry or Frances Harper of Zora Hurston or Nella Larsen or Bessie Smith; or Elizabeth Catlett, or Katherine Dunham, either—brings me to the title of this essay, "In Search of Our Mothers' Gardens," which is a personal account that is yet shared, in its theme and its meaning, by all of us. I found, while thinking about the far-reaching world of the creative black woman, that often the truest answer to a question that really matters can be found very close. 29

In the late 1920s my mother ran away from home to marry my father. Marriage, if not running away, was expected of seventeen-year-old girls. By the time she was twenty, she had two children and was pregnant with a third. Five children later, I was born. And this is how I came to know my mother: she seemed a large, soft, loving-eyed woman who was rarely impatient in our home. Her quick, violent temper was on view only a few times a year, when she battled with the white landlord who had the misfortune to suggest to her that her children did not need to go to school. 30

She made all the clothes we wore, even my brothers' overalls. She made all the towels and sheets we used. She spent the summers canning vegetables and fruits. She spent the winter evenings making quilts enough to cover all our beds. 31

During the "working" day, she labored beside—not behind—my father in the fields. Her day began before sunup, and did not end until late at night. There was never a moment for her to sit down, undisturbed, to unravel her own private thoughts; never a time free from 32 interruption—by work or the noisy inquiries of her many children. And yet, it is to my mother—and all our mothers who were not famous—that I went in search of the secret of what has fed that muzzled and often mutilated, but vibrant, creative spirit that the black woman has inherited, and that pops out in wild and unlikely places to this day.

But when, you will ask, did my overworked mother 33 have time to know or care about feeding the creative spirit?

The answer is so simple that many of us have spent 34 years discovering it. We have constantly looked high, when we should have looked high—and low.

For example: in the Smithsonian Institution in Wash- 35 ington, D.C., there hangs a quilt unlike any other in the world. In fanciful, inspired, and yet simple and identifiable figures, it portrays the story of the Crucifixion. It is considered rare, beyond price. Though it follows no known pattern of quilt-making, and though it is made of bits and pieces of worthless rags, it is obviously the work of a person of powerful imagination and deep spiritual feeling. Below this quilt I saw a note that says it was made by "an anonymous Black woman in Alabama, a hundred years ago."

If we could locate this "anonymous" black woman 36 from Alabama, she would turn out to be one of our grandmothers—an artist who left her mark in the only materials she could afford, and in the only medium her position in society allowed her to use.

As Virginia Woolf wrote further, in *A Room of One's* 37 *Own*:

> Yet genius of a sort must have existed among women as it must have existed among the working class. [Change this to "slaves" and "the wives and daughters of sharecroppers."] Now and again an Emily Brontë or a Robert Burns [change this to "a Zora Hurston or a Richard Wright"]

blazes out and proves its presence. But certainly it never got itself on to paper. When, however, one reads of a witch being ducked, of a woman possessed by devils [or "Sainthood"], of a wise woman selling herbs [our root workers], or even a very remarkable man who had a mother, then I think we are on the track of a lost novelist, a suppressed poet, of some mute and inglorious Jane Austen.... Indeed, I would venture to guess that Anon, who wrote so many poems without signing them, was often a woman....

And so our mothers and grandmothers have, more often than not anonymously, handed on the creative spark, the seed of the flower they themselves never hoped to see: or liked a sealed letter they could not plainly read.   38

And so it is, certainly, with my own mother. Unlike "Ma" Rainey's songs, which retained their creator's name even while blasting forth from Bessie Smith's mouth, no song or poem will bear my mother's name. Yet so many of the stories that I write, that we all write, are my mother's stories. Only recently did I fully realize this: that through years of listening to my mother's stories of her life, I have absorbed not only the stories themselves, but something of the manner in which she spoke, something of the urgency that involves the knowledge that her stories—like her life—must be recorded. It is probably for this reason that so much of what I have written is about characters whose counterparts in real life are so much older than I am.   39

But the telling of these stories, which came from my mother's lips as naturally as breathing, was not the only way my mother showed herself as an artist. For stories, too, were subject to being distracted, to dying without conclusion. Dinners must be started, and cotton must be gathered before the big rains. The artist that was and is   40 my mother showed itself to me only after many years. This is what I finally noticed:

Like Mem, a character in *The Third Life of Grange* 41
Copeland, my mother adorned with flowers whatever shabby house we were forced to live in. And not just your typical straggly country stand of zinnias, either. She planted ambitious gardens—and still does—with over fifty different varieties of plants that bloom profusely from early March until late November. Before she left home for the fields, she watered her flowers, chopped up the grass, and laid out new beds. When she returned from the fields she might divide clumps of bulbs, dig a cold pit, uproot and replant roses, or prune branches from her taller bushes or trees—until night came and it was too dark to see.

Whatever she planted grew as if by magic, and her 42
fame as a grower of flowers spread over three counties. Because of her creativity with her flowers, even my memories of poverty are seen through a screen of blooms— sunflowers, petunias, roses, dahlias, forsythia, spirea, delphiniums, verbena . . . and on and on.

And I remember people coming to my mother's yard 43
to be given cuttings from her flowers; I hear again the praise showered on her because whatever rocky soil she landed on, she turned into a garden. A garden so brilliant with colors, so original in its design, so magnificent with life and creativity, that to this day people drive by our house in Georgia—perfect strangers and imperfect strangers —and ask to stand or walk among my mother's art.

I notice that it is only when my mother is working in 44
her flowers that she is radiant, almost to the point of being invisible—except as Creator: hand and eye. She is involved in work her soul must have. Ordering the universe in the image of her personal conception of Beauty.

Her face, as she prepares the Art that is her gift, is a 45
legacy of respect she leaves to me, for all that illuminates and cherishes life. She has handed down respect for the possibilities—and the will to grasp them.

For her, so hindered and intruded upon in so many ways, being an artist has still been a daily part of her life. This ability to hold on, even in very simple ways, is work black women have done for a very long time. ⁴⁶

This poem is not enough, but it is something, for the woman who literally covered the holes in our walls with sunflowers: ⁴⁷

> They were women then
> My mama's generation
> Husky of voice—Stout of
> Step
> With fists as well as
> Hands
> How they battered down
> Doors
> And ironed
> Starched white
> Shirts
> How they led
> Armies
> Headragged Generals
> Across mined
> Fields
> Booby-trapped
> Kitchens
> To discover books
> Desks
> A place for us
> How they knew what we
> *Must* know
> Without knowing a page
> Of it
> Themselves.

Guided by my heritage of a love of beauty and a respect 48
for strength—in search of my mother's garden, I found my
own.

And perhaps in Africa over two hundred years ago, 49
there was just such a mother; perhaps she painted vivid
and daring decorations in oranges and yellows and greens
on the walls of her hut; perhaps she sang—in a voice like
Roberta Flack's—*sweetly* over the compounds of her village; perhaps she wove the most stunning mats or told the
most ingenious stories of all the village storytellers. Perhaps she was herself a poet—though only her daughter's
name is signed to the poems that we know.

Perhaps Phillis Wheatley's mother was also an artist. 50

Perhaps in more than Phillis Wheatley's biological life 51
is her mother's signature made clear.

Sight into Insight

ANNIE DILLARD

◆

Annie Dillard was born in 1945 in Pittsburgh, Pennsylvania, and educated at Hollins College near Roanoke, Virginia. She lived for nearly a decade in the Roanoke Valley, observing the natural landscape around Tinker Creek. She recorded her observations in Pilgrim at Tinker Creek *(1974), a book that was awarded the Pulitzer Prize for general nonfiction. Since 1973 she has served as a contributing editor to* Harper's *magazine and has written a column for* Living Wilderness. *She has also worked as a professor of English at Western Washington State University and writer-in-residence at Wesleyan University. Her books include a collection of poems,* Tickets for a Prayer Wheel *(1974), a volume of literary criticism,* Living by Fiction *(1982), and two meditations on the beauty and mystery in nature,* Holy the Firm *(1977) and* Teaching a Stone to Talk: Expeditions and Encounters *(1982). In "Sight into Insight," first published in* Harper's *in 1974, Dillard speculates on two kinds of "seeing"— one literal, one "a discipline requiring a lifetime of dedicated struggle"—by which human beings may hope to encounter and understand the unexpected in the world.*

When I was six or seven years old, growing up in Pittsburgh, I used to take a penny of my own and hide it for someone else to find. It was a curious compulsion; sadly, I've never been seized by it since. For some reason I always "hid" the penny along the same stretch of sidewalk up the street. I'd cradle it at the roots of a maple, say, or in a hole left by a chipped-off piece of sidewalk. Then I'd take a piece of chalk and, starting at either end of the block, draw huge arrows leading up to the penny from both directions. After I learned to write I labeled the arrows "SURPRISE AHEAD" or "MONEY THIS WAY." I was greatly excited, during all this arrowdrawing, at the thought of the first lucky passerby who would receive in this way, regardless of merit, a free gift from the universe. But I never lurked about. I'd go straight home and not give the matter another thought, until, some months later, I would be gripped by the impulse to hide another penny.

There are lots of things to see, unwrapped gifts and free surprises. The world is fairly studded and strewn with pennies cast broadside from a generous hand. But—and this is the point—who gets excited by a mere penny? If you follow one arrow, if you crouch motionless on a bank to watch a tremulous ripple thrill on the water, and are rewarded by the sight of a muskrat kit paddling from its den, will you count that sight a chip of copper only, and go your rueful way? It is very dire poverty indeed for a man to be so malnourished and fatigued that he won't stoop to pick up a penny. But if you cultivate a healthy poverty and simplicity, so that finding a penny will make your day, then, since the world is in fact planted in pennies, you have with your poverty bought a lifetime of days. What you see is what you get.

Unfortunately, nature is very much a now-you-see-it, now-you-don't affair. A fish flashes, then dissolves in the water before my eyes like so much salt. Deer apparently ascend bodily into heaven; the brightest oriole fades into leaves. These disappearances stun me into stillness and concentration; they say of nature that it conceals with a grand nonchalance, and they say of vision that it is a deliberate gift, the revelation of a dancer who for my eyes only flings away her seven veils.

For nature does reveal as well as conceal; now-you-don't-see-it, now-you-do. For a week this September migrating red-winged blackbirds were feeding heavily down by Tinker Creek at the back of the house. One day I went out to investigate the racket; I walked up to a tree, an

2

3

4

Osage orange, and a hundred birds flew away. They simply materialized out of the tree. I saw a tree, then a whisk of color, then a tree again. I walked closer and another hundred blackbirds took flight. Not a branch, not a twig budged: the birds were apparently weightless as well as invisible. Or, it was as if the leaves of the Osage orange had been freed from a spell in the form of red-winged blackbirds; they flew from the tree, caught my eye in the sky, and vanished. When I looked again at the tree, the leaves had reassembled as if nothing had happened. Finally I walked directly to the trunk of the tree and a final hundred, the real diehards, appeared, spread, and vanished. How could so many hide in the tree without my seeing them? The Osage orange, unruffled, looked just as it had looked from the house, when three hundred red-winged blackbirds cried from its crown. I looked upstream where they flew, and they were gone. Searching, I couldn't spot one. I wandered upstream to force them to play their hand, but they'd crossed the creek and scattered. One show to a customer. These appearances catch at my throat; they are the free gifts, the bright coppers at the roots of trees.

It's all a matter of keeping my eyes open. Nature is like   5
one of those line drawings that are puzzles for children: Can you find hidden in the tree a duck, a house, a boy, a bucket, a giraffe, and a boot? Specialists can find the most incredibly hidden things. A book I read when I was young recommended an easy way to find caterpillars: you simply find some fresh caterpillar droppings, look up, and there's your caterpillar. More recently an author advised me to set my mind at ease about those piles of cut stems on the ground in grassy fields. Field mice make them; they cut the grass down by degrees to reach the seeds at the head. It seems that when the grass is tightly packed, as in a field of ripe grain, the blade won't topple at a single cut through the stem; instead, the cut stem simply drops vertically, held in the crush of grain. The mouse severs the

bottom again and again, the stem keeps dropping an inch at a time, and finally the head is low enough for the mouse to reach the seeds. Meanwhile the mouse is positively littering the field with its little piles of cut stems into which, presumably, the author is constantly stumbling.

If I can't see these minutiae, I still try to keep my eyes open. I'm always on the lookout for ant lion traps in sandy soil, monarch pupae near milkweed, skipper larvae in locust leaves. These things are utterly common, and I've not seen one. I bang on hollow trees near water, but so far no flying squirrels have appeared. In flat country I watch every sunset in hopes of seeing the green ray. The green ray is a seldom-seen streak of light that rises from the sun like a spurting fountain at the moment of sunset; it throbs into the sky for two seconds and disappears. One more reason to keep my eyes open. A photography professor at the University of Florida just happened to see a bird die in midflight; it jerked, died, dropped, and smashed on the ground.

6

I squint at the wind because I read Stewart Edward White: "I have always maintained that if you looked closely enough you could *see* the wind—the dim, hardly-made-out, fine débris fleeing high in the air." White was an excellent observer, and devoted an entire chapter of *The Mountains* to the subject of seeing deer: "As soon as you can forget the naturally obvious and construct an artificial obvious, then you too will see deer."

7

But the artificial obvious is hard to see. My eyes account for less than 1 percent of the weight of my head; I'm bony and dense; I see what I expect. I just don't know what the lover knows; I can't see the artificial obvious that those in the know construct. The herpetologist asks the native, "Are there snakes in that ravine?" "No, sir." And the herpetologist comes home with, yessir, three bags full. Are there butterflies on that mountain? Are the bluets in bloom? Are there arrowheads here, or fossil ferns in the shale?

8

Peeping through my keyhole I see within the range of   9
only about 30 percent of the light that comes from the
sun; the rest is infrared and some little ultraviolet, perfectly apparent to many animals, but invisible to me. A
nightmare network of ganglia, charged and firing without
my knowledge, cuts and splices what I do see, editing it
for my brain. Donald E. Carr points out that the sense
impressions of one-celled animals are *not* edited for the
brain: "This is philosophically interesting in a rather
mournful way, since it means that only the simplest animals perceive the universe as it is."

A fog that won't burn away drifts and flows across my   10
field of vision. When you see fog move against a backdrop of deep pines, you don't see the fog itself, but streaks
of clearness floating across the air in dark shreds. So I see
only tatters of clearness through a pervading obscurity. I
can't distinguish the fog from the overcast sky; I can't be
sure if the light is direct or reflected. Everywhere darkness
and the presence of the unseen appalls. We estimate now
that only one atom dances alone in every cubic meter of
intergalactic space. I blink and squint. What planet or
power yanks Halley's Comet out of orbit? We haven't
seen it yet; it's a question of distance, density, and the
pallor of reflected light. We rock, cradled in the swaddling
band of darkness. Even the simple darkness of night whispers suggestions to the mind. This summer, in August, I
stayed at the creek too late.

Where Tinker Creek flows under the sycamore log   11
bridge to the tear-shaped island, it is slow and shallow,
fringed thinly in cattail marsh. At this spot an astonishing
bloom of life supports vast breeding populations of insects,
fish, reptiles, birds, and mammals. On windless summer
evenings I stalk along the creek bank or straddle the sycamore log in absolute stillness, watching for muskrats. The
night I stayed too late I was hunched on the log staring
spellbound at spreading, reflected stains of lilac on the
water. A cloud in the sky suddenly lighted as if turned

on by a switch; its reflection just as suddenly materialized on the water upstream, flat and floating, so that I couldn't see the creek bottom, or life in the water under the cloud. Downstream, away from the cloud on the water, water turtles smooth as beans were gliding down with the current in a series of easy, weightless push-offs, as men bound on the moon. I didn't know whether to trace the progress of one turtle I was sure of, risking sticking my face in one of the bridge's spider webs made invisible by the gathering dark, or take a chance on seeing the carp, or scan the mudbank in hope of seeing a muskrat, or follow the last of the swallows who caught at my heart and trailed it after them like streamers as they appeared from directly below, under the log, flying upstream with their tails forked, so fast.

But shadows spread and deepened and stayed. After thousands of years we're still strangers to darkness, fearful aliens in an enemy camp with our arms crossed over our chests. I stirred. A land turtle on the bank, startled, hissed the air from its lungs and withdrew to its shell. An uneasy pink here, an unfathomable blue there, gave great suggestion of lurking beings. Things were going on. I couldn't see whether that rustle I heard was a distant rattlesnake, slit-eyed, or a nearby sparrow kicking in the dry flood debris slung at the foot of a willow. Tremendous action roiled the water everywhere I looked, big action, inexplicable. A tremor welled up beside a gaping muskrat burrow in the bank and I caught my breath, but no muskrat appeared. The ripples continued to fan upstream with a steady, powerful thrust. Night was knitting an eyeless mask over my face, and I still sat transfixed. A distant airplane, a delta wing out of nightmare, made a gliding shadow on the creek's bottom that looked like a stingray cruising upstream. At once a black fin slit the pink cloud on the water, shearing it in two. The two halves merged together and seemed to dissolve before my eyes. Darkness pooled in the cleft of the creek and rose, as water collects in a well. Untamed, dreaming lights flickered over the sky. I saw hints of hulking underwater shadows, two pale

12

splashes out of the water, and round ripples rolling close together from a blackened center.

At last I stared upstream where only the deepest violet remained of the cloud, a cloud so high its underbelly still glowed, its feeble color reflected from a hidden sky lighted in turn by a sun halfway to China. And out of that violet, a sudden enormous black body arced over the water. Head and tail, if there was a head and tail, were both submerged in cloud. I saw only one ebony fling, a headlong dive to darkness; then the waters closed, and the lights went out. 13

I walked home in a shivering daze, up hill and down. Later I lay openmouthed in bed, my arms flung wide at my sides to steady the whirling darkness. At this latitude I'm spinning 836 miles an hour round the earth's axis; I feel my sweeping fall as a breakneck arc like the dive of dolphins, and the hollow rushing of wind raises the hairs on my neck and the side of my face. In orbit around the sun I'm moving 64,800 miles an hour. The solar system as a whole, like a merry-go-round unhinged, spins, bobs, and blinks at the speed of 43,200 miles an hour along a course set east of Hercules. Someone has piped, and we are dancing a tarantella until the sweat pours. I open my eyes and I see dark, muscled forms curl out of water, with flapping gills and flattened eyes. I close my eyes and I see stars, deep stars giving way to deeper stars, deeper stars bowing to deepest stars at the crown of an infinite cone. 14

"Still," wrote Van Gogh in a letter, "a great deal of light falls on everything." If we are blinded by darkness, we are also blinded by light. Sometimes here in Virginia at sunset low clouds on the southern or northern horizon are completely invisible in the lighted sky. I only know one is there because I can see its reflection in still water. The first time I discovered this mystery I looked from cloud to no-cloud in bewilderment, checking my bearings over and over, thinking maybe the ark of the covenant was just passing by south of Dead Man Mountain. Only much 15 later did I learn the explanation: polarized light from the sky is very much weakened by reflection, but the light in clouds isn't polarized. So invisible clouds pass among visible clouds, till all slide over the mountains; so a greater light extinguishes a lesser as though it didn't exist.

In the great meteor shower of August, the Perseid, I 16 wail all day for the shooting stars I miss. They're out there showering down committing hara-kiri in a flame of fatal attraction, and hissing perhaps at last into the ocean. But at dawn what looks like a blue dome clamps down over me like a lid on a pot. The stars and planets could smash and I'd never know. Only a piece of ashen moon occasionally climbs up or down the inside of the dome, and our local star without surcease explodes on our heads. We have really only that one light, one source for all power, and yet we must turn away from it by universal decree. Nobody here on the planet seems aware of this strange, powerful taboo, that we all walk about carefully averting our faces, this way and that, lest our eyes be blasted forever.

Darkness appalls and light dazzles; the scrap of visible 17 light that doesn't hurt my eyes hurts my brain. What I see sets me swaying. Size and distance and the sudden swelling of meanings confuse me, bowl me over. I straddle the sycamore log bridge over Tinker Creek in the summer. I look at the lighted creek bottom: snail tracks tunnel the mud in quavering curves. A crayfish jerks, but by the time I absorb what has happened, he's gone in a billowing smoke screen of silt. I look at the water; minnows and shiners. If I'm thinking minnows, a carp will fill my brain till I scream. I look at the water's surface: skaters, bubbles, and leaves sliding down. Suddenly, my own face, reflected, startles me witless. Those snails have been tracking my face! Finally, with a shuddering wrench of the will, I see clouds, cirrus clouds. I'm dizzy, I fall in.

This looking business is risky. Once I stood on a 18 humped rock on nearby Purgatory Mountain, watching through binoculars the great autumn hawk migration below, until I discovered that I was in danger of joining the hawks on a vertical migration of my own. I was used to binoculars, but not, apparently, to balancing on humped rocks while looking through them. I reeled. Everything advanced and receded by turns; the world was full of unexplained foreshortenings and depths. A distant huge object, a hawk the size of an elephant, turned out to be the browned bough of a nearby loblolly pine. I followed a sharp-shinned hawk against a featureless sky, rotating my head unawares as it flew, and when I lowered the glass a glimpse of my own looming shoulder sent me staggering. What prevents the men at Palomar from falling, voiceless and blinded, from their tiny, vaulted chairs?

I reel in confusion: I don't understand what I see. 19 With the naked eye I can see two million light-years to the Andromeda galaxy. Often I slop some creek water in a jar, and when I get home I dump it in a white china bowl. After the silt settles I return and see tracings of minute snails on the bottom, a planarian or two winding round the rim of water, roundworms shimmying, frantically, and finally, when my eyes have adjusted to these dimensions, amoebae. At first the amoebae look like *muscae volitantes*, those curled moving spots you seem to see in your eyes when you stare at a distant wall. Then I see the amoebae as drops of water congealed, bluish, translucent, like chips of sky in the bowl. At length I choose one individual and give myself over to its idea of an evening. I see it dribble a grainy foot before it on its wet, unfathomable way. Do its unedited sense impressions include the fierce focus of my eyes? Shall I take it outside and show it Andromeda, and blow its little endoplasm? I stir the water with a finger, in case it's running out of oxygen. Maybe I should get a tropical aquarium with motorized bubblers and lights, and keep this one for a pet. Yes, it would tell its fissioned descendants, the universe is two feet by five, and if you listen closely you can hear the buzzing music of the spheres.

Oh, it's mysterious, lamplit evenings here in the galaxy, 20 one after the other. It's one of those nights when I wander from window to window, looking for a sign. But I can't see. Terror and a beauty insoluble are a riband of blue woven into the fringe of garments of things both great and small. No culture explains, no bivouac offers real haven or rest. But it could be that we are not seeing something. Galileo thought comets were an optical illusion. This is fertile ground: since we are certain that they're not, we can look at what our scientists have been saying with fresh hope. What if there are *really* gleaming, castellated cities hung up-side-down over the desert sand? What limpid lakes and cool date palms have our caravans always passed untried? Until, one by one, by the blindest of leaps, we light on the road to these places, we must stumble in darkness and hunger. I turn from the window. I'm blind as a bat, sensing only from every direction the echo of my own thin cries.

I chanced on a wonderful book called *Space and Sight*, 21 by Marius Von Senden. When Western surgeons discovered how to perform safe cataract operations, they ranged across Europe and America operating on dozens of men and women of all ages who had been blinded by cataracts since birth. Von Senden collected accounts of such cases; the histories are fascinating. Many doctors had tested their patients' sense perceptions and ideas of space both before and after the operations. The vast majority of patients, of both sexes and all ages, had, in Von Senden's opinion, no idea of space whatsoever. Form, distance, and size were so many meaningless syllables. A patient "had no idea of depth, confusing it with roundness." Before the operation a doctor would give a blind patient a cube and a sphere; the patient would tongue it or feel it with his hands, and name it correctly. After the operation the doctor would show the same objects to the patient without letting him touch them; now he had no clue whatsoever to what he was seeing. One patient called lemonade "square" because it pricked on his tongue as a square shape pricked on the touch of his hands. Of another post-operative patient the doctor writes, "I have found in her no notion of size, for example, not even within the narrow limits which she might have encompassed with the aid of touch. Thus when I asked her to show me how big her mother was, she did not stretch out her hands, but set her two index fingers a few inches apart."

For the newly sighted, vision is pure sensation unencumbered by meaning. When a newly sighted girl saw photographs and paintings, she asked, " 'Why do they put those dark marks all over them?' 'Those aren't dark marks,' her mother explained, 'those are shadows. That is one of the ways the eye knows that things have shape. If it were not for shadows, many things would look flat.' 'Well, that's how things do look,' Joan answered. 'Everything looks flat with dark patches.' " 22

In general the newly sighted see the world as a dazzle of "color-patches." They are pleased by the sensation of color, and learn quickly to name the colors, but the rest of seeing is tormentingly difficult. Soon after his operation a patient "generally bumps into one of these colour-patches and observes them to be substantial, since they resist him as tactual objects do. In walking about it also strikes him—or can if he pays attention—that he is continually passing in between the colours he sees, that he can go past a visual object, that a part of it then steadily disappears from view; and that in spite of this, however he twists and turns—whether entering the room from the door, for example, or returning back to it—he always has a visual space in front of him. Thus he gradually comes to realize that there is also a space behind him, which he does not see." 23

The mental effort involved in these reasonings proves overwhelming for many patients. It oppresses them to realize that they have been visible to people all along, perhaps unattractively so, without their knowledge or consent. A disheartening number of them refuse to use their new 24 vision, continuing to go over objects with their tongues, and lapsing into apathy and despair.

On the other hand, many newly sighted people speak 25 well of the world, and teach us how dull our own vision is. To one patient, a human hand, unrecognized, is "something bright and then holes." Shown a bunch of grapes, a boy calls out, "It is dark, blue and shiny.... It isn't smooth, it has bumps and hollows." A little girl visits a garden. "She is greatly astonished, and can scarcely be persuaded to answer, stands speechless in front of the tree, which she only names on taking hold of it, and then as 'the tree with the lights in it.' " Another patient, a twenty-two-year-old girl, was dazzled by the world's brightness and kept her eyes shut for two weeks. When at the end of that time she opened her eyes again, she did not recognize any objects, but "the more she now directed her gaze upon everything about her, the more it could be seen how an expression of gratification and astonishment overspread her features; she repeatedly exclaimed: 'Oh God! How beautiful!' "

I saw color-patches for weeks after I read this wonder- 26 ful book. It was summer; the peaches were ripe in the valley orchards. When I woke in the morning, color-patches wrapped round my eyes, intricately, leaving not one unfilled spot. All day long I walked among shifting color-patches that parted before me like the Red Sea and closed again in silence, transfigured, wherever I looked back. Some patches swelled and loomed, while others vanished utterly, and dark marks flitted at random over the whole dazzling sweep. But I couldn't sustain the illusion of flatness. I've been around for too long. Form is condemned to an eternal danse macabre with meaning: I couldn't unpeach the peaches. Nor can I remember ever having seen without understanding; the color-patches of infancy are lost. My brain then must have been smooth as any balloon. I'm told I reached for the moon; many babies do. But the color-patches of infancy swelled as meaning filled them; they arrayed themselves in solemn ranks down distance which unrolled and stretched before me like a plain. The moon rocketed away. I live now in a world of shadows that shape and distance color, a world where space makes a kind of terrible sense. What Gnosticism is this, and what physics? The fluttering patch I saw in my nursery window—silver and green and shape-shifting blue—is gone; a row of Lombardy poplars takes its place, mute, across the distant lawn. That humming oblong creature pale as light that stole along the walls of my room at night, stretching exhilaratingly around the corners, is gone, too, gone the night I ate of the bittersweet fruit, put two and two together and puckered forever my brain. Martin Buber tells this tale: "Rabbi Mendel once boasted to his teacher Rabbi Elimelekh that evenings he saw the angel who rolls away the light before the darkness, and mornings the angel who rolls away the darkness before the light. 'Yes,' said Rabbi Elimelekh, 'in my youth I saw that too. Later on you don't see these things anymore.'"

Why didn't someone hand those newly sighted people   27
paints and brushes from the start, when they still didn't know what anything was? Then maybe we all could see color-patches too, the world unraveled from reason, Eden before Adam gave names. The scales would drop from my eyes; I'd see trees like men walking; I'd run down the road against all orders, hallooing and leaping.

Seeing is of course very much a matter of verbalization.   28
Unless I call my attention to what passes before my eyes, I simply won't see it. If Tinker Mountain erupted, I'd be likely to notice. But if I want to notice the lesser cataclysms of valley life, I have to maintain in my head a running description of the present. It's not that I'm observant; it's just that I talk too much. Otherwise, especially in a strange place, I'll never know what's happening. Like a blind man at the ball game, I need a radio.

When I see this way I analyze and pry. I hurl over logs   29
and roll away stones; I study the bank a square foot at a

time, probing and tilting my head. Some days when a mist covers the mountains, when the muskrats won't show and the microscope's mirror shatters, I want to climb up the blank blue dome as a man would storm the inside of a circus tent, wildly, dangling, and with a steel knife claw a rent in the top, peep, and, if I must, fall.

But there is another kind of seeing that involves a letting go. When I see this way I sway transfixed and emptied. The difference between the two ways of seeing is the difference between walking with and without a camera. When I walk with a camera I walk from shot to shot, reading the light on a calibrated meter. When I walk without a camera, my own shutter opens, and the moment's light prints on my own silver gut. When I see this second way I am above all an unscrupulous observer. 30

It was sunny one evening last summer at Tinker Creek; the sun was low in the sky, upstream. I was sitting on the sycamore log bridge with the sunset at my back, watching the shiners the size of minnows who were feeding over the muddy sand in skittery schools. Again and again, one fish, then another, turned for a split second across the current and flash! the sun shot out from its silver side. I couldn't watch for it. It was always just happening somewhere else, and it drew my vision just as it disappeared: flash! like a sudden dazzle of the thinnest blade, a sparking over a dun and olive ground at chance intervals from every direction. Then I noticed white specks, some sort of pale petals, small, floating from under my feet on the creek's surface, very slow and steady. So I blurred my eyes and gazed toward the brim of my hat and saw a new world. I saw the pale white circles roll up, roll up, like the world's turning, mute and perfect, and I saw the linear flashes, gleaming silver, like stars being born at random down a rolling scroll of time. Something broke and something opened. I filled up like a new wineskin. I breathed an air like light; I saw a light like water. I was the lip of a fountain the creek filled forever; I was ether, the leaf in the zephyr; I was flesh-flake, feather, bone. 31

When I see this way I see truly. As Thoreau says, I ₃₂
return to my senses. I am the man who watches the baseball game in silence in an empty stadium. I see the game
purely; I'm abstracted and dazed. When it's all over and
the white-suited players lope off the green field to their
shadowed dugouts, I leap to my feet, I cheer and cheer.

But I can't go out and try to see this way. I'll fail, I'll go ₃₃
mad. All I can do is try to gag the commentator, to hush
the noise of useless interior babble that keeps me from
seeing just as surely as a newspaper dangled before my eyes.
The effort is really a discipline requiring a lifetime of
dedicated struggle; it marks the literature of saints and
monks of every order east and west, under every rule and
no rule, discalced and shod. The world's spiritual geniuses
seem to discover universally that the mind's muddy river,
this ceaseless flow of trivia and trash, cannot be dammed,
and that trying to dam it is a waste of effort that might
lead to madness. Instead you must allow the muddy river
to flow unheeded in the dim channels of consciousness;
you raise your sights; you look along it, mildly, acknowledging its presence without interest and gazing beyond it
into the realm of the real where subjects and objects act
and rest purely, without utterance. "Launch into the
deep," says Jacques Ellul, "and you shall see."

The secret of seeing, then, is the pearl of great price. ₃₄
If I thought he could teach me to find it and keep it forever I would stagger barefoot across a hundred deserts after
any lunatic at all. But although the pearl may be found,
it may not be sought. The literature of illumination reveals this above all: although it comes to those who wait
for it, it is always, even to the most practiced and adept,
a gift and a total surprise. I return from one walk knowing where the killdeer nests in the field by the creek and
the hour the laurel blooms. I return from the same walk
a day later scarcely knowing my own name. Litanies hum
in my ears; my tongue flaps in my mouth, *Alim non*,
alleluia! I cannot cause light; the most I can do is try to

put myself in the path of its beam. It is possible, in deep space, to sail on solar wind. Light, be it particle or wave, has force: you rig a giant sail and go. The secret of seeing is to sail on solar wind. Hone and spread your spirit till you yourself are a sail, whetted, translucent, broadside to the merest puff.

When her doctor took her bandages off and led her into the garden, the girl who was no longer blind saw "the tree with the lights in it." It was for this tree I searched through the peach orchards of summer, in the forests of fall and down winter and spring for years. Then one day I was walking along Tinker Creek thinking of nothing at all and I saw the tree with the lights in it. I saw the backyard cedar where the mourning doves roost charged and transfigured, each cell buzzing with flame. I stood on the grass with the lights in it, grass that was wholly fire, utterly focused and utterly dreamed. It was less like seeing than like being for the first time seen, knocked breathless by a powerful glance. The flood of fire abated, but I'm still spending the power. Gradually the lights went out in the cedar, the colors died, the cells unflamed and disappeared. I was still ringing. I had been my whole life a bell, and never knew it until at that moment I was lifted and struck. I have since only very rarely seen the tree with the lights in it. The vision comes and goes, mostly goes, but I live for it, for the moment when the mountains open and a new light roars in spate through the crack, and the mountains slam.

A Modest Proposal

FOR PREVENTING THE CHILDREN OF IRELAND
FROM
BEING A BURDEN TO THEIR PARENTS
OR
COUNTRY;
AND
FOR MAKING THEM BENEFICIAL TO THE
PUBLICK

JONATHAN SWIFT

◆

Jonathan Swift (1667–1745) was born in Dublin, Ireland, and educated at Trinity College, Dublin. When his cousin, John Dryden, told him he would never be a poet, Swift reluctantly decided on a career in the church. He earned his M.A. at Oxford, was ordained an Anglican priest, and assigned a parish in Kilroot, Ireland. Swift soon resigned his position and began traveling to England to negotiate church business, to participate in political activities, and to plead for a special church assignment in London. He was forced to settle for a minor appointment, deanship of St. Patrick's Cathedral in Dublin. As demonstrated in his best-known book, Gulliver's Travels *(1726), Swift's real gift as a writer is as a satirist. His other writing includes attacks on the corruption in religion and learning (*A Tale of a Tub, *1704;* The Battle of the Books, *1704) and this preposterous parody of a solution to the difficulties between Ireland and England—*"A Modest Proposal" *(1729).*

It is a melancholly Object to those, who walk through this great Town or travel in the Country; when they see the Streets, the Roads and Cabbin-doors crowded with Beggars of the Female Sex, followed by three, four, or six Children,   1 all in Rags, and importuning every Passenger for an Alms. These Mothers, instead of being able to work for their honest Livelyhood, are forced to employ all their Time in stroling to beg Sustenance for their helpless Infants; who, as they grow up, either turn Thieves for want of Work; or leave their dear Native Country, to fight for the Pretender in Spain, or sell themselves to the Barbadoes.

I think it is agreed by all Parties, that this prodigious number of Children in the Arms, or on the Backs, or at the Heels of their Mothers, and frequently of their Fathers, is in the present deplorable state of the Kingdom, a very great additional Grievance; and therefore, whoever could find out a fair, cheap, and easy Method of making these Children sound and useful Members of the Commonwealth, would deserve so well of the Publick, as to have his Statue set up for a Preserver of the Nation. 2

But my Intention is very far from being confined to provide only for the Children of professed Beggars: It is of a much greater Extent, and shall take in the whole Number of Infants at a certain Age, who are born of Parents in effect as little able to support them, as those who demand our Charity in the Streets. 3

As to my own Part, having turned my Thoughts, for many Years, upon this important Subject, and maturely weighed the several Schemes of other Projectors, I have always found them grossly mistaken in their Computation. It is true, a Child, just dropt from its Dam, may be supported by her Milk, for a Solar Year with little other Nourishment; at most not above the Value of two Shillings; which the Mother may certainly get, or the Value in Scraps, by her lawful Occupation of Begging: and it is exactly at one Year old that I propose to provide for them in such a manner, as, instead of being a Charge upon their Parents or the Parish, or wanting Food and Raiment for the rest of their Lives; they shall, on the contrary, contribute to the Feeding and partly to the Cloathing, of many Thousands. 4

There is likewise another great Advantage in my 5

503

Scheme, that it will prevent those voluntary Abortions, and that horrid practice of Women murdering their Bastard Children, alas! too frequent among us; Sacrificing the poor innocent Babes, I doubt, more to avoid the Expence than the Shame; which would move Tears and Pity in the most Savage and inhuman breast.

The number of Souls in Ireland being usually reckoned one Million and a half; of these I calculate there may be about Two hundred Thousand Couple whose Wives are Breeders; from which number I subtract thirty Thousand Couples, who are able to maintain their own Children, although I apprehend there cannot be so many under the present Distresses of the Kingdom; but this being granted, there will remain an Hundred and Seventy Thousand Breeders. I again Subtract Fifty Thousand, for those Women who miscarry, or whose Children die by Accident, or Disease, within the Year. There only remain an Hundred and Twenty Thousand Children of poor Parents, annually born: The Question therefore is, How this Number shall be reared, and provided for? Which, as I have already said, under the present Situation of Affairs, is utterly impossible, by all the Methods hitherto proposed: For we can neither employ them in Handicraft or Agriculture; we neither build Houses, (I mean in the Country) nor cultivate Land: They can very seldom pick up a Livelyhood by Stealing until they arrive at six Years old; except where they are of towardly Parts; although, I confess, they learn the Rudiments much earlier; during which Time, they can, however be properly looked upon only as Probationers; as I have been informed by a principal Gentleman in the County of Cavan, who protested to me, that he never knew above one or two Instances under the Age of six, even in a part of the Kingdom so renowned for the quickest Proficiency in that Art.

I am assured by our Merchants, that a Boy or a Girl before twelve Years old, is no saleable Commodity; and even when they come to this Age, they will not yield above Three Pounds, or Three Pounds and half a Crown at most, on the Exchange; which cannot turn to Account either to the Parents or the Kingdom; the Charge of Nutriment and Rags, having been at least four Times that Value.

I shall now therefore humbly propose my own Thoughts; which I hope will not be liable to the least Objection. 8

I have been assured by a very knowing American of my Acquaintance in London, that a young healthy Child, well nursed is, at a Year old, a most delicious, nourishing and wholesome Food, whether Stewed, Roasted, Baked, or Boiled; and I make no doubt that it will equally serve in a Fricasie, or Ragoust. 9

I do therefore humbly offer it to publick Consideration, that of the Hundred and Twenty Thousand Children, already computed, Twenty thousand may be reserved for Breed; whereof only one Fourth Part to be Males; which is more than we allow to Sheep, black Cattle, or Swine; and my Reason is, that these Children are seldom the Fruits of Marriage, a Circumstance not much regarded by our Savages; therefore, one Male will be sufficient to serve four Females. That the remaining Hundred thousand, may, at a Year old be offered in Sale to the Persons of Quality and Fortune, through the Kingdom; always advising the Mother to let them suck plentifully in the last Month, so as to render them plump, and fat for a good Table. A Child will make two Dishes at an Entertainment for Friends; and when the Family dines alone, the fore or hind Quarter will make a reasonable Dish; and seasoned with a little Pepper or Salt, will be very good Boiled on the fourth Day, especially in Winter. 10

I have reckoned upon a Medium, that a Child just born will weigh Twelve Pounds; and in a solar Year, if tolerably nursed, increaseth to 28 Pounds. 11

I grant this Food will be somewhat dear, and therefore very proper for Landlords; who, as they have already devoured most of the Parents, seem to have the best Title to the Children. 12

Infant's Flesh will be in Season throughout the Year; 13

but more plentiful in March, and a little before and after; for we are told by a grave Author* an eminent French Physician, that Fish being a prolifick Dyet, there are more Children born in Roman Catholick Countries about Nine Months after Lent, than at any other Season: Therefore reckoning a Year after Lent, the Markets will be more glutted than usual; because the Number of Popish Infants, is, at least, three to one in this Kingdom; and therefore it will have one other Collateral advantage; by lessening the Number of Papists among us.

I have already computed the Charge of nursing a Beg- 14 gar's Child (in which List I reckon all Cottagers, Labourers, and Four fifths of the Farmers) to be about two Shillings per Annum, Rags included; and I believe no Gentleman would repine to give Ten Shillings for the Carcase of a good fat Child; which, as I have said, will make four Dishes of excellent nutritive meat, when he hath only some particular Friend, or his own Family, to dine with him. Thus the Squire will learn to be a good Landlord, and grow popular among his Tenants; the Mother will have Eight Shillings net Profit, and be fit for Work till she produceth another Child.

Those who are more thrifty (as I must confess the 15 Times require) may flay the Carcase; the Skin of which, artificially dressed, will make admirable Gloves for Ladies, and Summer Boots for fine Gentlemen.

As to our City of Dublin; Shambles may be appointed 16 for this Purpose, in the most convenient Parts of it, and Butchers we may be assured will not be wanting; although I rather recommend buying the Children alive, and dressing them hot from the Knife, as we do roasting Pigs.

A very worthy Person, a true Lover of his Country, and 17 whose Virtues I highly esteem, was lately pleased, in discoursing on this Matter, to offer a Refinement upon my Scheme. He said, that many Gentlemen of this Kingdom,

* Rabelais.

having of late destroyed their Deer; he conceived that the
Want of Venison might be well supplied by the Bodies of
young Lads and Maidens, not exceeding fourteen Years of
Age, nor under twelve; so great a Number of both Sexes
in every County being ready to Starve, for want of Work
and Service: And these to be disposed of by their Parents,
if alive, or otherwise by their nearest Relations. But with
due Deference to so excellent a Friend, and so deserving
a Patriot, I cannot be altogether in his Sentiments. For as
to the Males, my American Acquaintance assured me from
frequent Experience, that their Flesh was generally tough
and lean, like that of our School-boys, by continual Exercise, and their Taste disagreeable; and to fatten them
would not answer the Charge. Then, as to the Females,
it would, I think, with humble Submission, be a Loss to
the Publick, because they soon would become Breeders
themselves: And besides it is not improbable, that some
scrupulous People might be apt to censure such a Practice,
(although indeed very unjustly) as a little bordering upon
Cruelty; which, I confess, hath always been with me the
strongest Objection against any Project, how well soever
intended.

But in order to justify my Friend; he confessed, that 18
this Expedient was put into his Head by the famous Sal-
manaazor, a Native of the Island Formosa, who came from
thence to London, above twenty Years ago, and in Conversation told my Friend, that in his Country, when any
young Person happened to be put to Death, the execu-
tioner sold the Carcase to Persons of Quality, as a prime
Dainty, and that, in his Time, the Body of a plump Girl
of fifteen, who was crucified for an Attempt to poison the
Emperor, was sold to his Imperial Majesty's prime Minister
of State, and other great Mandarins of the Court, in Joints
from the Gibbet, at Four hundred Crowns. Neither indeed
can I deny, that if the same Use were made of several
plump young girls in this Town, who, without one single
Groat to their Fortunes, cannot stir Abroad without a

507

Chair, and appear at the Play-house, and Assemblies in foreign fineries, which they never will pay for; the Kingdom would not be the worse.

Some Persons of a desponding Spirit are in great Con- 19
cern about that vast Number of poor People, who are Aged, Diseased, or Maimed; and I have been desired to imploy my Thoughts what Course may be taken, to ease the Nation of so grievous an Incumbrance. But I am not in the least Pain upon that Matter; because it is very well known, that they are every Day dying, and rotting, by Cold and Famine, and Filth, and Vermin, as fast as can be reasonably expected. And as to the younger Labourers, they are now in almost as hopeful a Condition: They cannot get Work, and consequently pine away for Want of Nourishment, to a Degree, that if at any Time they are accidentally hired to common Labour, they have not Strength to perform it; and thus the Country, and themselves, are in a fair Way of being delivered from the Evils to come.

I have too long digressed; and therefore shall return to 20
my Subject. I think the Advantages by the Proposal which I have made are obvious, and many, as well as of the highest Importance.

For First, as I have already observed, it would greatly 21
lessen the Number of Papists, with whom we are Yearly overrun; being the principal Breeders of the Nation, as well as our most dangerous Enemies; and who stay at home on Purpose, with a Design to deliver the Kingdom to the Pretender; hoping to take their Advantage by the Absence of so many good Protestants, who have chosen rather to leave their Country, than stay at home, and pay Tithes against their Conscience, to an idolatrous Episcopal Curate.

Secondly, The poorer Tenants will have something val- 22
uable of their own, which, by Law, may be made liable to Distress, and help to pay their Landlord's Rent; their Corn and Cattle being already seized, and Money a Thing unknown.

Thirdly, Whereas the Maintenance of an Hundred 23
Thousand Children, from two Years old, and upwards,

cannot be computed at less than ten Shillings a Piece per Annum, the Nation's Stock will be thereby encreased Fifty Thousand Pounds per Annum; besides the Profit of a new Dish, introduced to the Tables of all Gentlemen of Fortune in the Kingdom, who have any Refinement in Taste; and the Money will circulate among ourselves, the Goods being entirely of our own Growth and Manufacture.

Fourthly, The constant Breeders, besides the Gain of Eight Shillings Sterling per Annum, by the Sale of their Children, will be rid of the Charge of maintaining them after the first Year. 24

Fifthly, This Food would likewise bring great Custom to Taverns, where the Vintners will certainly be so prudent, as to procure the best Receipts for dressing it to Perfection; and consequently, have their Houses frequented by all the fine Gentlemen, who justly value themselves upon their Knowledge in good Eating; and a skilful Cook, who understands how to oblige his Guests, will contrive to make it as expensive as they please. 25

Sixthly, This would be a great Inducement to Marriage, which all wise Nations have either encouraged by Rewards, or enforced by Laws and Penalties. It would encrease the Care and Tenderness of Mothers towards their Children, when they were sure of a Settlement for Life, to the poor Babes, provided in some Sort by the Publick, to their annual Profit instead of Expence. We should soon see an honest Emulation among the married Women, which of them could bring the fattest Child to the Market. Men would become as fond of their Wives, during the Time of their Pregnancy, as they are now of their Mares in Foal, their Cows in Calf, or Sows when they are ready to farrow; nor offer to beat or kick them, (as is too frequent a Practice) for fear of a Miscarriage. 26

Many other Advantages might be enumerated. For instance, the Addition of some Thousand Carcases in our Exportation of barrel'd Beef: The Propagation of Swine's Flesh, and Improvement in the Art of making good Bacon; so much wanted among us by the great Destruction of Pigs, 27 too frequent at our Tables, and are no way comparable in Taste, or Magnificence, to a well-grown, fat yearling Child; which, roasted whole, will make a considerable Figure at a Lord Mayor's Feast, or any other publick Entertainment. But this, and many others, I omit; being studious of Brevity.

Supposing that one Thousand Families in this City, 28 would be constant Customers for Infants Flesh, besides others who might have it at merry Meetings, particularly Weddings and Christenings; I compute that Dublin would take off, annually, about Twenty Thousand Carcasses; and the rest of the Kingdom (where probably they will be sold somewhat cheaper) the remaining Eighty Thousand.

I can think of no one Objection, that will possibly be 29 raised against this Proposal; unless it should be urged, that the Number of People will be thereby much lessened in the Kingdom. This I freely own; and it was indeed one principal Design in offering it to the World. I desire the Reader will observe, that I calculate my Remedy for this one individual Kingdom of Ireland, and for no other that ever was, is, or, I think, ever can be upon Earth. Therefore, let no man talk to me of other Expedients: Of taxing our Absentees at five Shillings a Pound: Of using neither Cloaths, nor Household Furniture, except what is of our own Growth and Manufacture: Of utterly rejecting the Materials and Instruments that promote foreign Luxury: Of curing the Expensiveness of Pride, Vanity, Idleness, and Gaming in our Women: Of introducing a Vein of Parsimony, Prudence and Temperance: Of learning to love our Country, wherein we differ even from Laplanders, and the Inhabitants of Topinamboo: Of quitting our Animosities, and Factions; nor act any longer like the Jews, who were murdering one another at the very Moment their City was taken: Of being a little cautious not to sell our Country and Consciences for nothing: Of teaching Landlords to have, at least, one Degree of Mercy towards their Tenants. Lastly, of Putting a Spirit of Honesty, Industry, and Skill into our Shopkeepers; who, if a Resolution could now be taken to buy only our native Goods, would immediately unite to cheat and exact upon us in the Price, the Measure, and the Goodness; nor could ever yet be brought to make one fair Proposal of just Dealing, though often and earnestly invited to it.

Therefore I repeat, let no Man talk to me of these and the like Expedients; till he hath, at least, a Glimpse of Hope, that there will ever be some hearty and sincere Attempt to put them in Practice. 30

But, as to my self; having been wearied out for many Years with offering vain, idle, visionary Thoughts; and at length utterly despairing of Success, I fortunately fell upon this Proposal; which, as it is wholly new, so it hath something solid and real, of no Expence and little Trouble, full in our own Power; and whereby we can incur no Danger in disobliging England: For this Kind of Commodity will not bear Exportation; the Flesh being of too tender a Consistence, to admit a long Continuance in Salt; although, perhaps, I could name a Country, which would be glad to eat up our whole Nation without it. 31

After all, I am not so violently bent upon my own Opinion, as to reject any Offer, proposed by wise Men, which shall be found equally innocent, cheap, easy, and effectual. But before something of that Kind shall be advanced in Contradiction to my Scheme, and offering a better; I desire the Author, or Authors, will be pleased maturely to consider two Points. First, As Things now stand, how they will be able to find Food and Raiment, for a Hundred Thousand useless Mouths and Backs? And Secondly, There being a round Million of Creatures in human Figure, throughout this Kingdom; whose whole Subsistence, put into a common Stock, would leave them in Debt two Millions of Pounds Sterling; adding those, who are Beggars by Profession, to the Bulk of Farmers, Cottagers and Labourers, with their Wives and Children, who are Beggars in Effect; I desire those Politicians, who dislike my Overture, and may perhaps be so bold to attempt an Answer, that they will first ask the Parents of 32 these Mortals, Whether they would not at this Day think it a great Happiness to have been sold for Food at a Year old, in the Manner I prescribe; and thereby have avoided such a perpetual Scene of Misfortunes, as they have since gone through; by the Oppression of Landlords; the Impossibility of paying Rent, without Money or Trade; the Want of common Sustenance, with neither House nor Cloaths, to cover them from the Inclemencies of the Weather; and the most inevitable Prospect of intailing the like, or greater Miseries upon their Breed for ever.

I profess, in the Sincerity of my Heart, that I have not   33 the least personal Interest, in endeavouring to promote this necessary Work, having no other Motive than the publick Good of my Country, by advancing our Trade providing for Infants, relieving the Poor, and giving some Pleasure to the Rich. I have no Children, by which I can propose to get a single Penny; the youngest being nine Years Old and my Wife past Child-bearing.

Politics and the English Language

GEORGE ORWELL

———————— ◆ ————————

George Orwell (a pen name for Eric Blair, 1903–1950) was born in Motihari, Bengal, where his father was employed with the Bengal civil service. He was brought to England at an early age for schooling (Eton), but rather than completing his education at the university, he served with the Indian imperial police in Burma (1922–1927). He wrote about these experiences in his first novel, Burmese Days. *Later he returned to Europe and worked at various jobs (*Down and Out in Paris and London, *1933) before fighting on the Republican side of the Spanish Civil War (*Homage to Catalonia, *1938). Orwell's attitudes toward war and government are reflected in his most famous books,* Animal Farm *(1945) and* Nineteen Eighty-Four *(1949). In "Politics and the English Language" (from* Shooting an Elephant, and Other Essays, *1950) Orwell characterizes those aspects of our language that have allowed politicians to defend the indefensible.*

Most people who bother with the matter at all would admit that the English language is in a bad way, but it is generally assumed that we cannot by conscious action do anything about it. Our civilization is decadent and our language—so the argument runs—must inevitably share in the general collapse. It follows that any struggle against the abuse of language is a sentimental archaism, like preferring candles to electric light or hansom cabs to aeroplanes. Underneath this lies the half-conscious belief that language is a natural growth and not an instrument which we shape for our own purposes.

Now, it is clear that the decline of a language must ultimately have political and economic causes: it is not due simply to the bad influence of this or that individual writer. But an effect can become a cause, reinforcing the original cause and producing the same effect in an intensified form, and so on indefinitely. A man may take to drink because he feels himself to be a failure, and then fail all the more completely because he drinks. It is rather the same thing that is happening to the English language. It becomes ugly and inaccurate because our thoughts are foolish, but the slovenliness of our language makes it easier for us to have foolish thoughts. The point is that the process is reversible. Modern English, especially written English, is full of bad habits which spread by imitation and which can be avoided if one is willing to take the necessary trouble. If one gets rid of these habits one can think more clearly, and to think clearly is a necessary first step toward political regeneration: so that the fight against bad English is not frivolous and is not the exclusive concern of professional writers. I will come back to this presently, and I hope that by that time the meaning of what I have said here will have become clearer. Meanwhile, here are five specimens of the English language as it is now habitually written.

These five passages have not been picked out because they are especially bad—I could have quoted far worse if I had chosen—but because they illustrate various of the mental vices from which we now suffer. They are a little below the average, but are fairly representative samples. I number them so that I can refer back to them when necessary:

(1) I am not, indeed, sure whether it is not true to say that the Milton who once seemed not unlike a seventeenth-century Shelley had not become out of an experience ever more bitter

in each year, more alien [*sic*] to the founder of that Jesuit sect which nothing could induce him to tolerate.

Professor Harold Laski
(Essay in *Freedom of Expression*)

(2) Above all, we cannot play ducks and drakes with a native battery of idioms which prescribes such egregious collocations of vocables as the Basic *put up with* for *tolerate* or *put at a loss* for *bewilder.*

Professor Lancelot Hogben (*Interglossa*)

(3) On the one side we have the free personality: by definition it is not neurotic, for it has neither conflict nor dream. Its desires, such as they are, are transparent, for they are just what institutional approval keeps in the forefront of consciousness; another institutional pattern would alter their number and intensity; there is little in them that is natural, irreducible, or culturally dangerous. But *on the other side,* the social bond itself is nothing but the mutual reflection of these self-secure integrities. Recall the definition of love. Is not this the very picture of a small academic? Where is there a place in this hall of mirrors for either personality or fraternity?

Essay on psychology in *Politics* (New York)

(4) All the "best people" from the gentlemen's clubs, and all the frantic fascist captains, united in common hatred of Socialism and bestial horror of the rising tide of the mass revolutionary movement, have turned to acts of provocation, to foul incendiarism, to medieval legends of poisoned wells, to legalize their own destruction of proletarian organizations, and

rouse the agitated petty-bourgeoisie to chauvin-
istic fervor on behalf of the fight against the
revolutionary way out of the crisis.

Communist pamphlet

(5) If a new spirit *is* to be infused into this
old country, there is one thorny and contentious
reform which must be tackled, and that is the
humanization and galvanization of the B.B.C.
Timidity here will bespeak canker and atrophy
of the soul. The heart of Britain may be sound
and of strong beat, for instance, but the British
lion's roar at present is like that of Bottom in
Shakespeare's *Midsummer Night's Dream*—as
gentle as any sucking dove. A virile new Britain
cannot continue indefinitely to be traduced in
the eyes or rather ears, of the world by the effete
languors of Langham Place, brazenly masquerad-
ing as "standard English." When the Voice of
Britain is heard at nine o'clock, better far and
infinitely less ludicrous to hear aitches honestly
dropped than the present priggish, inflated, in-
hibited, school-ma'amish arch braying of blame-
less bashful mewing maidens!

Letter in *Tribune*

Each of these passages has faults of its own, but, quite 4
apart from avoidable ugliness, two qualities are common
to all of them. The first is staleness of imagery; the other
is lack of precision. The writer either has a meaning and
cannot express it, or he inadvertently says something else,
or he is almost indifferent as to whether his words mean
anything or not. This mixture of vagueness and sheer incompetence is the most marked characteristic of modern
English prose, and especially of any kind of political writing. As soon as certain topics are raised, the concrete melts
into the abstract and no one seems able to think of turns
of speech that are not hackneyed: prose consists less and
less of *words* chosen for the sake of their meaning, and

more and more of *phrases* tacked together like the sections of a prefabricated henhouse. I list below, with notes and examples, various of the tricks by means of which the work of prose-construction is habitually dodged:

DYING METAPHORS

A newly invented metaphor assists thought by evoking a 5 visual image, while on the other hand a metaphor which is technically "dead" (e.g., *iron resolution*) has in effect reverted to being an ordinary word and can generally be used without loss of vividness. But in between these two classes there is a huge dump of worn-out metaphors which have lost all evocative power and are merely used because they save people the trouble of inventing phrases for themselves. Examples are: *Ring the changes on, take up the cudgels for, toe the line, ride roughshod over, stand shoulder to shoulder with, play into the hands of, no axe to grind, grist to the mill, fishing in troubled waters, on the order of the day, Achilles' heel, swan song, hotbed.* Many of these are used without knowledge of their meaning (what is a "rift," for instance?), and incompatible metaphors are frequently mixed, a sure sign that the writer is not interested in what he is saying. Some metaphors now current have been twisted out of their original meaning without those who use them even being aware of the fact. For example, *toe the line* is sometimes written *tow the line*. Another example is *the hammer and the anvil*, now always used with the implication that the anvil gets the worst of it. In real life it is always the anvil that breaks the hammer, never the other way about: a writer who stopped to think what he was saying would be aware of this, and would avoid perverting the original phrase.

OPERATORS OR VERBAL FALSE LIMBS

These save the trouble of picking out appropriate verbs 6 and nouns, and at the same time pad each sentence with extra syllables which give it an appearance of symmetry. Characteristic phrases are *render inoperative, militate against, make contact with, be subjected to, give rise to, give grounds for, have the effect of, play a leading part (role) in, make itself felt, take effect, exhibit a tendency to, serve the purpose of, etc., etc.* The keynote is the elimination of simple verbs. Instead of being a single word, such as *break, stop, spoil, mend, kill,* a verb becomes a *phrase,* made up of a noun or adjective tacked on to some general-purpose verb such as *prove, serve, form, play, render.* In addition, the passive voice is wherever possible used in preference to the active, and noun constructions are used instead of gerunds (*by examination of* instead of *by examining*). The range of verbs is further cut down by means of the *-ize* and *de-* formations, and the banal statements are given an appearance of profundity by means of the *not un-* formation. Simple conjunctions and prepositions are replaced by such phrases as *with respect to, having regard to, the fact that, by dint of, in view of, in the interests of, on the hypothesis that;* and the ends of sentences are saved by anticlimax by such resounding commonplaces as *greatly to be desired, cannot be left out of account, a development to be expected in the near future, deserving of serious consideration, brought to a satisfactory conclusion,* and so on and so forth.

PRETENTIOUS DICTION

Words like *phenomenon, element, individual* (as noun), *objective, categorical, effective, virtual, basic, primary, promote, constitute, exhibit, exploit, utilize, eliminate, liquidate* are used to dress up simple statement and give an air of scientic impartiality to biased judgments. Adjectives like *epoch-making, epic, historic, unforgettable, triumphant, age-old, inevitable, inexorable, veritable,* are used to dignify the sordid processes of international politics, while writing that aims at glorifying war usually takes on

7

an archaic color, its characteristic words being: *realm, throne, chariot, mailed fist, trident, sword, shield, buckler, banner, jackboot, clarion.* Foreign words and expressions such as *cul de sac, ancien régime, deus ex machina, mutatis mutandis, status quo, gleichschaltung, weltanschauung,* are used to give an air of culture and elegance. Except for the useful abbreviations *i.e., e.g.,* and *etc.,* there is no real need for any of the hundreds of foreign phrases now current in English. Bad writers, and especially scientific, political, and sociological writers, are nearly always haunted by the notion that Latin or Greek words are grander than Saxon ones, and unnecessary words like *expedite, ameliorate, predict, extraneous, deracinated, clandestine, subaqueous,* and hundreds of others constantly gain ground from their Anglo-Saxon opposite numbers.* The jargon peculiar to Marxist writing (*hyena, hangman, cannibal, petty bourgeois, these gentry, lackey, flunkey, mad dog, White Guard,* etc.) consists largely of words and phrases translated from Russian, German, or French; but the normal way of coining a new word is to use a Latin or Greek root with the appropriate affix and, where necessary, the size formation. It is often easier to make up words of this kind (*deregionalize, impermissible, extramarital, nonfragmentary* and so forth) than to think up the English words that will cover one's meaning. The result, in general, is an increase in slovenliness and vagueness.

MEANINGLESS WORDS

In certain kinds of writing, particularly in art criticism and literary criticism, it is normal to come across long passages 8

---

* An interesting illustration of this is the way in which the English flower names which were in use till very recently are being ousted by Greek ones, *snapdragon* becoming *antirrhinum, forget-me-not* becoming *myosotis,* etc. It is hard to see any practical reason for this change of fashion: it is probably due to an instinctive turning away from the more homely word and a vague feeling that the Greek word is scientific.

which are almost completely lacking in meaning.* Words like *romantic, plastic, values, human, dead, sentimental, natural, vitality,* as used in art criticism, are strictly meaningless, in the sense that they not only do not point to any discoverable object, but are hardly ever expected to do so by the reader. When one critic writes, "The outstanding feature of Mr. X's work is its living quality," while another writes, "The immediately striking thing about Mr. X's work is its peculiar deadness," the reader accepts this as a simple difference of opinion. If words like *black* and *white* were involved, instead of the jargon words *dead* and *living,* he would see at once that language was being used in an improper way. Many political words are similarly abused. The word *Fascism* has now no meaning except in so far as it signifies "something not desirable." The words *democracy, socialism, freedom, patriotic, realistic, justice,* have each of them several different meanings which cannot be reconciled with one another. In the case of a word like *democracy,* not only is there no agreed definition, but the attempt to make one is resisted from all sides. It is almost universally felt that when we call a country democratic we are praising it: consequently the defenders of every kind of régime claim that it is a democracy, and fear that they might have to stop using the word if it were tied down to any one meaning. Words of this kind are often used in a consciously dishonest way. That is, the person who uses them has his own private definition, but allows his hearer to think he means something quite different. Statements like *Marshal Pétain was a true patriot, The Soviet press is the freest in the world, The Catholic Church is opposed to persecution,* are almost always made with intent to deceive. Other words used in

* Example: "Comfort's catholicity of perception and image, strangely Whitmanesque in range, almost the exact opposite in aesthetic compulsion, continues to evoke that trembling atmospheric accumulative hinting at a cruel, an inexorably serene timelessness.... Wrey Gardiner scores by aiming at simple bull's-eyes with precision. Only they are not so simple, and through this contented sadness runs more than the surface bittersweet of resignation." (*Poetry Quarterly*)

variable meanings, in most cases more or less dishonestly, are: *class, totalitarian, science, progressive, reactionary, bourgeois, equality.*

Now that I have made this catalogue of swindles and   9
perversions, let me give another example of the kind of writing that they lead to. This time it must of its nature be an imaginary one. I am going to translate a passage of good English into modern English of the worst sort. Here is a well-known verse from *Ecclesiastes:*

> I returned and saw under the sun, that the race is not to the swift, nor the battle to the strong, neither yet bread to the wise, nor yet riches to men of understanding, nor yet favour to men of skill; but time and chance happeneth to them all.

Here it is in modern English: 10

> Objective considerations of contemporary phenomena compels the conclusion that success or failure in competitive activities exhibits no tendency to be commensurate with innate capacity, but that a considerable element of the unpredictable must invariably be taken into account.

This is a parody, but not a very gross one. Exhibit (3),   11
above, for instance, contains several patches of the same kind of English. It will be seen that I have not made a full translation. The beginning and ending of the sentence follow the original meaning fairly closely, but in the middle the concrete illustrations—race, battle, bread— dissolve into the vague phrase "success or failure in competitive activities." This had to be so, because no modern writer of the kind I am discussing—no one capable of using phrases like "objective consideration of contemporary phenomena"—would ever tabulate his thoughts in that

precise and detailed way. The whole tendency of modern prose is away from concreteness. Now analyze these two sentences a little more closely. The first contains forty-nine words but only sixty syllables, and all its words are those of everyday life. The second contains thirty-eight words of ninety syllables: eighteen of its words are from Latin roots, and one from Greek. The first sentence contains six vivid images, and only one phrase ("time and chance") that could be called vague. The second contains not a single fresh, arresting phrase, and in spite of its ninety syllables it gives only a shortened version of the meaning contained in the first. Yet without a doubt it is the second kind of sentence that is gaining ground in modern English. I do not want to exaggerate. This kind of writing is not yet universal, and outcrops of simplicity will occur here and there in the worst-written page. Still, if you or I were told to write a few lines on the uncertainty of human fortunes, we should probably come much nearer to my imaginary sentence than to the one from *Ecclesiastes*.

As I have tried to show, modern writing at its worst 12 does not consist in picking out words for the sake of their meaning and inventing images in order to make the meaning clearer. It consists in gumming together long strips of words which have already been set in order by someone else, and making the results presentable by sheer humbug. The attraction of this way of writing is that it is easy. It is easier—even quicker, once you have the habit—to say *In my opinion it is not an unjustifiable assumption that* than to say *I think*. If you use ready-made phrases, you not only don't have to hunt about for words; you also don't have to bother with the rhythms of your sentences, since these phrases are generally so arranged as to be more or less euphonious. When you are composing in a hurry—when you are dictating to a stenographer, for instance, or making a public speech—it is natural to fall into a pretentious, Latinized style. Tags like *a consideration which we should do well to bear in mind* or *a conclusion to which all of us would readily assent* will save many a sentence from coming down with a bump. By using stale metaphors, similes, and idioms, you save much mental effort, at the cost of leaving your meaning vague, not only for your reader but for yourself. This is the significance of mixed metaphors. The sole aim of a metaphor is to call up a visual image. When these images clash—as in *The Fascist octopus has sung its swan song, the jackboot is thrown into the melting pot*—it can be taken as certain that the writer is not seeing a mental image of the objects he is naming; in other words he is not really thinking. Look again at the examples I gave at the beginning of this essay. Professor Laski (1) uses five negatives in fifty-three words. One of these is superfluous, making nonsense of the whole passage, and in addition there is the slip—*alien* for akin—making further nonsense, and several avoidable pieces of clumsiness which increase the general vagueness. Professor Hogben (2) plays ducks and drakes with a battery which is able to write prescriptions, and, while disapproving of the everyday phrase *put up with*, is unwilling to look *egregious* up in the dictionary and see what it means; (3), if one takes an uncharitable attitude towards it, is simply meaningless: probably one could work out its intended meaning by reading the whole of the article in which it occurs. In (4), the writer knows more or less what he wants to say, but an accumulation of stale phrases chokes him like tea leaves blocking a sink. In (5), words and meaning have almost parted company. People who write in this manner usually have a general emotional meaning—they dislike one thing and want to express solidarity with another—but they are not interested in the detail of what they are saying. A scrupulous writer, in every sentence that he writes, will ask himself at least four questions, thus: What am I trying to say? What words will express it? What image or idiom will make it clearer? Is this image fresh enough to have an effect? And he will probably ask himself two more: Could I put it more shortly? Have I said anything that is avoidably ugly? But you are not obliged to go to all this trouble.

You can shirk it by simply throwing your mind open and letting the ready-made phrases come crowding in. They will construct your sentences for you—even think your thoughts for you, to a certain extent—and at need they will perform the important service of partially concealing your meaning even from yourself. It is at this point that the special connection between politics and the debasement of language becomes clear.

In our time it is broadly true that political writing is 13 bad writing. Where it is not true, it will generally be found that the writer is some kind of rebel, expressing his private opinions and not a "party line." Orthodoxy, of whatever color, seems to demand a lifeless, imitative style. The political dialects to be found in pamphlets, leading articles, manifestoes, White Papers and the speeches of undersecretaries do, of course, vary from party to party, but they are all alike in that one almost never finds in them a fresh, vivid, homemade turn of speech. When one watches some tired hack on the platform mechanically repeating the familiar phrases—*bestial atrocities, iron heel, bloodstained tyranny, free peoples of the world, stand shoulder to shoulder*—one often has a curious feeling that one is not watching a live human being but some kind of dummy: a feeling which suddenly becomes stronger at moments when the light catches the speaker's spectacles and turns them into blank discs which seem to have no eyes behind them. And this is not altogether fanciful. A speaker who uses that kind of phraseology has gone some distance toward turning himself into a machine. The appropriate noises are coming out of his larynx, but his brain is not involved as it would be if he were choosing his words for himself. If the speech he is making is one that he is accustomed to make over and over again, he may be almost unconscious of what he is saying, as one is when one utters the responses in church. And this reduced state of consciousness, if not indispensable, is at any rate favorable to political conformity.

In our time, political speech and writing are largely 14

the defense of the indefensible. Things like the continuance of British rule in India, the Russian purges and deportations, the dropping of the atom bombs on Japan, can indeed be defended, but only by arguments which are too brutal for most people to face, and which do not square with the professed aims of political parties. Thus political language has to consist largely of euphemism, question-begging and sheer cloudy vagueness. Defenseless villages are bombarded from the air, the inhabitants driven out into the countryside, the cattle machine-gunned, the huts set on fire with incendiary bullets: this is called *pacification*. Millions of peasants are robbed of their farms and sent trudging along the roads with no more than they can carry: this is called *transfer of population* or *rectification of frontiers*. People are imprisoned for years without trial, or shot in the back of the neck or sent to die of scurvy in Arctic lumber camps: this is called *elimination of unreliable elements*. Such phraseology is needed if one wants to name things without calling up mental pictures of them. Consider for instance some comfortable English professor defending Russian totalitarianism. He cannot say outright, "I believe in killing off your opponents when you can get good results by doing so." Probably, therefore, he will say something like this:

"While freely conceding that the Soviet régime exhibits 15
certain features which the humanitarian may be inclined to deplore, we must, I think, agree that a certain curtailment of the right to political opposition is an unavoidable concomitmant of transitional periods, and that the rigors which the Russian people have been called upon to undergo have been amply justified in the sphere of concrete achievement."

The inflated style is itself a kind of euphemism. A 16
mass of Latin words falls upon the facts like soft snow, blurring the outlines and covering up all the details. The great enemy of clear language is insincerity. When there is a gap between one's real and one's declared aims, one turns as it were instinctively to long words and exhausted

idioms, like a cuttlefish squirting out ink. In our age there is no such thing as "keeping out of politics." All issues are political issues, and politics itself is a mass of lies, evasions, folly, hatred, and schizophrenia. When the general atmosphere is bad, language must suffer. I should expect to find—this is a guess which I have not sufficient knowledge to verify—that the German, Russian and Italian languages have all deteriorated in the last ten or fifteen years, as a result of dictatorship.

But if thought corrupts language, language can also corrupt thought. A bad usage can spread by tradition and imitation, even among people who should and do know better. The debased language that I have been discussing is in some ways very convenient. Phrases like *a not unjustifiable assumption, leaves much to be desired, would serve no good purpose, a consideration which we should do well to bear in mind,* are a continuous temptation, a packet of aspirins always at one's elbow. Look back through this essay, and for certain you will find that I have again and again committed the very faults I am protesting against. By this morning's post I have received a pamphlet dealing with conditions in Germany. The author tells me that he "felt impelled" to write it. I open it at random, and here is almost the first sentence that I see: "[The Allies] have an opportunity not only of achieving a radical transformation of Germany's social and political structure in such a way as to avoid a nationalistic reaction in Germany itself, but at the same time of laying the foundations of a co-operative and unified Europe." You see, he "feels impelled" to write—feels, presumably, that he has something new to say—and yet his words, like cavalry horses answering the bugle, group themselves automatically into the familiar dreary pattern. This invasion of one's mind by ready-made phrases (*lay the foundations, achieve a radical transformation*) can only be prevented if one is constantly on guard against them, and every such phrase anaesthetizes a portion of one's brain.

I said earlier that the decadence of our language is

probably curable. Those who deny this would argue, if they produced an argument at all, that language merely reflects existing social conditions, and that we cannot influence its development by any direct tinkering with words and constructions. So far as the general tone or spirit of a language goes, this may be true, but it is not true in detail. Silly words and expressions have often disappeared, not through any evolutionary process but owing to the conscious action of a minority. Two recent examples were *explore every avenue* and *leave no stone unturned*, which were killed by the jeers of a few journalists. There is a long list of flyblown metaphors which could similarly be got rid of if enough people would interest themselves in the job; and it should also be possible to laugh the *not un-* formation out of existence,* to reduce the amount of Latin and Greek in the average sentence, to drive out foreign phrases and strayed scientific words, and, in general, to make pretentiousness unfashionable. But all these are minor points. The defense of the English language implies more than this, and perhaps it is best to start by saying what it does *not* imply.

To begin with it has nothing to do with archaism, with the salvaging of obsolete words and turns of speech, or with the setting up of a "standard English" which must never be departed from. On the contrary, it is especially concerned with the scrapping of every word or idiom which has outworn its usefulness. It has nothing to do with correct grammar and syntax, which are of no importance so long as one makes one's meaning clear, or with the avoidance of Americanisms, or with having what is called a "good prose style." On the other hand it is not concerned with fake simplicity and the attempt to make written English colloquial. Nor does it even imply in every case preferring the Saxon word to the Latin one, though it does imply using the fewest and shortest words

19

* One can cure oneself of the *not un-* formation by memorizing this sentence: *A not unblack dog was chasing a not unsmall rabbit across a not ungreen field.*

that will cover one's meaning. What is above all needed is to let the meaning choose the word, and not the other way about. In prose, the worst thing one can do with words is to surrender to them. When you think of a concrete object, you think wordlessly, and then, if you want to describe the thing you have been visualizing you probably hunt about till you find the exact words that seem to fit it. When you think of something abstract you are more inclined to use words from the start, and unless you make a conscious effort to prevent it, the existing dialect will come rushing in and do the job for you, at the expense of blurring or even changing your meaning. Probably it is better to put off using words as long as possible and get one's meaning as clear as one can through pictures or sensations. Afterward one can choose—not simply *accept*—the phrases that will best cover the meaning, and then switch round and decide what impression one's words are likely to make on another person. This last effort of the mind cuts out all stale or mixed images, all prefabricated phrases, needless repetitions, and humbug and vagueness generally. But one can often be in doubt about the effect of a word or a phrase, and one needs rules that one can rely on when instinct fails. I think the following rules will cover most cases.

(i)   Never use a metaphor, simile, or other figure of speech which you are used to seeing in print.
(ii) Never use a long word where a short one will do.
(iii) If it is possible to cut a word out, always cut it out.
(iv) Never use the passive where you can use the active.
(v)   Never use a foreign phrase, a scientific word, or a jargon word if you can think of an everyday English equivalent.
(vi) Break any of these rules sooner than say anything outright barbarous.

These rules sound elementary, and so they are, but they demand a deep change of attitude in anyone who has grown used to writing in the style now fashionable. One could keep all of them and still write bad English, but one could not write the kind of stuff that I quoted in those five specimens at the beginning of this article.

I have not here been considering the literary use of language, but merely language as an instrument for expressing and not for concealing or preventing thought. Stuart Chase and others have come near to claiming that all abstract words are meaningless, and have used this as a pretext for advocating a kind of political quietism. Since you don't know what Fascism is, how can you struggle against Fascism? One need not swallow such absurdities as this, but one ought to recognize that the present political chaos is connected with the decay of language, and that one can probably bring about some improvement by starting at the verbal end. If you simplify your English, you are freed from the worst follies of orthodoxy. You cannot speak any of the necessary dialects, and when you make a stupid remark its stupidity will be obvious, even to yourself. Political language—and with variations this is true of all political parties, from Conservatives to Anarchists—is designed to make lies sound truthful and murder respectful, and to give an appearance of solidity to pure wind. One cannot change this all in a moment, but one can at least change one's own habits, and from time to time one can even, if one jeers loudly enough, send some worn-out and useless phrase—some *jackboot, Achilles' heel, hotbed, melting pot, acid test, veritable inferno,* or other lump of verbal refuse—into the dustbin where it belongs.

20

ESSAYS
ON READING
AND WRITING

A Sweet Devouring

EUDORA WELTY

◆

Eudora Welty was born in 1909 in Jackson, Mississippi, and educated at Mississippi State College for Women, the University of Wisconsin, and, for a brief period, the school of business at Columbia University, where she studied advertising. During the Depression she returned to Mississippi to write for newspapers and radio stations and to photograph and interview local residents for the Works Progress Administration. Welty's photographs were exhibited in New York City in 1936. During the 1930s Welty also began to publish her short stories in such magazines as The Southern Review, The New Yorker, *and* The Atlantic Monthly. *She has continued to live in Jackson, where she has written an impressive body of fiction that evokes a strong sense of her "place." Her books include* Ponder Heart *(1954),* Losing Battles *(1970), and* The Optimist's Daughter *(1972), which was awarded the Pulitzer Prize. Welty's collection of essays,* The Eye of the Story, *appeared in 1977, and recently she published an account of the forces that shaped her own writing career,* One Writer's Beginnings *(1984). In "A Sweet Devouring," reprinted from* The Eye of the Story, *Welty describes her childhood addiction to reading "series" books.*

Our library in those days was a big rotunda lined with shelves. A copy of *V.V.'s Eyes* seemed to follow you wherever you went, even after you'd read it. I didn't know what I liked, I just knew what there was a lot of. After *Randy's Spring* there came *Randy's Summer*, *Randy's Fall* and *Randy's Winter*. True, I didn't care very much myself for her spring, but it didn't occur to me that I might not

1

care for her summer, and then her summer didn't prejudice me against her fall, and I still had hopes as I moved on to her winter. I was disappointed in her whole year, as it turned out, but a thing like that didn't keep me from wanting to read every word of it. The pleasures of reading itself—who doesn't remember?—were like those of a Christmas cake, a sweet devouring. The "Randy Books" failed chiefly in being so soon over. Four seasons doesn't make a series.

All that summer I used to put on a second petticoat (our librarian wouldn't let you past the front door if she could see through you), ride my bicycle up the hill and "through the Capitol" (shortcut) to the library with my two read books in the basket (two was the limit you could take out at one time when you were a child and also as long as you lived), and tiptoe in ("Silence") and exchange them for two more in two minutes. Selection was no object. I coasted the two new books home, jumped out of my petticoat, read (I suppose I ate and bathed and answered questions put to me), then in all hope put my petticoat back on and rode those two books back to the library to get my next two.

The librarian was the lady in town who wanted to be it. She called me by my full name and said, "Does your mother know where you are? You know good and well the fixed rule of this library: *Nobody is going to come running back here with any book on the same day they took it out.* Get both those things out of here and don't come back till tomorrow. And I can practically see through you."

My great-aunt in Virginia, who understood better about needing more to read than you *could* read, sent me a book so big it had to be read on the floor—a bound volume of six or eight issues of *St. Nicholas* from a previous year. In the very first pages a serial began: *The Lucky Stone* by Abbie Farwell Brown. The illustrations were right down my alley: a heroine so poor she was ragged, a witch with an extremely pointed hat, a rich, crusty old gentleman in —better than a wheelchair—a runaway carriage; and I set to. I gobbled up installment after installment through the whole luxurious book, through the last one, and then came the words, turning me to *unlucky* stone: "To be concluded." The book had come to an end and *The Lucky Stone* wasn't finished! The witch had it! I couldn't believe this infidelity from my aunt. I still had my secret childhood feeling that if you hunted long enough in a book's pages, you could find what you were looking for, and long after I knew books better than that, I used to hunt again for the end of *The Lucky Stone*. It never occurred to me that the story had an existence anywhere else outside the pages of that single green-bound book. The last chapter was just something I would have to do without. Polly Pepper could do it. And then suddenly I tried something—I read it again, as much as I had of it. I was in love with books at least partly for what they looked like; I loved the printed page.

In my little circle books were almost never given for 5 Christmas, they cost too much. But the year before, I'd been given a book and got a shock. It was from the same classmate who had told me there was no Santa Claus. She gave me a book, all right—*Poems by Another Little Girl*. It looked like a real book, was printed like a real book— but it was *by her*. *Homemade* poems? Illusion-dispelling was her favorite game. She was in such a hurry, she had such a pile to get rid of—her mother's electric runabout was stacked to the bud vases with copies—that she hadn't even time to say, "Merry Christmas!" With only the same raucous laugh with which she had told me, "Been filling my own stocking for years!" she shot me her book, received my Japanese pencil box with a moonlight scene on the lid and a sharpened pencil inside, jumped back into the car and was sped away by her mother. I stood right where they had left me, on the curb in my Little Nurse's uniform, and read that book, and I had no better way to prove when I got through than I had when I started that this was not a real book. But of course it wasn't. The printed page is not absolutely everything.

Then this Christmas was coming, and my grandfather in Ohio sent along in his box of presents an envelope with money in it for me to buy myself the book I wanted. 6

I went to Kress's. Not everybody knew Kress's sold books, but children just before Christmas know everything Kress's ever sold or will sell. My father had showed us the mirror he was giving my mother to hang above her desk, and Kress's is where my brother and I went to reproduce that by buying a mirror together to give her ourselves, and where our little brother then made us take him and he bought her one his size for fifteen cents. Kress's had also its version of the Series Books, called, exactly like another series, "The Camp Fire Girls," beginning with *The Camp Fire Girls in the Woods.* 7

I believe they were ten cents each and I had a dollar. But they weren't all that easy to buy, because the series stuck, and to buy some of it was like breaking into a loaf of French bread. Then after you got home, each single book was as hard to open as a box stuck in its varnish, and when it gave way it popped like a firecracker. The covers once prized apart would never close; those books once open stayed open and lay on their back helplessly fluttering their leaves like a turned-over June bug. They were as light as a matchbox. They were printed on yellowed paper with corners that crumbled, if you pinched on them too hard, like old graham crackers, and they smelled like attic trunks, caramelized glue, their own confinement with one another and, over all, the Kress's smell —bandannas, peanuts and sandalwood from the incense counter. Even without reading them I loved them. It was hard, that year, that Christmas is a day you can't read. 8

What could have happened to those books?—but I can tell you about the leading character. His name was Mr. Holmes. He was not a Camp Fire Girl: he wanted to catch one. Through every book of the series he gave chase. 9

He pursued Bessie and Zara—those were the Camp Fire Girls—and kept scooping them up in his touring car, while they just as regularly got away from him. Once Bessie escaped from the second floor of a strange inn by climbing down a gutter pipe. Once she escaped by driving away from Mr. Holmes in his own automobile, which she had learned to drive by watching him. What Mr. Holmes wanted with them—either Bessie or Zara would do—didn't give me pause; I was too young to be a Camp Fire Girl; I was just keeping up. I wasn't alarmed by Mr. Holmes—when I cared for a chill, I knew to go to Dr. Fu Manchu, who had his own series in the library. I wasn't fascinated either. There was one thing I wanted from those books, and that was for me to have ten to read at one blow.

Who in the world wrote those books? I knew all the time they were the false "Camp Fire Girls" and the ones in the library were the authorized. But book reviewers sometimes say of a book that if anyone else had written it, it might not have been this good, and I found it out as a child—their warning is justified. This was a proven case, although a case of the true not being as good as the false. In the true series the characters were either totally different or missing (Mr. Holmes was missing), and there was too much time given to teamwork. The Kress's Campers, besides getting into a more reliable kind of trouble than the Carnegie Campers, had adventures that even they themselves weren't aware of: the pages were in wrong. There were transposed pages, repeated pages, and whole sections in upside down. There was no way of telling if there was anything missing. But if you know your way in the woods at all, you could enjoy yourself tracking it down. I read the library "Camp Fire Girls," since that's what they were there for, but though they could be read by poorer light they were not as good. 10

And yet, in a way, the false Campers were no better either. I wonder whether I felt some flaw at the heart of things or whether I was just tired of not having any taste; but it seemed to me when I had finished that the last 11 nine of those books weren't as good as the first one. And the same went for all Series Books. As long as they are keeping a series going, I was afraid, nothing can really happen. The whole thing is one grand prevention. For my greed, I might have unwittingly dealt with myself in the same way Maria Edgeworth dealt with the one who put her all into the purple jar—I had received word it was just colored water.

And then I went again to the home shelves and my lucky hand reached and found Mark Twain—twenty-four volumes, not a series, and good all the way through. 12

Of Speed Readers and Lip-Movers

WILLIAM H. GASS

♦

*William H. Gass was born in Fargo, North Dakota,
and was educated at Kenyon College and Cornell
University. In 1950 he accepted a position as instructor of philosophy at the College of Wooster in
Ohio. In 1954 he moved to Purdue University, where
he taught philosophy and began to write fiction. It
was during this period that Gass won a Rockefeller
grant, which enabled him to complete his first novel,*
Omensetter's Luck *(1966), and his much-praised volume of short stories,* In the Heart of the Heart of the
Country *(1968). In 1969 he won a Guggenheim fellowship and accepted a position as professor of philosophy at Washington University in St. Louis. He is a
regular contributor to magazines such as* The Nation,
South Atlantic Quarterly, *and* The New York Times
Book Review. *His recent work includes a collection
of essays,* Fiction and the Figures of Life *(1970); a
novella,* Willie Masters' Lonesome Wife *(1971); a
philosophical meditation,* On Being Blue *(1975); and a
volume of literary criticism,* The World Within the
Word *(1978). In "Of Speed Readers and Lip-Movers,"
first published in* The New York Times Book Review
*in 1984, Gass contrasts the process of "speed reading"
with a slower and more meaningful reading process.*

I was never much of an athlete, but I was once the member of a team. Indeed, I was its star, and we were cham-
pions. During high school I belonged to a squad of speed
readers in Ohio, although I was never awarded a letter for
it. Still, we took on the top 10 in our territory and read as
rapidly as possible every time we were challenged to a
match, hoping to finish in front of that towheaded punk

from Canton, the tomato-cheeked girl from Marietta, or that silent pair of sisters, all spectacles and squints, who looked tough as German script and who hailed from Shaker Heights or some other rough neighborhood full of swift, mean raveners of text.

We called ourselves the Speeders. Of course. Every- **2** body did. There were the Sharon Speeders, the Steubenville Speeders and the Niles Nouns. They never won. How could they? I lost a match myself once to a kid with green teeth. And that's the way, I'm afraid, we appeared to others—as creeps with squints, bad posture, unclean complexions, unscrubbed teeth, tousled hair. We never had dates, we only memorized them; and when any real sports team went on the road to represent the high school, we carried the socks, the Tootsie Rolls, the towels for them. My nemesis with the green teeth had a head of thin red hair like rust on a saw; he revolved a suggestive little finger in his large fungiform ears. My God, I thought . . . and the shame of that defeat still rushes to my face whenever I remember it. Nevertheless, even today I possess a substantial, gold-colored medallion on which one sunbeaming eye seems hung above a book like a spider. Both book and eye are open—wide. I take that open, streaming eye to be an omen.

Our reading life has its salad days, its autumnal times. **3** At first, of course, we do it badly, scarcely keeping our balance, toddling along behind our finger, so intent on remembering what each word is supposed to mean that the sentence is no longer a path, and we arrive at its end without having gone anywhere. Thus it is with all the things we learn, for at first they passively oppose us; they lie outside us like mist or the laws of nature; we have to issue orders to our eyes, our limbs, our understanding: Lift this, shift that, thumb the space bar, let up on the clutch —easy! There go the gears!—and don't forget to modify the verb, or remember what an escudo's worth. After a while, we find we like standing up, riding a bike, singing "Don Giovanni," making puff pastry, puppy love or model planes. Then we are indeed like the adolescent in our eager green enthusiasms: They are plentiful as leaves. Every page is a pasture, and we are let out to graze like hungry herds.

Do you remember what magic the word *thigh* could 4
work on you, showing up in the middle of a passage suddenly, like a whiff of cologne in a theater? I admit it: The widening of the upper thigh remains a miracle, and, honestly, many of us once read the word *thigh* as if we were exploring Africa, seeking the source of the Nile. No volume was too hefty then, no style too verbal. The weight of a big book was more comforting than Christmas candy, though you had to be lucky, strike the right text at the right time, because the special excitement Thomas Wolfe provides, for instance, can be felt only in the teens. And when, again, will any of us possess the energy, the patience, the inner sympathy for volcanic bombast to read—enjoy—Carlyle?

Repeating was automatic. Who needed Gertrude Stein? 5
I must have rushed through a pleasant little baseball book called "The Crimson Pennant" at least a dozen times, consuming a cake I had already cut into crumbs, yet that big base hit was never better than on that final occasion when its hero and I ran round those bases, and he shyly doffed his hat to the crowd.

No one threatened to whack our rumps if we didn't 6
read another Nancy Drew by Tuesday; no sour-faced virgin browbeat us with "The Blithedale Romance" or held out "The Cloister and the Hearth" like a cold plate of good-for-you food. We were on our own. I read Swinburne and the "Adventures of the Shadow." I read Havelock Ellis and Tom Swift and "The Idylls of the King." I read whatever came to hand, and what came to hand were a lot of naughty French novels, detective stories, medical adventures, books about bees, biographies of Napoleon, and "Thus Spake Zarathustra" like a bolt of lightning.

I read them all, whatever they were, with an ease that 7

541

defies the goat's digestion, and with an ease that is now so easily forgotten, just as we forget the wild wobble in our bikes' wheels, or the humiliating falls we took when we began our life on spokes. That wind I felt, when I finally stayed upright around the block, continuously re-affirmed the basic joy of cycling. It told me not merely that I was moving, but that I was moving *under my own power;* just as later, when I'd passed my driver's test, I would feel another sort of exhilaration—an intense, ad-dictive, dangerous one—that of command, of my ability to control the energy produced by another thing or per-son, to direct the life contained in another creature.

Yes, in those early word-drunk years, I would down   8
a book or two a day as though they were gins. I read for adventure, excitement, to sample the exotic and the strange, for climax and resolution, to participate in other-wise forbidden passions. I forgot what it was to be under my own power, under my own steam. I was, like so many adolescents, as eager to leap from my ordinary life as the salmon is to get upstream. I sought a replacement for the world. With a surreptitious lamp lit, I stayed awake to dream. I grew reckless. I read for speed.

When you read for speed you do not read recursively,   9
looping along the line like a sewing machine, stitching something together—say the panel of a bodice to a sleeve —linking a pair of terms, the contents of a clause, closing a seam by following the internal directions of the sentence so that the word *you* is first fastened to the word *read,* and then the phrase *for speed* is attached to both in order that the entire expression can be finally fronted by a grandly capitalized *When* . . . while all of that, in turn, is gathered up to await the completion of the later segment that begins *you do not read recursively.* You can hear how long it seems to take—this patient process—and how confusing it can become. Nor do you linger over lan-guage, repeating some especially pleasant little passage, in the enjoyment, perhaps, of a modest rhyme (for example, the small clause, *when you read for speed),* or a particu-

larly apt turn of phrase (an image, for instance, such as the one that dealt with Green Teeth's thin red hair—like rust on a saw). None of that, when you read for speed.

Nor, naturally, do you move your lips as you read the 10 word *read* or the words *moving your lips,* so that the poor fellow next to you in the reading room has to watch intently to see what your lips are saying: Are you asking him out? For the loan of his Plutarch's "Lives"? And of course the poor fellow is flummoxed to find that you are moving your lips to say *moving your lips.* What can that mean? The lip-mover—O, such a person is low on our skill-scale. We are taught to have scorn for him, for her.

On the other hand, the speeding reader drops diago- 11 nally down across the page, on a slant like a skier, cuts across the text the way a butcher prefers to slice sausage, so that a small round can be made to yield a misleading larger oval piece. The speeding reader is after the kernel, the heart, the gist. Paragraphs become a country the eye flies over looking for landmarks, reference points, air-ports, restrooms, passages of sex. The speeding reader guts a book the way the skillful clean fish. The gills are gone, the tail, the scales, the fins; then the filet slides away swiftly as though fed to a seal. And only the slow reader, whose finger falters in front of long words, who moves the lips, who dances the text, will notice the odd crowd of images—flier, skier, butcher, seal—that have gathered to comment on the aims and activities of the speeding reader, perhaps like gossips at a wedding.

To the speeding reader, this jostle of images, this crazy 12 collision of ideas—of landing strip, kernel, heart, guts, sex—will not be felt, because it is only the inner core of meaning he's after; it is the gist she wants. And the gist is: Readers who read rapidly read only for the most gen-eralized, stereotyped sense. For them, meaning floats over the page like fluffy clouds. Cliché is forever in fashion. They read, as we say, synonymously, seeking sameness; and, indeed, it is all the same to them if they are said in one moment to be greedy as seals, and in another

moment likened to descalers of fish. They—you, I, we—
"get" the idea.

A speed-reading match had two halves. (I say "had"   13
because I believe these matches long ago lit their last
light.) The first consisted of the rapid reading itself,
through which, of course, I whizzzzed, all the while mak-
the sound of closing covers in order to disconcert Green
Teeth or the silent Shaker Heights sisters, who were to
think I had completed my reading already. I didn't wear
glasses then, but I carried a glasses case to every match,
and always dropped it at a pertinent moment.

Next we were required to answer questions about what   14
we claimed we'd covered, and here quickness was again
essential. The questions, however, soon disclosed their
biases. They had a structure, their own gist; and it became possible, after some experience, to guess what would
be asked about a text almost before it had been begun. Is
it "Goldilocks" we're skimming? Then what is the favorite
breakfast food of the three bears? How does Goldilocks
escape from the house? Why weren't the three bears at
home when Goldilocks came calling? The multiple answers we could choose from also had their own tired tilt
and, like the questions, gave themselves away. The favorite breakfast foods, for instance, were: (a) Quaker Oats
(which this year is paying for the prizes, and in this sly
fashion gets its name in); (b) Just Rite (written like a brand
name); (c) porridge (usually misspelled); (d) sugar-coated
curds and whey. No one ever wondered whether Goldilocks was suffering from sibling rivalry; why she had become a teenie-trasher; or why mother bear's bowl of porridge was cold when baby bear's smaller bowl was still
warm and Just Rite.

There were many other mysteries, but not for these   15
quiz masters who didn't even want to know the sexual
significance of Cinderella's slipper, or why it had to be
made of glass. I won my championship medal by ignoring
the text entirely (it was a section from Volume Two of
Oswald Spengler's "Decline of the West," the part that

begins, "Regard the flowers at eventide as, one after the other, they close in the setting sun. . . ." But then, of course, you remember that celebrated passage). I skipped the questions as well, and simply encircled the gloomiest alternatives offered. Won in record time. No one's got through Spengler with such dispatch since.

What did these matches, with their quizzes for com- 16 prehension, their love of literal learning, tell me? They told me that time was money (a speed reader's clearest idea); they told me what the world wanted me to read when I read, eat when I ate, see when I saw. Like the glutton, I was to get everything in and out in a hurry. Turnover was topmost. What the world wanted me to get was the gist, but the gist was nothing but an idea of trade— an idea so drearily uniform and emaciated it might have modeled dresses.

There is another way of reading I'd like to recom- 17 mend. It's slow, old-fashioned, not easy either, rarely practiced. It must be learned. It is a way of life. What!—I hear your hearts exclaim—is the old wart going to go on some more about reading? Reading? When we can see the rings around his eyes for every year he's worn them out . . . reading? When we are commencing from college, leaving books, book bags, bicycles behind like pretty scenes along the highway? Yes. Just so. That's true. Most of you *are* through. Farewell, chemistry. Farewell, "Canterbury Tales." Imagine reading *that* again. Or "The Faerie Queene" even the first time. Farewell, Sir Philip Sydney, and your golden lines:

Farewell O Sunn, Arcadias clearest light;
Farewell O pearl, the poore mans plenteous treasure:
Farewell O golden staffe, the weake mans might:
Farewell O joy, the joyfulls onely pleasure.
Wisdom farewell, the skillesse mans direction:
Farewell with thee, farewell all our affection.

Now "Paradise" is "Lost." Who cares if molecular ge-   18
netics has revolutionized biology? Farewell, philosophy.
Farewell, free love. From now on there will be an interest,
a carrying, a handling charge. Farewell, "A Farewell to
Arms." "Goodbye, Columbus."

You may have noticed that I am now speaking in sen-   19
tence fragments. The speed reader hates subordination,
qualification, refinement, deployment, ritual, decoration,
order, mother, inference, country, logic, family, flag, God.
Here is a little test: In that last list, what word will the
speed reader pick out to stand for the rest of it—to be its
gist? *God,* you guess? No. Wrong. Nor *flag,* though that's
appealing. *Mother* will be the word we want.

All right. I heard your hearts heave like a slow sea.   20
I'm adaptable. Let's talk about drinking. I belonged to a
drinking club once. Defeated the Fraternal Order of Eagles
on their own turf. The Chug-a-lugs, we were called. Inevitably. You don't plan, I'm sure, to give up drinking. Or
reading—not altogether—I imagine. Not the letters to
Penthouse. The inky pages of The Washington Post. TV
Guide. Legal briefs. Medical romances. Business lore.

Well, there is another way of drinking I'd like to recom-   21
mend. We've already dealt with the first way. Gulp. Get
the gist. And the gist is the level of alcohol in your blood,
the pixilated breath you blow into the test balloon. It
makes appropriate the expression: Have a belt. We can
toss down a text, a time of life, a love affair, that walk in
the park that gets us from here to there. We can chug-
a-lug them. You have, perhaps, had to travel sometime
with a person whose passion was that simple: It was *getting there.* You have no doubt encountered people who
impatiently wait for the payoff; they urge you to come to
the point; at dinner, the early courses merely delay dessert; they look only at the bottom line (that obscene
phrase); they are persons consumed by consequences;
they want to climax without crescendo.

But we can read and walk and write and look in quite   22
a different way. It is possible. I was saved from sameness

by Immanuel Kant. You can't speed-read "The Critique of Pure Reason." You can't speed-read Wallace Stevens. There is no gist, no simple translation, no key concept that will unlock these works; actually, there is no lock, no door, no wall, no room, no house, no world.

Reading is a complicated, profound, silent, still, very   23
personal, very private, very solitary yet civilizing activity. Nothing is more social than speech—we are bound together by our common sounds more securely than even by our laws. Nevertheless, no one is more aware of the isolated self than the reader, for a reader communes with the word heard immaterially in that hollow of the head made only for hearing, a room nowhere in the body in any ordinary sense. On the bus, everyone of us may be deep in something different. Sitting next to a priest, I can still enjoy my pornography, though I may keep a thumb discreetly on top of the title.

I've grown larger, if not wiser. My vices now are vision-   24
ary. That baseball book, "The Crimson Pennant," has become "The Crimson Cancan." What do I care if Father McIvie is reading about investments? Yet while all of us, in our verbal recreations, are full of respect for the privacy of our neighbors, the placards advertising perfume or footwear invade the public space like a visual smell; Muzak fills every unstopped ear the way the static of the street does. The movies, the radio, television, theater, music: All run on at their own rate, and the listener or the viewer must attend, keep up, or lose out—but not the reader. The reader is free. The reader is in charge and pedals the cycle. It is easy for a reader to announce that his present run of Proust has been postponed until the holidays.

Reading, that is, is not a public imposition. Of course,   25
when we read, many of us squirm and fidget. One of the closest friends of my youth would sensuously wind and unwind on his forefinger the long blond strands of his hair. How he read—that is how I remember him. Yes, our postures are often provocative, perverse. Yet these outward movements of the body really testify to the importance of

the inner movements of the mind; and even those rapid flickers of the eye, as we shift from word to word, phrase to phrase and clause to clause, hoping to keep our head afloat on a flood of Faulkner or Proust or Joyce or James, are registers of reason. For reading is reasoning, figuring things out through thoughts, making arrangements out of arrangements until we've understood a text so fully it is nothing but feeling and pure response, until its conceptual turns are like the reversals of mood in a marriage—petty, sad, ecstatic, commonplace, foreseeable, amazing.

In order to have this experience, however, one must 26 learn to perform the text, say, sing, shout the words to oneself, give them, with *our* minds, *their* body. Otherwise the eye skates over every syllable like the speeder. There can be no doubt that often what we read should be skimmed, as what we are frequently asked to drink should be spilled. But the speeding reader is alone in another, less satisfactory way, one quite different from that of the reader who says the words to herself, because as we read we divide into a theater: There is the performer who shapes those silent sounds, moving the muscles of the larynx almost invisibly, and there is the listener who hears them said and who responds to their passion or their wisdom.

Such a reader sees every text as unique, greets every 27 work as a familiar stranger. Such a reader is willing to allow another's words to become hers, his.

In the next moment, let us read a wine, since I promised 28 I would talk about drinking. We have prepared for the occasion, of course. The bottle has been allowed to breathe. Books need to breathe, too. They should be opened properly, hefted, thumbed. The paper, print, layout, should be appreciated. But now we decant the text into our wide-open and welcoming eyes. We warm the wine in the bowl of the glass with our hand. We let its bouquet collect above it just as the red of red roses seems to stain the air. We wade—shoeless, to be sure—through the color it has liquified. We roll a bit of it about in our mouths. We sip. We savor. We say some sentences of Sir Thomas

Browne: "We tearme sleepe a death, and yet it is waking that kils us, and destroyed those spirits which are the house of life. Tis indeed a part of life that best expresseth death, for every man truely lives so long as hee acts his nature, or someway makes good the faculties of himself. . . ."

Are these words not from a fine field, in a splendid 29 year? There is, of course, a sameness in all these words: *life/death, man/nature.* We get the drift. But the differences! The differences make all the difference, the way nose and eyes and cheek bones form a face, the way a muscle makes emotion pass across it. It is the differences we read. Differences are not only identifiable, distinct; they are epidemic: The wine is light, perhaps, spicy, slow to release its grip upon itself, the upper thigh is widening wonderfully, the night air has hands, words fly out of our mouths like birds. "But who knows the fate of his bones," Browne says, "or how often he is to be buried."

Yet as I say his soul out loud, he lives again; he has 30 risen up in me, and I can be, for him, that temporary savior that every real reader is, putting his words in my mouth; not nervously, notice, as though they were pieces of gum, but in that way that is necessary if the heart is to hear them. And though they are his words and his soul, then, that return through me, I am in charge. He has asked nothing of me; his words move because I move them. It is like cycling, reading is. Can you feel the air, the pure passage of the spirit past the exposed skin?

So this reading will be like living, then—the living each 31 of you will be off in a moment to be busy with, not always speedily, I hope, or in the continuous anxiety of consequence, the sullenness of inattention, the annoying static of distraction. But it will be only a semblance of living— this living—nevertheless, the way unspoken reading is a semblance, unless, from time to time, you perform the outer world within. Because only in that manner can it deliver itself to us. As Rainer Maria Rilke once commanded: "Dance the taste of the fruit you have been tasting. Dance the orange." I should like to multiply that charge, even past all possibility. Speak the street to yourself sometimes, hear the horns in the forest, read the breeze aloud and make that inner wind yours, because, whether Nature, Man or God has given us the text, we independently possess the ability to read, to read really well, and to move our own mind freely in tune to the moving world.

Writing

WILLIAM STAFFORD

———— ◆ ————

William Stafford was born in Hutchinson, Kansas, in
1914 and educated at the University of Kansas and
the State University of Iowa. During World War II
he completed his service as a conscientious objector
by working for the Brethren Service and the Church
World Service. After the war Stafford held faculty
positions at several universities before moving to
Lewis and Clark College in Portland, Oregon, where
he has taught since 1957. Although he published an
account of his experiences as a conscientious objector,
Down in My Heart *(1947), when he was 33, Stafford*
did not publish his first volume of poetry, **West of**
Your City *(1960), until he was 54. He is now con-*
sidered one of America's most gifted poets. Among
his other books are **Traveling Through the Dark**
(1962), **The Rescued Year** *(1966), and* **Someday Maybe**
(1973). In "Writing" (first published in **Field** *magazine*
in 1970) Stafford describes the receptivity, risks, and
revelations that are part of the writing process.

A writer is not so much someone who has something to 1
say as he is someone who has found a process that will
bring about new things he would not have thought of if
he had not started to say them. That is, he does not draw
on a reservoir; instead, he engages in an activity that
brings to him a whole succession of unforeseen stories,
poems, essays, plays, laws, philosophies, religions, or—but
wait!

Back in school, from the first when I began to try to 2
write things, I felt this richness. One thing would lead to

another; the world would give and give. Now, after twenty years or so of trying, I live by that certain richness, an idea hard to pin, difficult to say, and perhaps offensive to some. For there are strange implications in it.

One implication is the importance of just plain receptivity. When I write, I like to have an interval before me when I am not likely to be interrupted. For me, this means usually the early morning, before others are awake. I get pen and paper, take a glance out the window (often it is dark out there), and wait. It is like fishing. But I do not wait very long, for there is always a nibble—and this is where receptivity comes in. To get started I will accept anything that occurs to me. Something always occurs, of course, to any of us. We can't keep from thinking. Maybe I have to settle for an immediate impression: it's cold, or hot, or dark, or bright, or in between! Or—well, the possibilities are endless. If I put down something, that thing will help the next thing come, and I'm off. If I let the process go on, things will occur to me that were not at all in my mind when I started. These things, odd or trivial as they may be, are somehow connected. And if I let them string out, surprising things will happen.

If I let them string out. . . . Along with initial receptivity, then, there is another readiness: I must be willing to fail. If I am to keep on writing, I cannot bother to insist on high standards. I must get into action and not let anything stop me, or even slow me much. By "standards" I do not mean "correctness"—spelling, punctuation, and so on. These details become mechanical for anyone who writes for a while. I am thinking about what many people would consider "important" standards, such matters as social significance, positive values, consistency, etc. I resolutely disregard these. Something better, greater, is happening! I am following a process that leads so wildly and originally into new territory that no judgment can at the moment be made about values, significance, and so on. I am making something new, something that has not been judged before. Later others—and maybe I myself—will make judgments. Now, I am headlong to discover. Any distraction may harm the creating.

So, receptive, careless of failure, I spin out things on 5 the page. And a wonderful freedom comes. If something occurs to me, it is all right to accept it. It has one justification: it occurs to me. No one else can guide me. I must follow my own weak, wandering, diffident impulses.

A strange bonus happens. At times, without my insist- 6 ing on it, my writings become coherent; the successive elements that occur to me are clearly related. They lead by themselves to new connections. Sometimes the language, even the syllables that happen along, may start a trend. Sometimes the materials alert me to something waiting in my mind, ready for sustained attention. At such times, I allow myself to be eloquent, or intentional, or for great swoops (treacherous! not to be trusted!) reasonable. But I do not insist on any of that; for I know that back of my activity there will be the coherence of my self, and that indulgence of my impulses will bring recurrent patterns and meanings again.

This attitude toward the process of writing creatively 7 suggests a problem for me, in terms of what others say. They talk about "skills" in writing. Without denying that I do have experience, wide reading, automatic orthodoxies and maneuvers of various kinds, I still must insist that I am often baffled about what "skill" has to do with the precious little area of confusion when I do not know what I am going to say and then I find out what I am going to say. That precious interval I am unable to bridge by skill. What can I witness about it? It remains mysterious, just as all of us must feel puzzled about how we are so inventive as to be able to talk along through complexities with our friends, not needing to plan what we are going to say, but never stalled for long in our confident forward progress. Skill? If so, it is the skill we all have, something we must have learned before the age of three or four.

A writer is one who has become accustomed to trust- 8 ing that grace, or luck, or—skill.

Yet another attitude I find necessary: most of what I [9] write, like most of what I say in casual conversation, will not amount to much. Even I will realize, and even at the time, that it is not negotiable. It will be like practice. In conversation I allow myself random remarks—in fact, as I recall, that is the way I learned to talk—, so in writing I launch many expendable efforts. A result of this free way of writing is that I am not writing for others, mostly; they will not see the product at all unless the activity eventuates in something that later appears to be worthy. My guide is the self, and its adventuring in the language brings about communication.

This process-rather-than-substance view of writing in- [10] vites a final, dual reflection:

1. Writers may not be special—sensitive or talented in [11] any usual sense. They are simply engaged in sustained use of a language skill we all have. Their "creations" come about through confident reliance on stray impulses that will, with trust, find occasional patterns that are satisfying.

2. But writing itself is one of the great, free human ac- [12] tivities. There is scope for individuality, and elation, and discovery, in writing. For the person who follows with trust and forgiveness what occurs to him, the world remains always ready and deep, an inexhaustible environment, with the combined vividness of an actuality and flexibility of a dream. Working back and forth between experience and thought, writers have more than space and time can offer. They have the whole unexplored realm of human vision.

Rewriting

WILLIAM ZINSSER

◆

*William Zinsser was born in 1922 in New York City
and educated at Princeton University. During the
1940s and 1950s he was a feature writer, drama critic,
film critic, and editorial writer for* **The New York
Herald Tribune.** *In the 1960s he was a columnist for*
Look *and* **Life** *magazines. In 1970 he began teaching
a course in expository writing at Yale University. The
course, which grew out of his long career as a journalist, led to the publication of "an informal guide
to writing nonfiction,"* **On Writing Well** *(1976). Zinsser's other books include* **Any Old Place With You**
(1957), **Pop Goes America** *(1966),* **The Lunacy Boom**
(1970), and **Writing With A Word Processor** *(1983).
In this selection, taken from the second edition of*
On Writing Well *(1980), Zinsser explains how revision
can make a piece of writing more readable.*

Clutter is the disease of American writing. We are a so-　1
ciety strangling in unnecessary words, circular constructions, pompous frills and meaningless jargon.

Who can understand the viscous language of everyday　2
American commerce and enterprise: the business letter,
the interoffice memo, the corporation report, the notice
from the bank explaining its latest "simplified" statement?
What member of an insurance or medical plan can deci-
pher the brochure that tells him what his costs and benefits are? What father or mother can put together a child's
toy—on Christmas Eve or any other eve—from the instruc-

tions on the box? Our national tendency is to inflate and thereby sound important. The airline pilot who wakes us to announce that he is presently anticipating experiencing considerable weather wouldn't dream of saying that there's a storm ahead and it may get bumpy. The sentence is too simple—there must be something wrong with it.

But the secret of good writing is to strip every sentence 3 to its cleanest components. Every word that serves no function, every long word that could be a short word, every adverb which carries the same meaning that is already in the verb, every passive construction that leaves the reader unsure of who is doing what—these are the thousand and one adulterants that weaken the strength of a sentence. And they usually occur, ironically, in proportion to education and rank.

During the late 1960s the president of a major uni- 4 versity wrote a letter to mollify the alumni after a spell of campus unrest. "You are probably aware," he began, "that we have been experiencing very considerable potentially explosive expressions of dissatisfaction on issues only partially related." He meant that the students had been hassling them about different things. I was far more upset by the president's English than by the students' potentially explosive expressions of dissatisfaction. I would have preferred the presidential approach taken by Franklin D. Roosevelt when he tried to convert into English his own government's memos, such as this blackout order of 1942:

> Such preparations shall be made as will completely obscure all Federal buildings and non-Federal buildings occupied by the Federal government during an air raid for any period of time from visibility by reason of internal or external illumination.

"Tell them," Roosevelt said, "that in buildings where 5 they have to keep the work going to put something across the windows."

Simplify, simplify. Thoreau said it, as we are so often 6
reminded, and no American writer more consistently practiced what he preached. Open *Walden* to any page and
you will find a man saying in a plain and orderly way
what is on his mind:

> I love to be alone. I never found the companion
> that was so companionable as solitude. We are
> for the most part more lonely when we go
> abroad among men than when we stay in our
> chambers. A man thinking or working is always
> alone, let him be where he will. Solitude is not
> measured by the miles of space that intervene
> between a man and his fellows. The really
> diligent student in one of the crowded hives of
> Cambridge College is as solitary as a dervish
> in the desert.

How can the rest of us achieve such enviable freedom 7
from clutter? The answer is to clear our heads of clutter.
Clear thinking becomes clear writing: one can't exist without the other. It is impossible for a muddy thinker to write
good English. He may get away with it for a paragraph or
two, but soon the reader will be lost, and there is no sin
so grave, for he will not easily be lured back.

Who is this elusive creature the reader? He is a person 8
with an attention span of about twenty seconds. He is
assailed on every side by forces competing for his time: by
newspapers and magazines, by television and radio and
stereo, by his wife and children and pets, by his house and
his yard and all the gadgets that he has bought to keep
them spruce, and by that most potent of competitors, sleep.
The man snoozing in his chair with an unfinished magazine open on his lap is a man who was being given too
much unnecessary trouble by the writer.

It won't do to say that the snoozing reader is too dumb 9
or too lazy to keep pace with the train of thought. My
sympathies are with him. If the reader is lost, it is

generally because the writer has not been careful enough to keep him on the path.

This carelessness can take any number of forms. Perhaps a sentence is so excessively cluttered that the reader, hacking his way through the verbiage, simply doesn't known what it means. Perhaps a sentence has been so shoddily constructed that the reader could read it in any of several ways. Perhaps the writer has switched pronouns in mid-sentence, or has switched tenses, so the reader loses track of who is talking or when the action took place. Perhaps Sentence B is not a logical sequel to Sentence A— the writer, in whose head the connection is clear, has not bothered to provide the missing link. Perhaps the writer has used an important word incorrectly by not taking the trouble to look it up. He may think that "sanguine" and "sanguinary" mean the same thing, but the difference is a bloody big one. The reader can only infer (speaking of big differences) what the writer is trying to imply.

Faced with these obstacles, the reader is at first a remarkably tenacious bird. He blames himself—he obviously missed something, and he goes back over the mystifying sentence, or over the whole paragraph, piecing it out like an ancient rune, making guesses and moving on. But he won't do this for long. The writer is making him work too hard, and the reader will look for one who is better at his craft.

The writer must therefore constantly ask himself: What am I trying to say? Surprisingly often, he doesn't know. Then he must look at what he has written and ask: Have I said it? Is it clear to someone encountering the subject for the first time? If it's not, it is because some fuzz has worked its way into the machinery. The clear writer is a person clear-headed enough to see this stuff for what it is: fuzz.

I don't mean that some people are born clear-headed and are therefore natural writers, whereas others are naturally fuzzy and will never write well. Thinking clearly is a conscious act that the writer must force upon himself, just as if he were embarking on any other project that requires logic: adding up a laundry list or doing an algebra problem. Good writing doesn't come naturally, though most people obviously think it does. The professional writer is forever being bearded by strangers who say that they'd like to "try a little writing sometime" when they retire from their real profession. Good writing takes self-discipline and, very often, self-knowledge.

Many writers, for instance, can't stand to throw anything away. Their sentences are littered with words that mean essentially the same thing and with phrases which make a point that is implicit in what they have already said. When students give me these littered sentences I beg them to select from the surfeit of words the few that most precisely fit what they want to say. Choose one, I plead, from among the three almost identical adjectives. Get rid of the unnecessary adverbs. Eliminate "in a funny sort of way" and other such qualifiers—they do no useful work. 14

The students look stricken—I am taking all their wonderful words away. I am only taking their superfluous words away, leaving what is organic and strong. 15

"But," one of my worst offenders confessed, "I never can get rid of anything—you should see my room." (I didn't take him up on the offer.) "I have two lamps where I only need one, but I can't decide which one I like better, so I keep them both." He went on to enumerate his duplicated or unnecessary objects, and over the weeks ahead I went on throwing away his duplicated and unnecessary words. By the end of the term—a term that he found acutely painful—his sentences were clean. 16

"I've had to change my whole approach to writing," he told me. "Now I have to *think* before I start every sentence and I have to *think* about every word." The very idea amazed him. Whether his room also looked better I never found out. 17

Writing is hard work. A clear sentence is no accident. Very few sentences come out right the first time, or the 18 third. Keep thinking and rewriting until you say what you want to say.

Two pages of the final manuscript of this essay. Although they look like a first draft, they have already been rewritten and re-typed—like almost every other page—four or five times. With each rewrite I try to make what I have written tighter, stronger and more precise, eliminating every element that is not doing use-ful work, until at last I have a clean copy for the printer. Then I go over it once more, reading it aloud, and am always amazed at home how much clutter can still be profitably cut.

5 —

is too dumb or too lazy to keep pace with the ~~writer's~~ train of thought. My sympathies are ~~entirely~~ with him. ~~He's not so dumb.~~ If the reader is lost, it is generally because the writer ~~of the article~~ has not been careful enough to keep him on the proper path.

This carelessness can take any number of ~~different~~ forms. Perhaps a sentence is so excessively ~~long and~~ cluttered that the reader, hacking his way through ~~all~~ the verbiage, simply doesn't know what it ~~the writer~~ means. Perhaps a sentence has been so shoddily constructed that the reader could read it in any of ~~two or three different~~ several ways. ~~He thinks he knows what the writer is trying to say, but he's not sure.~~ Perhaps the writer has switched pronouns in mid-sentence, or ~~perhaps he~~ has switched tenses, so that the reader loses track of who is talking ~~to whom~~ or ~~exactly~~ when the action took place. Per-haps Sentence B is not a logical sequel to Sentence A — the writer, in whose head the connection is ~~perfectly~~ clear, has not ~~given enough thought to providing~~ bothered to provide the missing link. Per-haps the writer has used an important word incorrectly by not taking the trouble to look it up ~~and make sure~~. He may

think that ''sanguine'' and ''sanguinary'' mean the same

thing, but ~~I can assure you that~~ the difference is a bloody

big one ~~to the reader,~~ ^The reader^ He can only ~~try to~~ infer ~~what~~

(speaking of big differences) what the writer is trying to

imply.

⌐Faced with ~~such a variety of~~ ^these^ obstacles, the reader

is at first a remarkably tenacious bird. He ~~tends to~~ blame^s^

himself^.^ ~~He~~ obviously missed something, ~~he thinks,~~ and he

goes back over the mystifying sentence, or over the whole

paragraph,

6 —⌡

piecing it out like an ancient rune, making guesses and

moving on. But he won't do this for long. ~~He will soon run~~

~~out of patience.~~ The writer is making him work too hard,

~~harder than he should have to work~~ and the reader

will look for ~~a writer~~ ^one^ who is better at his craft.

⌐The writer must therefore constantly ask himself: What

am I trying to say? ~~in this sentence?~~ Surprisingly often,

he doesn't know. ~~And~~ Then he must look at what he has ~~just~~

written and ask: Have I said it? Is it clear to someone

^encountering^ ~~who is coming upon~~ the subject for the first time? If it's

not, ~~clear~~ it is because some fuzz has worked its way into

the machinery. The clear writer is a person ~~who is~~ clear-

headed enough to see this stuff for what it is: fuzz.

⌐I don't mean ~~to suggest~~ that some people are born

clear-headed and are therefore natural writers, whereas

^Others^ ~~other people~~ are naturally fuzzy and will ~~therefore~~ never

write well. Thinking clearly is ~~an entirely~~ ^a^ conscious act

561

that the writer must ~~keep forcing~~ force upon himself, just as
if he were ~~starting out~~ embarking on any other ~~kind of~~ project that
~~calls for~~ requires logic: adding up a laundry list or doing an
algebra problem~~, or playing chess.~~ Good writing doesn't
~~just~~ come naturally, though most people obviously think
~~it's as easy as walking.~~ it does. The professional

Acknowledgments

$\blacklozenge$

JAMES AUSTIN "Four Kinds of Chance" reprinted from *Saturday Review/World*, November 2, 1974, by permission.

CAROL BLY Pages 8–13, "Getting Tired," from *Letters from the Country* by Carol Bly. Copyright © 1981 by Carol Bly. Reprinted by permission of Harper & Row, Publishers, Inc.

JOHN BROOKS "Dressing Down," copyright © 1981 by John Brooks. By permission of Little, Brown and Company in association with the Atlantic Monthly Press.

ROBERT BRUSTEIN "Reflections on Horror Movies" reprinted from *The Third Theatre* by permission of the author.

RACHEL CARSON "The Obligation to Endure" from *Silent Spring* by Rachel Carson. Copyright © 1962 by Rachel L. Carson. Reprinted by permission of Houghton Mifflin Company.

JOHN CIARDI "What Is Happiness?" © 1964 Saturday Review Magazine Co. Reprinted by permission.

MALCOLM COWLEY "How Writers Work" from *Writers at Work: The Paris Review Interviews* by Malcom Cowley, ed. Copyright © 1958 by The Paris Review Inc. Reprinted by permission of Viking Penguin, Inc.

JOAN DIDION "Migraines" from *The White Album*, copyright © 1979 by Joan Didion. Reprinted by permission of Simon & Schuster, Inc.

ANNIE DILLARD "Sight into Insight" reprinted by permission of the author and her agent Blanche C. Gregory, Inc. Copyright © 1974 by Annie Dillard.

LOREN EISELEY "The Flow of the River," copyright 1953 by Loren Eiseley. Reprinted from *The Immense Journey*, by Loren Eiseley, by permission of Random House, Inc.

BOB EVANS "How to Get a Job as a 'Swing Dancer' in a Hit Broadway Show" copyright © 1964 by *Harper's* Magazine. Reprinted from the January 1965 issue by permission of the author.

E. M. FORSTER "My Wood." From *Abinger Harvest*, copyright © 1936, 1964 by Edward Morgan Forster. Reprinted by permission of Harcourt Brace Jovanovich, Inc. and Edward Arnold (Publishers) Ltd.

FORTUNE MAGAZINE "Riveters," reprinted from the October 1930 issue of *Fortune* magazine by special permission. © 1930 Time Inc.

WILLIAM GASS "Of Speed Readers and Lip-Movers" copyright © 1984 by The New York Times Company. Reprinted by permission.

ELLEN GOODMAN "The Chem 20 Factor" from *Close to Home*. Copyright © 1979 by the Washington Post Company. Reprinted by permission of Simon & Schuster, Inc.

DOROTHY PARKER "The Short Story, Through a Couple of the Ages" from *The Portable Dorothy Parker*, edited by Brendan Gill. Copyright 1927, renewed copyright © 1955 by Dorothy Parker. Originally published in *The New Yorker* Reprinted by permission of Viking Penguin Inc.

S. J. PERELMAN "Insert Flap A and Throw Away" from *The Most of S. J. Perelman* copyright © 1930, 1933, 1935, 1936, 1953, 1956, 1958 by S. J. Perelman. Reprinted by permission of Simon and Schuster, Inc.

MURRAY ROSS "Football Red and Baseball Green" by Murray Ross first appeared in *Chicago Review* Vol. 22 Nos. 2 and 3, copyright © by *Chicago Review*. Used with permission.

BERTON ROUECHÉ "The Causes of Alcoholism." Reprinted by permission of Harold Ober Associates Incorporated. Copyright © 1960 by Berton Roueché. First published in *The New Yorker*.

RICHARD SELZER "The Knife" from *Mortal Lessons*. Copyright © 1974, 1975, 1976 by Richard Selzer. Reprinted by permission of Simon and Schuster, Inc.

JEAN SHEPHERD "The Endless Streetcar Ride into the Night and the Tinfoil Noose" from *In God We Trust: All Others Pay Cash* by Jean Shepherd. Copyright © 1966 by Jean Shepherd. Reprinted by permission of Doubleday & Company, Inc.

WILLIAM STAFFORD "Writing" from "A Way of Writing," reprinted by permission of *Field* (Spring 1970).

WILLIAM STYRON "The Habit," from *This Quiet Dust and Other Writings*, by William Styron. Copyright © 1982 by William Styron. Reprinted by permission of Random House, Inc.

JUDY SYFERS "I Want a Wife" copyright Judy Syfers, 1971. Reprinted with the permission of the author.

ALEXANDER THEROUX "The Candy Man" copyright © 1979 by *Harper's* Magazine . All rights reserved. Reprinted from the August, 1979 issue by special permission.

LEWIS THOMAS "The Technology of Medicine" from *The Lives of a Cell* by Lewis Thomas. Copyright © 1971 by the Massachusetts Medical Society. Originally published in The New England Journal of Medicine. Reprinted by permission of Viking Penguin Inc.

BARBARA TUCHMAN "An Inquiry into the Persistence of Unwisdom in Government." Reprinted by permission of Russell & Volkening, Inc. as agent for author. Copyright © 1980 by Barbara Tuchman.

ALICE WALKER "In Search of Our Mother's Gardens" from *In Search of Our Mother's Gardens*, copyright © 1983 by Alice Walker. Reprinted by permission of Harcourt Brace Jovanovich Inc.

EUDORA WELTY "A Sweet Devouring" copyright © 1979 by Eudora Welty. Reprinted from *The Eye of the Story: Selected Essays and Reviews*, by Eudora Welty, by permission of Random House, Inc.

E. B. WHITE "Once More to the Lake" (page 40)—August 1941—in *Essays of E.B. White* (1977) by E. B. White. Copyright 1941, 1969 by E.B. White. By permission of Harper & Row, Publishers, Inc.

MARIE WINN   "The Plug-in Drug" from *The Plug-In Drug* by Marie Winn. Copyright © 1977 by Marie Winn Miller. Reprinted by permission of Viking Penguin Inc.

TOM WOLFE   "The Right Stuff" excerpt adapted from *The Right Stuff* by Tom Wolfe. Copyright © 1979 by Tom Wolfe. Reprinted by permission of Farrar, Straus and Giroux Inc.

VIRGINIA WOOLF "If Shakespeare Had Had a Sister" excerpted from *A Room of One's Own* by Virginia Woolf, copyright 1929 by Harcourt Brace Jovanovich, Inc.; renewed 1957 by Leonard Woolf. Reprinted by permission of the publisher, the Author's Literary Estate, and The Hogarth Press.

WILLIAM ZINSSER   "Rewriting" copyright © 1980 by William K. Zinsser. Reprinted by permission of the author from *On Writing Well*, 2nd ed. Harper & Row, publishers, Inc.

Index

———— ◆ ————

Connotative language in
persuasion and argu-
ment essay, 392–393
Conrad, Joseph, 99
Contrast, defined, 191
Cowley, Malcolm, 143, 144,
169–178, 190

Defining negatively in definition essay, 297
Definition essay
analyzing qualities in,
296
attributing characteristics
in, 296–297
audience for, 295–296
defined, 293–294
defining negatively in,
297
drawing analogies in, 297
examples in, 296
giving functions in, 297
points to consider regard-
ing, 330
prewriting exercises, 330–
331
purpose of, 294–295
strategies of, 296–297
three types of definition
in (dictionary/lexi-
cal, stipulative, ex-
tended), 293–294
writing topics, in class,
331–332
writing topics, out of
class, 333
Definition(s)
of cause and effect essay,
335–336
of *classify*, 237–238
of college reader, 1–2

of *compare*, 191
of comparison and con-
trast essay, 191–192
of *contrast*, 191
of definition essay, 293–
294
of descriptive essay, 95–96
dictionary, 293–294
of *divide*, 237–238
of division and classification essay, 237–238
extended, 294
lexical, 293–294
of narrative essay, 25–26
negative, 297
of *analysis*, 140
of *definition*, 293
of *describe*, 95
of *narrator*, 25–26
of persuasion and argu-
ment essay, 389–390
of *process*, 139–140
of process analysis essay,
140
stipulative, 294
Descriptive essay
appeal to the senses in,
97–98
arrangement of details in
pattern in, 98–99
audience for, 97
defined, 95–96
objective description in,
96
points to consider regard-
ing, 134
prewriting exercises, 135–
136
purpose of, 96
selection of details for, 98
special features in, 98